Skin Deep

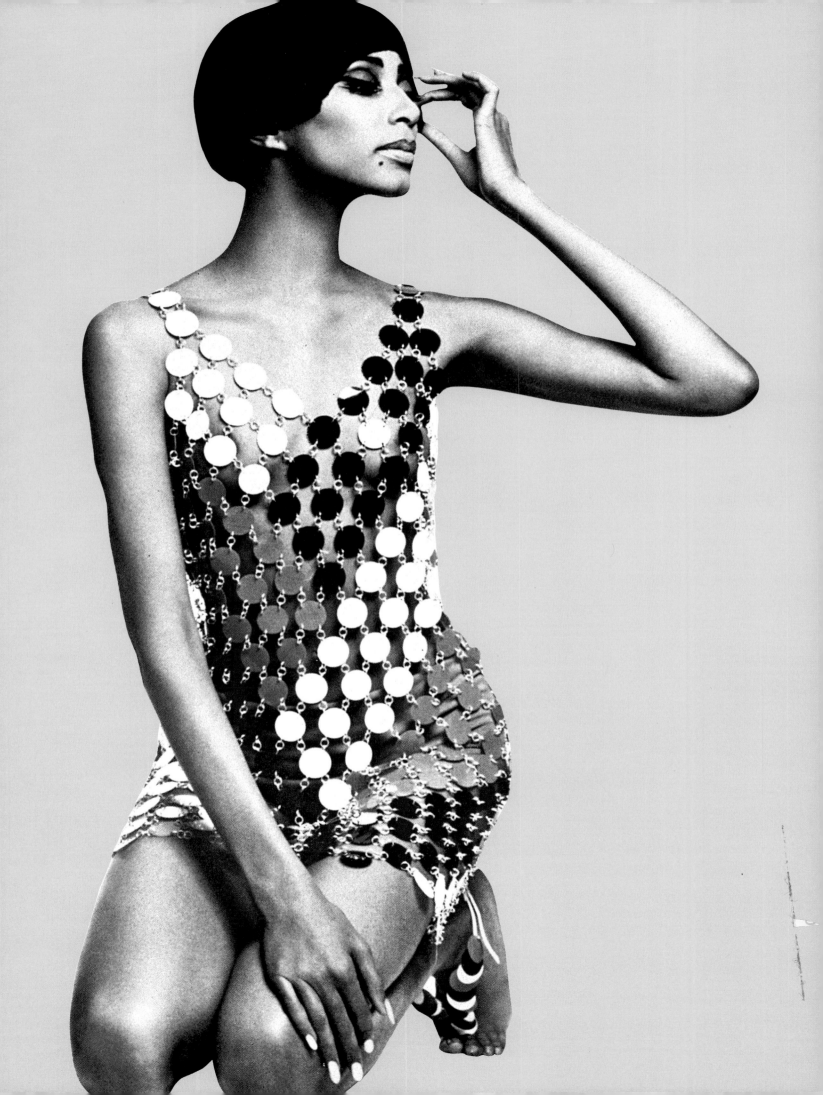

Skin Deep

Inside the World of Black Fashion Models

BARBARA SUMMERS

Amistad

Amistad Press, Inc.
225 Lafayette Street
Suite 806
New York, New York 10012

Distributed by:
St. Martin's Press c/oVHPS
175 Fifth Avenue
New York, New York 10010

Designed by Gilbert D. Fletcher

10 9 8 7 6 5 4 3 2 1

Library of Congress Cataloging-in-Publication Data

Summers, Barbara, 1944-
Skin Deep :Inside the World of Black Fashion Models / Barbara Summers
p. cm.
Includes index.
ISBN 1-56743-031-7 (hc.)
1. Afro-American models. I. Title.
HD8039. M772U58 1998
746.9'2' 08996073--dc21   98-28644
                                                                                  CIP

For the Girls

t is part of the curious language of a curious profession that women who model are called girls. Their chronological age does not matter, nor their life experience, hourly income or celebrity wattage in the media. In the business everyone refers to models as girls—including the models themselves.

Except in this book. In *Skin Deep*, all models are Girls with a capital G. Slightly adjusting the posture of this one word elevates these women above the belittling term which infantilizes them and insults their profession, all with the sweetest intentions.

Beauty is a power. Women know this. Black women in White societies, especially, know this. And Black people, so often misnamed and misjudged on appearance alone, know from personal experience that there must be more to Black models than meets the eye. They are right.

Simply because models are in the business of projecting their face and figure, none of us should be deluded into thinking that what we see is all they've got. Or that what we call them is all they are.

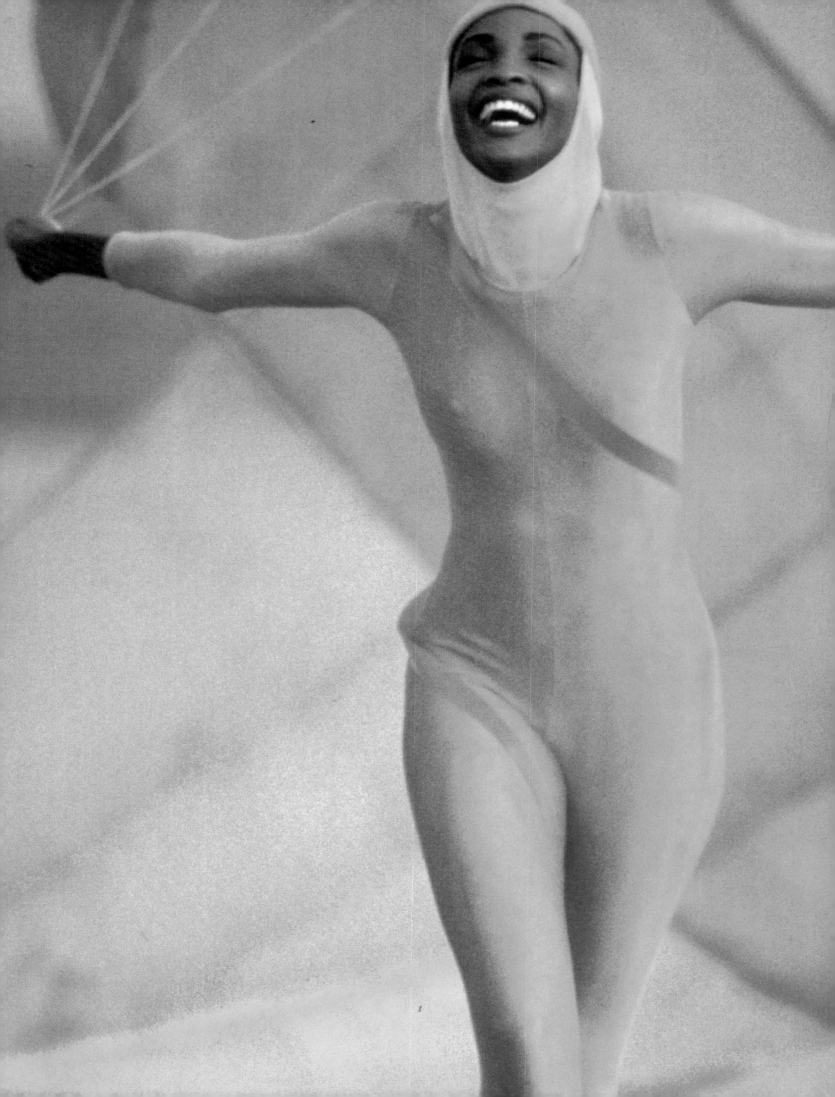

CONTENTS

Preface: Black & Beautiful
BOOK ONE: SEEING IS BELIEVING   1
1.   Breakthroughs   3
2.   Beginnings   14
3.   The Body Politic   41
4.   Navigating the Mainstream   64
5.   Leaving Home   84
6.   Sirens   106
7.   Being and Meaning   128
8.   Next   151
     Epilogue: Vision   172

BOOK TWO: CLOSE-UPS   185
Introduction: Self-Portrait   187
1.   Getting Down with Dorothea Towles   197
2.   Face Time with Joey Mills   204
3.   Patrick Kelly in the Present Tense   210
4.   In Her Own World: Pat Cleveland   219
5.   The Goddess Next Door: Beverly Johnson   224
6.   Images of Iman   231

BOOK THREE: TRAVELS & TRIPS   239
Introduction: Itinerary   241
1.   Milan   242
2.   Paris   251
3.   Tokyo   270

Portfolio   181
Acknowledgments   278
Photo credits   279
Index   282

This page: Roshumba
Frontispiece: Donyale Luna

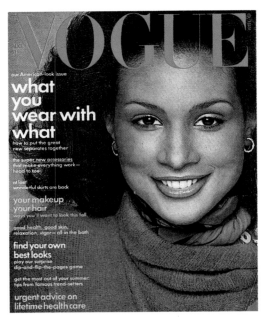

*If there is
to be change,
we are it.*

Clarissa Pinkola Estés

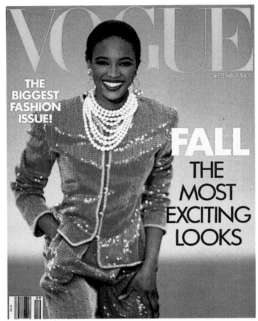

Transcending time, the beauty of
Beverly Johnson, 1974,
Naomi Campbell, 1989,
Kiara Kabukuru, 1997.

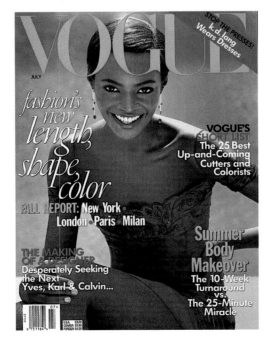

Black & Beautiful

It is a sign of their success that Black models are taken for granted today. At the end of the 20th century, these models stand tall because they are supported by the many women who preceded them, women of color who were pioneers in a special wilderness, the profession of fashion and beauty. Since the middle of this century, every generation has had its pathfinders and trailblazers, its novas and shooting stars, extraordinary women who shone with a special light. We have seen them, often admired and even idolized them, but rarely have we known them, and never have we examined their history.

Skin Deep seeks to name, know, and honor these women. Not for their existence alone, but for their persistence in the silently revolutionary acts that removed blinders, corrected our cultural vision, and expanded our definition of beauty.

During my many years as a model I saw much more than people acknowledged. But when I exultantly asked Eileen Ford, my long-time agent, for her opinion of a book project on the history of Black fashion models, her response was characteristically brisk and blunt.

"Well, Barbara," she said, "it's going to be a very short book."

Despite over four decades in the modeling business as one of the founders, innovators, and great success stories, Eileen Ford was wrong. Her response only fueled my determination to learn as much as I could about what I was certain would be a big, rich, and important story.

Historically, Black women in White America have been called many things: Mammy and mule, radical and religious, Sapphire and sexpot, whore and welfare queen. We have been many others on a too-long list. Beautiful was among the last.

We did not compile that list, yet that list helped to make us, to shape and define us in ways that continue today. Skin color, hair texture, facial features, body types, and much more were factors in a giant social audition whose lines echoed this perennial top tune:

If you're light, you're all right
If you're brown, stick around
If you're black, get back

And so we were cast.

Neither Jezebel nor Jemima, in a society that could not imagine whatever else they might be, Black models were women of rare presence. For their unique blends of elegance and innocence, the media had no convenient place. Cultural thieves had robbed us of pride in our looks and prejudiced us against ourselves, confusing us with imitations of life, bleached dreams, and fears of our own darkness.

Modern Black women could look only to each other for recognition. Art did not feature us nor celebrate our beauty in galleries lined with oil portraits and marble statues. Traditional African art and the Western arts of the 20th century have given us impersonal, stylized features, admirable in their strength and simplicity of line, perhaps, yet distant, dense, and often unlovely. There have been few images and fewer masterpieces. Queen Nefertiti, whose bust was sculpted in Egypt over three millennia ago, is one of the few that speaks directly to the eye and to the heart of who we might be. Contemporary entertainers, actresses, and eventually models became our Mona Lisas. As they claimed new images for themselves, they created new realities for all women of color.

Models are a special breed of women, and Black models are the most special of that breed. In the five decades since the end of World War II, they have insisted on recognition and respect in front of the camera and on the runway. They did not always get what they sought. They did not always give what was expected of them. But in their story lies a kernel of modern culture, ready to burst through the hull of desiccated clichés.

In the old days—that is before the 1970s—whenever we stumbled across pictures of these women in magazines, the shock of recognition was instantaneous. These faces were real. They looked like us. We hoped to look like them. When we saw their beauty, we could believe in our own. We hung their images in the galleries of our imagination and treasured them with inarticulate pride. For a long time there were so few. We felt as if we knew them, knew each Girl's tribe and relations. We felt as if we could interpret a model's personality from her photograph. Whenever one or two pictures or, amazingly, a multi-page spread appeared, we refocused and looked at it longer, harder, more tenderly, more critically. Even in a rare, languid beauty pose, a Black model leaped off the page, grabbed our attention, and insisted that we look again at who she was. She revealed to us our own potential: who we were, are, or could be.

Yet while we prided ourselves on knowing our models, while we thanked them silently for being there, we did not quite trust them. How real could they be, those smooth-skinned girl-women, all smiles, no thighs, and fat bank accounts? Then, too, they were always selling us things, programming us to part with our hard-earned money for things we might not need. Ultimately, no matter what products they sold, what we really bought from them was an image of ourselves, acknowledgment of our existence, our diversity, our power, our value.

What we could not see, however, were the rocky slopes these women climbed to reach the pasture of glossy ads and magazine spreads. We could not hear their thoughts when people slammed doors in their face or, somewhat more politely, kept them waiting for hours before saying no. We could not share their laughter when that magic job did come through or dry their tears when all seemed lost. We could not read their feelings as they walked down brilliant runways alone in front of hundreds of the most influential taste-makers in the world. And we did not know to care—or care to know—if they went home afterwards to empty hotel rooms to feel even more alone. They were beautiful and therefore, we thought, they did not feel joy and pain the same way we did. *Skin Deep* shows that we were wrong.

After the political upheavals of the '60s, more Black models moved successfully into the business. The few became many in the '70s and then too many—for some—in the '80s and '90s. Although fashion eras were and still are dominated by one or two superstars, at varying altitudes hundreds of women of color have worked as models. Standards of beauty could never again be rigidly corseted.

In terms of prestige and income, modeling ranks high on the list of dream jobs. While the money is great and the personal rewards grand, the daily stings of rejection are not for thin skins of any color. Dangerous detours into drug abuse and debilitating relationships are just as sensationalized as the glory path. Behind the pretty face may lie knots of personal identity, self-worth, and confused values. Underneath the sleek ad may lie thorny questions of corporate quotas, target marketing, and moral image. Models may not only wear a mask, they may also be a mask.

To find out who Black models really are *Skin Deep* looks below the surface and behind the scene, and speaks in the voices of the women themselves. Such is the irony of success that Black models and their stories are now in danger of being mistaken for granted. Some Girls are known by their first name alone, appearing as often in the gossip columns as they do in the fashion spreads. They publicize clothing styles, advertise products, and legitimize attitudes, all on a scale unforeseeable fifty years ago. Back then, many ads for skin creams and hair dressings—which provided some of the first opportunities for professional models—did not hesitate to moralize along these or similar lines: "It's a shame how many girls miss out on romance and good times because their complexions are unfashionably dark."

It is ridiculous to think that skin color could ever be in or out of fashion. And it is humbling to admit that Black people themselves were both part of the problem and part of the solution. The fact is that race remains an issue.

Concepts of beauty are more than skin deep. They are often attached to color codes, moral judgments, and dollar signs by strings we do not see or cannot comprehend. But what is beauty and who determines it? Men defined it for women, and Whites defined it for Blacks, until Black people and women started re-defining it for themselves.

Black fashion models were some of the first to make these new definitions and to see their effects. They helped to stretch a new canvas and expand the palette, but neither the picture nor the frame would change overnight. The early professional models of color in the 1940s were often light-skinned with European features, deviating only slightly from the White ideal. Even these deviations were a start, however. Given a shade, they eventually covered the rainbow. Today's fashion models advance assertively in all colors, with all kinds of features and cultural affiliations.

If we have heroines today, we must also acknowledge that we have had victims. Due to the racial prejudice of the past, the identity of the first professional Black model may never be known. She might have been passing for White. Nevertheless, as we honor the women we do know, *Skin Deep* also wishes to salute her, the first, an unknown soldier in an undeclared war.

Make no mistake about it. Beauty is a power. And the struggle to have the entire range of Black beauty recognized and respected is a serious one, no less so because it is bloodless, deals with a vague territory (aesthetics, morals, culture) and the planet's least powerful majority: women. Battles have been won, but the conflict—cosmetic though it may appear—continues.

Black models are living proof that beauty is more than skin deep. From the past to the present, their unique flair and impeccable style won them a place no social legislation could create or deny. Each step onto the runway, each click of the camera gave real form to what was only an abstraction. With each distinctive face, figure, and personality, they focused our awareness on their presence as individuals and their significance as a group. Whether they knew it or not, they were on a mission to redefine beauty and power. It was a mission that, in its own way, would change the world.

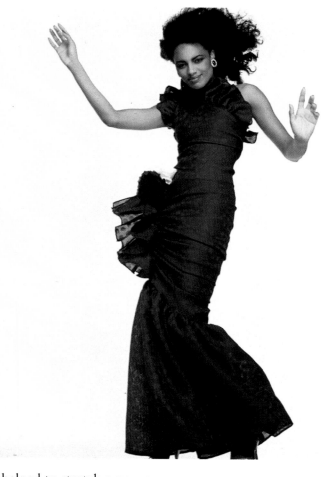

The feminine flair of
Wanakee.

Next page: **Grace Jones,**
fearless and fun.

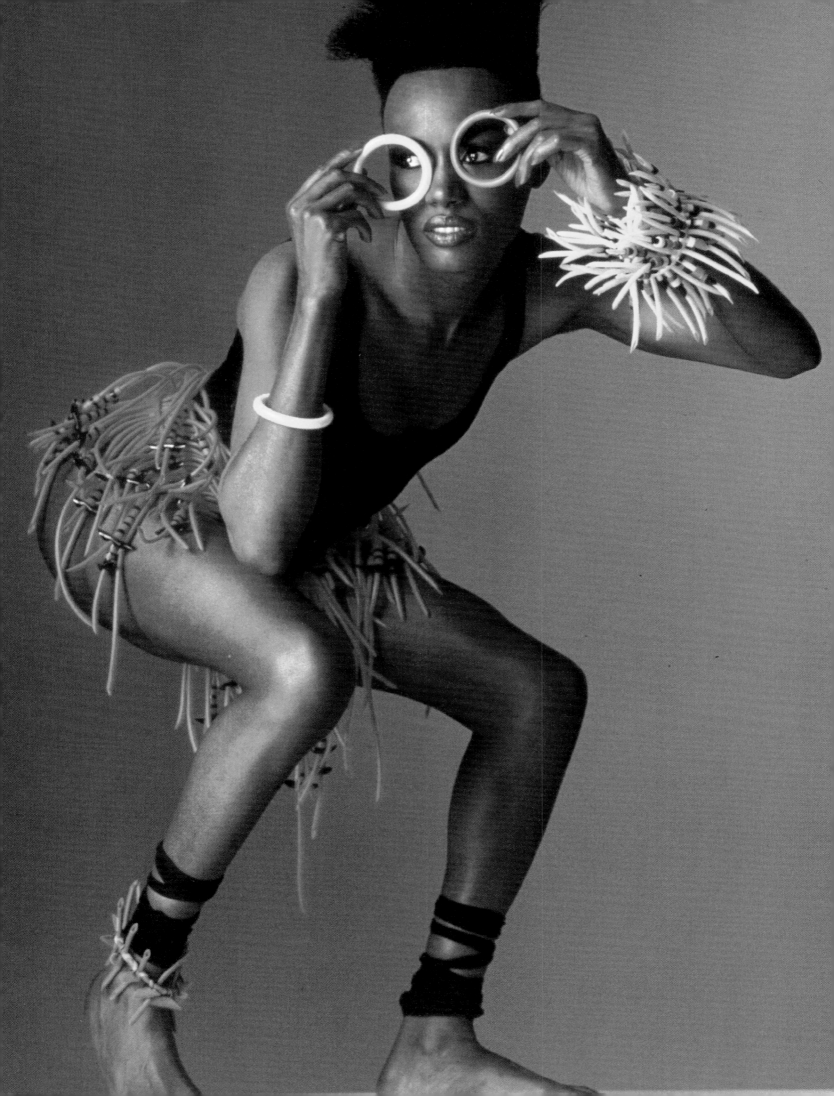

Book *1*

Seeing is Believing

It is only as we collectively change
the way we look at ourselves and the world
that we can change how we are seen.
bell hooks

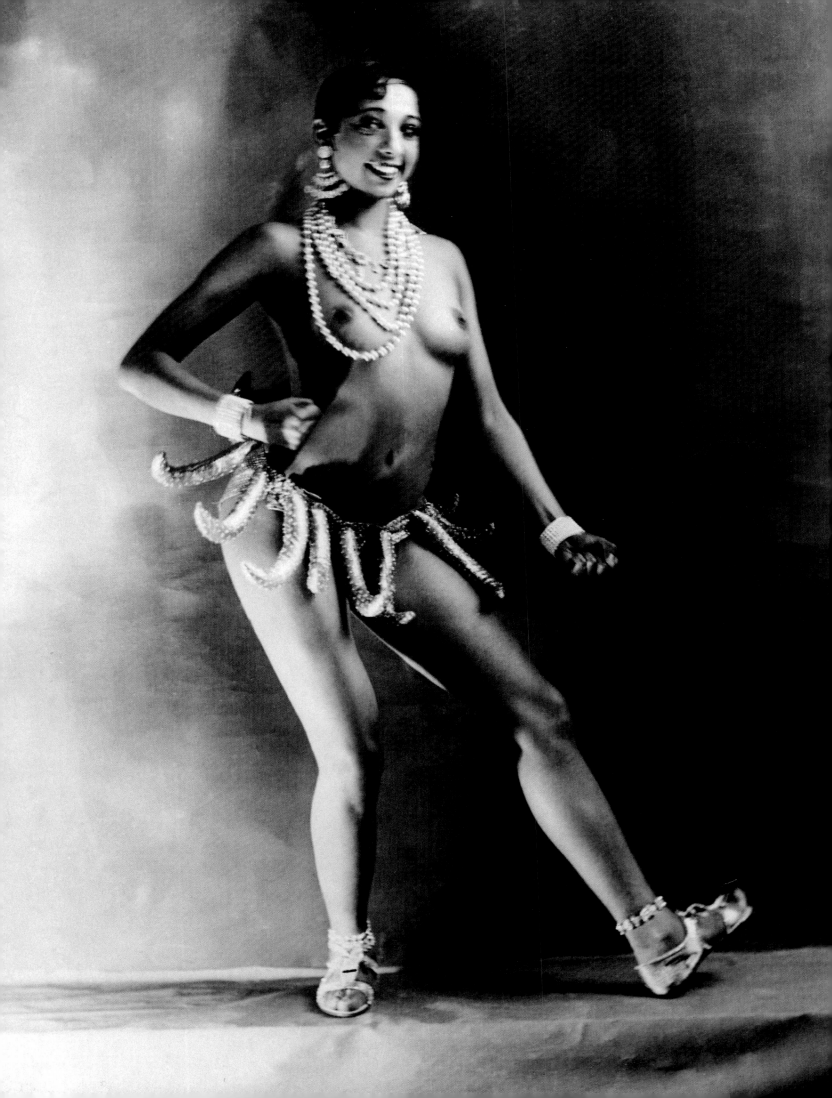

Breakthroughs
Versailles

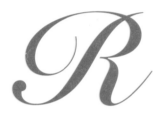

evolutions are often ascribed a defining moment, a time and a place where people can actually see change happening. For Black models the defining moment of change took place at Versailles on a date to remember: November 28, 1973. For the first time, a group of Black American models—no longer isolated, individual stars—walked off an unusually opulent runway and onto the pages of history. *En masse.* At last.

The scene was set: the stage of the Opera House at the Sun King's imperial chateau. To celebrate the restoration—partially financed by wealthy Americans—of Louis XIV's 300-year-old palace, five American fashion designers were invited to show their work along with five French couturiers. The home team: Pierre Cardin, Christian Dior, Hubert de Givenchy, Yves Saint Laurent, and Emanuel Ungaro. Their names alone were synonymous with the "*luxe, calme et volupté*" of exquisite confections in priceless fabrics created for the world's most elegant women. The visitors: Bill Blass, Stephen Burrows, Halston, Anne Klein, and Oscar de la Renta, well-known to the fashion-conscious of the States, but hardly international labels. And so it was the republicans—creative but often mass manufacturers—against the royalists—heirs to an elite tradition of custom-made finery.

Although the numbers were even, the match seemed to favor the Europeans. They were, after all, playing on their home court. They also benefited from a longer history and greater prestige in the market. But times and lifestyles were evolving and so were the clothes real people wanted to wear. Practical sportswear, tasteful but easy-to-wear separates, apparel that befit the increasingly independent working woman dominated the presentations. Against the odds, the Americans scored a resounding triumph.

As *Women's Wear Daily*, the fashion world's newspaper, crowed in its headlines: "Americans came, they sewed, they conquered." The front page article on the Battle of Versailles opened with this tactful surrender: "'It's about time the Paris couture got a good kick in the tail—and the Americans have done it,' said André Oliver, designer at Pierre Cardin." *WWD* then went on to quote the other French couturiers—Marc Bohan of Dior: "Perfect. Just the way it should be." Ungaro: "Extraordinary impact. I've seen those clothes in American stores but up there on the stage they had soul." Saint Laurent: "Fabulous.... Stephen Burrows has a great talent." Givenchy: "There's no other way to describe it than 'show business.' It moved so quickly. The black girls had such stage presence. We should have done more."

Americans came, they sewed, they conquered.

Women's Wear Daily

Josephine Baker in Paris, 1926. Her legacy of flamboyant sexuality, good-humored glamour, and plain hard work inspired many models.

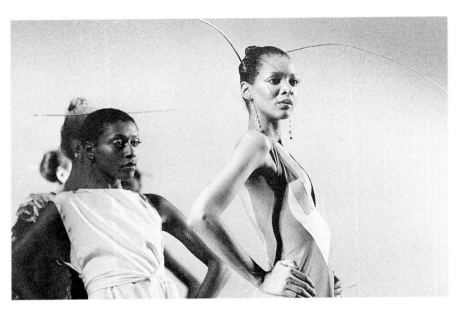

Bethann Hardison and **Ramona Saunders** wearing outfits by **Stephen Burrows** at Versailles, 1973.

And yet it was not a matter of doing more. Rather, it was a matter of being more. For the American designers had a secret weapon that even they did not fully appreciate: Black women. African American women were the surprise element, the shock troops on the runway. Billie Blair, Alva Chinn, Pat Cleveland, Norma Jean Darden, Charlene Dash, Bethann Hardison, Barbara Jackson, Ramona Saunders, and Amina Warsuma were among the two dozen mannequins selected to present the work of the American designers. These women of all shades of beauty brought their own special qualities to the work. In the words of one long-time fashion show director, they epitomized "spirit, energy, personality, music. The clothes were moving. Those Girls made that audience come alive. It was electric, exciting."

Although the American segment lasted only about a half hour, it was unquestionably a revolution. That it took place at Versailles was more than slightly ironic. For even if the dramatic events of the French Revolution were not uppermost on the minds of the Best Dressed at the fashion gala of 1973, certainly the symbolism of the Galérie des Glaces, the famed Hall of Mirrors, could not be overlooked. For centuries wealth and beauty had been reflected, even frozen in the image of European nobility—rich and White. In one unexpected evening those reflections were shattered.

"The most dramatic moment came when Bethann Hardison stalked down the runway in a tight-fitting yellow silk halter by Burrows holding a floor-length train by a tiny ring on her pinky," wrote reporter LaVerne Powlis. "When Hardison reached center stage, she made a dramatic turn and haughtily dropped her train. The audience exploded in a frenzy of approval. They stomped, screamed and tossed their programs into the air." Bill Cunningham, photographer and long-time chronicler of the fashion scene, wrote in the *New York Daily News*: "The bejeweled Paris audience was stunned by the showmanship of the black models from America (as well as with the no-fuss backgrounds and elegant wearability of the American sportswear)....The Parisian aristocrats were both frightened and thrilled."

Fashion was never to be colonized in the same ways again. And Black American models, who had moved over the previous twenty-five years from near invisibility to grudging recognition, now commanded center stage, never again to be ignored.

Alva Chinn described the Versailles gala as "a gift from God. Our side was so simple. We didn't have props and things. We just had us."

Norma Jean Darden added, "Stephen stole the show. People were just clapping for days."

Charlene Dash said simply: "We killed them."

While the American Girls were indeed "the stars of the show...applauded, praised and taken for professional show biz dancers," their material reward was little more than symbolic. After enduring "tears, fights, prima donna trips by both models and designers and 11 hours of rehearsing without food and little water," they had some priceless memories but little else. The models were in fact discussing the formation of a union once they returned to New York in order to upgrade their working conditions and improve their pay. The bare-faced reality was that these fabulous performers received the less than fabulous sums of $25 per day for spending money

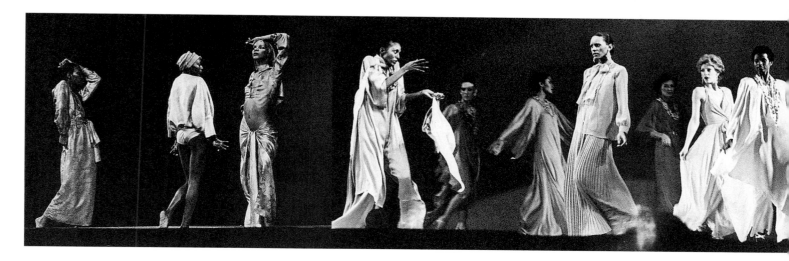

Versailles, 1973. Black models brought drama to the fashion stage.

and $300 in salary for the show. The French models earned even less.

Despite these skirmishes in the trenches, the Black Girls led the Americans to such an overwhelming, uncontested victory that one important American socialite present at the gala enthused: "Not since Eisenhower liberated Paris have the Americans had such a triumph in France."

If the Parisian fashionalities were both frightened and thrilled by this explosion of Black and American womanhood, there was one person on stage who must have found the uproar thoroughly familiar: Josephine Baker. A native-born American who became a French citizen, La Baker entertained during the French segment of the gala at Versailles. Undoubtedly aware of the significance of the Black models' success, she later said, "I'm so proud to be American. I was jumping like a jack-in-the-box." She had special reason to be proud. Almost fifty years earlier, in 1925, she had stunned Paris—both frightening and thrilling her audiences—while starring as a jazz dancer in *La Revue Nègre*, an unprecedented, all-Black musical imported from the States. A short while later at the Folies Bergère in 1926, she first wore the outrageous banana skirt—and little else—that remained a kind of comic, sexy signature for the rest of her long career.

In November, 1973, Josephine Baker was sixty-seven years old and had suffered a stroke earlier that year. Yet after a short recuperation, she was back on the road and the stage, performing tirelessly to support her large family of adopted children. She toured the United States playing to enthusiastic audiences in seventeen cities. She traveled to Israel to celebrate that country's 25th anniversary. And she spent time in Mexico with a man she considered a new husband, her fifth. Illness, like many other dangers, continued to threaten but did not stop her. When she sang at Versailles, her impact on the Black models was tremendous and very personal. She was old enough to be their grandmother. And with the respect due one's grandmother, Alva described La Baker as "one of the most generous persons I ever met in my life, generous in spirit. At one point she was sitting on the side and she said, 'I'm so proud of you Girls. I'm so happy to see all of you Black Girls here. You make me proud.' Was that not a special moment in time?"

Charlene also recounted a poignant story: "I was headed down some very steep stairs to go to the rest room when I saw a little old lady waiting by the stairwell. I asked if she needed help, and she took my arm. Only then did I realize it was Josephine Baker. She was absolutely incredible. She sang, she pranced around the stage with these heavy headdresses and heels five inches high, and then she sat perched on the piano. I could never do it. But right there and then, she was just a little old lady. She was her age, but she could act young. I think that's what killed her."

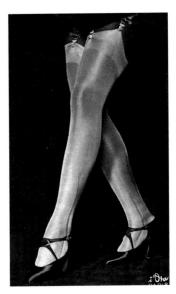

Josephine Baker's legendary assets: Her legs, her smile.

A year and a half later, on April 14, 1975, Josephine Baker died in Paris of a cerebral hemorrhage. A few days before she had celebrated yet another triumphant return to the musical stage at the Bobino Theatre. She fulfilled a dream that she had described when only twenty-one years old. "To live is to dance," she had written. "I would like to die out of breath, exhausted, at the end of a dance."

While La Baker was not a fashion model in the strictest sense of the word, she was, in the largest sense, one of the great models of the 20th century. As a highly paid entertainer and entrepreneur, she grew accustomed to luxurious clothes, maintaining for most of her life the lithe, gorgeous figure for which she was renowned. And with the skill of a consummate makeup artist, she was able to contour her life, highlighting real success, rouging the rough spots and deepening dramatic shadows.

The Nefertiti of Now

Josephine Baker was born in St. Louis on June 3, 1906. Family poverty and an adventuresome spirit led her away from her mother's house when she was still a young teenager. Twice married by the time she was sixteen, she had traveled on the TOBA—Theatrical Owners' Booking Association, more popularly known as Tough On Black Asses or the chitlin'—

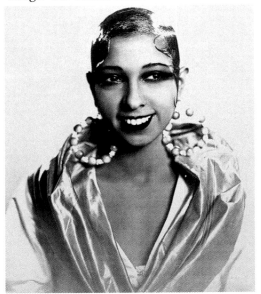

circuit with a Black vaudeville troupe. After stints with Eubie Blake and Noble Sissle's ground-breaking production *Shuffle Along*, and follow-ups in *Bamville* and *The Chocolate Dandies*, she took a chance, signing on for an overseas production organized by a wealthy White American woman, Caroline Dudley Reagan.

La Revue Nègre opened in October, 1925, at the Théâtre des Champs-Elysées on the Avenue Montaigne, in what was and still is a sophisticated neighborhood of luxurious hotels and exclusive fashion salons. Josephine's opening piece was a clowning, cross-eyed contortion in the vaudeville tradition which contrasted dramatically with her finale, the notorious *"Danse sauvage"* performed in a scanty, feathery costume with her male partner, Joe Alex. The show was an immediate *succès de scandale*.

Picasso called her "the Nefertiti of now." Influenced to some degree by African masks and newly discovered treasures in Egypt, the European at world was opening up to other ways of seeing. But, top hats and monocles aside, was *La Revue Nègre* art or vulgarity? More to the point, who was she? And with that short, slick hair, what was she? Was Josephine Baker an exotic primitive come to exorcise European morality of its pretensions and hypocrisies? Could it be that Europe's layers of civilization had been peeled back and its sexual center revealed by one nearly nude Black girl? Was she just the latest incarnation of the savage, this time simply sexual, forget the "noble"? Was the incredible success of the show the beginning of the end of white-skinned civilization? These and many other unanswerable questions ignited discussion in newspapers and cafés, all the while fueling business at the box office wherever she performed.

Throughout Europe people of color were caricaturized and treated with paternalistic disdain. Superior sexual prowess, cannibalism, and illiteracy were often alluded to in the satirical cartoons, commercial advertisements and product labels of the time. American jazz and African art were felt by many Whites to

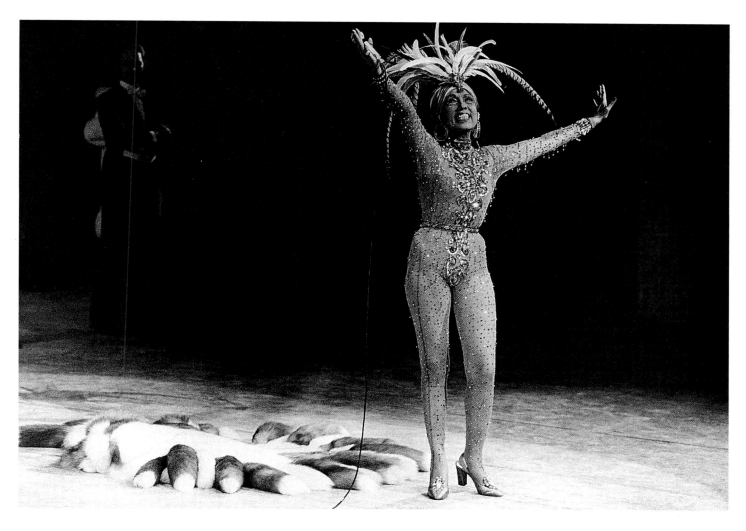

La Baker performing at Versailles, 1973.

spring from some naturally spontaneous source of creativity inherent in those distant peoples who lived so close to nature. Cultural condescension was in the air and in the attitudes. It would take wars and mass political movements for independence to change things. And it would take daring individuals who embodied and also challenged the stereotypes to give a name to the change. Josephine Baker was one of those pioneers. She did not start out that way. On stage she became a frankly artificial yet glamorous and exciting character. Off stage she was an idealistic, romantic charmer. For the daughter of a washerwoman who told tales of living in the East St. Louis community of abandoned railroad cars called Boxcar Town, she had come a long way.

In 1935, ten years after she had left the States she optimistically returned for the first time. She was engaged to dance and sing in the Ziegfeld Follies of 1936 in New York City. The show starred Fannie Brice and included the sensational young dancers, the Nicholas Brothers. It also featured music by George Gershwin and Vernon Duke, sets and costumes by Vincente Minelli, and choreography by George Balanchine. Bob Hope's name was paired with hers on the marquee. But despite this concentration of talent, Baker's reviews were mixed to disastrous. The segregated accommodations offended her. The unattractive wardrobe presented to her could not compare with the costumes she was used to at the Folies Bergère and the Casino de Paris. When she returned to France in 1936, she was disillusioned with American life. She was to spend most of the next four decades living out her own legend, embroidering on the gossamer fantasies of her career and the character—some say caricature—she had become. Beneath the glitter of entertainment, however, was always the dream of a peaceful world free of poverty and race tension. During World War II she joined the French resistance. As a fervent supporter of Charles de Gaulle, she did secret intelligence work in Marseilles and North Africa for which she was later awarded the Medal of the Resistance and the Legion of Honor. It was in the uniform of the Women's Auxiliary of the Free French Air Force that she attended the historic civil rights March in Washington in August, 1963.

In the '50s and '60s she created her famous Rainbow Tribe, adopting twelve children of different races, religions, and nationalities. Eventually bankrupted by her dreams, Josephine Baker was laid to rest in Monte Carlo in 1975.

If the legend of La Baker survives today it is due in large part to the irrepressible talent for glamour and show business that many 20th century Black women have epitomized. To a society over-eager to limit them to images of handkerchief-headed mammies and hot-blooded bad girls, these women often showed a completely different face. They

Josephine Baker, the elegant exotic.

A forceful combination of pose, props, and lighting would figure prominently in the developing art of fashion photography.

became less willing to play undignified roles for others' amusement.

Black fashion models could challenge such pernicious stereotypes precisely because they had no lines to read, no songs to sing, no dances to perform. They had only to be their beautiful selves. That simple recognition made their victory at Versailles complete. What few models and even fewer of the audience knew was the history that had brought them to such splendor and the future that they would help to shape.

Paving the Way

I got a start by giving
myself a start. I believe in push
and we must push ourselves.
Madam C.J. Walker

The models who caused such a sensation at Versailles in 1973 owed their success to many Black women of style and substance who paved the way for them. As free as the Girls appeared, they were firmly rooted in a tradition of working women—far older than professional modeling—which combined qualities of the flamboyant show girl, the dedicated entrepreneur, and the ageless beauty. Josephine Baker, Madam C.J. Walker, and Lena Horne would figure among their foremothers as women who dealt creatively and successfully with being Black and beautiful.

If beauty lies in the eyes of the beholder, why does the recorded history of Africans in America leave so many blank spaces? With a few scattered exceptions Black beauty—and images of the same—were kept a family secret until the Civil War of the 1960s. Who knew what Black beauty was? How could it be measured? What use did it serve? Despite cloudy answers to these questions, some saw opportunity in the confusion.

In the early years of the 20th century Black newspapers were crowded with the advertisements of beauty culturists and manufacturers of beauty products. Black-No-More, Fair-Plex, Cocotone Skin

Whitener, Golden Brown Ointment, and Complexion Wonder Creme were sold to Black men and women not only to lighten and brighten dark skin, but also to lighten and brighten one's social and professional prospects. Even more than skin color, however, problems with hair were likened to a crown of thorns. Paralleling advertisements for skin preparations, Black newspapers were loaded with information about anti-kink ointments, hair-growing preparations, special soaps and shampoos, combs, wigs, beauty parlors, and competing hair-dressing schools and systems. Kinkilla, La Creole Hair Restorer, and Ford's Original Ozonized Ox Marrow were just a few of the distinctively named products. While Kink-No-More—called Conk for short—was used by many jazz musicians and stylish men, the great majority of products and services were aimed at Black women.

As Harlem developed into the quintessential African American community during the second decade of the 20th century, successful beauticians rose to positions of wealth and social influence. Foremost among them was Madam C.J. Walker. She was not only the first Black millionairess; she was also credited with being the first self-made woman millionaire in the United States. In 1919 one writer commented that the "largest and most lucrative business enterprises conducted by colored people in America have been launched by women." It was no coincidence that these businesses were based on beauty.

Two Dollars and a Dream

Madam C.J. Walker was born Sarah Jane Breedlove two years after the end of the War Between the States on Dec. 23, 1867, in Delta, Louisiana. Seeking to escape miserable family conditions, she moved to Vicksburg, Mississippi, and married at age fourteen. By age twenty, however, she was a widow and the mother of a young daughter. Always seeking a better life, she moved upriver to St. Louis, where, like Josephine Baker who would follow, she worked as a washerwoman. Knowing that such back-breaking drudgery would

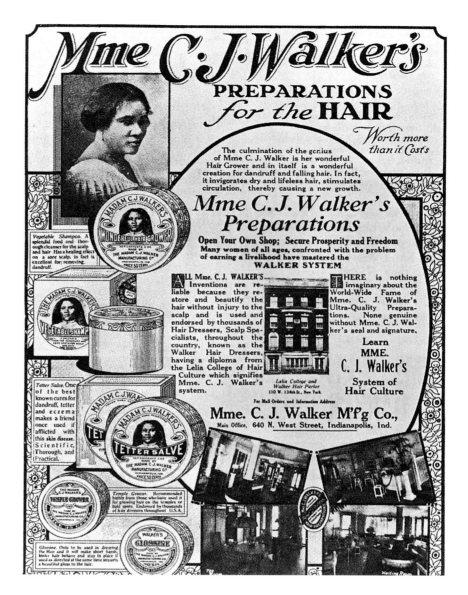

never provide the material security she craved and the social polish she admired, she set about formulating a hair treatment that would answer her own needs and those of other Black women. Her first products— Wonderful Hair Grower, Vegetable Shampoo, and Glossine—included ingredients which she claimed appeared to her in a dream. The treatment used botanical elements imported from Africa and tools which had originated in Europe, such as a heated iron comb and a curling iron— mentioned as far back as the first century A.D. by Petronius "to 'convert' non-Ethiopian hair to Ethiopian hair." Once she achieved the desired results she moved to a new frontier in Denver, Colorado, where she married newspaperman Charles Joseph Walker, whose journalistic expertise helped her business to expand greatly.

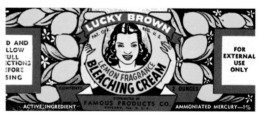

Madam Walker was her first model and her own best advertisement. The jars and tins which carried her likeness suggested to her customers that if an ordinary Black woman—who looked just like them—could turn her life around, they could do the same. In the process, women made fortunes for other women.

Bleaching creams testified to racial ambivalence.

A forceful saleswoman and intrepid entrepreneur, Madam Walker initially sold her products door to door. Later she traveled throughout the country's heartland, settling first in Pittsburgh and eventually in Indianapolis, where she established her manufacturing plant. Her advertisements in newspapers serving the Black communities generated a steadily increasing stream of mail orders from across the country. In person she journeyed to hundreds of communities selling her products, demonstrating her procedures, and above all exhorting women to go into business for themselves.

Her success was extraordinary. From "two dollars and a dream," she built a business whose factory covered an entire city block in Indianapolis and whose yearly payroll exceeded $200,000 in 1917. Headquartered in an elaborate townhouse in Harlem, she operated a network of beauty culture colleges extending from Washington, D.C. to Dallas, which advertised "low-cost, pay-as-you-go courses" along with her expanded line of hairdressings, ointments, and cosmetics.

The proof was in the profits. Hers became a household name throughout Black America. From there she extended her business into twenty-nine foreign countries in the Caribbean and Central and South America. In the Roaring Twenties, which she would not live to see, slicked-down short bobs became the style for women of all colors. In Paris Josephine Baker would promote a comparable hair pomade, Bakerfix, which White French women bought with enthusiasm. Imitation, the sincerest form of flattery, had thus come full circle, making some people enormously rich along the way.

While Madam Walker lived lavishly, she never forgot her humble origins. Her ultimate goal was to use her wealth to uplift her race. To this end she provided material support for struggling Black artists and schools, as well as for organizations headed by political thinkers as diverse as Booker T. Washington, W.E.B. DuBois, Mary McLeod Bethune, and Ida B. Wells-Barnett. A committed race woman, she respectfully tolerated divergent opinions as long as they worked for the betterment of Black people. Never shy of the public spotlight and indignant over the army's official policy of segregation during World War I, she was part of a delegation sent to protest that injustice before President Woodrow Wilson and to petition him—unsuccessfully—to make lynching a federal crime. At age fifty-one she was planning to attend the Versailles Peace Conference in 1919 as a representative of William Monroe Trotter's National Equal Rights League when her extraordinary life ended on May 25, 1919.

The bulk of her estate, estimated from one to two million dollars, was bequeathed to her only child, A'Lelia, who was later to play an important role as a socialite and arts patron during the Harlem Renaissance. Large sums were left to charities, old folks' homes, and educational and political institutions.

Even the great scholar and activist, W.E.B. Du Bois praised Madam Walker for transforming a people in a single generation by revolutionizing their personal habits and appearance. While subsequent generations continue to debate whether processed hair leads to processed minds, beyond dispute is the fact that before she died, Madam Walker employed thousands of people in her factories, laboratories, and schools. More than illusions, she gave tangible "dignified employment to thousands of women who would othwise have had to make their living in domestic service."

Statistics show that by 1920—the year that American women won the right to vote—almost 40% of Black women were working. One could argue that virtually 100% of Black women were working, in or out of their homes; domestic service in White households held the majority of them in neo-slavery. Emancipated by law, they were still the cooks, maids, nannies, and laundresses for others.

Financial independence was seen as the key to a better life. Often that key opened the door to a neighborhood beauty shop. In segregated America the route to economic advance was traditionally paved by businesses that serviced the Black community: barbering and hair-dressing, tailoring and dressmaking, catering and cooking, insurance and undertaking. More than a few of the leading families of African-American heritage today owe their beginnings to such enterprises.

Madam C.J. Walker appeared at a propitious moment in history with an auspicious program. She trained sales agents who dressed neatly in white shirt-waists and long black skirts as they went door to door selling and demonstrating hair growers, pressing oils, salves, and shampoos. Most of the women who bought these products did so not out of mere vanity—a luxury which hardly fit within their budget—but with the ultimate goal of finding a better job and improving living conditions for their family. The Walker motto: "Look your best to succeed." If contemporary Black women—and models in particular—can fling their hair around with confident abandon, much credit must go to Madam Walker and her colleagues, beauty culturists and keepers of the flame. They never confused their income with their identity. They understood what Black women needed to progress and what America demanded as the price of that progress.

After World War I mass migration from the rural South to the urban North was moving at high speed. African Americans competed for jobs and housing with newly-arrived European immigrants. Established Whites who resented the influx of assertive Blacks—and especially, returning veterans who had served victoriously in the European war—scandalized the nation with a reign of lynching and murder during the Red Summer of 1919. In defiance of entrenched and violent opposition, the Black middle class was growing, organizing, and making its voice heard. New political organizations sprung up, and to spread the word they published periodicals. Whatever their ideology, they all—including *Opportunity* (Urban League), *The Crisis* (NAACP), and *The Messenger*—appealed to the eye and featured attractive Black women on their covers. Pretty faces were used to sell the politics of the day.

Lena, Helena, and Light Egyptian

Perhaps no single woman has been a more enduring representative of Black beauty than Lena Horne. Her career as a singer and actress for over sixty years has given her a unique platform from which to view the world—and to be viewed. The flawless copper complexion, the long, silky hair, the glistening smile, the sophisticated manner, all animated a beauty that seemed somewhere to be making fun of itself. While cabaret and movie audiences gasped at her irresistible appeal, the Black world shouted Yes, at last, one of us. She was the first glamorous Black Hollywood star.

Lena Horne, the ingenue.

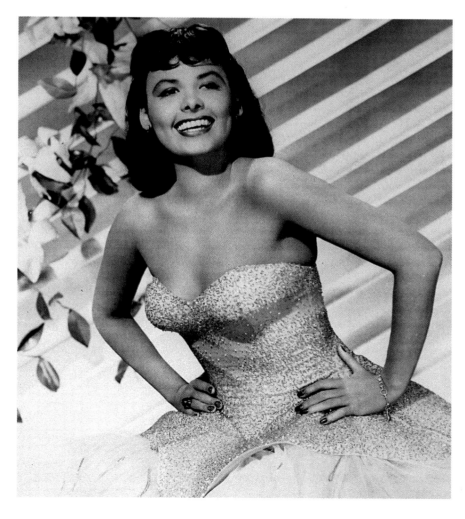

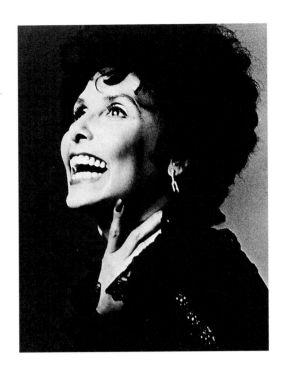

Lena Horne, the survivor. Her life is proof that beauty can endure and commitment can enrich.

Lena Horne was born on June 30, 1917, in Brooklyn, New York, at the confluence of several historical tides. The United States had just entered the Great War in Europe against Germany. African Americans from the South were migrating in record numbers to the industrialized, liberalized North and the virgin Western states only to find that all was not paradise beyond the Cotton Belt. The NAACP organized a protest parade in which 10,000 Black people marched down New York's Fifth Avenue in total awe-inspiring silence to protest the murderous persistence and spread of lynching.

As her daughter Gail Lumet was to write many years later, "Baby Lena Horne was already an NAACP cover girl at the age of two and a half. She starred in the October 1919 issue of the NAACP Branch Bulletin" as one of the youngest members of the fledgling fire-brand organization.

Other political pressures in the States were building up advocating women's rights and the prohibition of liquor. Still another note was sounding. Despite the death of ragtime composer Scott Joplin and the closing of the notorious Storyville district in New Orleans—both in 1917—jazz was percolating all across the country, enough so that the next decade would be named in its honor. The 20th century was rushing headlong into dramatic change.

Raised by paternal grandparents, emotionally distant, proud members of Brooklyn's light-skinned Black bourgeoisie, Lena lived in a household run with "a kind of polite ferocity." The Do's included standing straight, speaking clearly, and sitting still. The Don'ts forbade cringing, sulking, crying, and, most of all, being like her mother, who had done the unthinkable. She had gone on the stage. When Grandmother Horne died, Lena went there also.

Sixteen when she joined the chorus line at the segregated Cotton Club in Harlem, Lena worked three shows a night, seven days a week, earning a hefty $25 during the depths of the Depression. After a short run on Broadway as a quadroon in what she called "a silly

thing" about voodoo, Lena went on tour as the girl singer with the Noble Sissle Society Orchestra. Sissle helped refine her image into a romantic, "somewhat shy and serious soubrette," and suggested changing Lena into Helena, a stage name with more class. As a singer at the defiantly integrated Café Society in Greenwich Village, the Little Troc in Los Angeles, an other important cabarets, and as a film actress under contract to Metro-Goldwyn-Mayer, she was to alternate names as she alternated personalities and identities.

No matter what name she used, however, the figure, and the style became immediately identifiable. Her appearance in *Cabin in the Sky* and *Stormy Weather*, Black musicals of the early '40s, helped to make them excitingly successful films. Already a darling of the Black press, she reached a new level of celebrity appearing in *Time*, *Life*, and *Newsweek* magazines all in the same week early in 1943. She became a crossover sex-symbol, the dream woman men of all colors loved to fantasize about and a popular pin-up for Black GIs fighting in the still-segregated American armed forces. She became a model of elegance for women to imitate. And she became a weapon—her film career a test case which the NAACP used to pressure the Hollywood studios for better roles. "No maids or jungle types" for her, she insisted, with her father and the NAACP backing her up in front of movie mogul Louis B. Mayer. Yet no romantic heroines were scripted for her either.

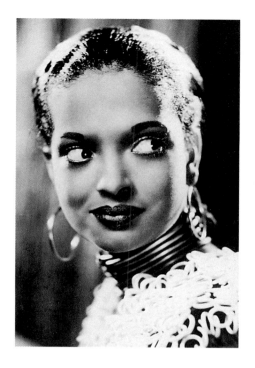 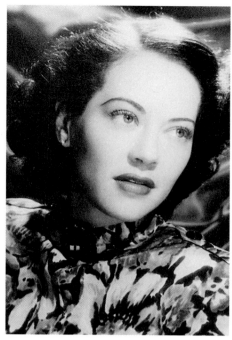 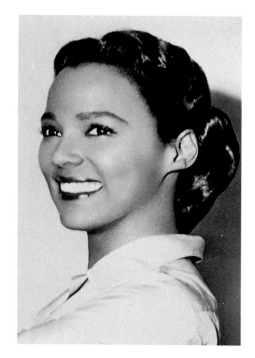

As with Nina Mae McKinney, Fredi Washington, and Dorothy Dandridge, Hollywood never quite knew what to do with Lena Horne. Neither stereotypically Black nor passably White nor hypocritically Other, she fit no traditional role and inspired no revolutionary one. Her first screen test after signing with M-G-M was a disaster. The makeup used on her gave the grotesque impression of "some white person trying to do a part in blackface." Consequently Max Factor himself was called in to help create a more realistically colored makeup base. The result was a beautiful shade called "Light Egyptian." Ironically, her "color" was successfully used to paint White actresses for Black or mulatto roles. As her lonely star continued to shine in limbo in the Hollywood sky, she complained that her basic screen posture consisted of being "pasted to a pillar to sing [her] song." And often that song segment would be cut for the film version shown in Southern theatres.

While she continued to evolve her own style as an entertainer, the emotional reserve and apparent aloofness she had developed as a child served to protect her from the racial and sexual harassment she had to endure. This protective shell also served to isolate her from the whole-hearted support and recognition of Black people, who confused her charmed life on screen with her real life as a Black woman. It took her thirty years—from first setting foot on the stage of the Cotton Club in 1933 to "the long, hot summer of 1963" and the

Civil Rights Movement—to establish her own identity as a validly lovable and loving human being.

As young people began to challenge American racism through their courageous protests at lunch counters, on school campuses, and in the streets, she began to awaken. Despite her fears of being misunderstood and rejected by Black people, Lena went South for the first time in decades. The prodigal daughter returned to the bosom of Black America where she flowered like an autumn rose with revitalized confidence and artistry. In 1981, almost fifty years after her Cotton Club debut—and a painful decade after the deaths of her father, mother, husband, and son—Lena hit the stage again in a spectacular production, part song, part self, all forcefully alive with feeling. *The Lady and Her Music* became the longest-running one-person show on Broadway. In 1994, ten years after she closed in London, Lena Horne released a heartfelt new album of songs, *We'll Be Together Again*. She has continued to be discovered by the generations who have grown up after the Movement and re-discovered by thousands who knew—or thought they knew—who she was. She has surprised them all. By being strong and tender, funny and sentimental, angry and accepting, but most of all, by being so miraculously alive, she left no doubt that the beautiful Black woman could survive with body and soul intact.

Nina Mae McKinney. With *Hallelujah* in 1929, she opened Hollywood's door to actresses of color only to find follow-up quality roles nonexistent.

Fredi Washington. Although she played a tragic mulatto in the 1934 blockbuster *Imitation of Life*, she refused to pass for White in real life and helped organize the Negro Actors Guild.

Dorothy Dandridge. For her fiery role in 1954's *Carmen Jones*, she became the first Black woman nominated for an Academy Award as Best Actress.

Beginnings
First Steps

To limit me would be a blunder

For I can make the seven wonders wonder

And I haven't even gotten started yet.

*Beah Richards
for Audrey Smaltz*

Models are made, not born. They do not exit the womb with perfect complexions, enviable hair, and long, thin bodies. Holograms of *Vogue* covers do not glow auspiciously above their heads. They come out squalling and wrinkled like everybody else. And then they grow. They grow up in circumstances as unique as their careers become. In big cities and small towns, in poor families or well-to-do, with one parent, two parents or several generations in a household. There is no feeding formula that guarantees beauty, or more importantly, success in the business of beauty.

While many models were educated in the performing arts, modeling itself was not considered one. Combining elements of dance, drama, and perhaps sculpture, modeling did not share the social recognition and respect that were accorded these art forms—quite the contrary. Fashion models, latter-day descendants of artist's models, were often considered kissing-kin to prostitutes. No amount of accredited training could eliminate that moral shadow in some people's minds. To complicate matters even further, Black women have always had to bear the onus of being considered promiscuous, oversexed, and irresponsible. In the first centuries of American society, the rape of Black women by White men was not uncommon, and yet the victims were portrayed as the perpetrators.

This double punishment of Black women—firstly, the crime done against them; secondly, the unjust conviction of guilt—has helped to thwart aspirations on many levels. Some repressive internalized authority, a sad legacy of slavery, decided the parameters of our existence from what we could wear to who we could be. Edward S. Green's *National Capital Code of Etiquette Dedicated to the Colored Race*, published in 1920, urged Black women to say little, to strive to be inconspicuous, to wear dark colors and black stockings. Red was for bad girls, we were told. Dark girls couldn't— or shouldn't—wear bright colors. If we could manage to escape domestic service, we should aim to educate ourselves to be teachers, nurses, social workers or just plain good wives to good men. What would give a young Black woman raised in that environment the idea—and the nerve to even have the idea—that she could be a model?

Dorothea Towles, the first fully professional Black model, answered that question with one of her own: "Why can't I do this?" In the United States of the late '40s there were probably more reasons why she could not than why she could. But she let none of the negatives deter her. In the course of developing a unique international and national fashion career Dorothea Towles paved the way for future generations of ambitious, creative women.

The question remained: Just what did a model do, after all, but display her face and body with no apparent technique?

Each model would find her own answer to that question, answers that probably changed with time and experience. At the start of her career, however, all a model needed to do was be: be fresh, be new, be interesting, be different, and most important, be herself.

Models' backgrounds revealed a tremendous diversity of self-awareness, family support, conscientious planning, and courage, yet there always seemed to be a surprise element, an unexpected opportunity, or a moment of discovery. Many models were tapped on the shoulder while they were pursuing totally different objectives.

As a child in Haiti in the 1950s, Jany Tomba's "greatest fantasy was to be a doctor and to work in Africa." In the United States, she became a medical assistant, and while working in a doctor's office in the late '60s, met an editor from *Glamour*. Although she "had no ideas about modeling," this chance encounter led to a career that lasted for over two decades. "It's strange how life turns out," she said.

Other models could say the same, Veronica Webb, among them. She came from Detroit to New York in the late '80s "to do a double major of fine art and environmental design at Parsons. Eventually, I got interested in something else and I changed my major. In the meantime, I had taken a semester off and was working as a cashier in this store in SoHo. This man came in who looked like a biker and asked me if I was a model. I said, 'No, of course not.' To me he was like some kind of Pepe LePew character. I didn't really pay any attention even when he gave me his card with the address of the Click agency. When you're not in the business, you've only heard of Elite and Ford.

"In high school I was very into magazines. But when you looked through them, especially American magazines, you didn't see many pictures of Black women. The most popular Girls were exotic White beauties; they had dark hair and big lips and that was the only reason I identified with them so strongly. But the other women didn't look so different. There was a continuity, like the look could be duplicated. I knew I didn't look like any of those people, and I didn't look like any movie star in the past. At the time I started, there was really no aesthetic vein for me to fall into. It seemed

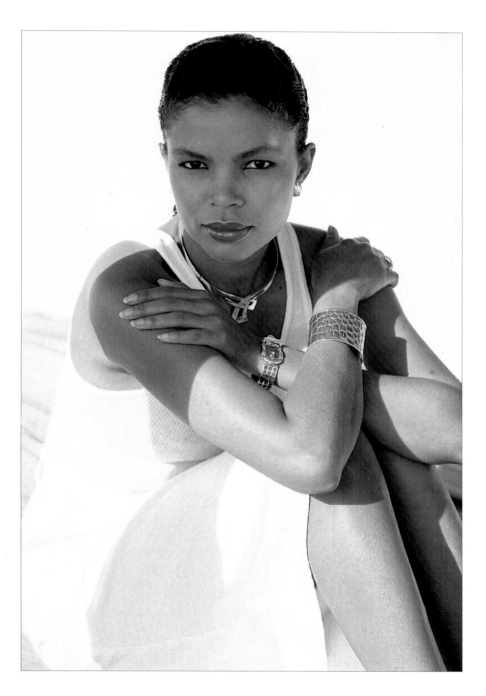

Jany Tomba. She was discovered working in a doctor's office.

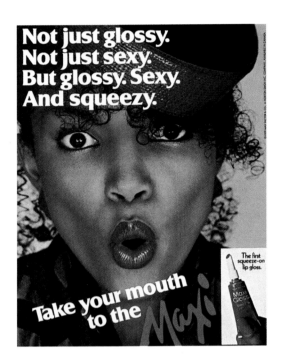

Not just glossy.
Not just sexy.
But glossy. Sexy.
And squeezy.

The first
squeeze-on
lip gloss.

Take your mouth
to the *Maxi*

Two views of **Jany Tomba**. Her natural, versatile good looks were the foundation of a long-lasting career.

so improbable. I had never met anybody who was a model." After more persuasion, Veronica took the plunge. Within a few years she would become one of the most sought-after models in the world both in print and on the runway.

Some young Black women were surrounded in their youth by compliments, affirmations, and encouragement. As a matter of family pride as well as individual initiative, they were groomed to perform in public, learning early to project their personality and to control the intensity of their light. Such preparation still did not make them models or mean that they even wanted to model.

For Sheila Johnson, "acting started even before modeling. I was serious. I was a drama major at Emerson College before I transferred to study with Lee Strasberg in New York in the late '70s. I was going to be an actress no matter what." Suddenly the opportunity came for her to model. Superstar Beverly Johnson was pregnant. "I had been at Elite for about a month and a half and Tony Barboza, the photographer, believed in me. He got on the phone with two of his best clients, *Essence* and Avon." Sheila's first bookings: a cover and an eight-page spread in *Essence*; a two-day ad shoot for Avon which

turned into a commercial; and a Max Factor ad. "I had carte blanche," Sheila said, "the whole hair and makeup. I had never seen myself made up like that. It was great."

During her girlhood days near Cape Cod, Sheila described herself as "your typical adventure girl. All the plays, all the beauty contests, prom queen, Miss Duxbury. My mother started pushing me from then. She knew I was going to be something." Sheila had been trained to win, and as a model she continued to do so.

When Robin Townsend, a native of Pasadena, California, entered the Tournament of Roses pageant in the '80s she was participating in the sister act of an all-American New Year's Day tradition the nationally televised Rose Bowl football game. "It wasn't like a beauty pageant where you wear bathing suits and anything like that," she said. "It was very conservative. They choose contestants not only for their looks, but also for their intelligence, how well they speak, how well they walk, how they present themselves. Over seven hundred girls tried out and in the end there were only seven on the court. The last time we got together was in front of the media; the newspapers, all the networks, parents,

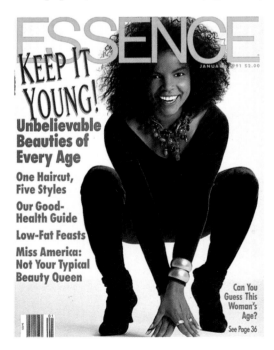

friends, Tournament of Roses Associates, the President, the Grand Marshal. I was the last girl to be named. And I was the only Black woman in the court."

Traditionally, the last girl named is the Queen. The *Los Angeles Times* and other publications called to do interviews with Robin because they had gotten "wind of the fact that she was actually chosen queen" but had been removed. The Tournament of Roses wasn't "ready for a Black queen," she said and yet refused to give them the story "about what really happened." Years later she was still reluctant to talk about it. "It was not a very good time in my life because that's the first time I'd ever been hit with prejudice. It was very difficult for me to accept, but there was nothing I could do about it. I was only seventeen or eighteen years old."

Time and conditions had changed by the time Sheila Johnson and Robin Townsend came along in the '70s and '80s, when they could make the splash that they did by winning—or almost winning. Twenty or thirty years earlier people of color claimed victory by simply being allowed to integrate the competition. Winning meant being allowed to run.

Audrey Smaltz, "born, bred, buttered, jellied, jammed, and honeyed in Harlem," described her experiences in the '50s with her usual flamboyant confidence: "It seems as though I was born six feet tall. I was tall before my time. Models were not tall when I was modeling; most were 5′5″ 5′6″ 5′7″ And I didn't say I was six feet. I said I was 5′11″, 'cause six feet, that was a bit much. My first modeling assignment was a job as a 'Say Hey' kid for Willie Mays's Day at Giant Stadium in 1954. I won two or three beauty contests, Miss Transit, Miss Medina which led up to Miss Shriner. I made *Time*, *True*, and *Life*, all these magazines. It was fabulous. Through Ophelia DeVore and her modeling agency, I was the first Black they allowed in the Miss New York City contest—that led to the Miss America contest. I did this wonderful skit that Beah Richards, the actress, wrote and taught me. It was called *You Wanna Bet*:

Ladies and gentlemen,
There's something I must tell you
And I hope it will compel you
'Cause your attitude
has got me in asnit.
To limit me would be a blunder
For I can make the seven wonders wonder
And I haven't even gotten started yet.

"A Black columnist with the *Amster-*

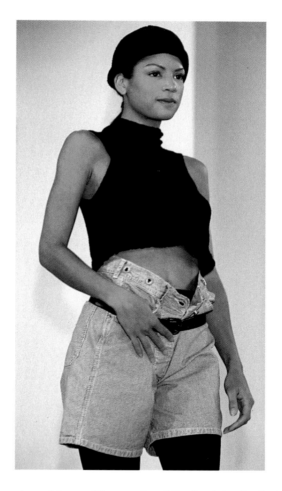

Veronica Webb. She made the improbable world of fashion her own.

dam News, Thomasina Norford looked White, so the judges didn't know who she was. And the judges, Thomasina told me, because she later wrote it up, they really wanted me in the worst way to be the winner, to be Miss New York City. But those White folks said that I could not be the winner. I was one of the runner-ups." Audrey smiled with philosophical acceptance and said, "It was a good experience for me."

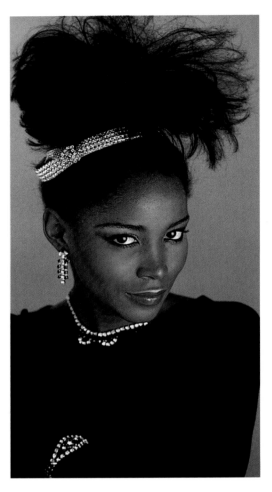

Magic Jordan. She let no obstacle deter her.

If winning top prize was out of the question for that time period, a winning attitude shows up again and again in models' stories. Long before Vanessa Williams, a blonde, blue-eyed African American, was crowned Miss America in 1983—a historic first—Black women were competing against each other in pageants. These intraracial competitions were as revealing of the judges' criteria and the contestants' fortitude as the later interracial contests would be.

Magic Jordan, who hit the New York modeling scene at the end of the '70s, was determined never to let any obstacle—White racism, Black prejudice or even a major material loss—keep her out of the competition. "In my senior year in high school in Orlando, Florida, I was first lieutenant to the queen. The judges liked me but I was too dark, so the light-skinned girl with the long hair won. When I started to get into college activi-

ties, I was head majorette, I was campus queen, and I was Miss Black Atlanta."

As Sharon Jordan, she moved from Orlando to Atlanta to attend Morris Brown College, eventually graduating from the Art Institute as a fashion merchandising major. In the meantime she caught a dose of fashion fever that changed her name. "The name Magic came from a wonderful black chiffon dress that I wore in a show put on by some designers in Atlanta. I really worked this dress, and the commentator said, 'We're going to call her Magic.' The name stuck."

The week she was to enter the Miss Black Atlanta contest a fire destroyed her apartment. "I had nothing at that time, only the clothes on my back. But all my friends helped me. I had shaved my hair so it was just laid back, short hair. I was the last one they expected to win because everybody was fair with long hair. Everybody. I was number thirteen, and I won. In the Georgia state competition I was first runner-up but the girl that won was fair-skinned and had long hair, too.

"I came to New York in 1979 for an international model contest at the Waldorf Astoria. All the agency people were there, including Zoli and Wilhemina. I won across the board for everything."

After they have gone on to expanded careers many models must chuckle inwardly, restraining the desire to say "I told you so" to the doubters and disbelievers they've met along the way. But many were just as ignorant of their beauty, considering themselves nothing exceptional.

"Modeling was not something I ever wanted to do," said Gamiliana, a native of Chicago who started traveling on the international show circuit in the late '80s. "I dabbled as a young child but I was really goofy-looking, with glasses and the whole works. Nobody ever told me I should model. I was going to the Art Institute of Chicago, studying fashion. My measurements were very close to the dress forms that we used. We couldn't just always work on these dress forms, so every now and then we'd have a live

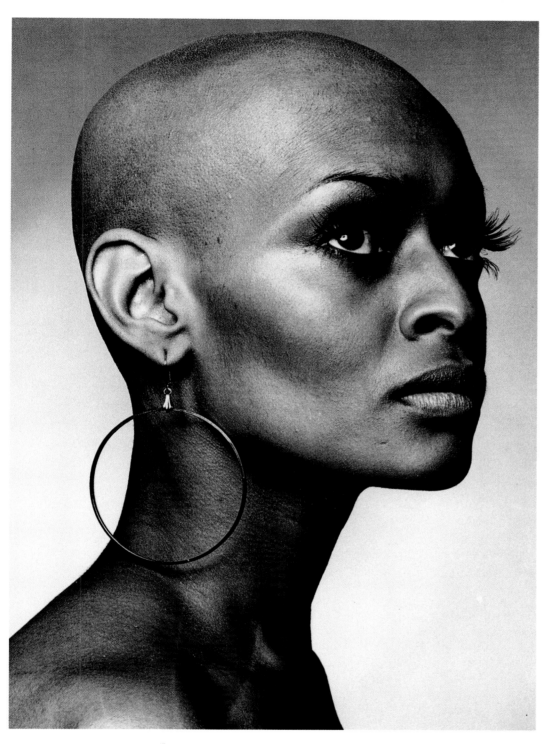

Pat Evans. She made the most daring physical statement of any model.

model. I would do fittings for the other students, but it got to be a problem because it interrupted my work and interfered with my studies. I couldn't say No because I knew the struggle. I was struggling, too. So my instructor said, 'OK, we're going to make a job out of this.' And once a week I started doing that. It still wasn't a thing of, 'Oh, you're so beautiful, you should model.' It was just a mathematical situation. Then as the art students graduated from school, they kept me in mind and asked me to do different shows for them, or wanted me to

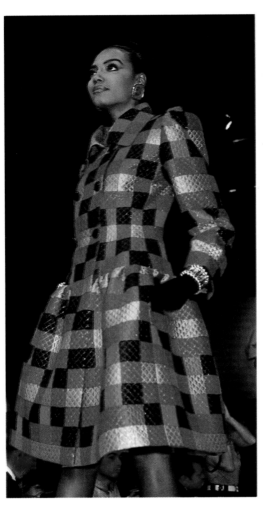

Lu Sierra wearing **Givenchy** couture.

a girl, and I was the first born so I was definitely given the ultimate. The name Iman means a lot in the Islamic religion. It means faith, it means everything that's good, it means strong. That's as much as I know about how special I was.

"From then on it went down the hill. I could never get a date. My father and my brothers paid this guy. Not this guy, my cousin! How bad is that? They paid my cousin to take me to my high school prom. He didn't want to, he had to be paid. I was in a school with 450 kids. Eighty of us were girls, the rest were boys. Every girl had like 15 guys to choose from. Me, not one. Never had any dates.

"I come from a very beautiful people, very beautiful. Though I looked just like a Somali, I felt different. Always I was the odd one out."

Although Iman could shrug off her feelings of being different and separate, other models like Pat Evans, were not so secure. The insults she suffered in her early years left lasting scars on her personality.

"As a child," she said, "I was never told, you look nice or anything. I was always thought of as homely. I have a sister who was very pretty. When I was little, she used to tease me by saying, 'You have a chicken butt nose.' I grew up with low self-esteem. People used to say, 'Pat, you always walk with your head down.' Even when I modeled, the head may be up but the eyes would be down. I never had the confidence." Yet during the height of her popularity in the late '60s, Pat Evans made one of the most powerful physical statements ever dared by any model: she was bald. Her outrageous look helped her become the highest earning model at her agency.

document their clothes in photographs. I was doing a lot of things as favors, and for clothes. Gradually a book started building, and one of these young designers was so bold as to encourage me to actually go to an agency and become a model. And that's just what I did."

Contrary to popular belief, not all women who became instantly recognizable world-famous beauties spent their youth adored by their peers for their special looks. Iman, born in Somalia and educated in Egypt, laughed a husky, heart-felt laugh as she described what might have been a bitter beginning. "My name, Iman, is a man's name in my country. I was named Iman because I was the first girl in three generations of boys. In my country boys are looked up to, but after three generations my family had had it up to here with boys. They wanted

Many women from all generations—Sara Lou Harris, Bethann Hardison, Norma Jean Darden, Carol LaBrie, Sherry Brewer, Sheila Johnson, Naomi Campbell and others—crossed over to the fashion spotlight from the stage. They trained as artists and entertainers, acting, singing, and dancing, long before becoming models.

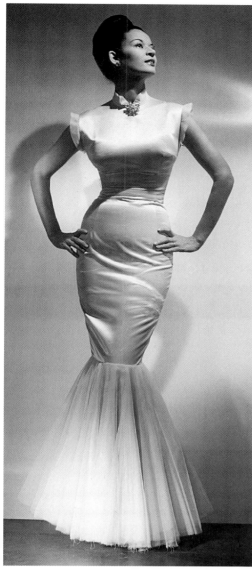

Sara Lou Harris attended Bennett College in Greensboro, N.C., a liberal arts college for Black women with a highly polished reputation that emphasized the importance of upper-class etiquette and social graces. Typically, Bennett girls were required to wear a hat and gloves when off campus. After graduation in the mid-1940s, Sara Lou taught elementary school for a year and then set her sights on a master's degree at Columbia University in New York. But her postgraduate education had more to do with Harlem than Morningside Heights. Having sung with the Sy Oliver Orchestra in college, she continued to perform and even worked as a cashier at the famed Savoy Ballroom. She got a job singing with Fritz Pollard's Harmonettes, traveling for ten months entertaining American troops in Europe. When she returned to the U.S., Sara Lou signed up with Brandford Models, becoming one of the twelve women who formed the nucleus of the first licensed Black model agency in the United States. Well educated, perfectly groomed, and professionally seasoned, she launched a strikingly successful career as a model, winning distinction as the first woman of color to appear in national advertisement campaigns.

Another woman who graduated from entertainment to modeling was Bethann Hardison. She recalled how important dance was to her Brooklyn childhood in the '50s and to her developing sense of drama.

"From nine years old I was well known as a tap dancer. We had television early in our house. In fact, my mother got me a TV to help take care of me when she and my grandmother went to work. I'd watch all the variety shows and old movies and all the dancing. I started tap dancing with Duke Baldwin who'd take me to ballrooms where people were having dances. I'd go out in the middle of this big dance floor with two other little girls and we'd do team dancing. Sometimes when the other kids couldn't make it I'd do it by myself, 'cause I was the lead dancer. It was against the law for a child to work in that way so they would throw money to me. I did that for many years. So it was very natural for me to go on a runway and perform because I sort of knew what it was all about."

Quite a number of dancers made careers for themselves on the runway. Norma Jean Darden, a '60s graduate of Sarah Lawrence College, studied with the legendary Martha Graham for six years and started an acting career before becoming a model. Seven years of ballet helped Carol LaBrie decide to leave her secretarial job on Wall Street and move to Los Angeles where she started dancing at the popular disco Whiskey-a-Go-Go in the late '60s. Nineties superstar Naomi Campbell, born and raised in London, claimed her dancing shoes from her mother, a contemporary ballet dancer from Jamaica who lived for a while in Geneva. Naomi was attending the London School of Performing Arts when a chance encounter steered her toward fashion. "My mom wanted me to be a

Sara Lou Harris. A Bennett graduate and Brandford model, she epitomized well-bred elegance during and after her career.

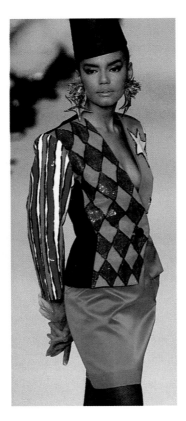

Lu Sierra in **Yves Saint Laurent**. Her parents linked lofty goals to a practical foundation.

dancer. So she shoved me into this school to study dance. I loved it. My agent in London discovered me on the street after school. I started modeling a month before I turned sixteen."

In modeling even the lucky intersection of chance and choice does not automatically guarantee a victorious outcome. A beautiful, intelligent young woman with years of arts training and even some modeling experience can still find the road to success a rocky one.

In the mid-'80s a young girl growing up tall in Hollywood, Florida, was trying on a dream. Lucelania Sierra had finished high school as an honor student at sixteen and was headed to college, eventually to study medicine. But after four years of ballet and three years of tap, singing, and drama lessons, another voice was speaking to her; she wanted to model in New York City.

Supported by encouraging but realistic parents, she made a deal. "I had to save $5,000 in the bank in Florida in case I had to come back and start over. I had to take $5,000 with me, and they had to find a place for me to stay. My father believed in going for your dream. That's all he's ever asked of us. My mother also had real high goals for us. I worked three jobs to save the money. Finally, I packed my bags, bought a New York newspaper, and when I got to New York moved into the Martha Washington Hotel for women. That was part of the agreement. Mom said I had to stay in an all-women's hotel until one of them came up to help me find an apartment. When my father came I found a really cute small apartment midtown, but only stayed a couple of months because it was too much money and I didn't have a job.

"All the agencies rejected me. That was hard. I had been modeling in Florida and I had done quite a number of shows for department stores and luncheons for women's organizations. To come to New York and find everyone saying no, that was hard.

"I got a job as a waitress to support myself. I even took a job as a limousine driver but that became very difficult.

Finally, I got a little showroom work for a swimwear house, Gottex of Israel.

"Right before I was going to give up and go back to college—I had been in New York about a year—I did a show for a friend. After the show a woman from Zoli invited me to work with her agency." From that unglamorous beginning Lu Sierra became one of the most popular runway models on the show circuit. "I believe that God has a plan," she said. "He gave me the strength to go through the disappointments and build a stronger character. I always asked Him to give me the knowledge to know what's next."

Once the decision has been made to try to become a model and pursue a career in modeling, what did a young woman do, especially if she was not supported by understanding friends and family, prepared by arts training, and disciplined by experience? One aspiring model told a story of struggle that did not have the silver-lined endings recounted so far, but one that might be much more typical than we would like to imagine.

Angela Baptiste, a graduate of private schools and Cornell University, Class of '89, was the product of conservatively ambitious West Indian parents. Although she received her degree in business management and marketing, she decided that she "could not stand to work a nine-to-five on Wall Street." She found a modeling agency in New York but her "parents were really against it. They knew I had been interested in modeling even before high school, but they knew that I wouldn't dare to pursue it. As a matter of fact, my father told me that if I didn't get a job on Wall Street or in one of those big companies, I would have to find my own apartment. So I left."

Her independence plunged her into a world she had never known. From an ad in the *Village Voice* she rented a cheap room in a dubious hotel populated by prostitutes, crackheads, and drug dealers. "It was horrible."

Determined to model, Angela spent the first few months at her agency "testing, testing, testing"—getting her book together. "To learn from testing you have to be doing it constantly. And if you want to get good tests with a decent photographer, you have to pay. Some photographers you just pay for the film, which is fair. But some charge you hundreds of dollars, and you may not even get a shot that you can use for your book!"

As far as concrete work, Angela did not get much of it. While she wanted to do runway, she later realized that her agency was not well-connected to fashion show clients. She eventually landed odd jobs in showrooms and "a couple of print things, but they didn't pay."

Meanwhile, she needed to support herself. She worked at night in an investment banking company to keep her days free for modeling. Then she started waitressing at the Rainbow Room at Rockefeller Center. The money was good, but her original priorities were in danger of being lost.

"I want to do the shows. That's my passion. I'm interested in print, of course, because nowadays your work in print can get you more shows." At the time she was speaking Angela had left New York and found work in a Parisian showroom "just to pay the rent. I have so many other goals that I want to pursue, but right now I can't get this modeling thing out of my system. I really want to get over it. It sounds contradictory, but I want to get over it. I want to have done it. I don't want to waste my life away being a wannabe."

Enter the Agency

I had a mission to focus our image in the way we wanted people to see us.

Ophelia DeVore

No one would want to waste a life trying to achieve an impossible goal. One of the advantages of modeling being such a high-performance, high-visibility field was that a newcomer could tell when and if she was reaching the necessary markers along the road to success. Those early markers were,

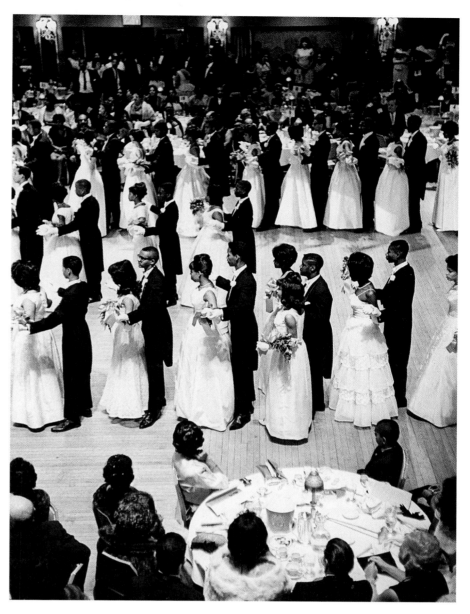

Black debutantes in a cotillion at the Waldorf Astoria Hotel, New York City, 1950.

inevitably, one of two things: joining a reputable agency or doing reputable, paid work. Although it did not matter which came first, agency representation was essential and inevitable. A beautiful woman could not sell herself; she needed a respectable intermediary. Enter the agency.

A modeling agency was not to be confused with a modeling school, that descendant of the neighborhood charm school where girls learned grooming, posture, table manners, and other prerequisites of proper ladyhood. While many models from Dorothea Towles to Barbara Smith recounted only positive experiences with them, modeling schools could sometimes mislead insecure young women into believing that if they paid enough for training and a portfolio of photographs, they were qualified to work as models. Schools could only teach.

They could not guarantee work. Disreputable schools often blurred the line between becoming a model and learning to look like one, bilking women out of hundreds or thousands of dollars in the process.

In Black communities around the country, however, modeling and charm schools have long been societally approved cultural academies where young people were taught important social graces and potentially professional skills. In Detroit, the fastidious Maxine Powell applied the lessons she taught at her finishing school to Motown's legendary girl groups of the '60s. Grooming the Supremes, the Marvelettes, Martha and the Vandellas, and others was one way of educating an entire generation of newly assertive Black women.

Emily Miles

One of the most enduring of such establishments in the New York area was the Belle Meade School of Charm and Modeling, run by the indomitable Emily Miles, in Newark, New Jersey.

Emily Miles has been around forever—at least, since the '40s—and successfully so, coaching generation of beauty contestants, cotillion debutantes, bridal parties, and men and women of all ages and social exposure. After the doors of Seventh Avenue repeatedly closed on her own dreams of being a model, she turned her disappointment into design. Hats became her specialty, and church and society benefits became her showcase. She soon expanded into clothing and, bolstered by regular attendance at the New York and Paris shows, developed the entertaining theatrical style that was her trademark. "What Miles produces," wrote one New Jersey newspaperwoman, "is a personal extravaganza, a production in which all the clothes are her own designs, all the models trainees or graduates of her own Belle Meade Modeling School." And all the energy was generated by a seemingly inexhaustible resource: herself. At an undisclosed—and unidentifiable age—Miles was often the star model in the dozens of shows she presented around the country. "I always tell my models, 'If you want to act up and be a fool, I can do it better.' I'll get out there, and I'll do it myself. So I am the diva," she stated with no appreciable hint of self-mockery.

Social graces—"how to sit, how to stand, how to speak well, how to present yourself"—were the foundation of her school. "What we try to do is build self-esteem, because if you don't have self-esteem, you can't do anything. So you have to teach this and believe this. I want to be first, and I want the best."

Being the best meant refining her fashion instincts by working as a fit model on Seventh Avenue, studying at the New York School of Costume Design, FIT, Parsons, and McDowell, as well as learning from NYU, "everything about stage and lights and how to use the smoke. So all of that dramatic stuff is what I insert into these shows."

A typical show would be a fund raiser with an audience of five hundred to three thousand people where ten models would present one hundred and eighty outfits.

Maintaining the Belle Meade Models and her school required tremendous stamina over the years. How did she do it? "Because I majored in physical education, I'm a stickler with my body, food, and health. So all of that kept me together at this age." In Emily Miles discipline and dream combined to fashion an ageless prima donna who kept the flame of style ablaze.

As modeling shaped itself into an authentic full-time profession, the rules came to be more defined. Fashion was foremost a big-city phenomenon. From all across the country girls eager for the dream arrived wide-eyed in the nearest metropolis. Eventually or directly, they came to New York. In need of guidance and protection, they sought admission to an established agency.

Veronica Webb described the breathless anticipation she felt on entering Click, her first agency. "All of a sudden you ride up this elevator, and you walk down this hallway, and you don't know what's awaiting you, and you go into this whole new world where phones are ringing and people are speaking all these different languages and talking really loud. Models were sashaying in and out, talking in weird accents, wearing weird hair cuts and really nice clothes. It was astounding, like stepping onto a technicolor set."

The agency combined elements of a nunnery—a single sex devoted to a single cause—with a stable. Like thoroughbreds, Girls were groomed to compete for high stakes. In return for a sizable percentage—from 10% in the good ol' days to 20% or more—of a model's earnings, the agency—actually the owner or head plus a staff of bookers and bookkeepers—sent the model on interviews to photographers, advertising agencies, magazines, and catalog houses. From these go-sees the agency would coordinate whatever jobs resulted and insure that the models actually got paid. Although the system worked well in general, there was room for honest error as well as creative bookkeeping and outright fraud. Outside of the United States, the situation could be even more complex.

Veronica, who left New York for the adventure of Paris soon after starting to model, said "I got a one-way ticket and stayed for two and a half years. I didn't know what was going to happen. I couldn't speak French. I didn't know anyone. All I knew was an agency there. By the time I left Paris, I was with another one, because in any agency there're always financial problems and staff problems. You are only as good as the people you work with. Models get robbed. Basically, we are glamorous migrant workers. We may get all the fame, but we just follow the work. We don't speak the language. We operate outside the law most of the time. We have to trust these people who represent us to be completely honest. And let's face it, money is a very seductive thing. Most of us just can't get enough of it."

Regardless of geographic location, model agencies took only the Girls who they thought would work, who would provide the look that they knew their clients wanted or might be interested in experimenting with. But agencies also had their own look, a certain image they aimed for, as well as a reputation to maintain.

At its peak in the '60s and '70s, the Ford agency, founded in 1947 by Eileen and Jerry Ford, was not only the largest of the half-dozen or so major New York agencies, but it was also the one known to specialize in the so-called All-American Girl, the pretty blonde with blue eyes. In the late '70s Johnny Casablancas and his transplanted Parisian agency, Elite, successfully challenged the Fords' primacy with more varied and sophisticated-looking models. During that period an influx of European models and photographers avid for a share of the big American fashion and beauty campaigns swept into town. An international image became more exciting and in some markets actually more sellable.

Decades before this trend, however, big-city agencies already had an indigenous pool of talent which they consistently rejected: Black women. As in most other areas of American life in the '40s and '50s, model agencies were segregated. Where was a beautiful young woman of color who aspired to be a model to go?

In New York City, she went to the Colored agencies. One of the most famous was run by the legendary Ophelia DeVore who founded the Grace del Marco agency in 1947. Organized by five friends—who lent the initials of their first names, Marie, Albert, Rupert, Charles and Ophelia, to their enterprise—the agency was really the story of one woman's life: Ophelia DeVore, considered to be one of the first professional models of color in the United States.

Ophelia DeVore

Born in South Carolina in the early '20s, Ophelia came from a family that was proud of its mixed African, European, and Native American ancestry. Proud enough to fight. She recalled the racial tensions that framed her early days. "The Blacks would call us names,

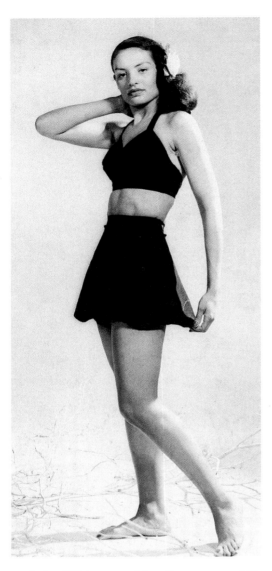

Ophelia DeVore, considered the first model of color in the United States, in the '40s.

"I was very young, about fourteen, when I went to modeling school in New York. Unbelievably, I photographed White. I found out later they basically thought I had a suntan, which was what White people got when they wanted a little color. I had no idea. I just thought they knew what I knew. That was my naïveté." Although her main desire was to be a dancer, her parents refused to let her enter the dangerous world of show business. Her second choice was modeling which "had no reputation at all, whereas show business had a bad reputation. But in those days they were not entertaining the idea of Black people as models. The were looking for the Nordic type. I photographed like a Northern European. So if my photograph went out and they selected me on that basis, they never questioned what I was.

"I didn't model very long. I only stayed in the business about two years because the challenge was gone. I saw how we were being rejected as a people. The newspapers and magazines would always have us written up in a stereotyped manner, in a negative position, hanging from a tree or scrubbing floors. I didn't want to live in that kind of world. My direction changed. I decided to get some Black women, start an agency, and sell the idea of Black models to the advertising industry. Then I found out that nobody was trained. I never thought of that. So I had to open a school to train the models. Before I could sell a product, I had to develop the product, and then create the market for it. I learned just by exposure, by people liking me. And I was lucky that I got so much support.

"I felt that Black people had to get another image. We couldn't be shown with a rag on our head or shooting craps in the street. We had to show the other side. We were well-groomed, well-spoken, well-presented, and there were plenty of people who represented that. My mother was a school teacher. I've never come out of a ghetto situation. But to get us in the image of America I had to get vast exposure. We had to be seen in mass media. I wanted to sell the industry on using women of color in their ads."

and the Whites would call us names. We had to fight both. We had to learn to survive very young. We had to find a place for ourselves." That struggle gave her an enduring strength. "We learned to have a great deal of confidence and respect in ourselves. I have no problems any place I go because I deal from a standpoint of merit and responsibility."

The modeling profession, however, was never so philosophical. It was based entirely on appearance. In a 1969 article in *Sepia* magazine, Ophelia was quoted as saying, "Black has always been beautiful but you had to hide it to be a model." Forty years after she started she was a living legend in an industry whose business was to create living legends on a regular basis.

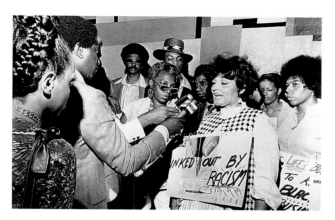

Ophelia DeVore became an institution. She developed a fashion column for the *Pittsburgh Courier*, at the time one of the most highly respected and widely circulated of the Black weeklies. She used her column to showcase models and advertise designers and stores. Although the major New York City department stores had never done so before, they lent her clothes for Black models to wear in photographs for the paper. "Some stores would shoot the models. Others would get me to do it, and I'd hire a photographer, either Rupert Callendar or Al Murphy. I wrote for the *Courier* for years in order to get that forum for expression and experience."

Doing what no others had done before on such an ambitious level, she refined her skills and expanded into public relations, fashion shows, and television. "I started putting on contests so the models could get experience walking on a runway and on stage to develop stage presence. We put on all kinds of local fashion shows in nightclubs. Ralph Cooper, who was the long-time M.C. at the world-famous Apollo Theater, and I had a TV show, which was one of the first for Blacks, on ABC. Then I developed national contests and took the Girls overseas."

In 1959, and again in 1960 and 1961, her protégées were crowned Queen of the International Film Festival in Cannes. Cecilia Cooper "was the first American girl, not just the first Black girl," insisted Ophelia, "to win. When Cecilia won she had the seat of honor over all the top movie stars. United Press

International almost died because a Black American had won the title. I went to Cannes again and won again. This time it was LeJeune Hundley; the next time it was Emily Yancy. I went to Europe and got acceptance. Then when I came back to America I had it made."

"Her specialty is polishing black diamonds," declared one newspaper article. Ophelia's visible successes were backed up by even more significant, if less visible, achievements in the boardrooms of major companies. "I became a marketing consultant, because once I talked clients into using Black models, then I had to tell them how to use them. They didn't know. I had to deal with the client, work with the advertising agencies, work with the TV stations, develop television commercials, and talk with the community organizations. I had to work on all levels: to develop the product, to find a need for the product, and to show the consumers who needed the product how to use it."

Her best weapons were her models and perhaps the very best of her models was Helen Williams. "God was good to her," said Ophelia. "She had that

Ophelia DeVore protesting the advertising industry's status quo.

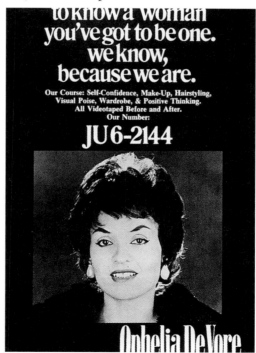

to know a woman you've got to be one. we know, because we are.

Our Course: Self-Confidence, Make-Up, Hairstyling, Visual Poise, Wardrobe, & Positive Thinking. All Videotaped Before and After. Our Number:

JU 6-2144

Ophelia DeVore

Teacher, agent, and promoter, **Ophelia DeVore**'s specialty was polishing black diamonds.

smooth, gentle skin and wonderful bone structure, and she used it to her best advantage. She was a fantastic person, a sweetheart. She wanted to be the best and to do the best, and she was a hard worker. Elitists in our group would laugh at somebody if they were totally Black. You've heard the expression: 'If you're Black, stand back.' And when she came along, she was very self-conscious because she was dark. But Helen influenced people. She gave people who were Black—and I don't mean brown—the opportunity to know that if they applied themselves they could reach certain goals that they thought were not reachable."

Ellen Holly who became a pioneering television actress, was another one of Ophelia's models. "Ellen was extremely talented and artistic, but she had the opposite effect. Because she was fair, people would laugh at her and talk about her. She was taunted by her own people, yet she could have passed if she wanted to. She didn't want to. She wanted to be who she was inside. I think it hurt her a lot. Just like Helen was hurt by people throwing jibes at her, Ellen got the same thing because she was light. We so often hurt our own people ourselves."

"I went into business because I had a mission to focus our image in the way we wanted people to see us. I used to fight all the time against ideas that were not complimentary to Blacks.

"I've kept our reputation squeaky clean. I have no interest in anything that's going to sell my people in a negative light. I wanted to share with my people the idea that if you apply yourself, many opportunities will open up to you."

Spreading the News

Show me a man or a woman who's satisfied with what he's got and I'll show you a man or woman who's not going to get anything else.

John H. Johnson

When segregated America restricted the material means available to its citizens of color, it assumed it could limit their aspirations as well. It was wrong. Like other realistic dreamers, Black models worked for Black people before they worked for anyone else. Having little choice, they made the most of what choice they had. They appeared in local church benefits and sorority "Fashionettas," in talent contests and beauty pageants, wearing tastefully tailored clothes and confident attitudes that had nothing of the second-best about them.

Ruth King

Ruth King was one of the most photographed models in Harlem during the 1940s and '50s. She typified the many women who made names for themselves—but not a profession—out of fashion. Fresh out of high school and a business school course, she joined the Abyssinian Baptist Church, one of the largest and most prestigious congregations—socially and politically—in Black America. In 1942, Adam Clayton Powell Jr., the charismatic preacher and Congressman, became her first boss. Ruth recalled with undiminished delight, "He had a great influence on me. Can you imagine how I felt as a teenager starting out with a man of his tremendous stature? Great!"

Cecilia Cooper, the first American crowned Queen of the International Film Festival in Cannes, 1959.

A few years later she joined Sepia Art Models which advertised itself as an agency dedicated to "creative art and photography, highly imaginative, but within the limits of good taste." Soon she was starring in fashion shows and balls. She won so many contests—Miss Sweater Girl, Miss East Coast, Miss press Photographer—that she was asked to step aside from competing and give other Girls a chance. When well-known New York designers Lois Bell, Ann Harris, and Millicent Taylor sponsored shows, Ruth with her 21½″ waist was at the top of their model roster. "They paid us a minimal wage. It wasn't a great salary, maybe $20 or $25. We knew there were not great financial benefits, but we were so happy to be modeling and to be exposed because this was very new to us. We were pioneers breaking into the field. I loved runway modeling. I had such a love affair with the audience. I was just in my heaven. I had a strut that was fantastic. I was not a model to go out and show a gown with a cold face. No, I was smiling, very dramatic. In fact, they would practically have to pry me off the stage because I never wanted to get off. I had the audience in the palm of my hand and I loved it."

While the models' appearance in gala social events most often took place in localized communities, the photographs of these affairs were not so restricted. Publications geared to people of color were eager to spread the news. By 1943 the Negro press included 164 newspapers and weeklies with a combined circulation of close to two million people, and an active readership of many more. The influence of such papers as the *Pittsburgh Courier*, the *Baltimore Afro-American*, the *Chicago Defender*, New York's *Amsterdam News*, the *Norfolk Journal and Guide*, and *The Freeman* in Indianapolis spread far beyond their city limits. But it was not until the end of World War II—which had unified and energized the United States but left paper, among other basic goods, scarce—that opportunity knocked and savvy entrepreneurs answered. It was then that a

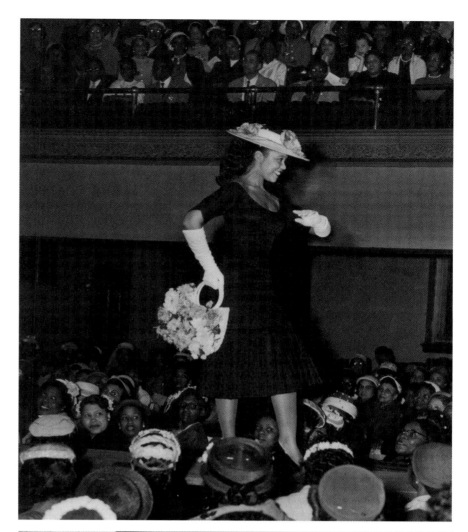

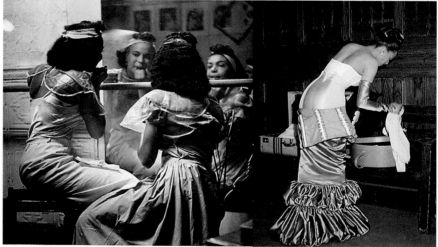

national Black press allowed people across the country to see for themselves how notable individuals of color had created successful lives. And it was not until the monthly magazine *Ebony* appeared that these lives were reproduced on the slick paper and in the gorgeous color of the best-selling mainstream periodicals such as *Life* and *Look*. Publisher and editor in chief, John H. Johnson pledged in the inaugural issue of November, 1945,

Ruth King had a love affair with her audience.

Scenes of amateur models preparing for a show.

that *Ebony* would "try to mirror the happier side of Negro life."

Aimed at educating as well as entertaining, early articles featured among many others Eslanda Goode [Mrs. Paul] Robeson writing about a journey to Africa, Marva [ex-Mrs. Joe] Louis, Lena Horne, Gordon Parks, Katharine Dunham, and "The Man in the Ads," Maurice Hunter.

A native of South Africa, Hunter had been a model since 1918. Although the most money he earned was $25 a job, he was considered very successful in his portrayal of butlers, chauffeurs, and porters in ads primarily for cigarettes and liquor. He also posed nude for art classes at Pratt Institute for twenty years.

"From beautiful to bony," female models—whether of the fashion, artist or

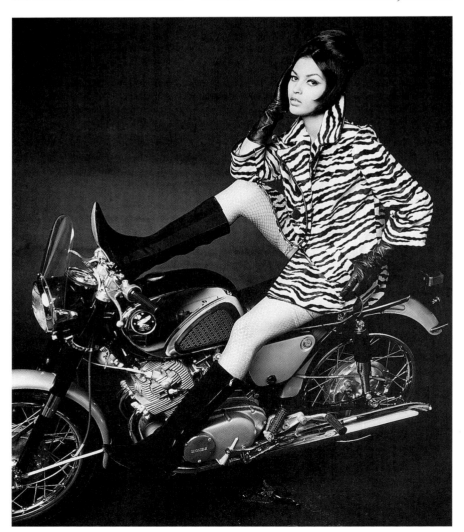

LeJeune Hundley. After winning Miss Cannes in 1960, she zoomed into a fashion career.

contest variety—were often depicted in *Ebony*. That Black Americans were conflicted about their appearance and standards of beauty was nothing new. Ebony merely helped to showcase the contradictions. While an article preached that "Rose-Meta campaigns against the idea that Negroid hair is inferior," advertisements on neighboring pages blared just the opposite. "Don't be 'Wire-Haired Willie,' the man nobody loves." Have "Handsome Hair the Amazing, New Snow White Way." Along with full-page ads for Madam C.J. Walker's products and beauty colleges, there might be an article on "Hair attachments," which estimated that "4,000,000 Negro women use an average of 2 cranial falsies each year." Black photographic models posed and were paid for ads which promised a nearer paradise for those who looked closer to White.

Ebony was not alone. In April, 1946, *Our World*, "A Picture Magazine for the Negro Family," published its first issue with a color cover of MGM singing star Lena Horne. A regular column entitled "Know Your Own People" featured an illustrated history quiz. Yet placed next to serious articles relating, for example, to post-World War II adjustment was the perpetual moan-and-groan issue, "What Shall I Do About My Hair?"

The October, 1946 issue of *Our World* with Dorothy Dandridge on the cover included a long article on the Brandford Girls. Created for a dual purpose, the Brandford Agency was dedicated to "helping interested firms get to the Negro market by using decent copy" and "getting a fair break for Negroes in a major $5,000,000 industry," advertising. Marie-Louise Yabro, then the fashion director of the Brandford Agency, "urged the trade to use Negroes in human, dignified roles" in regular ads as well as high-visibility billboards.

Eight years later in 1954, a significant article in *Ebony* addressed the issue of the future of Black models in more depth. It maintained that "the best that the average colored model could hope for prior to 1944 was an occasional stipend for posing as a servant in an ad." Due to

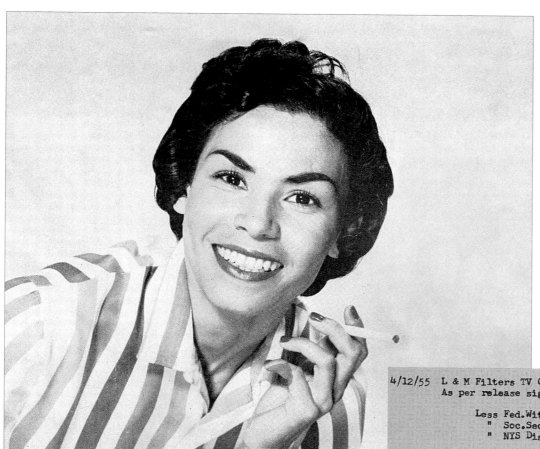

Barbara January. A typical pose and pay stub.

4/12/55	L & M Filters TV Commercials As per release signed Apr.5,1955		$100.00
	Less Fed.With.Tax	$18.00	
	" Soc.Sec.	2.00	
	" NYS Dis.Ins.	.07	20.07
			$79.93

the growth of Negro newspapers and magazines, job openings for them expanded so that ten years later approximately two hundred women were working, at least as part-time professionals, in the field. Ads promoting cigarettes and liquor, products of dubious benefit which were nevertheless associated with an affluent lifestyle, employed relatively large numbers of Black models. Billie Allen sold Chesterfields while Tina Marshall, an artist's model, was sketched and rendered as a White woman in Marlboro ads.

Despite daunting obstacles, this growing clan of models was composed of "notoriously optimistic creatures." Even though they were making slow progress overcoming negative stereotyping, limited opportunities, and irregular pay, *Ebony* indicated "straws in the wind that predict that colored models will someday be completely integrated at the top levels."

The irony was that this integration could not take place within the Black publications which had provided their initial opportunities. These same magazines and newspapers, which were important tools of communication in the Black community, had only minimal

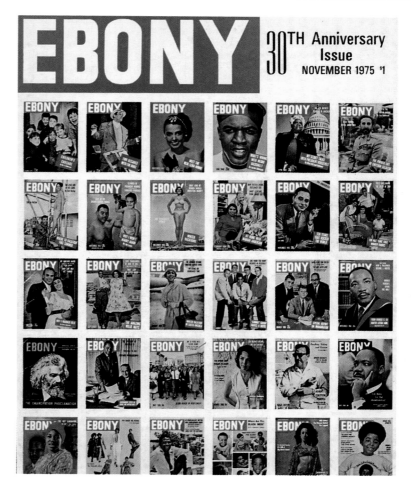

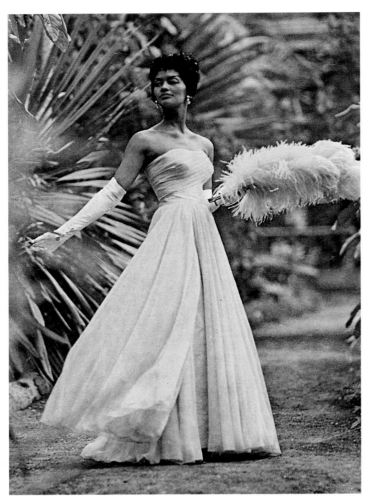

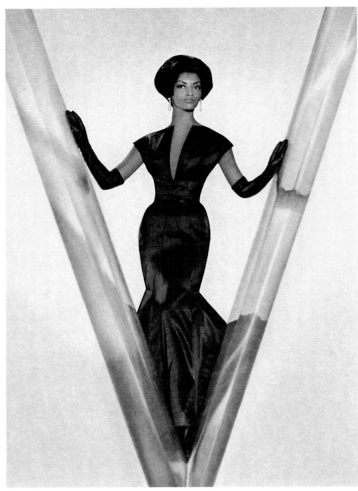

The incomparable
Helen Williams.

Ads exuding such unalloyed glamour were—and still are— rare. These were used for feminine hygiene products.

impact in the White world. To be "completely integrated at the top levels" meant—in plain and simple language— working in the White world. And in a country that had to use the Supreme Court to overturn the doctrine of "separate but equal" in 1954, the chances looked painfully slim.

Helen Williams

The face of Helen Williams launched the dreams of an entire generation growing up in the '50s. Exquisite in its finely chiseled features, it seemed to be the prototype of the mythical Greek beauty whose face launched a thousand ships. Helen Williams was, however, a very real person. After graduating from high school in New Jersey, she studied dance, drama, and art. Her first job at Pagano Studios, one of the largest commercial photography houses in New York, was as an artist, but she claimed that she was "too fidgety to stay at the drawing board for so many hours." In the studio she learned to be a stylist working with models. It was at the suggestion of Black entertainers, such as Lena Horne and Sammy Davis, Jr., who

came there to be photographed for ads that she crossed over to the other side of the camera.

The change was not easy. Until the late '60s, the big model agencies were closed shops. When she started modeling in 1954, Helen Wiliams was a Black beauty before the times had a name for her. At one major agency, she was kept waiting for two hours only to be told that they had "one Black model already, thanks." Although she signed with Ophelia DeVore and later with White-owned companies, the agency hurdle was only the beginning. She was the most photographed model of color of her era. Yet despite major ads and extensive work in Black publications, her pictures did not appear in White newspapers, magazines, and catalogs. Nevertheless, she was "determined to make it." Tired of being rejected for jobs, tired of time passing without a breakthrough, she changed her strategy and took her story straight to the newspapers. Influential columnists Dorothy Kilgallen and Earl Wilson championed her cause, and she soon began to see material results in more and better jobs in mainstream publications.

Helen persisted in making her career a success. She kept testing, trying new approaches with lighting, makeup, and wardrobe. "I was pushy and positive in my approach. I was determined to do a job and to do it well. If I was rejected, I knew I would return. Every year I would get up to the semi-finals in the Miss Rheingold contest"—which some people considered the second largest election after the presidency—"and each time they'd tell me, 'That's as far as you can go.' I'd simply wave and smile and say, 'See you next year.'"

Travels to Europe gave her another perspective. "In France I was called '*la belle américaine*,' and I loved it." Europe helped her realize that she was not the problem—something about America was.

It took twenty years before *Ebony*'s prediction—that the top ranks of models would be integrated—became a near reality. In 1974, twenty years after Helen Williams's debut, the refreshingly beautiful and undeniably brown face of Beverly Johnson appeared on the cover of American *Vogue* magazine.

"By spotlighting the Negro market," wrote John H. Johnson in his 1989 autobiography, *Succeeding Against the Odds*, "we helped create new jobs for Blacks in advertising and related fields. We're accustomed today to Black advertising agencies, Black advertising specialists, and Black models But back then, a mere forty years ago, there were no Black ad agencies or Black models.... We helped change all that....We stressed the importance of using Black models. Most companies resisted this idea. Wild as it may seem now, many companies were opposed to showing Black models washing clothes, although advertising managers knew full well that Black women had been washing clothes in America for centuries."

If there was resistance to pictures of Black models *washing* everyday clothes, we can only imagine the depth of resistance to photographs showing Black women *wearing* beautiful clothes.

The two main avenues open to mod-

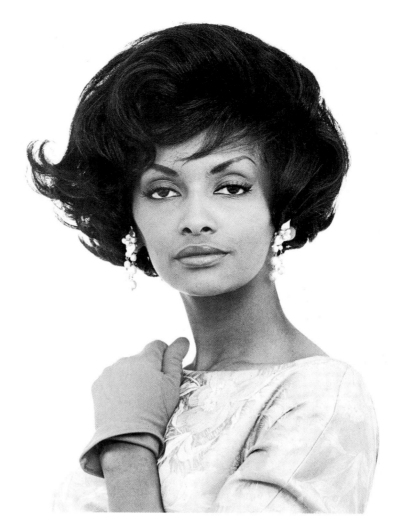

Helen Williams. A classic beauty equipped with the determination to succeed.

els—fashion and advertising—were only beginning to develop into the mega-industries they are today. In the middle of the 20th century no one could know what the changes would bring. But Black models were determined to be an undeniable presence, if not a powerful force, in whatever the future brought.

First Bookings

You are your own woman in the hope of being just what someone else is looking for.

Barbara Kruger

Designers' showrooms were the first places where professional Black models could work in fashion on a regular basis. Perhaps because designers themselves were often individuals of unusual character and aspirations, they were the first to appreciate what was new, different, and inspiring about Black models. Then, as the fashion establishment began to open its doors in the '60s to designers of other than European-

American heritage, Black models again found work with Black designers. Both groups would advance in exposure, prestige, and popularity.

The showroom was a special place providing the ideal stylistic atmosphere for the designer's clothes. In this setting department store buyers and privileged individual clients viewed selected garmentas up close, either hanging on racks or worn by house models. Viewing led hopefully to buying. Enter, or perhaps, exit the Black model. For while a designer might espouse politically liberal beliefs, the clientele might not share them. Good personal intentions sometimes made for risky business.

The public face of the showroom stopped at the threshold to the private domain, the back room, where the real design work went on. Only the model worked in both. For a designer to be worth a label, his or her hands had to do some of the work. And some of it on a live model. The intimate nature of the relationship could be misleading, especially as more men came to prominence in the design profession. The designer must objectify the model's body, learning its particular angles and curves the better to style and fit a garment. Despite the constant personal interaction, however, there was an invisible barrier between the professional touch and the erotic feel. Perhaps homosexuality, so wide-spread in the business as to be the norm and no longer a notorious taboo, has aided in the creative interchange between women's desires and men's designs. Released from traditional roles, both men and women were able to communicate better, more freely and more frankly, and to become more completely who they wanted to be.

Although male designers have dominated women's fashion for many decades, a woman was credited with being the first top New York designer to employ a Negro model on a permanent basis. She was Pauline Trigère, a French designer who moved to the United States in the '40s and won the American Fashion Critics' Award in 1949, a precursor of the Coty Awards. In 1961, she hired an elegant twenty-three-year-old, Beverly Valdes.

In 1962, *Life* magazine devoted a major photographic spread to "Negro Models—a Band of Beautiful Pioneers." The story, shot by Gordon Parks, the first Black photographer to work at *Life* and *Vogue* magazines, quoted Miss Trigère as saying: "I didn't choose Beverly to make history. I chose her because of her good features." Good features evidently made good history.

History, however, often required updating and revision. Mozella Roberts, another model featured in the *Life* article, stated that Beverly Valdes "was the first to get all of the publicity for being the first model hired on Seventh Avenue." The significant but missing detail was that Mozella was already there. "People always forgot about me," she claimed. "You know why? They never put me into the category that I belonged, which was that of a Black woman. They always made me something else. If a Black woman did come on the scene and if she did have any success, she herself never owned up to being Black, because had she, she would not have worked." Mozella never denied who or what she was, although for many others in the business tactful evasion was standard procedure when it came to matters of race.

Mozella Roberts

When I came on the scene in 1960, everybody had heard that there was this Negro Girl that people were making such a fuss about. Some of them knew her name, some of them didn't. People made statements that they would never use a Black Girl. Chuck Howard was designing at the time for Mr. Klein, who owned Townley. When he first saw me, Chuck just fell in love with me, and he wanted to hire me. But Mr. Klein had said that he would never use Negroes in the showroom. No, No, out of the question. Chuck booked me, but he did not tell Mr. Klein that I was the Negro Girl that everybody was talking about. A year later a conversation came up, and Mr. Klein mentioned to Chuck, 'Whatever

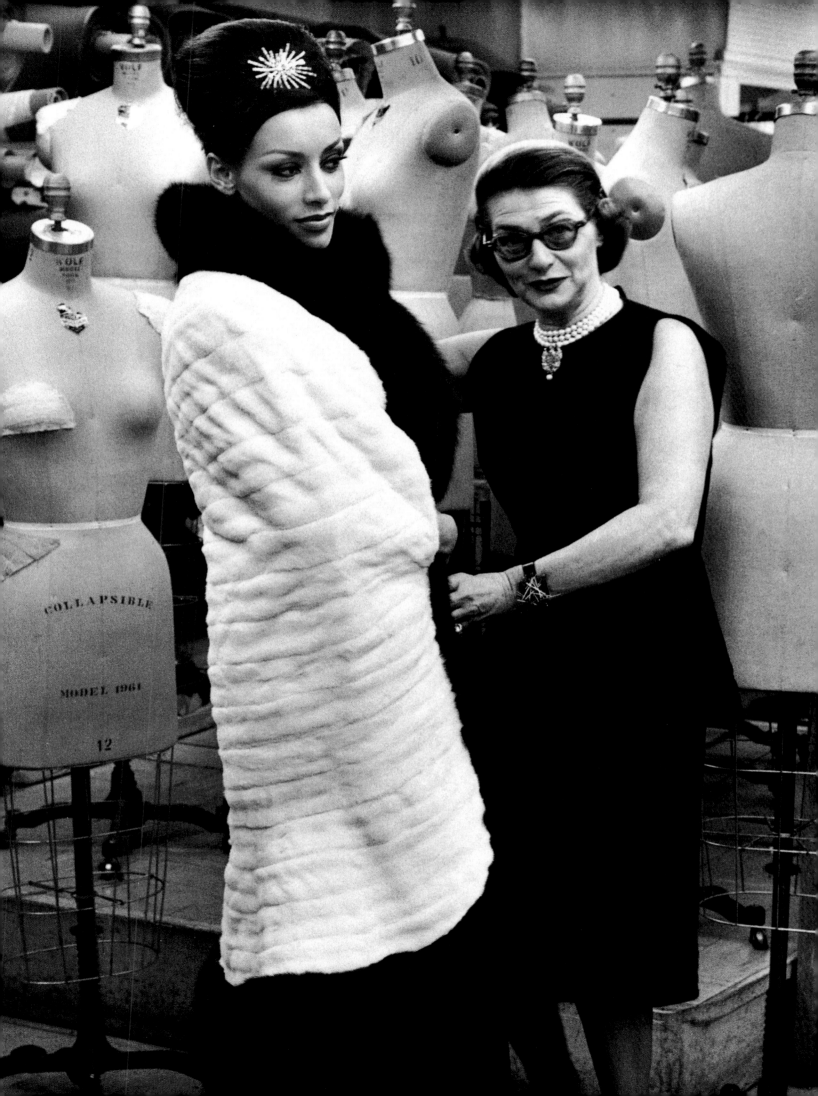

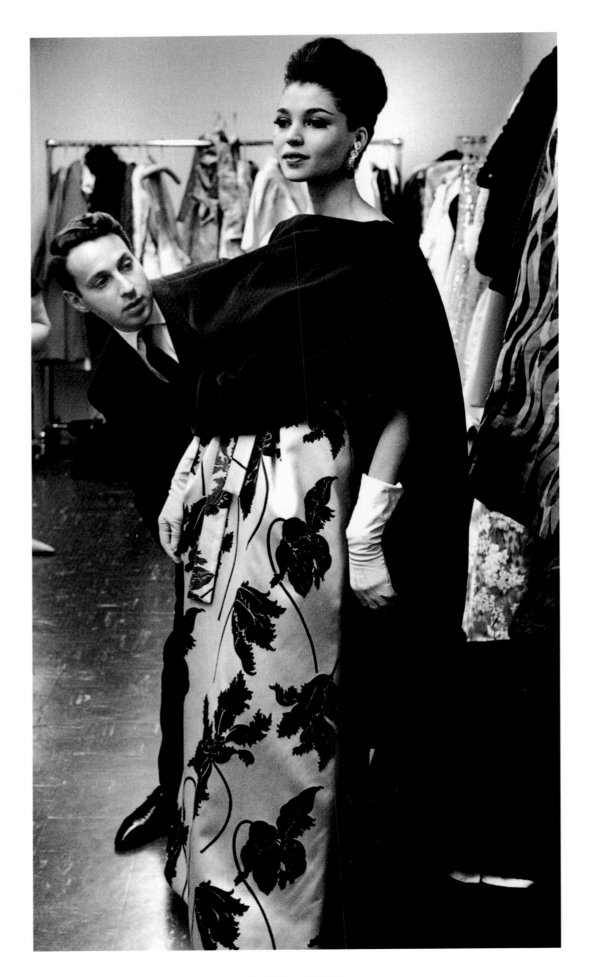

Mozella Roberts with
Arnold Scaasi.

happened to that Negro Girl you once wanted to use?' Chuck said, 'We use her.' And Mr. Klein said, 'She's Negro?' I'd been working with him for a year, and he didn't know it. I was just one of the Girls."

Mozella Roberts did not start out being just one of the Girls. A native of North Carolina, she arrived in New York City via Pittsburgh, the mother of two small children and the pampered wife of a successful entertainer whose close friends included Lena Horne, Pearl Bailey, Count Basie, Duke Ellington, and Billy Strayhorn. When her marriage ended, she found herself without marketable talents or skills. A job in the rug department at Gimbel's department store did not last long. During one fateful lunch hour at B. Altman's, she watched an in-store fashion show and was fascinated by the models, their poise, grooming, and style. "Of course, they were all White. But all I could remember was that these Girls all had long, false eyelashes on. I came out of that store flying. I was going to find some false eyelashes somewhere. I bought the eyelashes at a little makeup place, and then I went to Woolworth's where I picked out the darkest makeup base that they had at that time, a peach color, and a bright red rouge, and a nut brown power. I took all this stuff home and I played with that makeup. By night, I had perfected a look. When I got through, I was floored by my own self! I was pretty. Wow, I was proud! I had never had color in my life, and here I was brown and gorgeous. I had gone to beauty culture school so I could do hair, but as far as makeup went, I would wear a little lipstick and sometimes I'd take the lipstick and put a dot on the cheek and then rub it around. And that was about it. But after I had perfected this makeup, I thought I could do what I saw those White Girls doing. That's what the makeup was saying in my mind.

"I never took into consideration that your feet had to move, too, that you had to know how to arch your body and how to present clothes. All I knew is that I could look like they looked so, therefore, that would allow me to become a model.

I bought the *New York Times* for that Sunday and it seemed like all of Seventh Avenue was in there; everybody needed a showroom model. There was not a showroom on Seventh Avenue—the heart of the garment district—that I did not cover. I only wanted a job. Of course, I was turned down by everybody. I was Black. It was very simple. It was a thing of fear to hire me. It took me, I guess, a couple of weeks to cover the whole of Seventh Avenue. My feet were killing me. And then I started looking for work on Broadway. I wound up going into Maidenform, which had been famous for bras. That year they had just gone into bathing suits. There was a Japanese girl working as the designer's assistant. She liked me a lot, and she told me to be patient. It took three weeks, but I finally did land the job. My first modeling job was with swimwear at Maidenform, and I stayed with them for about three or four months."

Informal but persistent networking expanded her contacts and landed her a coveted spot in a prestigious fashion show. "All of the leading models were there. I did the show, in fact I broke it up because I really did not know how to model. So I did everything that everybody else wasn't doing. I smiled, and in those days, you did not smile. I came out in the most beautiful gowns that the show's director had pulled from different Girls and given to me. And I smiled so hard and so much that my cheeks hurt.

"I met Gillis MacGil at that show, and she was so impressed with me that she wanted me to join her agency, Mannequin. All of the top models were with her. She said that I had great potential and that she would like to pass me off as Polynesian. I said no. I said, 'I am Negro.' I did not want to be anything else but what I was. Long before 'Black is beautiful' came in, I always felt very proud of who I was. You were taught to be somebody. Southerners always had a pride about them. I'm not putting down the Northerners because they have their thing, too. But down South, you are taught to be proud of who you are, to work hard to achieve. I believed in myself as far as becoming successful. I knew that once I got one foot in, I would get the other one in, and I would win over everybody who felt that they did not want Negroes wearing their clothes.

"I really did believe that it would happen, and I was willing to work hard to make it happen. I used to come in from work as a model, and I would stay up to two and three o'clock in the morning working my feet in front of the mirror to make sure that I could do what I saw the White women do and to do it better. When they said pivot, child, please! I used to take a chiffon gown and almost make it come up over my head.

"I worked for everybody who was anybody: Norman Norell, James Galanos, Arnold Scaasi, Donald Brooks, Bill Blass, Bob Mackie, Oscar de la Renta, Junior Sophisticates, DuPont, you name it. There's nobody in the modeling world during the '60s that had shows that I didn't work with and for. Some shows were in the showroom, some were on runways in big hotels. When I started working in 1960, clients were having as many as ten to fifteen shows per season. I was never without work. I've never done anything other than model to pay my bills.

"In the beginning, I can remember walking in to the dressing room, saying hello to the other models and staff and nobody speaking back. I remember sitting and crying. But that's the name of the game. If you want to do something and you believe in yourself and believe that you can do it, you'll shed your tears, and you'll still get the job done. My determination was that I was going to outwork everybody. I was going to show them that when you work a runway, you really work it, and that's what I did. And I did it out of frustration a little bit. I chose the runway and showrooms over photography because I liked people. I liked to reach out and touch, smile and wink.

"Now, when you're working with a camera, you've got to love that camera, because it really does pick up everything it sees. It leaves nothing. To me, the cam-

era is cold. I get no feedback from it. You have to do everything you can to be exciting to the camera. In other words, you've got to be a darn good actress. For me the camera was OK. It was good to me. The pictures that came back were not unpleasant, but I just preferred the runway. I guess I liked to show off. That applause just meant so much. I was an only child so, I think, when you're an only child you are always seeking approval anyway, because you have no siblings to cling to, to cry to, to hug up.

"I wanted the audience to love what I had on. I knew how to get to them, and I loved doing it, too. I've watched some Girls walk down a runway. They would have on the most beautiful outfit that you could imagine but the audience would be so cold. And then I'd come out, and the atmosphere would change completely. I had designers who used to say to me, 'Mo, this is a dog. I'm giving it to you.' And I'd say, 'Honey, give it here. I'll work it.' Sometimes their dog would become the best seller of the whole collection. If a model is good, she's always going to work. As long as she doesn't get so grand that she becomes grander than her profession she will always work.

"It was fun. Lots of wonderful things happened during those years. The first fashion show that was ever done in the White House, I was a part of it. It was about '67, and Lyndon Johnson was president.

"To model I think you have to have a great sense of humor. You have to love people, because as a model, you're dealing with all types of people simply to work. I was not born a model. I was born to wear clothes. But to model, no. I was a nervous wreck. My stomach was jelly. But after that fifth year, everything changed for me. I knew who I was. I knew that I was wanted. And my competition was White, not Black. So I knew that I had to be better than they were because I could be dropped just like that. I knew I was the cream of the crop. Not bragging, but that was the attitude, you know? You have to have an attitude to be a successful anything, and to be a successful model, especially."

Rene Hunter

In 1964, Rene Hunter, a college student studying to be an English teacher, cut a class to try to see Seventh Avenue designer Donald Brooks, whom she had met the night before at the Coty Awards. Brooks wasn't in yet but she chanced upon the office of Jacques Tiffeau and thus landed not only a job but also a career.

"Tiffeau was a French designer, very modern, one of the best of the '60s. He worked in beautiful colors and interesting fabric. His clothes were very simple, simply cut, very architectural. He didn't like bust darts, so he didn't use them. He used a kind of side panel that made the dress fit over the bust. They were very simple, clean clothes. Tiffeau liked Girls who were different, and he wasn't afraid of Girls who were ethnic. I'm a city Indian, an urban Indian, without the hunting and fishing part, although my brothers learned how to do that. Outside of Southampton, Long Island, there's a reservation for Indians called Shinnecock. I spent all of my summers there. My grandparents and my family were there. Having had that experience you're very aware of being a Native American. People weren't quite sure what I was. They'd say, 'What are you? Are you from some exotic island?' And I'd say, 'How about Long Island?'

"At first, my folks weren't thrilled. Originally, modeling wasn't something that someone like me should be doing, they'd say, 'with your brain and your mind.' I told them that it was not going to hurt my mind to put makeup on my face.

"I started out being a showroom model at Tiffeau. I worked very closely with him. Originally he even fit the collection on me. He liked the proportions of my body. He liked women who were broad-shouldered, narrow-hipped. But he liked bosoms, which was interesting. Tiffeau was one of the first people to say no underwear, no girdles.

"It started out as one of those things where you were in the right place at the right time. Then I worked at it, worked very hard at it.

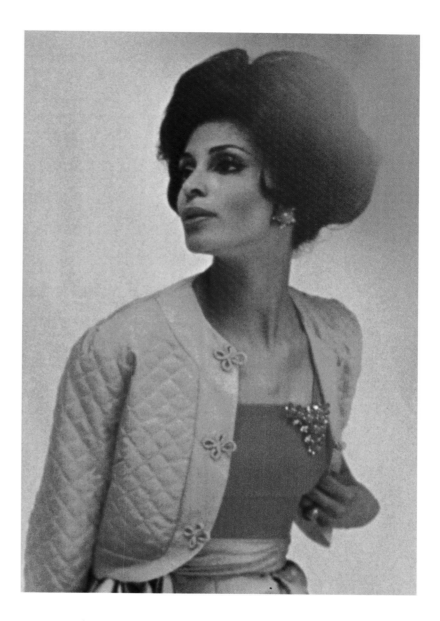

"People started to ask me to do other shows. Bergdorf Goodman was one of the first. At that time department stores used to have fashion shows once a week. Bergdorf Goodman, Franklin Simon, Stern's, Saks, A&S. Gimbel's used to have half-hour lunch shows, at twelve-thirty and one o'clock. So you'd do an hour, two little mini-shows back to back for the working person. You'd get booked for a week to do all of these shows. It's not like what we have now. There was a lot of work.

"In season, you're talking September, October, you would do department stores. Then in November you would do

Liz Campbell, one of the "Band of Beautiful Pioneers" in 1962. The daughter of noted cartoonist **E. Simms Campbell**, she married ground-breaking photographer **Gordon Parks**.

the designer collections. December, there wasn't much work, but it didn't matter. Then, if you were a fitting model, like I was, you started to fit again in January for the new collection that was shown in March.

"When I was working in the show season, I would start at eight o'clock in the morning and work until seven-thirty or eight o'clock at night. I would do that five days a week, April, May, and June. Then you would do the fittings which would take you through the summer. Then the department stores would start their shows again in September and October. Then you go back to Seventh Avenue in November. I worked probably eleven or twelve months a year since I was a fitting model also. But if you didn't fit, you could work at least eight months.

"I did a few things for print, but I did a lot of TV, those early morning shows: Johnny Carson, Virginia Graham, Sonny Fox. They'd have different designers and three or four models and they'd talk about whatever the fashion was for that season. They would have a little five or seven-minute fashion segment. That was a very important part of how people sold things.

"I knew I was different. I wasn't like the White models. People walked with a stiff style, what they called Dior turns, very formal. There was a whole group of us who brought a whole new kind of easy way of looking at clothes and a great sense of fun and personality. It didn't exist before when they were doing that rigid Dior walk. I came in on the fringe of it. I was loping around the stage. They'd say, 'She walks like a guy.' I'd say that I spent my life walking between my brother and my father. My father was six feet tall, and my brother was six feet six, plus I have a long stride. Why would I be mincing along growing up with these two people? I had to keep up.

"I quit modeling in 1971 and went to work at Bloomingdale's in the fashion office. I stayed there for six years and then I went on to become a buyer at Saks Fifth Avenue. I went to Europe, did the European buys. It was like completing the circle, seeing modeling from the other side. I knew what it was like backstage, the excitement a show could generate. And later I was quite content sitting on the other side watching. We are each fabulous in our own way. I felt so much pride at being part of a chain, part of a continuum. I loved that period of time in Europe when you'd go to a major show, and 80% of the models would be Black, all shades of Black. They were stunning, just fabulous.

"Versace would open the show, and there'd be ten gorgeous Black women lined up. You could hear the audience gasp. That whole White audience has got to perceive the people they see around them differently. They have to. The impact! When the Black models would come down with their walk and the music, then the White Girls started doing the same thing. When did you see White Girls get behinds? And lips? All of a sudden now all of the White Girls have big full lips and they've got nice little behinds and everybody's jiggling and wiggling. I think it was great. It was much needed. I never felt better or prouder than to watch all of those Girls come down the runway."

Before this epiphany of break-throughs in the '60s and '70s, however, very few Black women were seen on runways in the States, not to mention Europe. There was one major exception: the Ebony Fashion Fair. Founded in 1958 by Mrs. Eunice W. Johnson, the wife of publisher John H. Johnson, the Fashion Fair was "probably the best introduction to runway modeling that one could have," according to June Murphy, who made her modeling debut in the annual three-month benefit. "You worked in all varieties of circumstances. You toured on a bus with stage managers. You were in town for one or two days. You had long runways, you had short ones, you had ones where you could only take two steps, others where you had to walk a mile and come back. And you wore the most gorgeous clothes because Mrs. Johnson went to Paris and bought the couture. It was pretty exciting that the first really big shows you did were the real deal."

The Body Politic
Style and Survival

Style represented a challenge to nonexistence. Ever since Africans were stolen or sold away from the Mother Continent and hijacked from their cultures, they have used every means to insure the survival of what remained. Some could separate body from soul and sacrifice one for the other. Many could not, and suffering defined their totality. Although they bent under the load and often the lash, their numbers in the New World have never ceased to grow. There were more Black people in the present than there ever were in the past.

And there were more Black people in more places doing more things considered inconceivable until they were actually achieved. They have survived, propagated, and often prospered despite an unrelenting system that has tried to legislate, overwork, starve, lynch, inoculate, brainwash, and otherwise wipe them out of existence. Outnumbered and overpowered, they fought the *guerrilla*—the little war—of life on their private, personal battleground, on the only thing they could be said to possess: their body. In slavery, when they did not own even that, and out of slavery, when they rented it out for a job, they used their appearance every day to affirm their existence.

Style said I am. No matter what.

Clothing and accessories spoke their own languages with their own alphabets, signs, and symbols. Colors, textures, shapes, and functions made themselves felt in ways beyond words, for the wearer and the looker. In all societies there existed cultural dictionaries and private codes for dressing. There were the Do's and the Don'ts, what's in and what's out. There were club rules and anti-club rules. And, of course, there were anti-rules.

Black people continuously redefined the rules. Individual style has been perhaps one of the most basic and unexplored survival skills of Africans in the Americas, one of the most obvious and undervalued tools of resistance, and one of the most successful strategies of the subversive. Whether standing out or blending in, a Black person with style did it better. Style could resound in quiet details: the perfect insouciance of an immaculate pocket square in the breast pocket of a sober double-breasted suit or the ritual intricacy of corn-rowed hair woven into ancestral patterns forgotten by all but the nimblest fingers. Or style could startle in grand-scale images: a tall dark woman dressed in a billowing white bridal gown or undressed in a minimal neon monokini. Style said surprise.

It was not that absolutely every Black person had it. And it was certainly not that every one looked like a fashion photo, that is, dressed in the latest style. What did evolve was a critical number of individuals who developed, maintained, and communicated a critical amount of the Real Thing, so that Black people as a whole

God created black people and black people created style.

George Wolfe

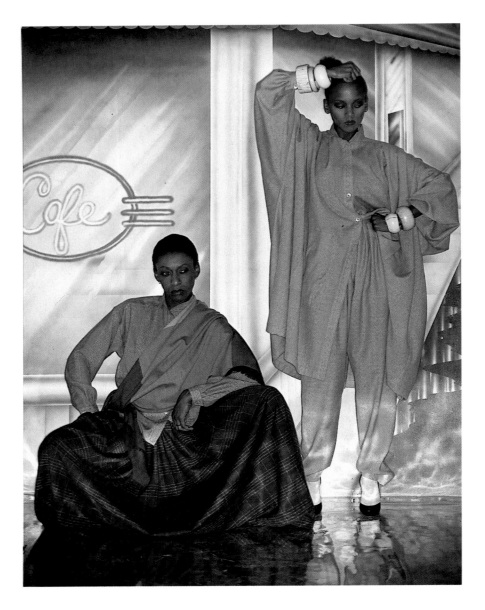

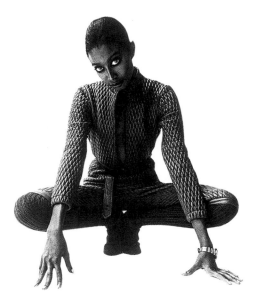

tion for style. And through a uniquely efficient combination of capitalism, racism, sexism, and homosexual buddy-ism, it has resulted by no coincidence that almost all of the leading designers in the fashion world were White homosexual men—the females of their gender, the Blacks of their race, survivors who cannot reproduce.

Black homosexuals were considered doubly endowed stylistically at the same time that they were doubly punished biologically. Their contributions as designers, consumers, and models could not be denied. Gay men were here and, despite AIDS and preventable diseases such as homophobia, they were here to stay.

And so were Black people and their style.

One tradition maintained that eleven o'clock Sunday morning was the most segregated hour in America. Another tradition claimed that the same time was the most fashionable hour in Black America. Church-goers wore their finest to praise the Lord and press the flesh, to see and be seen. Our dress on the Sabbath was material testimony to God's good grace rewarding us with yet another week of survival.

Model Toukie Smith described childhood visions: "No one dresses more than we do when we go to church every Sunday. Even if you're just sitting on the

Bethann Hardison and **Toukie Smith**. From *East Meets West* by **Issey Miyake**.

Donyale Luna. Her name was as inventive as her style.

were perceived as creative and original dressers. And it was not that White people absolutely did not have it. But since they were the ones who profited the most from the style industries—fashion and beauty—they were perceived more as acquisitions experts, buyers and sellers, the manipulators and *marchands* rather than the makers of style.

The exception to this generalization consisted of homosexuals. Like Black people in predominantly White societies, homosexuals were persecuted for being other, different, dangerous, and on the increase. Also like Black people, they were perceived as having a genetic predisposi-

steps, you're looking at a fashion show when you're young. On Easter, especially, oh honey, it was fashion time. Everybody in the neighborhood got dressed up." Extra care was taken with the cleaning and pressing of garments. Hence, the words "clean" and "sharp", meaning particularly well-dressed. Adornments in the form of scrupulously matching accessories took on ritual aspects. We had to look right to be righteous.

The conventions of Sunday morning worship were further spotlighted by another church function: the charity fashion show. At these seasonable events—well-organized and enthusiastically attended—local dressmakers and milliners enjoyed a special opportunity to showcase their designs: hats that soared in flights of fancy, smartly tailored business suits, glittering cocktail dresses, and glamorous evening gowns. These outfits were embellished by precise hand-worked details, for quality craftsmanship was always a point of pride. On temporary runways set up in the center aisle prominent church and club members played glamour girl. For the most part these women were not fashion models, for this tradition existed long before the current term or the modern profession. Rather they were role models, real women whose influence on real people was often profound. Thus, part of Black style was not about breathlessly aspiring to an impossibly grand life but about confidently, proudly, spreading around the knowledge and polish we already possessed.

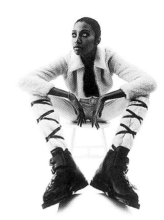

Donyale Luna.

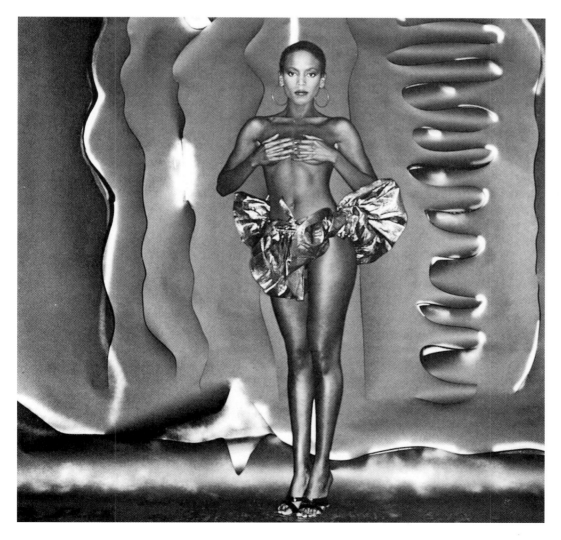

Toukie Smith. From *Black Borders* by **Anthony Barboza**.

Tony Barboza combined an acutely commercial eye with a unique artistic vision to become the most successful Black photographer of his generation.

THE BODY POLITIC

Norma Jean Darden, whose father, Walter T. Darden, was a well-respected doctor in an established New Jersey suburb, described how traditions of family, church, and fashion combined in her early years: "When I was in college I worked the Black fashion circuit. Every year we did the Abyssinian Baptist Church. My father put on a big fashion show to raise money for the NAACP, and it became an annual extravaganza. All the models of that era would come over—

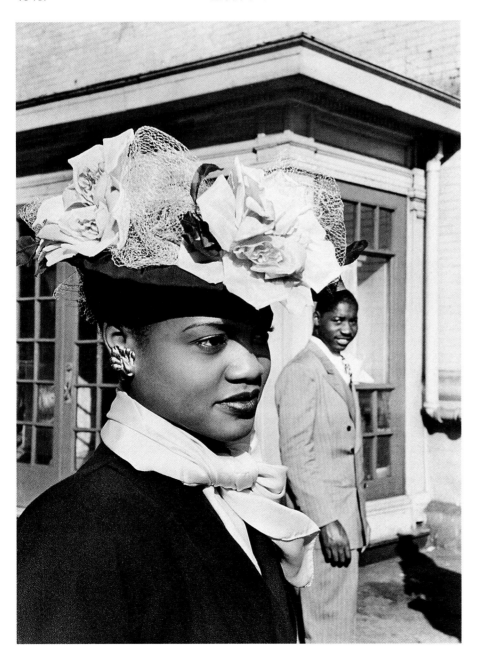

An Easter hat blooms in Harlem, 1946.

Helen Williams, Dorothea Towles, Etta Mae [Mrs. Sugar Ray] Robinson. Sammy Davis Jr. came over. He loved models. My father was quite dapper. My mother was very practical—she liked slacks and blouses long before they were popular. She liked ease and comfort. She was not at all what we'd call clothes conscious or a clothes horse. I had an aunt who was the opposite of my mother. Every year I was sent to spend the summer with her in North Carolina. She was a club woman and the epitome of a clothes woman. She had an outfit for every occasion along with the hat and the bag, the gloves and the shoes—everything totally coordinated. She loved my little fashion career."

Healthy, down-home Southern roots combined with Northern big-city sophistication to provide Norma Darden with a solid appreciation of who she was and what she could be. But lifestyle and material foundations were not foolproof predictors of success. A totally different kind of environment surrounded Toukie Smith and her brother, Willi. It was not the grand life or even a comfortably bourgeois family that inspired them. Although there was pain and near-poverty, Toukie described an essential, abiding feeling of love. "My mother was a silent alcoholic, but I could still talk to my mother. I could also talk to my grandmother, my aunts, and sometimes my uncles, although I didn't want to talk to them because they always wanted to correct me, and they were right. I was a wild child, real wild. All this energy. I had all this curiosity, and I still have it.

"When my mother was working—she worked in a factory—she would do a sketch on our lunch bags every morning. When my parents used to go to cabarets on Saturdays we would stay with the neighbors, and it was fine 'cause it was like ten kids all together. It was fun.

"My mother had a blue chiffon dress with blue bugle beads on top. She dyed her shoes sapphire blue. She sprayed her hair sapphire blue. She had earrings that had little sapphire blue stones. And they'd go to see someone like Stan Getz. The dressing up, it wasn't about *Vogue*. It was the Sundays at church. It was going to see

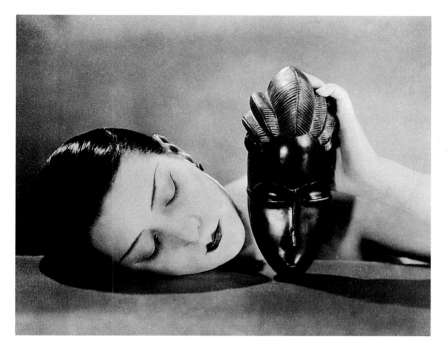

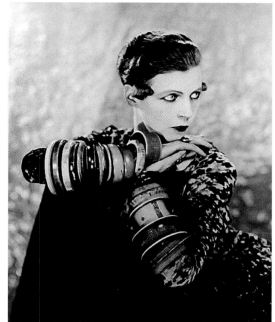

the jazz musicians or Lena Horne or Josephine Baker. How could you not be affected by that?

"Willi and I would dress up. We'd take the sheets and make clothes out of them. It wasn't about how much you paid for what you got. It was how you made it work. My parents didn't have money to buy the most expensive clothes, but baby, those clothes worked, and they were glamorous and wonderful."

Black style has always encompassed extremes—just as the Saturday night show-stopper could turn up the following Sunday morning as the compleat church lady.

No matter where you went in Black America, music—in all its denominations—was religion. At jazz clubs and after hours spots, at formal dances and house parties, people dressed up to get down, sometimes in loud colors to loud sounds. A timeless, generic rhythm and blues song said: "Put on your red dress, baby, 'cause we're going out tonight."

What would the jazz musicians of the '30s—in zoot suits with the reet pleat, 31″ at the knee tapering down to 12″ at the ankle, swinging 5′ long gold pocket chains—think of the rap musicians of the '90s—in wide baggy pants, wide-shouldered jackets and ropes of gold around their neck? Would we catch a nod of recognition, a smile saying Yesss? From our *fin de siècle* vantage point we could see that both styles were somehow connected to an African tradition of voluminous drape and easy movability:

what, in another context, Duke Ellington might have called swing. Black to the future, indeed.

And what would the lindy-hopping sisters of the '40s with flared skirts flipping over their heads think of the Lycra tights and dare-to-bare bustiers of their present-day granddaughters out on the neon dance floor? Imagine these intergenerational, transoceanic dialogues taking place in family closets and attics. Imagine us trying on the old and them trying on the new, all of us sharing and tearing up false, wear-dated distinctions. The place might be unfamiliar and the language totally different, but if we listened closely to the lyrics, if we succumbed and hummed along and patted our feet, we learned what we've always known: the beat goes on.

Actress Carol Cole had poignant stories to tell about her family and their sometimes conflicting sense of style. When her biological parents died, she was only four years old. "The plan was for me to be adopted by my great aunt, Dr. Charlotte Hawkins Brown, the founder of Palmer Memorial Academy. My aunt, Marie Hawkins, who later changed her name to Maria, had just married the illustrious Nat "King" Cole. They say it was Nat who first suggested adopting me. A tug-of-war ensued between the Coles and Dr. Brown. They all went to court for the custody of yours truly, and the Coles won. Soon after, I was moved from Massachusetts to the West Coast and we integrated the famed all-Anglo neighborhood of Hancock Park

CONJUGATING CULTURE, 1926.

Black and White. An elegant symmetry of opposites.

Shipping heiress **Nancy Cunard** wearing her collection of ivory bracelets.

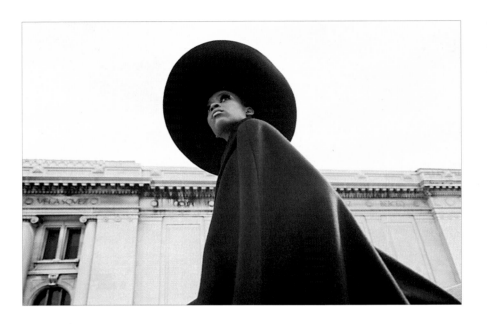

PUBLISHING FIRSTS.

Naomi Sims became the first identifiably Black model to appear on the cover of the *New York Times* supplement, *Fashions of the Times*. August, 1967.

Harper's Bazaar was the first American fashion magazine to feature the image of a Black woman—this sketch of **Donyale Luna**—on its cover. January, 1965.

in L.A. In one fell swoop my destiny was altered. Mother Maria was always fashion conscious. In an odd way, I think Dr. Brown, whom I called Lala, encouraged snobbism among her nieces and students. Lala picked up a number of priceless frocks for her wards in Paris and wrote one of the first books of etiquette for Blacks, *The Correct Thing—To Do, To Say, To Wear*, published in 1941. Seen in the context of her times, her stance was perfectly understandable; she was out there beating the band for equality and digesting European sensibilities.

"Anyway, Mother Maria was well schooled in the finer things of life. Maria probably set new standards in fashion consciousness all on her own. She was determined to 'bring some class' to what she considered to be the tacky and ignorant and glitzy world of show biz. Ah, she had conservative, but exquisite taste.

"There's no one who will dispute the fact that she radically altered Dad's taste in clothes. He was sporting some cool zoot suits when they met, and a sparse mustache. Very flash, very Be-Bop. The zoot suits were replaced. With Maria's influence, he was impeccable, setting standards of his own. He was suave, understated. White America could be comfortable and comforted by this Black velvet man."

True proponents of original style always worked their own magic, whether the elements were based on elegant, bourgeois conventions or on rugged, even ragged improvisations from cultures and classes which were scorned for, supposedly, having no culture and no class.

Style stealing was nothing new in fashion. If imitation was the sincerest form of flattery, it has also become one of the surest routes to fortune. It no longer involved the privileged classes copying each other. Status seekers of all colors and ethnicities have always dressed up. At the end of the 20th century their offspring, in cautious revolt, were dressing down with a high-priced vengeance. "Varnished barbarism" became a staple at staid fashion houses while patchwork with unfinished seams received pounds of press.

Acknowledgment was another issue entirely. "When I look at fashion," said Mikki Taylor, a former model and the current Beauty Editor of *Essence* magazine, "and I look at how trends come and go, worldwide cues are taken from Black folk. But very few will come out and say it. It's like the best-kept secret. They find other words to make it palatable to sell it to this one, to sell it to that one. But to tell the truth, who's going to tell the truth? That's what we're trying to do."

Black women's very survival depended on continuous re-invention. One hundred years ago they were barely more than a

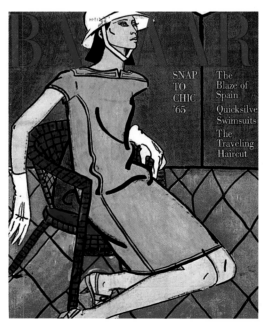

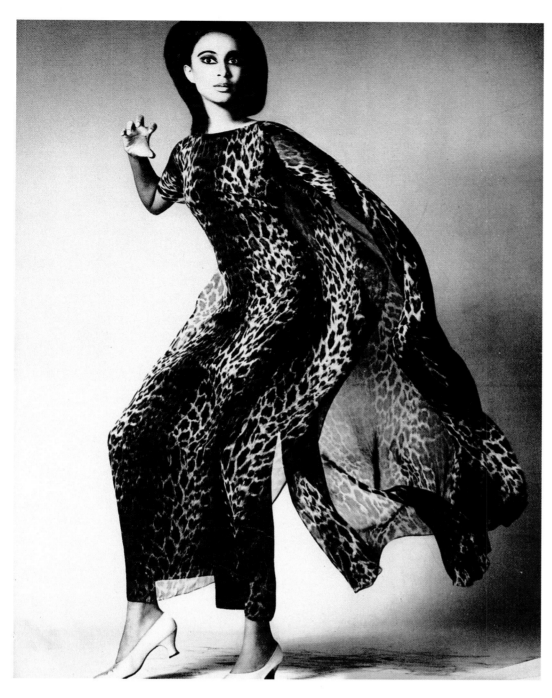

Initiating a new era, **Donyale Luna** defied fashion's genteel conventions of pose and presentation.

generation removed from slavery. As Black families undertook the exodus from the rural unreconstructed South, Black women were obliged to expand their education, augment their professional skills, and hone their survival instincts. As they did so, they began making a more serious investment in their wardrobe. Skirt hemlines gradually rose with the early decades of the 20th century, increasing women's mobility. Tightly structured corsets, multi-layered petticoats, and buttoned boots, gave way to flexible panties and brassieres, body-liberating shifts, and open shoes. Clothes, always a label of identity, now became a signal of aspiration. The apparent status of a higher social class was within reach of whoever could afford—or create—the apparel.

Americans have long been making clothes and making social statements with them. Among them are historical figures prominent behind the scenes of White society. The first great Black dressmaker of record, Elizabeth Hobbs Keckley, not only designed for President Abraham Lincoln's wife but also supported her financially after her husband's assassination. Ann Lowe, the daughter and granddaughter of dressmakers who sewed for the first families of Montgomery, Alabama, came to be known as both the "Dean of American Designers" and "society's best-kept secret." Her customers

One dressmaker, who was perhaps short on style but long on survival, actually changed the course of modern political history. It started on the evening of December 1, 1955. The beginning of Christmas rush was always a busy season, and she was tired after working at a department store in Montgomery, Alabama doing men's alterations. But as she said, she "was tired every day." Going home on the bus, she found a welcome seat in the back section reserved for Colored people just behind the section allotted for Whites. As the bus filled up, the bus driver asked the Black people to give up their seats so that standing Whites could sit. Fully aware of the penalty if she did not comply, she nonetheless refused and was arrested. Her court case challenged the system of legal segregation, led to the successful boycott of the Montgomery bus system that lasted for over a year, and eventually ignited a nationwide movement for civil rights. This seamstress, known affectionately as the Mother of the Civil Rights Movement, was Rosa Parks.

Evolution

The high cost of our color
is sometimes our freedom.

Naomi Sims

While no other single fashion person has had the far-reaching and directly political impact of dressmaker Rosa Parks, people of African descent continued to influence the style and substance of modern life. The social revolution which started in the '50s sparked an evolution in fashion and beauty that led to the increased presence and significance of Black models. The women of the early '60s, however, found themselves in an unusual situation. Each one was a unique beauty, yet each one represented a whole people. Their individual recognition and personal success were markers on a larger record of achievement. They were, perhaps, far from being card-carrying Freedom Fighters. But as political barriers were

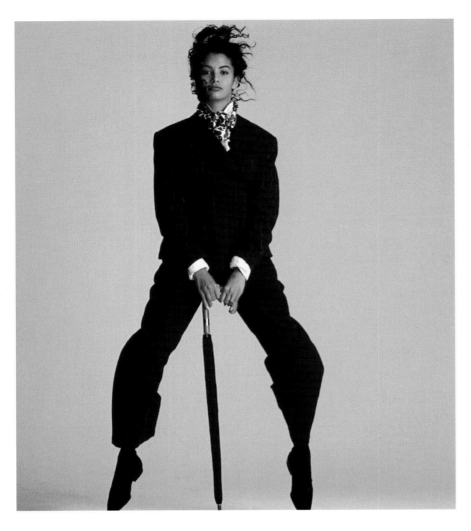

Kara Young.

Women helped liberate menswear, and menswear helped liberate them.

included two and three generations of American aristocracy, the DuPonts, Roosevelts, Posts, Biddles, Rockefellers, and Auchinclosses. "An awful snob," according to her own testimony, she was never interested in sewing for café society or social climbers. She sewed for families listed in the Social Register where her own name also appeared. Yet even she was not granted the full recognition she deserved. Her most famous creation—the wedding dress Jacqueline Bouvier wore when she married Senator John Kennedy—was not publicly acknowledged. While the *New York Times* described the bride's dress at length in its account of the Bouvier-Kennedy marriage at Newport, R.I., Sept. 13, 1953, it neglected to name the designer. That designer, who had also provided fifteen gowns for the bridal party, was Ann Lowe.

breached by new laws, non-legislated social barriers and unspoken moral codes —the real supports of society—showed their ugly strength. And models, just like all the others who dared, rose to challenge them.

Individual perseverance—an occupational requirement—did pay off for some models, like the regal Helen Williams. The most successful model of her day, she had been confined to Black publications until an ad for Loom Togs appeared in the *New York Times* in 1959. Subsequent appearances in *Life* and *Redbook*, newspapers and catalogs, were the long-awaited proof that "there was a dark model who could make it."

But most dark models continued to exist in a glamorous limbo working a dependable day job while waiting for that special call. If living in suspension had been a common condition among Black models, the decade of the '60s saw the limbo game begin to change.

The sleek Black beauties in their chic chignons photographed for *Life* magazine by Gordon Parks in 1962 presented an elegantly sophisticated image. With full-page fanfare they were described as having "graduated from specialized modeling for Negro fashion magazines and stores to the elite fashion salons" of New York City. Said to "have a special flair for wearing clothes of exotic design or color," they were pictured in opulent creations by Pauline Trigère, Pierre Balmain, and Arnold Scaasi. This acceptance into the highest echelons of American couture made good press, but it worked better as publicity than as a statement of significantly improved opportunities. True, a handful of women, generally very light-skinned, were employed in the showrooms of a handful of daring designers and seen by a privileged few journalists and buyers at their shows. But the fashion magazines and their advertisers had yet to take the leap. The magazine audience which counted millions of readers remained in the dark.

The later '60s were years of critical political upheaval around the world. In the United States fiery rebellions in Los Angeles, Newark, Detroit, and other large cities forced the philosophy of non-violent resistance of the Southern Civil Rights Movement into new directions. American college students linked Black demands with protest against the Vietnam War, capitalism, and conformism. Thousands of miles away, students in China carried the cultural revolution into the countryside while students in Prague and Paris confronted the steel-clad forces of law and order with flowers and street stones.

Only after history was made in the street did identifiably Black models hit the page as well as the stage. Black models also developed a stronger style and projected a stronger image. They already stood out. To become the best in the business they had to become outstanding. Whether they were born with the instinct for style or whether they learned it on the job, Black models were obliged to make themselves better than good. Helping to harness this potential, more Black-oriented agencies opened in New York City—Elaina Adams, American Models, and Black Beauty welcomed good Girls that White agencies often still rejected.

In their relentless pursuit of the new, the fashion makers of the '60s pounced on a creature who transcended Negro, Black, and any of the other racial categorizations, present and past. Her given name: Peggy Anne Donyale Aragonea Pegeon Freeman. Her chosen name—Donyale Luna—was as unusual as her appearance. Gauzed in leopard-spotted silk or sheathed in field flowers on the pages of *Harper's Bazaar* in 1965, she was described as having "the tall strength and pride of movement of a Masai warrior." *Time* called her "a spindly siren from Detroit...[who] stalked onto the fashion scene and became an overnight success." Fashion chronicler Bill Cunningham wrote, "The curtain parts, and the white-model dominated fashion world is confronted by the first ethereal African queen image. Her body moves like a panther, her arms, the wings of an exotic bird, the long neck suggests a black trumpet swan. The audience responds with shattering applause.... It is the birth of a new fashion era.... The new star on the horizon is Donyale Luna [whose] arrival...was

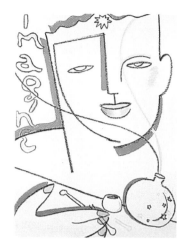

DRAWING ON STYLE.

An invitation to imagine, by **Harvey Boyd**.

The firebird spirit of fashion, as captured by **Antonio**.

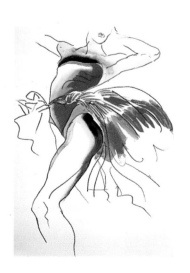

greeted in both the photography and runway worlds of modeling with a success unknown to blacks at that time. She cast a spell of exotic movement over the once-ladylike attitudes."

Launched into the fashion strato-sphere, Donyale Luna rocketed through the pages of *Bazaar*, *Paris Match*, and *Queen*, as well as the American, British, French, and Italian editions of *Vogue*. She quickly left the States for Europe. Her departure created a void of excitement that was soon to be filled by modeling's first Black superstar.

Naomi Sims

No one model was more representative of her era than Naomi Sims. She personified the slogan "Black is Beautiful" with equal emphasis on deep color and high value. None of the previous models—the "Band of Beautiful Pioneers"—of the early '60s was as tall, as thin or as dark. Naomi was the first to prove that dark Black was unquestionably beautiful, unexpectedly exciting, challenging, desirable, and profitable.

Born in Oxford, Mississippi in 1949, Naomi Sims was sent to Pittsburgh in the early '60s to better her education. By the age of thirteen she had shot up to 5'10 ½". In the Catholic schools she attended, she described herself as being "rather a loner, teased and intensely disliked. I could have developed a neurosis, but instead I learned to walk with dignity. I carried pride and confidence. I equate height with power. Most of the boys were tall, and they seemed to have most of the power in school. So I felt very good to be as tall as they.

"We were a family of women who adored beauty and makeup and fashion. At age fourteen I went door-to-door—I was raised in a primarily White neighborhood—to my White neighbors, and I sold Avon products. So I got my first hands-on experience with cosmetics and skin care products at the age of fourteen."

While still in Pittsburgh Naomi won a scholarship for modeling, publicly declaring her intentions of becoming a high fashion model and then going into the beauty industry. Staking a claim to her destiny, she moved to New York City to fulfill it. By day she studied design at the Fashion Institute of Technology, by night psychology at New York University. But she quickly ran out of money. When her college career counselor suggested that she

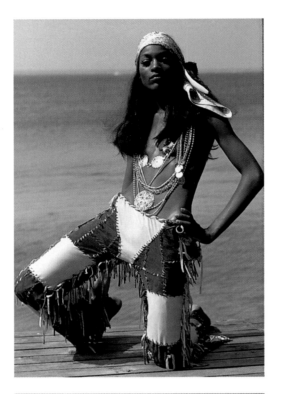

AMERICAN FUR— THE SEAL COAT

BLACK SEAL, WHITE MINK AND WHITE LEATHER

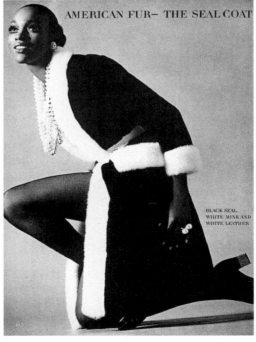

Naomi Sims. No matter what she wore, she carried pride and confidence.

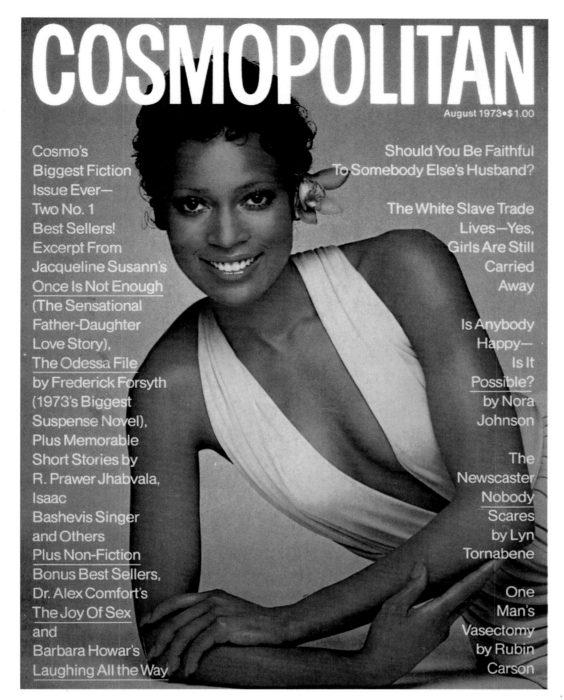

Naomi Sims's seductive finale as a model signaled a fresh start as an entrepreneur and author, as well as a wife and mother.

try modeling, she began working for fashion illustrators who sketched her for Macy's ads. At age seventeen she was making an impressive $20 an hour and gaining in experience and stamina.

Her big breakthrough came in 1967 by way of Gus and Pat Peterson, the innovative husband and wife team who photographed and edited the influential fashion supplement of the *New York Times*. In August she landed on the cover of the *Fashions of the Times* in a sweeping black cape and hat. It was the first time a Black model was seen on the cover of a major fashion magazine.

Naomi thought she would have little

difficulty signing with one of the leading model agencies, but, instead, she faced one rejection after the other. Undeterred, Naomi became her own agent. She sent out copies of her work to every art director and fashion concern in the industry's advertising guide. "I asked Wilhemina if I could use her telephone number, and she demurred. But I said, 'What have you got to lose? If anybody calls, you'll get a commission.' I was a saleswoman even at a very early age. And she said all right, reluctantly, and I went home to bed in a fit of depression.

"When a telegram arrived, I thought, Oh my God, what have I done? I've done

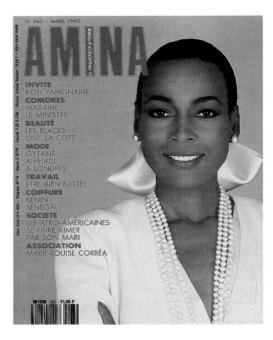

Naomi Sims. Her image and her products reached an international market. *Amina*, March 1992.

something wrong. I didn't read it. Then a second telegram arrived a second day, and I still didn't read it. I left them lying on the floor. Finally, a third telegram arrived, and I opened it. It said, 'Dear Naomi, stop, we have many many bookings for you, AT&T, General Electric, and *Vogue* magazine. Please call.' And my career started from there. I was off and running."

Photographers launched her and designers loved her. Just what was it that made her the star? "I modeled to death. I was very unique and original in my movements. And I loved the clothes, I loved the atmosphere, I loved the environment, and I loved the people. I felt like a fish being thrown back into the water. I loved it!"

Naomi enjoyed unprecedented recognition and success. Although, by her color alone, she was "considered revolutionary" and by her size strictly high fashion, she made important forays into all sectors of America via the magazine covers of *Ladies' Home Journal* and *McCall*'s as well as *Life* and *Cosmopolitan*. The heartland saw her smile and forgot their anxiety.

But what fashion conservatives feared Naomi represented was true. She was revolutionary. Not in dramatic political rhetoric or action. Merely in her being. As the first indisputably Black model on the pages of *Vogue* and other publications, she seemed to magnetize all attention. Near her White models literally paled into insignificance. And in that era, when fashion drew inspiration from so many different ethnic sources—Native American, North African, Black African, Indian—as well as from futuristic, space-age fantasies, Naomi was a perfect fit. Like Donyale Luna, her great inspiration, she could do it all. For her favorite editorial shoots, "nothing was too good for a picture. I always wanted more fantasy. I gave them elegance and regality. I was reaching for the stars." At fashion shows where the atmosphere was already electric with anticipation, she dazzled the audience, and left devoted fans and recent converts alike screaming with applause.

Pleasant memories of the good old days were not the only ones she had. She found out early on that modeling had other aspects to it that tended to disrespect her intelligence and sensitivity. "I found it boring," she said candidly. She found another disappointing aspect to the fashion business was "that people expected you to be your image all the time. I resented that."

If she resented being locked into the full-time role of fashion model, she did accept the responsibility of being the exemplary professional Black woman, dressing carefully and with dignified style. Always racially conscious and outspoken, she was determined to "give something back" to the Black community. What she gave was an image of beauty, freedom, and success, a combination all too rarely seen at that time by "young people who were hurt, confused, and angry."

After just six fast-paced years as a model, Naomi went into phase two of her career plan. "I was ready to go into business. I used modeling as a stepping stone into the business arena. It was never my ultimate goal to be a model. I had to make a name for myself so I could put it on my products." In the early '70s, the spirit of the '60s was being eroded by the war in Vietnam, economic uncertainty, and the new Republican politics. "Dark-skinned models were on the wane and light-skinned models were at a premium," said Naomi. Sensing that the Afro was evolving and Black women would be looking for more variety in their hairstyles, she looked at the wig market, and what she found was opportunity. She saved her money, studied, experimented, and eventually sold her ideas to a manufacturer. In its peak year of business, her wig company grossed about $7,000,000.

Nevertheless, Naomi was no more content settling down as a wig entrepreneur than she was as a model. She authored four books on health and beauty, and marketed a fragrance. In the mid-'80s after ten years of research and development she brought out her own skin care and cosmetics line. As founder, chairman of the board, and spokesmodel for Naomi Sims Beauty Products Ltd., she continued to maintain an active schedule traveling and making personal appearances.

"In 1988, only three years after founding her firm and barely two years after her line of cosmetics and skin-care products was launched in 100 department stores, Naomi Sims Beauty Products grossed about $5 million," reported *Black Enterprise* magazine in March, 1989. In the years since, the company has managed to survive serious inroads being made in Black cosmetics by White companies.

Naomi Sims has always advised women to secure a good education, to be prepared for the future, and not to "look for a rich man to take care of you. Black women work longer, and while we age benignly, we must keep our eyes and ears open and think of ways to support ourselves."

A certain bounce-back perseverance characterized her, whether she was speaking of her public life as a model and entrepreneur or of her personal life as a wife and mother. Success for her was "a sense of accomplishment. It's like a story well told. It has a beginning, a middle, and an end. The beginning is the dream or the desire. The middle is the impetus. And the end is when you've caught your golden ball, you've got your earth on a string."

Naomi Sims was a hard act to follow, but even during the years of her modeling career, there were other Black models on the scene. The presence of a dozen or so of these women—each one outstanding and unique—informed magazine editors, fashion designers, advertising clients, and catalog marketers that there were more where Naomi came from. Ironically, though, her very success left many decision-makers smug about their brand of good-hearted tokenism.

Norma Darden described an experience from the late '60s. "When I first started modeling they just had Naomi Sims, and every place I went they'd say, 'Oh, we've got Naomi,' as if that were the answer to everything. They'd go into this long explanation of how they weren't prejudiced themselves but they could understand the Southern point of view. We'd been through all that for years. I remember going to *Vogue* and asking the model editor, 'Isn't it time that *Vogue* opened its pages up to the Black model?' She said, 'Oh, I'm sorry but we're interested in the White woman here.' And I said, 'Do you think that's fair?' Then she said, 'That's one of the inequities of life.' One of the inequities. I'll never forget it. That's a direct quote. It was brutal. Very few people today realize what we had to go through to get other people hired. Only rarely did the first to beat the door down get the job."

One model who was able to profit from others' experiences was Charlene Dash. In 1968, a recent high school graduate still living at home in Long Island City, she went into the Ford agency. The timing was right, as well as her look of wide-eyed caramel innocence. Before she knew it, her plans to be a teacher were discarded—she was working as a model. On her first appointment to see Diana Vreeland, the legendary fashion editor and style setter at *Vogue*, Charlene said, "Mrs. Vreeland never even looked at my book. She used two pairs of glasses to watch me walk. My first pictures were six pages in *Vogue* with photographer Gianni Penati. That was so exciting. Once you worked for *Vogue*, then you worked for everybody."

Manifestly "not a fashion person and not caught up in the glamour and glitz" of the business, she was sometimes paired with a model of quite opposite tempera-

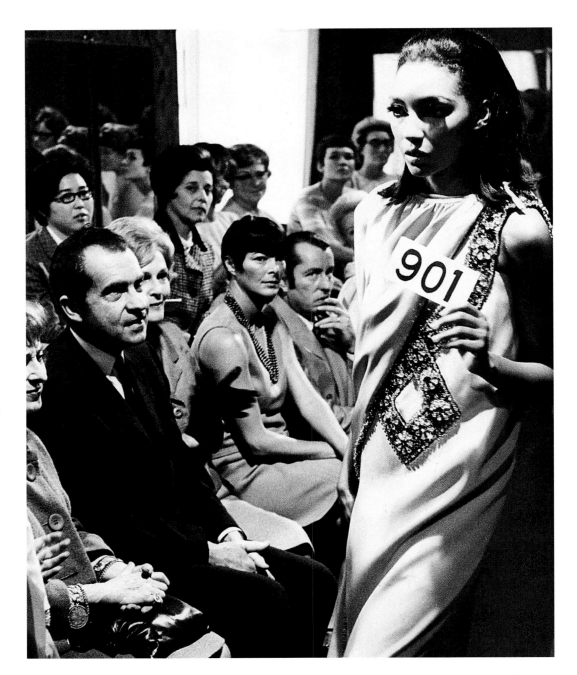

Kellie showing Parisian couture in 1966 before an audience which included **Pat** and **Richard Nixon**, who would be elected president of the United States in 1968.

One of the first Black models to develop a career in Europe, **Kellie** was a prize-winning graduate of the School of the Art Institute of Chicago. She maintained her home base in London, where she died unexpectedly of cancer at age 31 in 1973, at the height of her career.

ment, Naomi Sims. "I didn't get my name in the paper like Naomi," said Charlene, still upset about the rumors of competition between the two of them decades ago. But she worked regularly doing mostly catalog from which she earned a comfortable living and considerable respect.

Just as the fashion doors—oiled by blood sacrifice and pressured by social change—creaked open to allow the integration of Black models, another challenge soon followed: diversity. In 1969, *Time* magazine headlined an article on fashion, the "Black Look in Beauty." Despite the lump-it-all-together title, there was obviously no automatically predictable, monolithic Black look. No longer restricted to one skin shade or one set of facial features, the six models photographed for the article—Carmen Bradshaw, Charlene Dash, Jolie Jones, Yahne Sangare, Naomi Sims, and Jany Tomba— showed a wide range of style, personality, and marketability. Emphasis was put on recognizing tangible changes made in a "fashion industry that has started thinking black." There were now a variety of Black models in formerly all-White agencies, on the pages of all-White magazines, and in television commercials.

During these heady times, mere words carried tremendous weight. The language of the news and fashion articles was symptomatically ambivalent. The Girls were Negro models while the look in beauty was Black. And where women of obvious African descent were once refused work because they were too dark, at this moment in time some were refused because they were not dark enough. When June Murphy heard that excuse one too many times, she quipped, "'That's OK, hire me like I'm White then.' Of course," she added gleefully, "the clients almost passed out when I said that, right?"

Runway Radicals

You know you're not what they want to see. You're not what they ever saw before.

Bethann Hardison

The fashion show possessed a reality that photography could only represent. For White clients and journalists, Black people could be a convenient sociological abstraction. But Black models—in the flesh—were undeniable. When the Girls of the late '60s began strutting in all their glamorous variety down the runways of designers and department stores, the audience response was not always warmly enthusiastic. Face to face with a confused and sometimes hostile audience, only the strongest—models and designers—would survive.

Bethann Hardison

I was a performer and was lucky enough that I came along when the rhetoric was beginning to affect the system with 'Black is Beautiful.' People were very much searching for Black faces. I didn't photograph well but I was clever, and I chose to face the market of fashion designers and

skip the photo. Where all the other Girls, because they were nice looking, worked hard to be photogenic, I didn't do that. So it gave me my in. I was the first dark Girl that was un-Colored looking, so to speak. There was no one who looked like me. I had very, very short hair and big, big eyes. And I was not particularly attractive—attractive but not what they considered beautiful or passable.

"It's foolish sometimes that little girls have to be taught they're beautiful. Growing up, I never had a problem thinking I was unattractive because I was so successful as a person. I never had time to think about, 'Oh, you're not attractive.' I had succeeded so well in high school. I was the first Black to be a cheerleader, to be senior high school president, the first to do so many things.

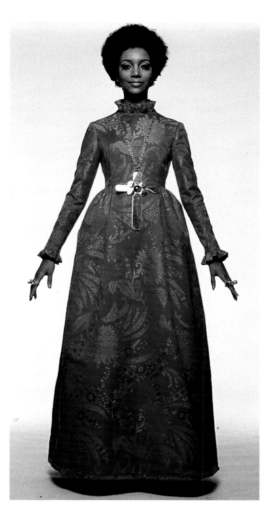

Charlene Dash. Her look and her timing were right.

"But when you start going into the world of modeling, when they start rejecting you....Chester Weinberg, who's gone now, was the one to give me my first big professional job. He was great because he knew that he was taking a chance—the audience could just turn against him, too. Every time I came back, he knew there was this groaning out there, but he kept telling me how beautiful I was. To their eyes, I was a problem. To Chester, it was like, This Girl has got something.

"We helped to change all that, and we became successful. The Black Girl made the selling of clothes so much more believable, so much more attractive from the standpoint of entertainment. The White Girl didn't know how to do that. Not only did we prove we could do it and do it better, even White people believed it when they saw it, and they began to focus on it. So five to ten years later, if enough people look and watch long enough they can learn how to do it, too. So they've learned how to do it now. They know how to walk.

"Now it's become a time where things are not as radical. What allowed us then was that people did go against something. There was a lot of 'I won't take it any more!'"

Paco Rabanne

When Paco Rabanne first presented Black models in his collection in July, 1964 in Paris, little did he suspect that his choice of models would be as controversial a subject as his choice of plastic and metal "fabrics". Nor did he think that the opposition would be so fierce and last so long.

In the spring of 1990, he had just won the Golden Thimble award, *le Dé d'or*, France's highest accolade for a fashion designer. The road had been long and lonely. Born in Spain and educated in France in architecture, Rabanne had been designing clothes in Paris since the early '60s. After twenty-five years on the innovative fringes of the industry, to be recognized by its establishment brought back bitter memories. He claimed that he was ostracized—placed in virtual internal exile—because he was the first European designer to use Black models.

"Here is the first Black model in Paris, Kellie," he declared with complete authority. "There were Kellie and Donyale Luna, whom I presented to Salvador Dali, who shot her in his films. But Kellie is really the first Black mannequin, and it's because of her that the American press spit in my face. Literally, splat.

"I was back in the dressing room. I watched them coming, the girls from American *Vogue* and *Harper's Bazaar*. 'Why did you do that?' they said. 'You don't have the right to do that, to take those kind of Girls. Fashion is for us, White people.' They spit in my face. I had to wipe it off." Asked if the French were any more tolerant, Rabanne answered with a hesitant and conditional yes.

Rabanne felt that as a Spaniard designing in Paris, friendly with talented young people of diverse nationalities, he wanted to be inclusive of many different looks in his collections. "To give a universal aspect to fashion, it was normal to have blondes and brunettes and women of color. There weren't any Asian models in the business, otherwise I would have had Asian Girls, too. The idea was to be universal, that's all. But the press reaction was so violent. And violent for what reason? Because I showed plastic dresses worn by

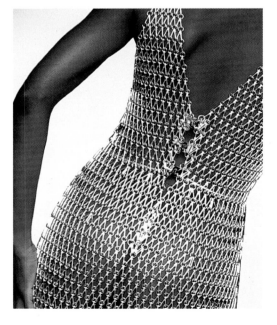

Metal dress by **Paco Rabanne**.

Black Girls—and with music in the background—for the first time!

"In the '60s, you know, fashion shows took place in silence with a woman in each salon shouting out the number of each outfit. I found that terribly boring. So I played music, and the Girls danced. And at the time the Girls went barefoot, because I didn't have enough money to buy shoes. It was a scandal."

Rabanne contended that he was punished by powerful French fashion authorities for using "*négresses*" in his collections. That punishment involved being consistently denied positive press and access to the usual show venues. He felt that he was banished to a kind of fashion Siberia until Black models became popular and, indeed, indispensable.

Rabanne was careful to discern cultural differences between different groups of Black models. "Black Americans are hyper-professional, super, supra-professional, whereas the West Indian Girls are very soft, very sweet, even sugary. African models are straight, with a lot of elegance and rigidity. The American has more feeling, while the African has none. She has a gravity, that spinal column. By using Girls of different ethnic origin I am trying to show different aspects of womanliness. The Black woman has a way of carrying herself that is different from the Asian woman, for example, who is completely boxed in. She walks with her head down because the Asian woman is submissive. She submits to male domination [Rabanne used the word "*machisme*"]. And Asian *machisme* is more ferocious than the *machisme* of Black Africa, for example. But I also like the attitude that woman can have, because in fashion I'm looking to express all kinds of moods.

"I taught my models not to smile, because during a certain period all models were smiling. And I said, 'You are not whores. You're not selling anything. You're not selling your body. Those people in the audience who are looking at you, look at them with disdain. You are ten times more beautiful than they are, so scorn them.'

"There was a moment at the beginning of the '80s when suddenly everybody

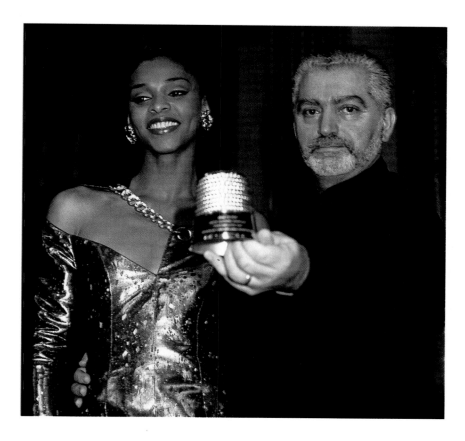

used Black Girls, and then just as suddenly, they decided that Black Girls were out of style. Well, I said to myself, I didn't see how a skin color could be a matter of style, and I kept on using them. Today it has become a given, that is, a natural thing, like breathing. You can take an Asian, a blonde, a brunette, an African, etc., and it's fine. But it wasn't easy. How many times did my family say, 'Stop it, cut it out, let them go, you're going to lose everything?' And I did suffer."

So what gave him the fortitude to persist? "The confidence of the Girls themselves," he answered, the confidence they had in their own talent and in his proven ability to showcase them no matter which way the political winds blow.

Stephen Burrows

When Naomi Sims and the other Black models of her generation started down American runways in the late '60s, they were challenging a small but significant corner of society. But they also were supported by a mass movement for political change and by key individuals

Kathy Jean-Louis accompanying **Paco Rabanne** when he won the Golden Thimble award. Paris, 1990.

in the fashion field. Not the least of these were Black designers just beginning to make names for themselves. One of the brightest, loudest, and most enduring of them was Stephen Burrows.

During the fall of 1993, the Costume Institute of the Metropolitan Museum of Art hosted an exhibit underwritten by Halston Enterprises, "Versailles 1973", in honor of "the epic fashion show where American designers challenged the French domination of fashion for the first time," and which provided the general public with the opportunity to see a few of Stephen Burrows' classic color block and lettuce-edged designs.

Despite two Coty awards—which he won in 1973 and 1977—financial backing had always been difficult to find. Invesment bankers and venture capitalists, even supposedly sympathetic Black investors, would not listen to his proposals. He called them "Black traitors. They want you to have the business already. And then they want to take that business in order to invest in you. If I could be White for just a minute and at least get my foot in the door to get that money, and then turn back again…," he trailed off in fantasy. But the reality of the bottom line brought him back. "I'm going to be out of business again if I don't get it now."

Burrows had been there before. After graduating from the Fashion Institute of Technology in 1966, he went to work on Seventh Avenue designing women's blouses. Then he started his own business, O Boutique in '68. "I did everything myself: sketch, design, make the pattern, and sew." He derided the current big-name fashion houses who use a fail-safe team approach to design. "How can you go wrong?" he asked. "You have twenty people in a room sketching, and you can pick and choose, saying this will be hot and this will not. Black style may be the only style left. At least there is adventure in putting pieces together. It may not work, but I am taking a chance."

The chances he took early in his career were inspired by a family environment where artistic ability, love of intense color, and sophisticated style were taken for granted. Both of his grandmothers were sample hands, the seamstresses who actually put the sample garments together, who worked for designer Hattie Carnegie. "They were friends, and that's how my parents met. My father was an illustrator who did caricatures of people in the bars in Harlem. And my mother had to be among the best-dressed to go to the Abyssinian Baptist Church."

Bias cuts, bright color combinations, matte jerseys and stretch chiffons, surplice wraps and lettuce edges, patchworks and fringes, all came to be part of Burrows' design signature. And, eventually, part of the iconoclastic look of the '60s. Fire Island figured as "a major inspirational place," where gay men, models, and many of the less visible but more powerful fashionalities could socialize across race and gender lines.

"When O Boutique ended in 1969, Joel Schumacher, who was the visual director at Henri Bendel, made an appointment for me to show my work to Geraldine Stutz, who was then the president of the 57th Street store. As a department store Henri Bendel was known to be a fashion innovator. When she said, 'I'll give you a boutique on the third floor. You'll start on Monday,' it was like a dream."

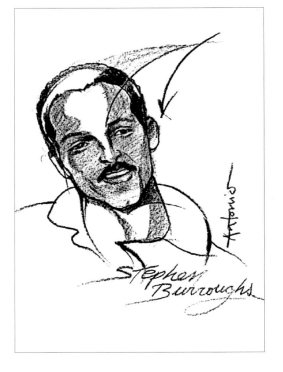

Stephen Burrows by **Antonio**.

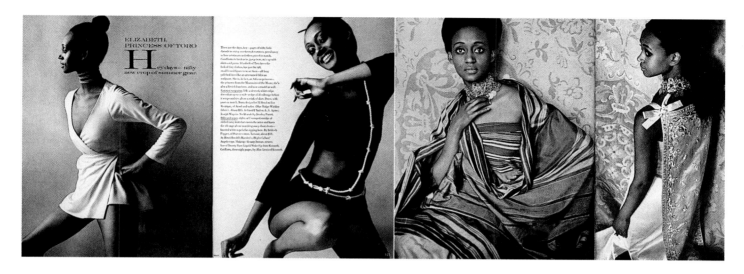

When it came to models he "used whoever I liked. Sometimes the show would be all Black, and then even I would say No, we've got to have some White Girls."

A meteoric year for Burrows was 1973. It was the third time that he was nominated for the Coty Award, and this time he won. Six years earlier at his graduation from FIT he had told his teachers and friends, "See you at the Cotys. It was a big thing for us as students. We used to sneak into the Cotys." National attention turned international when he was invited to Versailles that fall.

Soon afterward Max Factor launched a signature perfume under the name Stephen B. Although he claimed that he "hated the fragrance" during the test marketing, it did $3½ million worth of sales "before any customer ever smelled anything." According to Burrows, the manufacturer "then sold $3½ million to drugstores and discount retailers, and the prestige stores promptly returned their merchandise. It was a dream come true and a nightmare. What do you do? Have a nervous breakdown? That's not going to solve anything. You try to figure out what happened so it won't happen again. I had my time. But my time is now again."

Admitting that he could not handle both the creative and the financial ends of the business, he showed his financial plan for the '90s to people with extensive experience in the garment district. It was no secret that he "despises Seventh Ave-nue. That mentality is ruining the country," he insisted. "Everybody is in the business for short-term greed, not even long-term greed. If people want to back you, it's only for three years." Dubbed "the phoenix and firebird of New York fashion," Burrows had spent some long, quiet years in the '80s out of the limelight. "People ask me what was I doing. I was sewing for friends, which is what I did before I started the business. Just because they didn't see me didn't mean I wasn't doing anything."

Back together again—for the third time—with Henri Bendel in 1993, Burrows seemed calmer, more secure, almost stabilized. He paced the stage of the Grace Rainey Rogers Auditorium, comfortably recounting his life story to the audience at the Metropolitan Museum of Art. If the poetic and gracious introduction by Richard Martin, curator of the museum's Costume Institute, had set the tone for his "disestablishment sensibility," Burrows' hot pink jacket and flipped-up dark glasses provided the appropriate visuals. He was charming and funny, and in the company of photographer Charles Tracy and model Alva Chinn, he appeared relaxed. As they finished each other's sentences and filled in the missing details of certain scenes, the trio's slide show took on some of the better qualities of a family describing a special vacation. But this trip has lasted for twenty-five years. And as a few models showed outfits from then and now, it seemed as if Stephen Burrows was

Elizabeth, princess of Toro. Between a career in law or fashion, she chose modeling to best project Black culture.

still on an adventure, continuing to put original pieces together and take a chance.

Roots

Joyce Walker. Best known for her Afro and youthful demeanor, she enjoyed one of the most profitable careers of the period.

Diane Washington with an all-American Afro.

Image is what colonizes the mind.

John Henrik Clarke

Revolution was not only in the air in the '60s, it was also in the hair. Everybody grew it long, wild, different. From the young counter-culture Whites, who wanted to break away from the schizophrenia of a democratic and yet racist society, to the newly re-enfranchised Blacks, who wanted to burn, earn or vote their way into a freer society, people spoke through their hairstyles. And photography—whether of the news or fashion genre—helped disseminate their messages.

Black American women, long used to regarding their naturally thick and tightly curled hair as a problem began in their own small ways to redefine history, aesthetics, and their personal values. They returned, literally and figuratively, to their roots. As the newly independent countries of Africa took their place on the world stage, they generated pride in Blackness and the African heritage of their New World relatives.

Elizabeth of Toro

Elizabeth, princess of Toro, part of modern Uganda, was the living embodiment of the African queen. Shortly after she graduated from Cambridge University with a law degree, she was photographed in London by Norman Parkinson wearing both traditional Ugandan garments and a couture gown by Guy Laroche. The article accompanying the shots which appeared in *Vogue* in 1967 bore the poetic title, "The Princess from

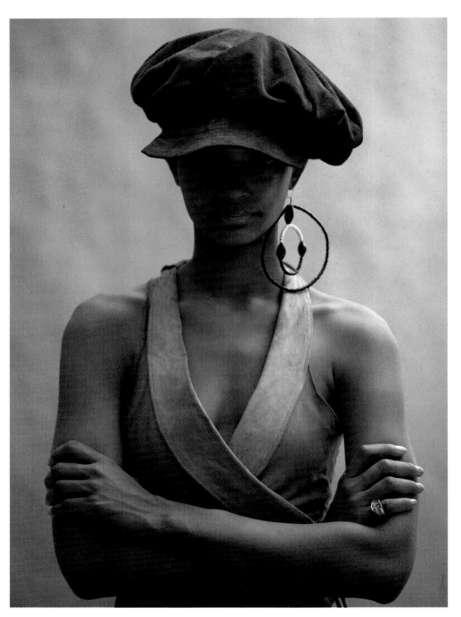

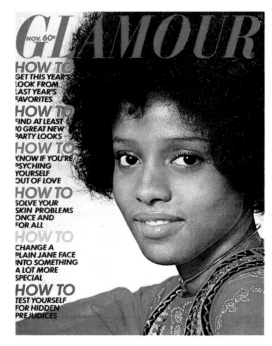

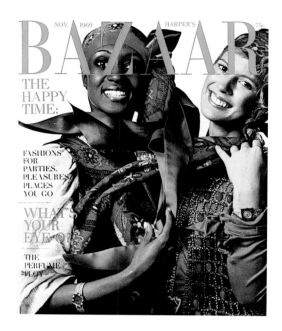

the Mountains of the Moon." Elizabeth was soon faced with a difficult career choice between two conflicting and demanding professions: law and modeling. In her autobiography, *African Princess*, she wrote, "My sole consideration in the making of the decision was which of the two careers would be the most effective way of symbolizing, projecting and thereby preserving the torch of my black culture. The language of clothes, of fashion and its attendant publicity, is a significant one. And I was utterly determined to utilize such a powerful weapon...." Photographs of her appeared in British *Vogue*, *Harper's Bazaar*, and *Queen*, while advertising jobs took her on location all over Europe.

In the United States, she signed with the Ford agency. Features for top American magazines such as *Life*, *Look*, and *Ebony* soon followed. "The crowning moment" of her modeling career came with her photograph on the cover of *Harper's Bazaar* in 1969. It was the first time a Black woman had been so honored, although the honor was dubious. Type fractured her face. A White sidekick diluted her presence, proof that White people were still perplexed by the newness of Black beauty.

While Elizabeth of Toro wore her hair in a modified African style, pulled back with a little hook of hair twisting upward,

other "do's" appeared. Tall, bushy Afros, close-cropped naturals, bejeweled braids, and precise cornrows, all found their fanciers, along with intricate cloth head wraps and, later, dreadlocks. Women wearing these styles did not receive total acceptance, however. Naturally straight and straightened hair were still preferred by many. Conservatives in the Black community thought the new styles were going too far, threatening the assimilationist status quo which encouraged Black people to look and act as much like proper Whites as possible in order to get ahead.

But the new heads of the '60s wanted progress on their own terms, or at least with fewer personal compromises. By the end of the decade many different looks were not only being worn, they were being analyzed and debated. When politics dressed fashion, fashion made the news.

Joyce Walker

One model whose signature hairstyle was the Afro arrived on the scene at this time. Joyce Walker, a native New Yorker, had a unique career based on a uniquely identifiable look. But the route to and through that career was full of twists and turns. Although her initial dream as an intellectually precocious, advanced high school student was to become an architect, she explained, "I went to Bennett College, as my father hoped, to become a lady. They made you wear white gloves and all this stuff, and I had to get out of there. So I came back and went to Long Island University. I started taking philosophy because I wanted to know how the world came to be. I knew I couldn't do anything with that. I just didn't know what I wanted to do. I had been dancing professionally since I was fourteen years old, and I had not really acted but my brother was at the Negro Ensemble Company. NEC had just started, this was '68. One day they called saying they need a Sister. So I auditioned for them, and I got the part. A few months after that, I auditioned for *Hair* on Broadway, and I got into *Hair* after four auditions. I was called a swinger, which is like an understudy. So I was actually an actress—and a dancer and singer—before

Harper's Bazaar takes a tentative step in the right direction. November, 1969.

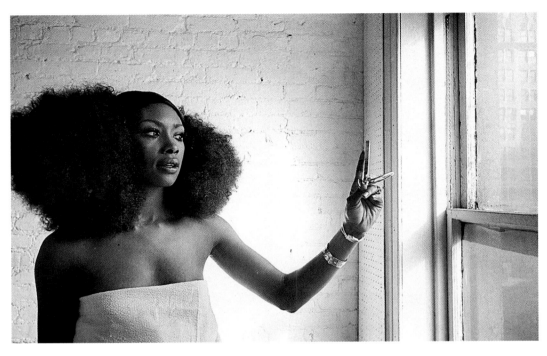

Arlene Hawkins in Afro puffs.

I started modeling at the tender age of nineteen.

"I didn't want to model. I didn't think I could, and I thought it was kind of silly to just stand there and pose. So if you notice in most of my pictures I'm smiling. It's really my shyness coming out. What happened is that I went to the Stewart agency first, and Stewart said, 'We already have a Black Girl.' Then a friend took me to Ford, and they took me right away. They hated my pictures because I had all these wigs on that this friend and the photographer said I should wear, because nobody had an Afro at this time. But I couldn't walk through the streets in the wig, so I went in there looking like me. I started working that week, and I just took off."

A special issue on Black beauty in *Look* magazine gave her four pages of exposure. The cover of *Seventeen* added to the momentum. "One of the interesting things when I started was that they would take me out of pictures to put on a wig for the Midwest. I'd be wearing the same outfit, and I'd have an Afro for the East and the West coasts, but a wig for the Midwest. It was so funny.

"I knew the Afro was a statement. I was not militant, but I was certainly politically aware. Still, the clients were hiring me. They could have put green balloons on my hair as far as I was concerned. It was a costume. I saw myself as a Black woman but the rest was part of the business, not my life. To me modeling is a serious profession. It's a lot of work, and it is so grating on the ego and the person that you have to be compensated, which is why you get paid a lot."

Pat Evans

While Joyce Walker represented the "right on" Sister, Pat Evans stunned an ever-hungry business with her hard-edged look. Not only was she Black, she was bald. Her clean-shaven head demanded recognition of a totally different kind of woman, one unafraid to strip to the bare essentials of her humanity.

Raised in the Sugar Hill section of Harlem, where upwardly mobile Black people could look over if not quite down on other folks, she came from a struggling family. As a dancer with Olatunji, she started wearing an Afro in 1957. "The whole group had Afros. We were the only people with them. In 1966 when I went to join an agency, they said, 'Well, you can't wear your hair in an Afro. You'll have to straighten it and carry an Afro wig.' And I got really mad about that, because all of my life it's been good hair, bad hair, you know. That same day I saw a little girl about seven years old skipping down the street with a sweater on her hair. I thought, my sister and I used to do that when we were little. It was a game called White girl. I said to myself, this means nothing has changed. And I shaved my head."

A failed marriage left her with two small children to support. Reluctantly, she went on welfare, but not long afterward, she told herself, "I can't just sit here. To get on your feet, you have to get up off your ass." She joined the Stewart agency and moved on to Wagner, taking her children with her to bookings, "one in a stroller, the other hanging onto my dress. Once when I was doing a fitting for Stephen Burrows, he had this dress that was a size two. The dress was so tight that when I took it off my wig came off, too. He said, 'Pat, your head!' I begged him not to tell my agency. But he said, 'Oh, no, I want you to do my show like that.' And overnight I became a success with a bald head. I kept my shaven head for ten years. Everything just took off. I did all the TV shows, all the magazines. People were coming from Japan and Germany to photograph me.

"It was different. It was the right time. It was the most psychedelic look. There were maybe only twelve Black models at the time, and we covered the market. Everybody was an individual."

As a model she became best known for the elegant ads she did for Astarté, a line of cosmetics for Black women. Her unadorned profile made the ultimate point: all kinds of Black—including bald—were beautiful.

But Pat Evans was not to leave the business before dropping a bombshell. It took the form of an article she wrote and published in *Essence* in 1972, that opened with this explosive statement: "Black modeling is just another form of prostitution." She went on to criticize racist attitudes prevalent among White modeling agencies. But White people were not the only ones she lambasted. "Black photographers [who] use their job as an excuse for sex" and "plastic" Black models also came under fire. If, as she wrote, "the

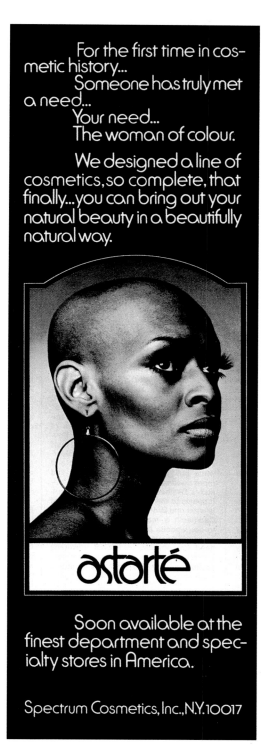

For the first time in cosmetic history...
Someone has truly met a need...
Your need...
The woman of colour.

We designed a line of cosmetics, so complete, that finally...you can bring out your natural beauty in a beautifully natural way.

astarté

Soon available at the finest department and specialty stores in America.

Spectrum Cosmetics, Inc., N.Y. 10017

Pat Evans issued a call for more Black-owned businesses and Black-owned minds.

Black model business is like slave trading—only more refined," her prescription for change was adamant. Modeling would never be an open profession for Black people "until we get more BLACK-OWNED products, ad agencies, magazines, and most of all Black-owned minds."

Navigating the Mainstream

Launched

> *Fortune brings in some boats that are not steer'd.*
>
> William Shakespeare

Despite the warnings of experienced professionals and despite the resistant core of racism at the heart of America, the late 1960s saw more Black models than ever before come into the business, stay longer, and achieve wider success. Challenge was nothing new to them, but the substantial examples set by models earlier in the decade gave them a surer footing on which to base their own success. No longer would the narrow straits of the Black community confine the most ambitious talents. No longer would the narrow minds of the White community relegate them solely to the backwaters of the back pages. Models, designers, photographers, and all the accessory personnel of fashion—among whom were found more and more people of color—sought their fortune in the mainstream.

In the 1970s the world opened its eyes to Black people not just as tortured victims, crowd-pleasing entertainers, and grittily romanticized revolutionaries. In the new models the world saw another image of womanhood, beautiful, spirited, sophisticated, independent, and original. In the States the majority of Black models made careers in photography, while in Europe and elsewhere abroad, Black models were more frequently used in shows. In either branch of the business, they became financially self-supporting, able to treat modeling as a full-time career, not just a part-time fantasy. Success was not simply one Black woman being allowed to enter the field. It was a rush of dozens competing for the highest stakes.

Images of Black beauty were moving into the mainstream of American and, thus, world culture on a monthly basis. Slowly but steadily, the major women's magazines began to feature Black faces on their covers. The struggle now was to find the "right" faces for them. Under the leadership of editor Ruth Whitney, *Glamour* found its first Black cover Girl in Katiti Kironde II, an African college student in Newfoundland.

Perhaps, the popular magazine realized it did not have to travel outside of the States to find an acceptable example of young Black womanhood as fourteen months later, Katiti was followed by Daphne Maxwell, a freckle-nosed African American, college student, bride, and in *Glamour*'s words, "new Renaissance girl."

Known today as Daphne Maxwell Reid, the familiar television actress, she did not realize that she was making history in 1969. It came with so little fanfare. A Merit scholarship winner from New York City's High School of Performing Arts, she was pursuing a degree in interior design and architecture at Northwestern University in Chicago. "During my freshman and sophomore years," she recalled, "Amy Green, who was a wonderful fashion editor for *Mademoiselle* and then for *Glamour*, kept flying me back and forth from Chicago to New York just to work for one-day jobs. During the course of several trips we must have done three or four cover tries, but they all had weird hair. One day Amy told me to put my hair simply to the side in a pony tail. We all worked real fast, and I was back at school by that afternoon.

"A few months later I was stunned to see my picture on the cover. It was like an out-of-body experience. I felt like I was a separate person from the one on the cover. At school nobody paid it any attention. I expected some sort of cataclysm, but I had already been Homecoming Queen, and people already knew me as me."

The first model of color on *Mademoiselle*'s cover was Jolie Jones, the green-eyed daughter of music celebrity Quincy Jones. Less than a year later, Haitian-born Jany Tomba appeared in the coveted spot. *Harper's Bazaar* enthroned Princess Elizabeth of Toro on the cover of its November, 1969 issue, although with a White co-regent. Even *Cosmopolitan*, which had been more closed to the presence of beautiful Black women, featured Jane Hoffman on its cover in June, 1969, and again in May, 1971. Although *Cosmo* took pride in its frank explorations of sex and the single girl, romantic fantasies coupled with race seemed too risky a combination for this commercial magazine to deal with regularly. Jane's covers were special coups.

If the political protests of the 1960s forced America's eyes open to the undeniable presence and varied beauty of Black people, the '70s consolidated that vision. In the publishing world two events stood out: the launch of a new Black women's magazine in 1970, and the presence of the first Black woman on the cover of *Vogue* in 1974.

In the same month that twenty-five-year-old *Ebony* featured four Black models on its cover—Naomi Sims, Princess Elizabeth of Toro, Avis McCarther, and Madelyn Sanders—and asked the question "Have Black Models Really Made It?", a new magazine was born which answered the question in its own way. By daring to exist.

Essence, the first Black women's magazine, published its first issue in May, 1970. If it was a product of its times, it also helped to produce those times, by providing images, interpretations, and evaluations of Black people by Black people for Black people. In his inaugural Publisher's Statement, Edward Lewis wrote: "You, the Black woman in America, are wrestling with your own identity and undergoing a process of change.... Above all, *Essence* is launched to delight and to celebrate the beauty, pride, strength and uniqueness of all Black women." Without excuses and apologies. Without complexes and hangups, subtexts and second thoughts. With Black women

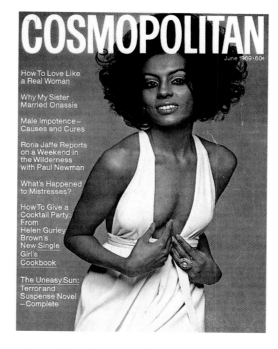

Jane Hoffman, the first *Cosmo* cover Girl of color. June, 1969.

Black is beautiful, and sexy.

pictured on the cover and in editorials and ads. Needless to say, many of these Black women belonged to a new professional elite, the models.

Ebony's question, however, was still a legitimate one. Its 1970 article stated: "Beautiful though Black is, and despite the fact that it seems to be 'busting out all over,' as one major magazine recently proclaimed, still there are only two or three Black models who command top rates" of $60/hour, possibly $1,000/week. Naomi Sims and Elizabeth of Toro were named to that short list. Other well-

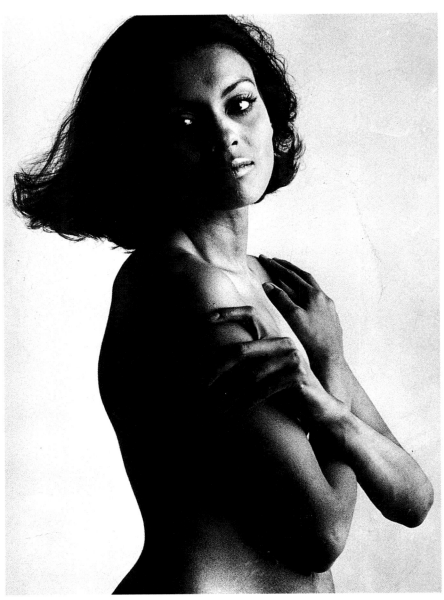

Jane Hoffman projected a caring kind of sensuality.

hoped to gain was experience, wider contacts, and those all-important tear sheets. At *Essence* she could have high hopes for she would be working with some of the most exciting names in the business. At the top of its masthead was the legendary Gordon Parks as editorial director. The first fashion spreads were shot by such notable photographers as Francesco Scavullo, Gösta Peterson, Anthony Barboza, Helmut Newton, and Deborah Turbeville. This magazine "dedicated to today's Black woman" was not going to be short-changed on talent on either side of the camera. The Black Girls who appeared in *Essence* could be proud of their work.

Yet during its initial two years, four editors came and went trying to establish the magazine's identity. *Essence* soon ceased to be a fashion-first publication. An article in the *New York Times* stated that publisher "Lewis credits Ms. [Marcia] Gillespie, who served as editor until 1980, with defining the magazine's direction and taking *Essence* from the fashion magazine its young founders first envisioned to a broader life-style and service publication."

The high-spirited fashion spreads that initially set the pictorial tone soon fizzled into a standard sameness. But Black models' loss was perhaps Black *women*'s gain. The woman on the street could see not only her likeness on the magazine's pages; she could actually be the model. "What we're all trying to do here," said beauty editor Mikki Taylor, "is to give Black women in America the correct vision of themselves, because through all these years that's not been happening. Subliminally, we are fed things that are not in keeping with us, both inner and outer. Where there's only one standard, there's no choice. And that's the message we have to keep sending home: that there are choices."

When asked about her choices for covers and beauty stories, she replied, "Very seldom do you see the top Girls on our pages because it's in keeping with that thing about the standard. Who has the right to say? I see them all in the same way, whether it's a top model or somebody I found in the subway, because we're

known working models cited in the same article were Charlene Dash, Tamara Dobson, Jane Hoffman, Ann Jones, Marcia McBroom, Candy Mitchell, Julie Poteat, Elizabeth Robinson, Rose Waldron, and Kellie Wilson. Each worked her own combination of print—magazine editorials, catalogs, and advertisements—and runway—showroom, shows, and department stores—to support herself.

As crucial as the issue of pay was the issue of exposure. No magazine, White or Black, paid the commercial rates of ads and catalogs that could soar into four-figure sums by the end of the work week. From editorial work, the most a model

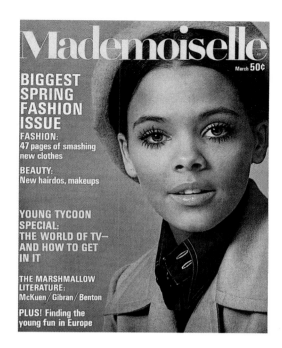

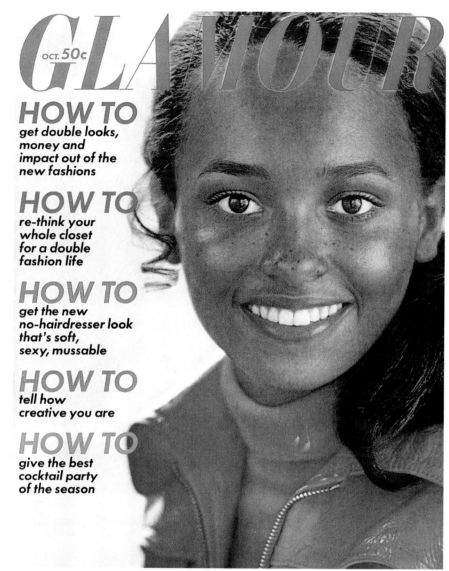

trying to do a bigger job. We're trying to give our audience what it wants, what it needs, and maybe what never occurred to it before. That's the beauty of being a service magazine. As the beauty editor, I am careful to make sure that over the course of twelve months we're never on one note in terms of complexions or types or ages."

One particularly controversial cover in the mid-'80s with model Marguerite Erasme provoked a surprising amount of anger and canceled subscriptions. Mikki explained her basic philosophy of choice. "We don't have the right to judge one another. How Black is Black? She's Black with blue eyes, and she's still one of us. Who sets the standard? Not you. Not any of us. And if you love *Essence*, then you have to love it when we get down to the light end of the spectrum, too. You can't only love it when it's chocolate and it's rich and it's a texture you understand. You have to love it when it's the other way. And maybe love her even more 'cause the Girl could have said she was White and not come this way. I just get so upset with us because we do the very same things that we insist we won't allow or say we wish weren't done to us."

Before she became the editor in chief of *Essence* in 1981, Susan Taylor was its beauty editor and fashion editor for ten years. During that time she brought yet

another perspective to the choice of models used in the magazine. "I would go to the shows in Paris, and I would see these Girls on the runway who were average-looking women. I mean, they had the fiercest bodies and knew how to carry those clothes down runways and dazzle an audience, but they would rarely be photographed by anyone. Someone like Ramona Saunders. Billie Blair and Pat Cleveland were not models whom you would see in the other women's magazines. Even Rashida Moore, Yvette Flowers, who ended up being a real favorite of mine, and Grace Jones. If you looked at women's magazines in 1970, '71, '72, you wouldn't see Grace Jones in

Jolie Jones, the first Black *Mademoiselle* cover Girl. March, 1969.

Daphne Maxwell, the first African American on the cover of *Glamour*. October, 1969.

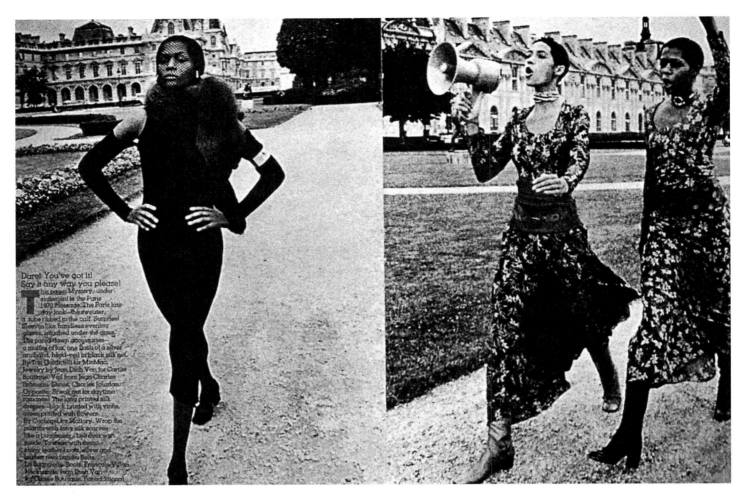

the White women's magazines, but you'd see her in *Essence*. We used women who certainly knew how to present themselves but weren't the same types that were being projected as the beautiful Black women in America. That was so exciting. We took these women who were superbly confident and incredibly dynamic on the runway and gave them an opportunity to present themselves in still photography. And the kinds of things they did! Absolutely dramatic! They were actresses who had a sense of themselves and their beauty. Every shoot was a joy. Do you know what else was joyous? The models used to tell me this all the time, 'Oh, we love working for *Essence* because the only time we get to work together is when we come to *Essence*.' That was great too, being able to provide an opportunity for all of the women to work together."

Susan took pride in having the power to say, "This is the kind of face that, if we don't put it on the cover or feature her, all the Sisters who look like her will never see their beauty."

The irony, of course, is that in over-valuing the girl-on-the-street, the decision-makers at *Essence* undervalued committed, professional Black models. Instead of

finding a safe—if always temporary—haven at the only seriously respected Black magazine for women, ambitious, qualified, and uncompromisingly beautiful Black models were left to suffer a kind of reverse bias. The unfortunate outcome meant that the White magazines—ever reluctant, ever quota-conscious—were still the major platform for the most striking photography and the most varied, challenging, and pulled-together fashion looks. It was in their pages that Black models most wanted to appear.

Maybe it was all a mirage in the first place, envisioning a Black women's magazine of quality ideas *and* quality images. It was a basic fact of business life that magazines were dependent on advertisers, who rarely enjoyed sterling reputations for using representative images of people. Advertisers bought space where they thought readers would buy their products. The Black consumer market, however, was often taken for granted and allotted smaller advertising campaigns and fewer ads specifically targeted toward it. Complicating this attitude was the instability of economic forces. "When money is tight," said *Essence* publisher Ed Lewis in the *New York Times*, "and these

Carol Hobbs (left). **Carol LaBrie** and **Carol Hobbs** in full stride as *Essence*, in its first year of publication, boldly stakes its claim to style.

days money is tight for many advertisers, we are often the first to be dropped."

Still, the basic issue of quality could not be avoided. The fashion/style/beauty forefront was ours to claim, even if we did have to compete for it. One long-time fashion philosopher suggested that—more by its promise than its performance—*Essence* helped defuse the anger among Black women and among Black models. But where did that anger go? Into providing Black women with the skills and tools to navigate the mainstream more successfully; into information that ranged from celebrity profiles to political reportage. In other words, into words. Images lost importance. The democratization of beauty eased imperceptibly into a benevolent acceptance of mass taste. Afraid, perhaps, of exerting their own potential and aiming to serve in the name of a greater good, *Essence* and other publications geared to Black women abandoned the challenge to re-envision them as style leaders, not fashion followers. And in those pages, at least, the best Black models seemed to be abandoned.

On Course

Today's shocks are tomorrow's conventions.

Caroline Heilbrun

In August, 1974, the same month that President Richard Nixon resigned over the Watergate scandal, *Vogue* magazine showed a Black woman on its cover, breaking one of the most formidable barriers to mainstream acceptance of Black beauty. Cautious optimists dared to predict that a new order was beginning.

Beverly Johnson became the most famous Black model the business had ever known and one of the most identifiable women in the world. Women of all races and backgrounds wanted to look like her. She was the Black Goldilocks of the era. Not too dark, not too tall, not too exotic, she was just right: tan, tall enough, and terribly, romantically pretty. But BJ, as she came to be known in her early days, was no overnight success. She had already

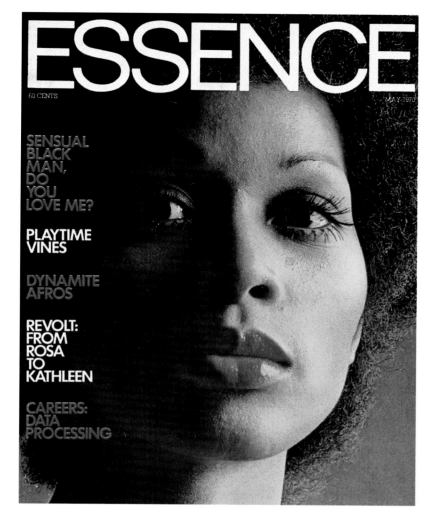

appeared on the cover of *Glamour* in March, 1972, and by the time of her *Vogue* cover had been modeling for three years. Hers seemed to be yet another classic story of going for the gold and winning it. The twist was that she won, lost, and had to win it back again.

If Beverly Johnson dominated her era as Naomi Sims did hers, that certainly did not mean that other Black models were not working, and working well. Cassandra, Barbara Cheeseboro, Pita Green, Gail Kendrick, Cynthia King, Jan Maiden, Maria McDonald, Mouchette, June Murphy, Romney Russo, Von Gretchen Shepard, Barbara Smith, Jany Tomba, Marcia Turnier, Joyce Walker, and Julie Woodson were the names behind some of the most popular faces. And the show Girls who had swept the French off their feet at Versailles in 1973 were busy expanding their own lucrative careers.

Alva Chinn

Among them was Alva Chinn, a third generation Bostonian whose tumultuous family circumstances made her, in her own words, "a very independent

Barbara Cheeseboro on the cover of the inaugural issue of *Essence*. May, 1970.

Essence was the first magazine "dedicated to today's Black woman." Its success as a publication provided the basis for expansion into popular music and television events.

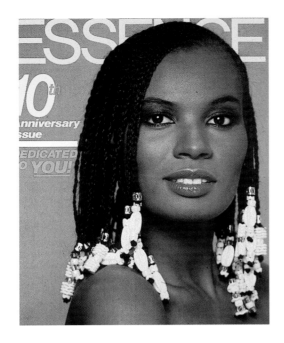

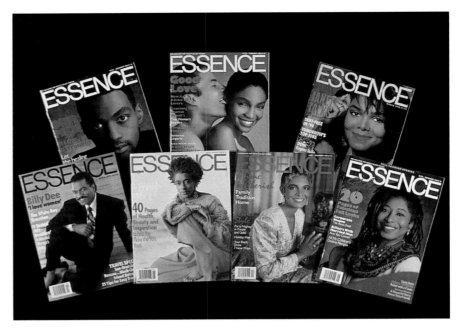

Julie Woodson, a top catalog Girl, helps celebrate the 10th anniversary of *Essence*.

Essence developed into a wide-ranging service magazine.

person at a very early age." Her mother's nervous breakdown resulted in an unhappy life with her father and later with relatives to whom she was boarded out. She was a "very good child, but very angry underneath the goodness." As a teenager she was thrown into culture shock when she moved into a Black neighborhood and high school. "I hated it. The kids were street tough, which I wasn't. They scared me, and it took me a while to adjust. I talked people into believing that I was more savvy than I was." She attended the University of Massachusetts where dance and poetry were her main interests, although she admitted that she had no clue to what she wanted to do after graduation. Appearance in the college issue of *Mademoiselle* in 1972 gave her some inkling of modeling possibilities. Her cousin, Henry Chinn, was living in New York and provided a handy landing spot when she decided to leave school and make the big move.

"I spent one year really struggling," said Alva, whose wavy light brown hair and hazel eyes were legacies from Florida Indian and mulatto grandparents. "I came at a time when it was better to be browner, right after Naomi Sims. And I was a misfit. Not a miss, not a junior. I was too tall and too sophisticated looking. So they had a problem: Where do we put this person? I was always told that I wasn't Black enough. In one movie audition I told them, 'I can get street if I want to, but what's the point? That's not really the way I speak. That's your idea of a Black person. But we come in all shades and varieties just like you do.'"

Her first job in New York was a show in 1973 for Stephen Burrows, whom she met through photographer Charles Tracy. "Stephen liked my body. I had such a little body, perfect for his matte jersey. For the first show I was so nervous and I walked so fast that none of the pictures taken of me indoors were in focus. Only when I got outside in the street would I relax." Photographer Bill Cunningham, well known for shooting outdoors, managed to capture her energetic spirit, and those pictures eventually came out in *Women's Wear Daily*.

Her initial nervousness disappeared as Alva became one of the most sought-after runway models, working for top designers on the American and European circuit. One of the first Black models to work for Valentino, she went to Rome where she did his couture collection. Part of the couture tradition meant not only wearing the most glamorous clothes but also carrying a numbered card identifying each outfit. Alva recalled, "I had an aversion to numbers, being numbered, being called a number, being thought of as a number. Eventually I stopped doing couture." But she more than compensated by working the burgeoning ready-to-wear market.

"The freedom you experience on the runway in Europe is what I liked. Here in the States the attitude in person was more friendly, but on the runway they're more strict. In Europe you could do whatever you wanted, whatever your fantasy was. You'd go out on stage, and it was like a party. The moment I treasure was when we brought some life to a show. Basically I have taken a human hanger walking down a runway and transformed that into a moment of energy that other people can relate to. I loved feeling that you could give to somebody else, that's why I liked going to Europe.

"Black models have a different energy on the runway. At least, we did. I don't know if we do anymore. There was never an edge against each other; a change came later on. I remember Carol Miles elbowed me in Milan and almost sent me flying off the runway. I know it was intentional. That never used to happen. But it's not an isolated incident. I know of people going to a designer and saying not to use a certain person. In Paris a lot of the Girls work in the *cabine* and have more clout. They can be against you or for you.

"In New York I got into a head where I did a lot of photography—mostly catalog—to make money. But I also did some editorial pictures that I will always love. There was something in that moment between myself and the photographer, a feeling that just starts to happen, and that's when you know it's right.

"A lot of my resentments had to do with Caucasians telling me who I am and what's right for me, what's right for my hair. That's where I went off. I think I went through a big period of trying to make people realize I was Black because a lot of people kept trying to deny it. They would say, 'What island are you from?' And I'd say, 'I'm from the island of Boston, Massachusetts.' I went through a lot of that, where you can't be American. I may be a mixture, but on my birth certificate, that's what it says I am. That's the way I was brought up, and I'm proud to be that.

"I think it's wonderful to see the variety of women of color that you see today. It was time. They had to admit we existed in various shades. I was persistent. Pat Cleveland was persistent, and no one does it like her. I find that many of the young models coming up think it started with them. But, as they say, the past is prologue."

The Girls who specialized in fashion shows were not the only ones to prosper. The number and variety of print Girls also expanded greatly in the '70s, as did their work opportunities. The Black Girl-next-door who might have first appeared in magazine editorials was now earning real money in catalogs and advertisements. Catalogs—at first for huge national chains, then for upscale department stores, and later for direct mail companies—became big business. They also provided the major percentage of a print model's income regardless of her color.

Sherry Brewer

Sherry Brewer came from Chicago to New York to study classical ballet with the Harkness Company. As a child she had well-rounded training in performance and dance, because as she explained, "In the Midwest when you go to a dance school, you learn everything: acrobatics, tap, jazz,

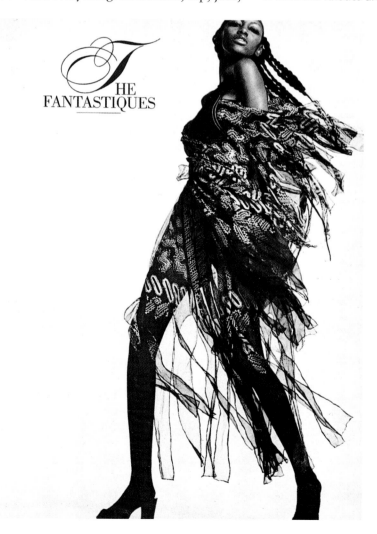

Amina Warsuma, "marvelously ethereal," according to *Bazaar*, in a Zandra Rhodes dress.

THE FANTASTIQUES

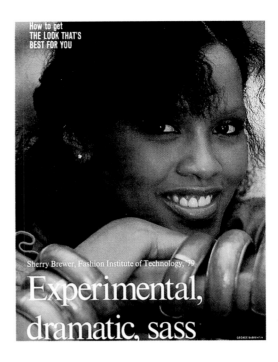

Sherry Brewer, Fashion Institute of Technology, '79

Experimental, dramatic, sass

GEORGE BARKENTIN

ballet, and everything." After enrolling in the Goodman Theatre in Chicago, hoping to major in acting, she had a revelation. The dancing and acting that seemed so abstract and insecure as professions became realistically attainable. "When Alvin Ailey came to Chicago, I could see that dance was very real. Those people were very real, their craft and their talent. And there were magazines and articles that helped me discover that the world was bigger than the South side of Chicago."

The first stop toward that bigger world was New York. "When I got here the timing was right, and that made all the difference. I started working immediately, performing in *Hello Dolly* and modeling. One of the first things that I did when I came to New York was to go to the famous Public Library on Fifth Avenue. There I met these actors. Later I picketed with them on Park Avenue against BBD&O, a prestigious advertising agency, and Lever Brothers because they had unfair hiring practices against Blacks in commercials. Little quiet me, right? I was probably one of the most militant people you'd ever meet. I believed that if there was something that I wanted to pursue, then I had the right to pursue it."

For Sherry, combining acting and advertising "was almost like a novelty. I was the junior model who had talent — and talent that they could visibly see. This made people feel more comfortable with me. If I didn't get one modeling job, I always felt there was another coming that would be better for me. I had a positive outlook. I felt that modeling was a bonus, because I didn't come to New York to pursue a modeling career. I came to pursue an acting career. And I never allowed modeling to take over. I knew how fortunate I was.

"It was a very tricky time. People weren't always as kind and as respectful of each other as they should have been. Even though we were Black, the models were all still faced with whether we were Black enough, the right shade of Black. Which segment of the Black population did we really represent? Here I was with what I considered proper training in order to

pursue a very healthy theatrical career, and all of a sudden I'm told that I'm not Black enough."

Sherry had an active career beyond print modeling in an extremely lucrative field slowly opening up to contemporary images of Black women: television commercials. "I did everything: paper towels, baby diapers, mouthwash, pantyhose, hair products, soap, dishwashing detergents, margarines, soft drinks. Most of the things I did involved action or dancing or there was a lot of dialogue. I worked an enormous amount. I don't think I suffered socially, and I don't think I missed anything."

Darnella Thomas

Another Chicago native came to New York in the '70s, but stopped off in Philadelphia for a couple of years, "because New York was very intimidating to me," Darnella Thomas explained. Working for the Wharton School of the University of Pennsylvania as an administrative assistant, she lucked into two opportunities: an on-campus spread in *Glamour* and an appointment with John Fairchild, the highly influential and opinionated publisher of *W* and *Women's Wear Daily*, whose lecture on marketing she happened to attend.

"When you're naive, you don't know about these things. I just knew I wanted to be a model. So when Fairchild granted me an interview, I came to New York. I was very excited. He said, 'I don't know why you want to get into this business, but if this is what you want to do, I'll call some of the designers.' I finally got to do a

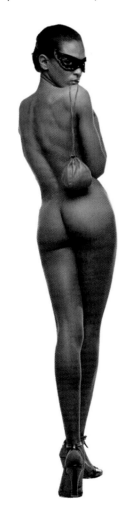

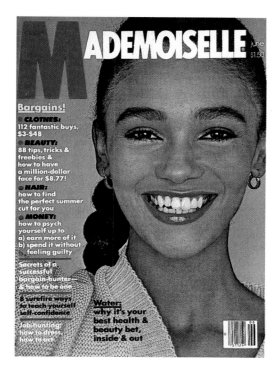

Cover Girl **Mouchette**
became senior fashion editor
at *Mademoiselle.*

Pierre Cardin show. I must have looked like a frightened chicken doing that first show. My false lashes were upside-down; I was real skinny and petrified, but I was happy to be there, and I ended up doing a second show. Then I used John Fairchild's name to death trying to get into the agencies, and I finally got into Stewart. But I was still commuting back and forth to Philadelphia."

The more Darnella got to know the city, the less intimidating it became. She finally made the move to New York with her close friend, rising star makeup artist Joey Mills. Although she started off doing runway and preferred doing shows, she found herself booked more and more for catalog. It was still a struggle. "In Philadelphia I was considered a little superstar. I did all the television things, I did all the newspapers, and I was with the top agency there. So when you come to New York, you figure you're going to have an easier time of it, but you don't, because the people who come here have also been at the top in their area of the country, and you're competing against these women. It's hard.

"When I first came I'd go on auditions, and I would be in awe of all the top stars in their fur coats and jeans, their silk blouses and diamond earrings. They all had a certain look, a certain grace and elegance, and they just stood out. I had to have a fur and diamonds, too, and when I got them I finally felt that I fit in.

"Before then I lost a lot of self-confidence. After one particular audition I

started thinking that my nose was too big, that I was too skinny and too tall. I started experiencing rejection that I never had before. That's when I read all the books I could on positive thinking and transcendental meditation.

"I was into modeling, but I was a model who came home and stuck her head in a book and got out the dictionary and was also trying to grow. I don't feel that I ever really made it because I think I was too busy *trying* to make it. I never appreciated what really happened to me. I always felt a little shy and introverted."

It was this shy and introverted model who hooked one of the biggest beauty campaigns of the '70s: confident, fast-striding, quintessentially all-American and always blonde Charlie. "I had to work my way into that," Darnella admitted. "It took a period of growth. When Joey and I saw Shelly Hack doing the Charlie ads, Joey said, 'That's you! You can do those ads!' It was great. I had learned about positive thinking on my own, and I knew how to plan. I had grown up not really understanding that the keys to life and success were to plan your life, go after your goals, and take the steps necessary to reach those goals. That was something I had to learn as I went along.

"So we started testing my book toward that Charlie look where the girl was walking—the most all-American image you could possibly imagine. I had my tennis shots and my outdoor looks in my portfolio because advertisers cannot visualize; they have to see. Then when it came time for the advertising agency to start looking for a Black Charlie, I began to realize that I would get it. You don't just walk in and get a campaign. People don't realize that. I had thought it out and planned for it.

"I always felt that a lot of Girls resented my relationship with Joey, because they thought that whatever I got, Joey helped me get it. Well, he was doing my makeup, and he helped me get photographers to photograph me. We were friends. What was he supposed to do? *Not* help me? I mean, he helped me with the Charlie ads as far as doing my makeup, but I was the one who hustled.

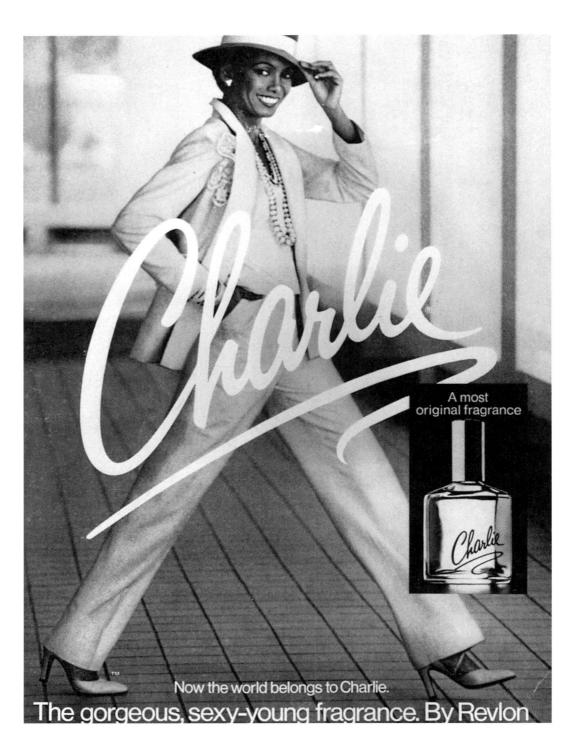

A most
original fragrance

Now the world belongs to Charlie.

The gorgeous, sexy-young fragrance. By Revlon

Darnella Thomas was the first to break the mold of the blonde Charlie girl.

The Girls should have been happy that there was a Black man helping me get something. Instead they had resentment. I don't blame them so much because there was so little work for us. We were always pitted against each other. But at the time it really limited my friendship with a number of the Girls, because you always feel that you're competing against someone you'd ordinarily like to know. Even when I got the Charlie ad, I found out that there were people whom I knew who were still trying to get it and take it away from me."

Although Darnella shot at least four ads for the Charlie campaign, she was not signed to a contract. "Every time I did a shoot for them I would get paid whatever the day rate was; it was never a contract. A contract would have entailed them giving me the television commercials, which is what I really wanted. I know for a fact that the reason I did the second, third, and fourth ads was because they got a lot of letters about me. I wouldn't have continued to do them if they weren't successful. It was interesting, too, that I didn't see some of the ads. When you photographed, you shot two or three ads. I don't know how many they used, or

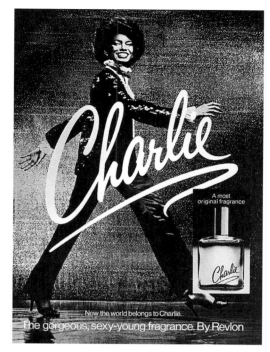

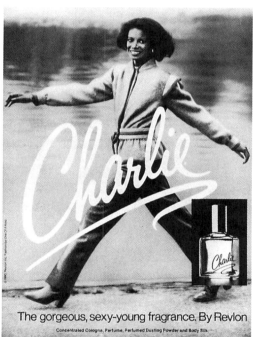

have been doing. But I realized that the way our society is, I was very fortunate to do what I did, because at Revlon, that was a big deal. Still, you look for more. You want more."

Designing Women

For me, the body is the most important part of fashion.

Issey Miyake

Models have always served not just as the subject but also as the muse of creative artists. As clothing design, advertising, and style magazines developed into big businesses during the '70s, fashion models continued this tradition, inspiring imaginative designers and photographers to accomplish their best work. Although all Black models gained in visibility and prestige after Versailles, very few print models enjoyed the close partnerships with photographers that runway models had with designers. Many advertisers were still too color- and class-conscious to risk identifying their products with Black faces. And many magazines were quick to pat themselves on the back for their few, well-intentioned covers.

The clothing world was different. It needed bodies first, faces second. With their lean physique and personal flair, Black models became valued associates, trusted to make significant contributions during the development of a designer's collection as well as to add the final flourish in the showroom, on the runway, and, eventually, in photographs. Models became designing women, indispensable adjuncts in the creative process.

In 1975, the role of the Black model was again spotlighted, this time in a hopelessly grade-B movie which became, nevetheless, a smash hit and a landmark film. *Mahogany*, starring the diva supreme Diana Ross, portrayed a struggling fashion designer, who became a couture model and then an international star, lost in a world of freeze-frame glamour until she was redeemed by true love, in the form of a politically correct Chicago activist

Darnella Thomas
shot several ads for the Charlie campaign.

where. The ads ran in some parts of Africa and Latin America, but they didn't tell me all that. I didn't know. I wasn't supposed to know, obviously. Who thought that far? I was only looking for *Essence*, you know? But they used my ad in *Vogue* and *Glamour* also.

"It was very exciting for me. But again, you're still struggling, so you don't have time to really absorb it. If you're Black, let's face it, most of us are always struggling for the next. I didn't have time to think about the figures. I just knew I was doing quite well. Still, I was disappointed about the commercials because it was something that I really felt I should

played by heart-throb Billy Dee Williams. Little about the film rang true. If the characterizations were laughable, the clothing designs were even more ludicrous. The movie's appeal, however, lay in the fact that it was the first—and only—drama centered on a wildly successful Black mannequin. In *Mahogany* Diana Ross's celebrity lent authenticity to the barely-articulated dreams of a generation of young girls in love with fashion.

As a high school teenager, Diana Ross had been one of those girls, having majored in fashion design and costume illustration. In a 1971 article in *Harper's Bazaar*, she recalled going "to beauty school in the evenings and on Saturdays to Hudson's Department Store in Detroit for modeling class. They gave me a little hat box and I felt very grand coming home every day with that little hat box in my hand and, in my mind, all the things I had learned." She proudly admitted that "modeling was my first love.... I thought it was the most beautiful business."

For real models that business had little to do with Hollywood's flamboyantly dressed fairy tale except to share the source of its dreams.

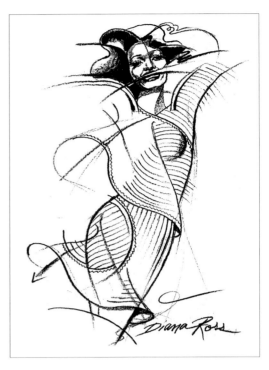

Diana Ross, as seen by **Antonio**. The music diva portrayed a celebrity model and designer in the pioneering 1975 film *Mahogany*.

Toukie Smith

In the early '70s, Willi Smith was making a name for himself on Seventh Avenue as a designer of inventive low-priced sports clothes that became instant classics. First at Digits, then at his own Seventh Avenue house, WilliWear, Smith brought perky, affordable, mostly cotton separates to the attention of young working women who wanted to maintain the free spirit of the '60s while looking capable and confident on their jobs in the '70s. WilliWear fit the bill in more ways than one. Loose pants with adjustable wrap waists and room for realistic thighs, easy, swingy skirts, soft jackets—all in mix-and-matchable earth tones—soon found their way into big department stores and, eventually, into customers' closets.

Willi's favorite model was his sister, Toukie. Not surprisingly, for they had always been a team.

"Willi was six years older than I was. I always had him as an absolute guide. But there was a ton of tension between us because our personalities were different. I'm very outward, Willi was inward. When your parents are alcoholics, there's always one child who takes the responsibility of seeing that everything is right for everyone. That was my relationship with Willi, taking care of him and watching out for him. Then, as we got older, the role was reversed. When I came to New York, he watched over me and took care of me. Then the roles reversed again when we started to work together, when I got more into the business and he was totally into design. My loft got turned into the stock room, and Willi's loft got turned into the sewing room."

Willi, the idea man, once said, "Inspiration comes from anything I enjoy. Movies. Music. Even browsing in a bookstore stimulates what I do." A discerning collector of modern art and African sculpture, he kept a fresh American focus on useful ideas imported from the Third World. Toukie also helped to keep him focused. He admitted, "She brings up things that I wouldn't even think of. She's brought me out of the model trip to design for the real girl."

Together Willi and Toukie were a public relations phenomenon. Separately,

Toukie found it more difficult to establish a professional identity. "I've always been blessed," she insisted. "But you know what? When it comes to modeling, you can be the sister of or the girlfriend of, but if the clients don't want you, they don't want you. If I had pulled the extra strings in a manipulating way, I would have been at another stage. I didn't. I didn't have my brother call up the magazines and say, 'This is my sister. I want her on the cover.' That never happened. What happened was they saw us as a team working together. When they came to us, they had to separate us. Willi was different, I'm different."

And different she was. She had scalp-close hair, no eyebrows, and a fully-endowed body. "When I was thirteen and fourteen Willi used to tease me because I was really skinny until that time. He'd say, 'Oh, you're never going to have any bust. You're never going to have any hips.' Then, wham! I had everything and a lot of it. I've taped it down, taped it around. I've worn support hose. I've starved. I've fainted. That's why I'd like to see more real women with real bodies in the magazines. I got a big bust, I got a small waist, and I got a big booty, OK? People don't like themselves. I like myself. Wilhemina said to me, 'Never lose who you are. Never lose your personality. Anybody who doesn't want to work with you doesn't deserve to work with you.' She said, 'Never forget that no matter how rough it is, be who you are.' I was blessed.

"I used to feel bad when certain designers didn't use me. But then you learn from that, and it makes you stronger. You learn that it's a business. The moment I realized that things change so quickly is when I realized that I had to keep changing. When I was twelve years old Naomi Sims came to Philadelphia. She amazed me. She was so tall, so thin, so regal, so in control, I was wrecked. I said to myself, What is this? A goddess from Egypt? Do you know what she said to me? 'When you want to model, just make sure you use it only as a stepping stone.' And she was absolutely right: to know that it's not going to last forever, and to know the signals. We all know what it's like to have

that season when you're not booked much anymore. You have to get to the next stage before that happens. My instincts, my gut, and my curiosity saved me. I wanted something else, too. If I was going to stand up there and have somebody else's clothes on, I wanted to have a say in it. I used to have the biggest arguments with Willi about clothes because I would change every single thing he put on me. But at a certain stage, you really cannot have a say because they are not your clothes, and you are just a product. And I wanted to be more than a product."

Black models and Black designers made a natural alliance in the early '70s. Norma Jean Darden was proud to say, "Jon Haggins was the first to hire me, then Scott Barrie and Stephen Burrows. I loved working for Willi Smith. I was more interested in working for Black designers because I knew that they were the fashion of the moment, which was more than they knew about themselves."

Norma felt that Black designers should take advantage of their identity to forge closer bonds with a guaranteed clientele, Black women. The designers did not necessarily see things the same way. She said, "Stephen had a chance to do a picture with all Black models in his clothes on a double-page spread in *Vogue*. And he didn't do it. He said that he wanted to be a designer for all women, not just Black women. And I said, 'Stephen, get that page

The young **Smith** siblings, **Willi** and **Doris** (aka **Toukie**), became a phenomenon.

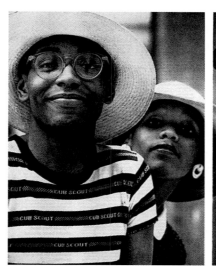
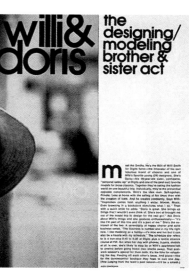

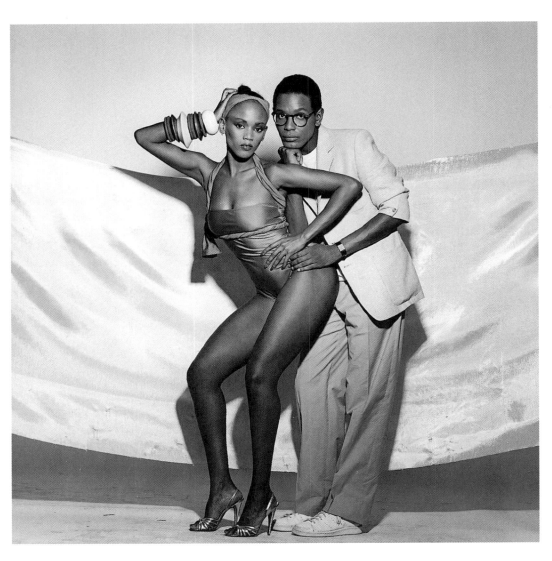

Toukie and Willi. The sheen of success.

and you'll be in Black women's minds for years to come.' He didn't want to listen. He did not want to be a Black designer. He wanted to be a designer, an American designer.

"Few people would listen. Jon wouldn't listen. I told him to make sure that he was in *Ebony* and *Jet* so that if anything happened people could call him directly. 'No, no,' he said.' They just didn't know. They had little consciousness of being Black. Some of them didn't really like Black people. They hadn't heard of Malcolm X or Frederick Douglass. They had little understanding of Black history. Their sense of the visual was so heightened that their whole thing was fashion."

Pal Henry

One model who happily devoted most of her career to one designer was Pal Henry. Her remarkable relationship with Adolfo, a Cuban-born American who preferred to call himself "a dressmaker," lasted for over twenty years, during which time she worked as his fitting model,

runway model, print model, salesperson, advice giver, and all-around team member.

Born in Puerto Rico and raised in New York, Palmira worked her way through nursing school by modeling. A lucky tip from the photographer of her yearbook got her started the summer she graduated from high school. "In the late '60s I was the only Black nursing student at Lenox Hill in a class of about thirty. The school made allowances for me and said that if I didn't miss important lectures, or an anatomy or physiology class, or my rotation in the operating room, then I could book out. So I would accept modeling assignments that wouldn't conflict with my studies.

"I married the chief surgical resident, who was the only Black American doctor there. Then he was drafted by the army. He owed Uncle Sam three years after his residency and internship, so we moved over to North Africa for two years and that's where my daughter, Lisa, was born, in Tripoli. So she's a true African, born there. It was really great. Then when we got back, instead of going into nursing, I went back into modeling. I did a lot of photography for the big companies; the cosmetics companies were very, very good at that time. And I did commercials, maybe one every year, but they would be national commercials. Things would be good for a few months. But you knew the modeling business was not a steady thing. I needed to know if there was anything else in between.

"I went up to see Gillis MacGil at Mannequin, and as I learned, the collections were very definite, as far as time, space, and periods of the year. It must have been in the fall when the Coty awards—which are like the Academy awards for fashion—were being handed out when I spoke with her. She suggested that I go to the Metropolitan Museum where all the designers were who had won their awards and just walk around and see what's going on. She said, 'Just acclimate yourself to the surroundings. Make sure to take an hour walking around and looking and smiling at people, and after an hour, you call me.'

"So I went the following day when the designers were selecting models. The models had already been booked, but they were fitting the models to the clothes and trying to put the show together. I walked in and looked around and Mr. Adolfo said, 'You, over here, please, please come here.' And he put me into something. The other Girls were supposed to be there but I just went to look and see what was going on. Gillis MacGil was a really smart lady. She knew. And that's how I started in runway fashion, and that's how I started with Adolfo, because he had won the Coty award that year. We have worked together ever since. We are very close, and it's like a real team.

"After that I worked with Victor George, Chester Weinberg, Don Simonelli, people that other people today don't even know existed. I did Geoffrey Beene, I did Blass and Oscar. I did bridal couture. I was very, very lucky. I would do all of them with the same look, which was really incredible. I've worn my hair this way—pulled straight back into a chignon—for the last twenty years. They just ate it up.

Somebody once told me that my hairstyle didn't detract from their clothes. That's what I was there for, to sell their clothes, and that's what I did. They kept booking me, and I kept working."

"I went to Europe first with Fashion Group. We went to Paris and all the Scandinavian countries. On the following trip we went to Greece and the Mediterranean. Then we went to Japan, which was wonderful, really fabulous. In the early '70s that was still quite a thing. Not too many people even dreamed of going or had the wherewithal to go all the way to Japan. That was very exciting. Before I decided to go exclusively with Adolfo, I'd go over to Europe and do a few collections a year for several of the top designers over there. Then more Girls started going over, and it became better for the Black Girls and really a great showcase for them.

"European designers are the starters. I would describe them as the key, and we're the car. They are the trend setters, they literally start fashion. Then we take over, and we make it go or we don't make it go. But we're good, very good, so they can't take anything away from the Americans. The world hasn't started to look to America for new ideas in high fashion yet. It's still working the other way. The world looks to Europe but America has all the stores, all the representatives and their big entourage going to the collections. They may start, but we take the ball and run with it.

"Since about 1979 I've been working exclusively with Adolfo, doing his ads and publicity. He just said, 'Pal, I need you to help me out.' It's like everything else in my life. I just started coming in every day and working with him, and I never had time for anybody else. I didn't want to really, because it's a nice team to work with. To be asked my opinion is something precious to me. I give it as honestly as I can. They trust it and follow it. It's very nice to feel that somebody appreciates what's inside your head and what you feel, and that you're not just a machine or a robot or that you do what you're told and that's it. They never tell me what to do. Including Mr. Adolfo. On the contrary. He

"It's very nice to feel that somebody appreciates what's inside your head."

Pal Henry

says, 'Pal, what are we going to do?' I say, 'What are we going to do? We?' So we laugh a lot. But he's very special. He's a very sensitive man. He was born and raised in Cuba, and what he says, which is very nice, is that he's an American out of choice. He loves America like nobody else I've ever seen. His shop is like the United Nations. We have people from South America, from China, from Japan. It's a tiny little team. But still, he listens to you, and he's not all full of himself. He's real and down to earth.

"When Adolfo asks for my advice on fashion and style and the season and everything, it just comes from inside. I might say that something's nice, that it works and why not do this. Then at the end of the season, he'll say, 'You know, that was a very good idea.' It's a mutual thing. We don't believe in titles. He just does everything, from the vacuuming to setting the alarm at night, and I do everything else.

"I still fit the entire collection from the bolt of fabric till the day of the show. And I still open up the show, twenty years later. His clothes make me feel young and pretty. That's really what a woman wants. She doesn't want to look dowdy or half put-together. She wants to know that when she buys something, she feels great in it. That's why you buy clothes.

"I'm a size six. God has been very good to me. He knew that I had to put a child through school by myself, because I'm divorced, and so He lets me eat whatever I want whenever I want. How I work it out, God only knows. I just don't gain any weight. I'm not an exercise person. I am abusive with food. I love good food; that's my vice. I love cooking, the presentation and everything. It makes me feel so good to put on a gorgeous table and then to sit down and enjoy it. One of these days I'm going to wake up, and I'm going to weigh four hundred pounds. I'm going to open my eyes and look from side to side, and I'm going to say, Girl, you deserve every inch of it. I ate it, it's true.

"I'm so lucky. But I know that once my daughter Lisa graduates from Brown something is going to happen then. She's really a very nice young woman, and I'm very, very lucky. She was never a crybaby or a tag-along or a gripper, a grabber, you know. She let me have my space, and I let her have hers. She's the one who pushed me to achieve and to be good and to do well. I never tell anybody, but she was the rock that really steadied me.

"I think my life is made up of happy accidents. I'm a Catholic. I thank God every day. I go to church just about every day. It's good for the soul. It helps me out a lot. You sit there quietly, and it sort of brings you back to reality. Life is fun when it's good. But it's also serious and sad.

"I look at myself and I say, Hmmm, it's going to blow up any second, you know. It's going to go poof or something's going to happen, that this is just not real. Why should I act like such a star when who knows what's going to happen tomorrow? You like me or you don't like me, but at least you make the choice based on who I am, not these airs.

"Things change. Models get very close to a lot of the designers. They're loyal, they book you from season to season. The continuity of it all is very important. That affected us because we could be assured of enough work to pay the rent and take care of our bills. But a lot of companies opened and closed and now they're non-existent. From the '60s into the '90s, they're not even here. It's scary."

Palmira Henry died in June, 1990, of a cerebral hemorrhage. She was forty-four years old, a quiet legend who had found an elegant niche within a clamorous business.

Crosscurrents

We grin and bear it while we're trying to change the tide.

Bethann Hardison

As successful as some individuals were, Black models on the whole wanted more. They wanted more because the could see so clearly the disparity between their job opportunities, pay, and career advancement and those of their White counterparts. Sometimes the inequality was blatant, as in the case of the

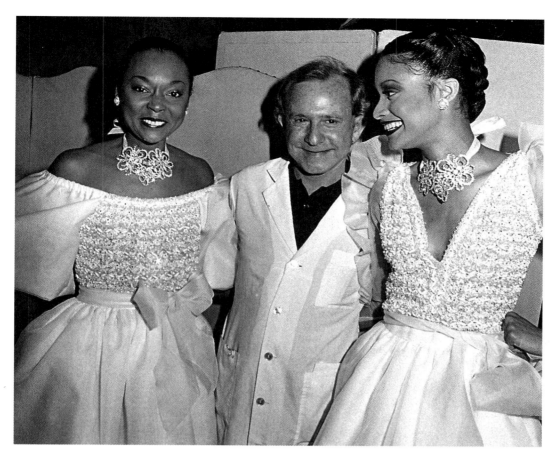

Pal Henry (left) with Adolfo and Vodi. Pal worked closely with Adolfo for twenty years.

two Charlie Girls. Sometimes it was less obvious, as in the standard practice of underbooking "ethnic" models. Generally, the darker models simply signed their booking vouchers and went on, if not quite merrily, at least contentedly, to their next job. Success was a relative measurement. Compared to the Black models of the past, the mainstream Girls of the '70s were prosperous and secure enough to appear to go with the flow. They could handle the crosscurrents that would inevitably emerge.

Despite appearances, however, many women retained a determination — nostalgic or simply hard-nosed—not to let the fiery spirit of the '60s burn out totally. Bethann Hardison acknowledged that more often than not Black models were "happy to get what they could get. They knew they were not getting a certain amount—of money and respect—because they were dark. So we grin and bear it while we're trying to change the tide. I believe in being more radical. We should and we can and we must demand more. Models can help young girls stop dreaming about being a model and think in larger terms of getting jobs that affect the business. We need as many vehicles as possible."

New Girls were constantly entering the business, constantly expanding the very concept of the mainstream. Some of these women came from nations whose African roots were strong. Some embodied cultural mixes never before acknowledged without shame or insecurity. They brought with them a distinctively modern authenticity that enriched the range of images of Black women as a whole. But they also confronted novel subtleties in uncharted waters.

The Crossover

One model, afraid of professional repercussions, told this story. The daughter of a West Indian dentist who had moved his family into exile, she began working in New York with Glamour when she was eighteen. When she went to Europe with two *Glamour* covers and book full of editorial and advertising to her credit, she was told that "there was no Black market," and consequently did not do the amount of work she anticipated. Disappointed but not defeated, she returned to the States where she went on to win the Miss Black Velvet contest in 1978.

"I won $25,000, but I should have really earned $250,000 from related bookings that year. When I didn't earn the money that I expected, I asked questions."

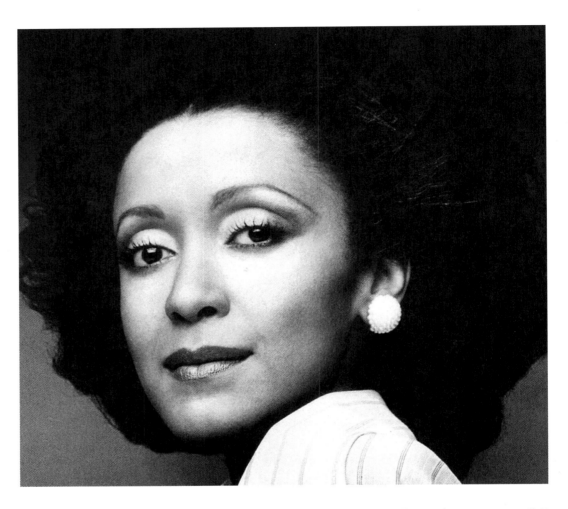

Norma Jean Darden. A graduate of Sarah Lawrence, she brought an entertainer's talent and a gifted intelligence to her work.

As it turned out, an ex-customer wrote a vicious letter to the company, labeling Black Velvet a "nigger-drinking booze" and stating that he would no longer buy the brand. "So that's the excuse they gave for canceling the billboards and the campaign," advertising outlets that would have vastly increased her income.

"It's very frustrating to hear that. That's the inequality, the worthlessness that I felt at times. My agents told me to be happy that I was working and not to rock the boat. But sometimes somebody has to take a stand. I'm going into the future, and I don't want my child to have to deal with those mind games that people play. I want people to know that we are, yes, equal and intelligent. I want all the things that are due me."

Print and television advertising were her mainstays. "I've been called an uppity nigger. I seem not to fit the stereotypical image that people have of Black women. I did not know what color I was until I reached America when they started saying, 'You are Black, I am White,' and all that nonsense. You get insulted a lot, and a lot of times you have to rise above it. I'm a Black woman with an accent, with culture. I've done a lot of shootings where they didn't publish the pictures because they said I was too strong. Until this day, I don't know what 'too strong' means because I think I'm just a normal person."

The racial and economic politics of modeling in the United States and Europe did not appear to differ much from the realities of her longest running contract which took her, ironically, to the heart of whitest Africa. "I was a spokesperson for Lux soap for over ten years in South Africa. I felt no guilt in having to go work in South Africa, because they were the people who were paying my rent. It was a question of survival. If you ask me, having been on both sides of the fence, there was no difference between Johannesburg and New York City in the '80s. I was treated the same way in New York that I was in Johannesburg. There were beautiful people in South Africa just like there were in America. And just like in America, there were neighborhoods where Blacks could not walk without being killed.

"I think modeling was a good opportunity. I've been happy. But you also know when you are not getting equal pay for equal work. That's all I'm wishing for.

"When you are Black, no matter where you go in the world, it's like you cannot erase that color. People have a preconceived idea of what you are, of who you are supposed to be. And when they see that you are different, automatically you have to prove yourself. I consider myself a lady. I don't feel like I have to do certain things to be accepted. In Europe, for example, Black Girls were expected to be the life of the party. And because I was not, perhaps I did not work as much as I should have. My career lasted because I worked at *working*."

Esther Kamatari

In the '70s, a decade after Elizabeth, princess of Toro, made her fashion debut in London, Esther Kamatari, born into the royal family of Burundi, made parallel pioneering moves in Paris. Esther's uncle, the last great king of Burundi, had reigned for fifty years. But after the assassination of her father, the country's political situation became unstable. In 1969 she emigrated to France where she studied law at the University of Lille until someone suggested that she try modeling. Her skepticism was well-founded. "At the time all you saw in magazines were blondes with long hair," she said. She couldn't imagine how she—"a Black girl with short, unstraightened hair and without false eyelashes"—could ever be a model. But after one interview with the friend of a friend who had an agency, she was off and running. Rather, walking.

Princess Kamatari made her mark early among the fashion royals when she swept down the runway of one of the oldest and most consistently distinguished couture houses in Paris. "I was the first Black bride at Lanvin. It was 1976. I wore a huge gown and a bridal crown made of stalks of grain. I was so emotional that the stalks were trembling. Afterwards, the journalists told me they thought there was a battery in the headdress to make it shake. But it was my nervousness, my fear. It was almost like a consecration. Lanvin was a very conservative house, and for them it was a revolution."

Esther flourished as a model, working for everyone in Paris: couturiers Dior, Givenchy, Rabanne, Saint Laurent, Scherrer, and Ungaro and stylistes Azzedine, Beretta, Montana, Mugler, and Rykiel. The big exceptions to her client list were those design houses that used no Black models at all. "At the time, people's responses were shocking. They didn't wear kid gloves to tell you that they did not use Black models." And yet, she felt that "in Paris you really don't feel racism. It's one hundred times less than in the United States."

Hers was not an abstract judgment, but rather the result of two and a half years of experience. "Going to the United States was the biggest mistake of my life," Esther declared. "You get this idea, I'm going to make my fortune in America. It was a complete mistake. I should have stayed in France where I was at the top of my profession. I didn't have a Black American look at all. I wasn't marketable. I wasn't commercial. I couldn't do catalog. I was a part of New York high society but I wasn't making any money. It was horrible."

To complicate matters, a broken ankle required that she stay longer than planned in New York. When she returned to Paris, she said, "I had to distance myself from the business and think about my future. I had been a big star, but staying so long in the States made it difficult for me to pick up where I left off in Europe. I wasn't on the front page anymore. I'd left the scene, and someone else had come along and taken my place. Plus, it was a different era. In the late '70s and early '80s, there was much more competition. I didn't work in the States, but on the other hand when the Black American Girls came to France they worked."

Leaving Home
Daring

Creatures of constant reinvention, models found travel essential. Location trips, lasting from a few days to a few weeks, became a privileged form of working vacation. International show seasons kept the best Girls on the go for months at a time. Star models came to be in demand all over the world. Having already left, in many cases, both hometown and native country, they were free to work wherever they were hired and to settle wherever they wanted for as long as they wanted, renaming, reshaping, and reevaluating themselves.

It was not for Black models alone that Versailles had been an eye-opener in 1973. Most models who worked in the United States—especially those with close ties to Seventh Avenue—saw that fashion was financed, manufactured, and worn there, but somehow it was not created and appreciated in the States the way it was in the privileged enclaves of Europe. Women who were even further from international currents had even fewer illusions. Whatever their origin, all models came to understand that true fashion, high fashion ,was created by European aristocrats whose names

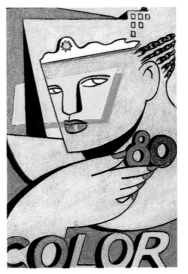

were difficult to pronounce, whose luxurious lives were impossible to penetrate, and yet whose prejudices were often less rigidly exclusionary.

But as the last gasps of '70s liberalism were smothered by an international sweep of political conservatism in the '80s, the fashion industry witnessed a surprising development: the phenomenal explosion of status designers. Led by the French and Italians, able to capitalize on their long couture tradition, and followed by the market-wise Americans and Japanese, designers were suddenly elevated to first-name icons of style and entertainment. They became pillars of the creative and financial establishments world-wide. The price of their fashion produce soared as their seasonal presentations developed into large-scale multi-media productions and international ad campaigns.

At the same time, large numbers of more ambitious Girls dared to leave the comforts—and constrictions—of home. The tidal wave of models who debuted during the '80s reflected and often embodied this international style. Among them were Akure, Karen Alexander, Amalia, Aria, Rebecca Ayoko, Cynthia Bailey, Naomi Camp-

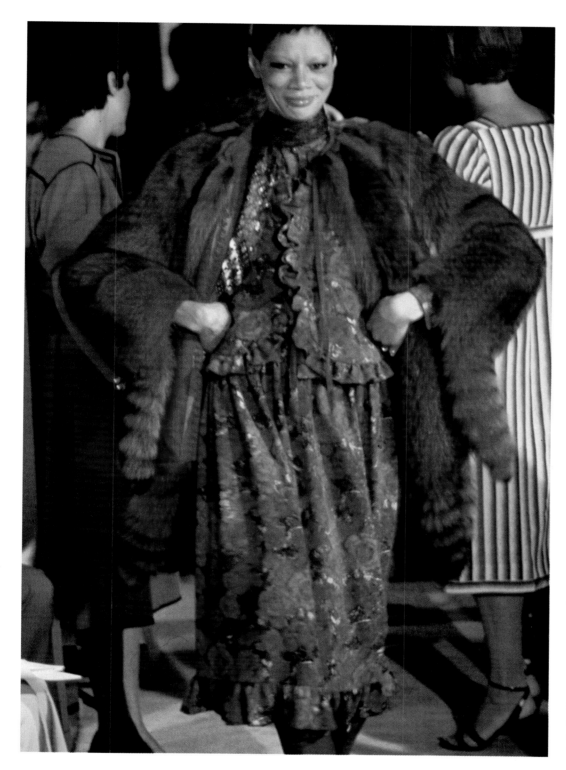

Jacquelyne Matisse left Tennesse and traveled to Germany, England, and France before settling in Paris in 1968. By day, she modeled chez **Balenciaga**, **Saint Laurent**, **Ungaro**, and others. By night, she danced under the direction of **Roland Petit** at the Casino de Paris. She married into a famous French family.

Color 80, by **Harvey Boyd**.

The '80s issued in the spectacular globalization of the fashion industry. More models became bigger celebrities, while designers became icons of style and their labels, passports to power.

bell, Sonia Cole, Katoucha, Khadija, Gail O'Neill, Carla Otis, Beverly Peele, Stephanie Roberts, Roshumba, Louise Vyent, Wanakee, Veronica Webb, and Kara Young. No matter where they were born and raised, most eventually came to New York City. But once they asserted their claim to American territory—with more or less success—they often sought to extend their careers overseas.

Part of what they discovered abroad led them to a radical redefinition of their basic professional identity. What had long been hard and fast separations between print Girls and show Girls crumbled, and Black models of a previous generation were among the first to lead the way. In 1980, a *Los Angeles Herald Examiner* report, estimating that 1,000 models deluged Paris during one show season, analyzed the change: "This year the high-voltage charge from the electric runway drew photographic models Iman and Beverly Johnson to Paris in an intriguing

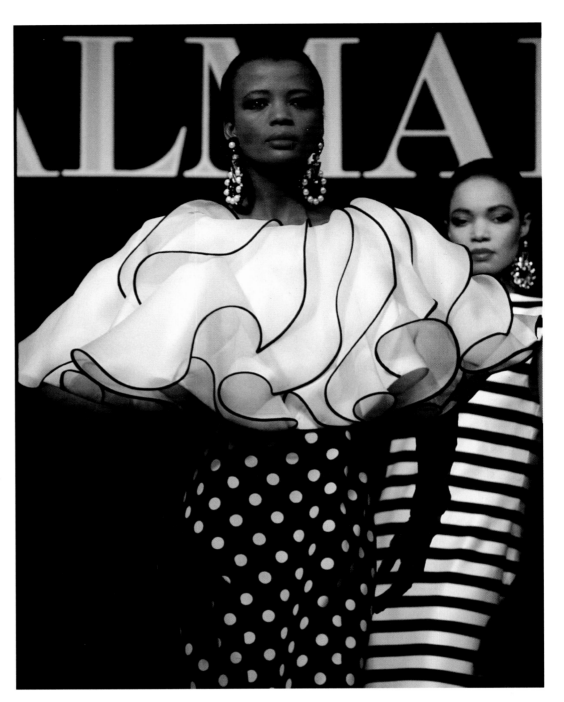

Rebecca Ayoko in Balmain.

Increased numbers of elegant African women moved assertively onto the fashion stage.

role-switch, though other magazine cover girls Rene Russo and Cheryl Tiegs still refuse to join the Paris Follies. 'They couldn't care less,' says agent [Eileen] Ford."

After savvy models—*and* agents—calculated the potential for income and career advancement, however, they made a complete about-face. Working Girls of the '80s and '90s aimed to do both pictures and *défilés*. It was all part of the creative whirlwind that modeling had become. As the quantity and quality of models increased dramatically in these decades, they could not afford to wait for golden opportunities to come their way. Black models, like other assertive women, squared their shoulders, packed their bags, and actively pursued success. In many cases they had little to lose and all the world to gain.

Europe

I wanted to go to the center
of the fashion world: Paris.

Dorothea Towles

Europe has always been a beacon. For those coming from the Old Country, it was a storehouse of fond or desperate memories. For those going, it was a sophisticated paradise free of petty restrictions. Paris, in particular, has emanated the glow of unlimited promise. As the capital of fashion, the City of Light attracted many moths to its flame.

Aspiring models from all over the world have landed there, bewildered, ecstatic, and often in need of a job. Black models, especially, found the lure of Paris irresistible, with its legendary combination of the most fashion with the least prejudice. Decades after Dorothea Towles first disembarked in 1949, Black models were still arriving as if for the first time, full of guts and dreams. Although everyone who made the trip did it her own way, Carol LaBrie's must rank as one of the most unique, for no one went to Paris as she did: on her honeymoon and quite happily alone.

Carol LaBrie

With the help of Hollywood film director Bob Rafelson, Carol LaBrie left her career as a dancer in L.A. and Las Vegas in the late '60s and started another as a model. "He called Nina Blanchard, the top Los Angeles agent, and when she saw me, she said, 'Great, let's do some pictures.' So I got pictures done, and my first job was a TV commercial. From that, clients saw me and booked me in New York. I came to New York, met a Frenchman through Fernando Sanchez, the designer, and after three days, we got married."

How could she marry someone she had known for only three days? "He was gorgeous. He couldn't speak any English, and I couldn't speak any French, and it was great. We got married in New York, and on my wedding night I flew to Paris. Yves Saint Laurent wanted to see me, but my husband had to stay to take care of his business as an art dealer.

"Yves wanted to put me under contract to be a house model. But that meant that I couldn't do anything else, so I refused. Then I started making the rounds with my book. When I saw the people at French *Vogue*, they flipped out, and I got twelve pages there. I started working constantly.

"I had tried to work in New York, but I couldn't make it. I was too light. That was during the late '60s, the Naomi Sims period when they wanted dark models. They never gave me a reason, they just wouldn't book me. So I said, Forget it, I'm going to Paris, and I made it very big there. The French treated me as an equal. There was no color involved. When they booked me, they booked me as a model, not as a Black model. To them I was just a very beautiful woman who reminded them of

Lynn Watts and **Hubert de Givenchy** shared a close professional relationship.

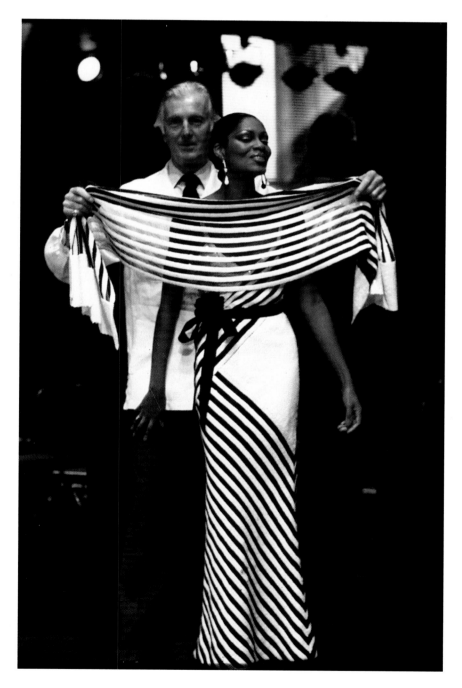

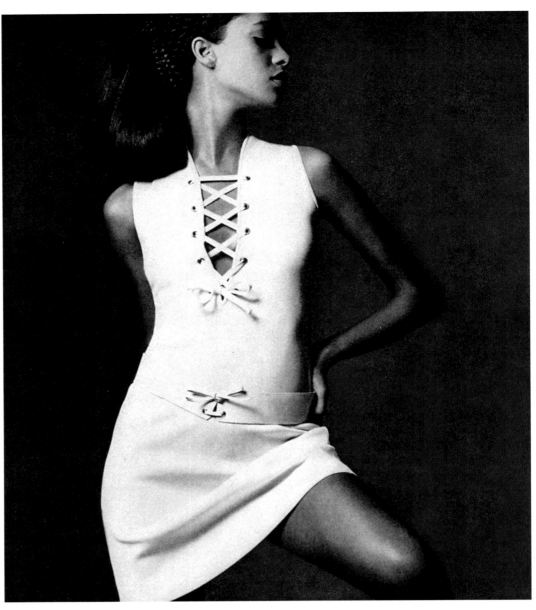

A sprightly personality and valuable friends propelled **Carol LaBrie**'s career.

Josephine Baker." Carol LaBrie became the first Black model on any *Vogue* cover, when she appeared on the cover of the Italian edition in August, 1971.

Liberated from the rules of conservative good taste and geared toward a younger generation of educated professional women, fashion was fast becoming an international phenomenon. Black models from all over the world were eager to be a part of it, and certain designers were just as eager to hire them. Hubert de Givenchy was among the first who traveled outside of his home base in France to find them.

Givenchy, who was used to dressing the rich and royal of the world, was traveling across the United States in 1978 doing charity shows for his American clients. On this trip he discovered a half dozen little-known Black models and

invited them back to Paris. Their first appearance with his fall '78 collection made it one of the best in his twenty-five-year career, according to fashion journalists. Bill Cunningham wrote: "The women were an inspiration, reigniting the creative fuse that had become dormant over the years of making good-taste clothes for understated aristocrats."

Nancy Clark

Nancy Clark was one of the lucky Girls picked by Givenchy, and just in the nick of time. "Prior to that," she said, "I was destitute. I had gotten my eviction notice. My phone was about to be cut off. I was really struggling. A few weeks before, I had gone home at Christmas and told my grandmother that I didn't know how long I could pursue this dream of modeling because it was just not working out. Everybody was rejecting me. They'd

Letter from a friend in deed.

say I was too short or I didn't look Black enough. It was just ridiculous. I thought I might have to return to Detroit to be a social worker again. But my grandmother said, 'Just hang on a little longer. I know someone's going to see you and something's going to happen.' Within a couple of months Givenchy came and changed my life. I went off to Paris with just that one show for him but I was so happy to be going that I decided I would make it work."

Sandi Bass

Sandi Bass was also one of the chosen ones. She had been modeling in Los Angeles for a year, "still not quite doing the best shows," when Givenchy asked her to go to Paris. Her excitement was tempered when she found out that the contract was for six months. She had only been married for two years and refused to consider such a lengthy separation from her husband, Jacob Wheeler. But Jacob's response surprised and encouraged her. "He told me, 'Sandi, we'll have the rest of our lives together. Of course, you can stay for six months. I'm not going to be the one to stand in the way of your doing anything you want to do.'"

Sandi Bass became part of Givenchy's historic all-Black *cabine*, a phenomenal first for the fashion world. The other models included Michele Denby, Jacqueline Miller, Regina Richardson, Diane Washington, and Lynn Watts. Their incomparable blend of sophistication and sass, elegance and energy made Givenchy

a new man. "They have changed my life," he was reported to say. His team of models became the envy of other designers. They spurred a new wave of Black Girls in Paris as they also elevated the status of runway models throughout the business.

"This all took place in 1978, so the French weren't really ready for us," said Sandi. "We were the spirited Americans. As far as giving Givenchy feedback about the designs, we did what the French Girls had never really done. We had our own opinions, and we expressed what we felt. They were not really used to that, so we caused quite a tremor over there. But Givenchy loved every minute of it. He loved us and our spirit. He loved how exciting we were on the runway. We gave him inspiration."

Lynn Watts

Another Cinderella tale starred Lynn Watts. Selected from a group of aspiring models at a modeling school in Chicago, Lynn was chosen by a French coiffeur to do a hair show there. "After the show, he asked me to come and work in Paris. I thought that wasn't a bad idea. I mean, everybody who wanted to model was going to New York, so why didn't I go to Paris? Although I thought that I would never hear from this man again, two weeks later he telephoned to say that I was confirmed for the Jean Patou show.

"I didn't know who Patou was or that I was going for good. I thought I was going just for this one show. Christian Lacroix was designing there at the time. During the show I saw all the photographers, and I thought, Wow, this is serious business! I was real happy. Then when the show was finished, the Patou people called me up and asked me to do a shoot for them for *Vogue*. So I went and did the shooting. But while I was changing, a photographer was in the dressing room. As I took my jacket off, I remember him flashing. I thought, What's he doing that for? Come to find out that I had a big beautiful picture in *Vogue* from the show, but on the next page was me taking my jacket off with my breasts in the air.

"Do you know what I did? I sued

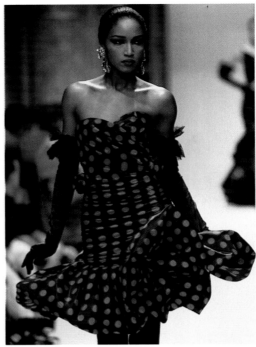

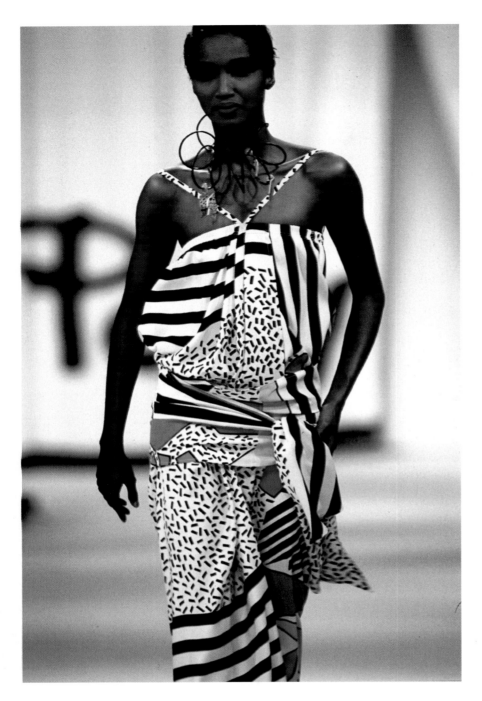

Two views of **Katoucha**. She ran away from her home in Senegal to model in Paris, and then the world.

them and won the suit. It wasn't really about suing them, because they knew they were wrong. They gave me money to just shut the whole thing up. So, there I was, rich in Paris, but I never worked for Patou again."

Acting on a recommendation, Lynn went to see Givenchy at his salon on Avenue Georges V. When she got there, she recalled, the receptionist told her plainly, "'Oh, we don't need any more Black Girls.' So I said, 'Well, thank you for being so nice about it.' When I turned to go down this winding staircase, I saw a big, tall man coming up the stairs. After we passed each other, he turned, looked at me, and said, 'My lord, you're so

beautiful.' And I thought to myself, Is he out of his mind?

"He asked if I was coming to see about the show. I didn't know who Givenchy was. I used to call him 'Gavinchie.' He said to come back and try on a dress. Then he turned to say something in French to the woman at the desk, and the next thing I knew, I had on an evening dress.

"Givenchy asked me to walk for him, and I said, 'Of course,' and I did the walk. Then he said, 'OK, can you start tomorrow in the *cabine*?' The next day I signed the contract. He made the whole collection on me for the press show that was coming up. I stayed in the *cabine* for three years, but I worked for him for seven years. I did all of his collections, photo shoots, TV spots, everything.

"I first came here at the end of the '70s, and for a while I was, like, I can't believe this is happening. My whole life here has followed exactly the same pattern. The same thing happened with Hanae Mori. For years I went to the casting, and they threw me out of the door like I was an old shoe, saying, 'No Black Girls.' But again, just by chance, at Hanae Mori her assistant came in at the same time that I was leaving. That's the only way you're going to get booked for shows, if you see the designer directly.

"At Givenchy the receptionist would just sit there and turn people away, Girls I knew he would like. Sometimes I would sneak a Girl in the back door. When everyone else was out to lunch, I'd tell her,

'Be here at two-fifteen sharp.' Then I would take her running upstairs to see him, and he would take that Girl every time. I knew what he liked, because you don't stay and do fittings for someone without knowing what he wants. I even told Givenchy one day that the best way to choose his mannequins was to let the other models choose them."

Lynn Watts also benefited from what she called "a chain," a network of friendly competitors who introduced her to an expanding circle of clients in Europe and Asia. "Every time you do a show, there's somebody who will come in and ask you if you want to do *their* show. That's what made me stay in Paris, because I knew that the base, the whole collection industry begins in Paris."

Being chosen is one way to leave home. Choosing to leave can be drastically different. Katoucha, a young Senegalese woman, was, in fact, running away from her home in West Africa. "My parents wanted me to be a historian and an archaeologist like my father. But I didn't want to continue my studies, and I ran away to Paris. I told them I'd be famous, that I'd be a big star. They said that I'd end up a whore. My parents were angry for a long time because they thought I didn't set

a good example in the family. But they forgave me and became very proud." They had good reason to be. From the late '80s to the mid-'90s Katoucha was one of the show models most in demand around the world. "I was very lucky," she said, "tremendously lucky."

Unpredictable yet indispensable, Lady Luck shone on many models who reached for the dream. Sonia Cole, another runway star in Europe, the United States, and Japan, had worked in a Las Vegas casino with her husband until a fortuitous meeting provided her with a real-life Godfather. "I used to work at Caesar's Palace dressed as Cleopatra. I would walk around handing out money to the big winners, giving directions, greeting people at the door, working in private parties. Then I met Bill Cosby. He asked me what I *really* wanted to do, and I told him: I wanted to go to Paris to model. So he sent me. Within two weeks of meeting him I was in Paris doing the shows. I was lucky. I was there at the right time."

In the late '80s Dor-Tensia and Lor-Tensia Hayes, twins from Detroit, stated that everyone had encouraged them to go abroad. "So we jumped from Detroit to Paris with no kind of experience whatsoever. We learned to walk watching 'Style' with Elsa Klensch on TV.

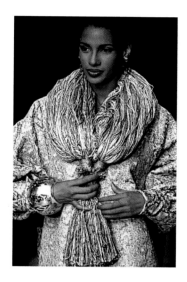

Entertainer and educator **Bill Cosby** sponsored **Sonia Cole**'s debut in the Paris collections.

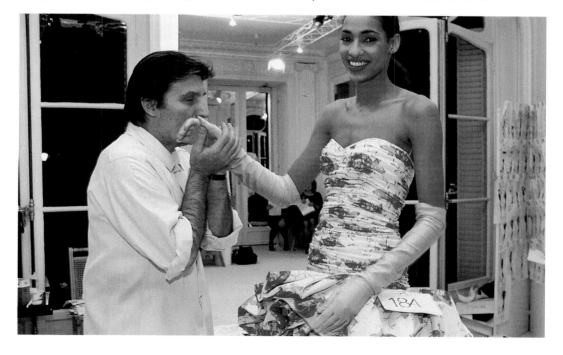

Sonia Cole with a courtly **Emanuel Ungaro**.

"Karin, a Parisian agency, came to Detroit scouting, and they decided they wanted to take us. Then over the telephone they told us they'd decided No. We were so disappointed, but we said we're going to go over there anyway. Who cares what these folks say? We came over with our books, went into Karin's anyway, and here we are." Although they did only one show in their first season—bad boy Jean-Paul Gaultier—it was enough to get them launched. They eventually switched agencies, broke into print work in the smaller London market, and have continued to develop careers in both branches of the business on both sides of the Atlantic.

Identical twins **Dor-Tensia** and **Lor-Tensia** Hayes left Detroit without even the assurance of an agency in Paris.

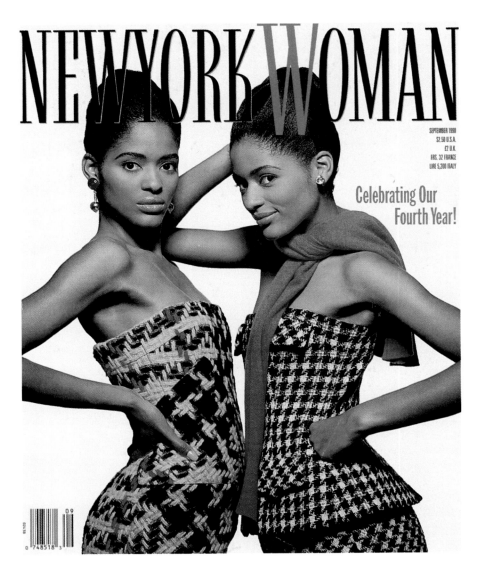

NEW YORK WOMAN

SEPTEMBER 1990
$2.50 U.S.A.
£2 U.K.
FRS. 32 FRANCE
LIRE 5,200 ITALY

Celebrating Our
Fourth Year!

While Europe could be a cradle for many models at the beginning of their career, it could also be a crucial testing ground for more established models. *Vogue* cover Girl Sheila Johnson went on her own initiative in the '80s. "The agency didn't think I needed it because I was already working so much. But I said, 'I want to go.' I went, and it never happened. I realized that in Paris, for a Black Girl, it wasn't going to be the same as in New York. I had a month and a half of go-sees. My book didn't mean anything because I was shorter than the runway Girls, the big Girls. I actually did do some runway, and I ended up staying for two months. In a way, I was a little disappointed. I expected so much. But I had it good in the States. I came back to the States only to return to Europe to work for Italian *Bazaar*. I realized that the States was going to be the thing that made me and would take me abroad, and that I'd rather do it that way than on my own."

Jade Brown

Even with contacts and encouragement, however, the move to Europe was always a big one, moreso if you were coming from places far off the beaten track. Born in Capetown, South Africa, to a Colored South African mother and a Greek father, Jade Brown's birth certificate identified her as 'Cape Colored'. While a teenager she moved with her family to Australia. The gift of a trip to Europe on her twenty-first birthday inspired her to leave her bank job and try modeling. Six months after signing with Vivian, Australia's largest agency, she was well on her way to local success.

"People kept telling me, 'You should go to Paris and work there.' And I kept saying No. I was scared, I guess. Then this French Girl came to work in Australia, and I became friendly with her so that when she went back to Paris, she took a mini-book of mine back to her agency. Once she had given it to them, they called me up and said, 'Come, get on the plane right away.'

"I left Sydney on the 29th of December, and I arrived in Paris literally on the 31st of December. For two days I had been up and down with landing and taking off again from the airports. When I arrived I was so exhausted, my skin was battered. It was too much with all the time changes and the flying, just too many things. I arrived at the agency, and the woman looked at me and went, 'My God, you're beautiful, but go to the dermatologist right away!' I went immediately, and that weekend my skin cleared up. Then I went in to see Jean-Louis Scherrer the next day, and I started working for him. And I've never stopped working since.

"I live between Paris and L.A. I do Milan, then Paris, then I go to L.A. for a week, then I go to Tokyo. I may go to Barcelona and New York and Sydney, where I still have my house. For work so far it's good, but it's hard to travel. I started with a number of other Girls, who haven't had the work flow coming that easily. You can't say why that is because you can't really put your finger on it. But I think a lot of good things happen to good people."

Leaving one home often opened the door to another. Work, the basic motivation, became only one element in the evolution of young lives. Exploring personal creativity was also important.

Veronica Webb

Veronica Webb described a particularly rich period in her life when she lived with the designer Azzedine Alaïa in Paris. "Azzedine is an extraordinary person. I lived in his house on the second floor. I really was like part of the family, like one of his kids. We would work all day together in the studio, fitting the clothes, talking together, looking at pictures and in books, getting ideas, cutting things out and hanging things up. And we'd sit up most of the night together. He would be on one side of his desk, and I'd be on the other, watching old movies and drawing shoes and dresses. He would give me all these clothes to try on, one incredible garment after another. I've seen him draw and stitch and sew and put together all these garments. I had an intimate knowledge of everything I had on. He creates from a very spiritual basis. You

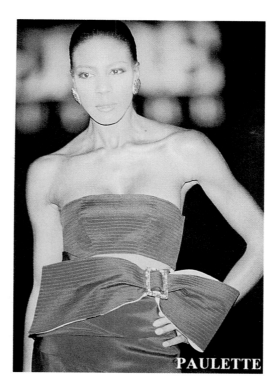

PAULETTE

Paulette James credits her shoulders for her success, especially as a fit model for **Giorgio Armani.**

really feel his craftsmanship and his spirit when you put his clothes on.

"Often people would come by and visit him late at night. Tina Turner would come by at two in the morning, and other artists and actors and filmmakers. There was this incredible entourage, this three-ring circus that flocked around him full of information and intrigue and drama.

"The same goes for Karl Lagerfeld, continuing in this kingly tradition. At one point I was working for him doing all his shows and his campaigns. I was his fitting model. I lived in his house with him. I had absolutely wonderful jobs. It was great getting to meet these people who are so creative and so geniused and so lost and absorbed in their talent."

Peggy Dillard, a three-time *Vogue* cover Girl who combined a successful show career with a long and continuing print career gave her thoughtful perspective on working abroad. "I think, more than anything, the designers wanted you to bring life to the clothes, sexuality to the clothes. Let's face it, we're usually showing swim suits at a time when they're not in season. So, even if we don't have a tan, we still come off darker and healthier.

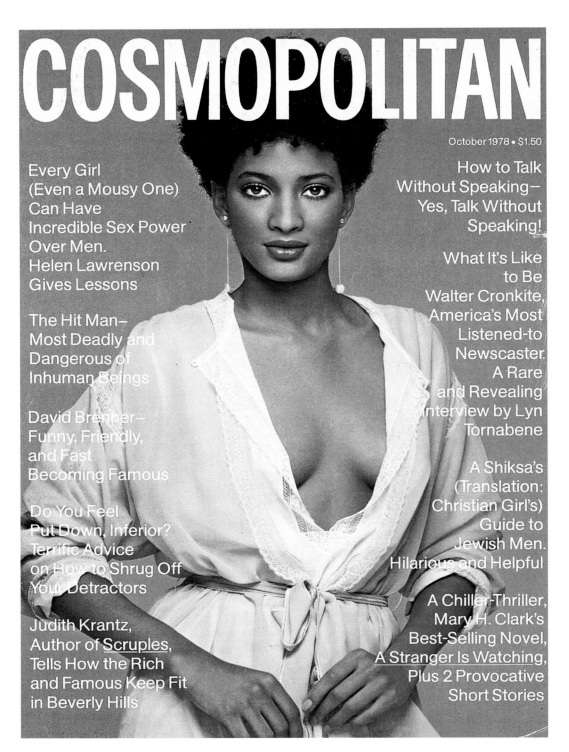

Peggy Dillard.
Cosmopolitan October, 1978.

In Italy where Black women have always been very popular, they're like the cream of the crop. But even though a woman was Black and a certain sexuality came along with that, each individual always added something different. She had her own personality.

"There was one season in Italy where I did forty-one shows in one week. When you're doing forty-one shows and you're averaging four pieces each show, to be able to bring a different experience to each outfit, you have to dig deep and search for something other than just walking straight down the runway. Otherwise it gets terribly boring."

The era when a Black model was booked for several dozen shows during collection season came to a sharp halt. Peggy Dillard recalled, "When Ronald Reagan came into office there was an article in *Women's Wear Daily* that said that the runways of Paris were beginning to look like 125th Street in Harlem. That one sentence had a greater effect on the Black model's income than any other phrase, I think, in my career. The next season you saw less than half of the Black

Girls that you had seen the season before. The season that followed that, you saw even less. It had a great effect on what we meant in the fashion industry."

A backlash against Black models in Europe was bound to come. And when it hit, it hit hard. Sandi Bass was there. "I remember when I first went to Italy for the collections. It was a very dangerous time because foreign models weren't allowed to work there. The Italian Girls were not happy. They're a little bit more vicious than the French. And we had umpteen jobs, so much work. I mean, people were pulling us off the street because Black Girls were really, really hot then, and they couldn't get enough on the runway. Early '80s, '79, '80, that's when it was. It was really very dangerous. They could take models to jail if we did not have working papers. Today, the agencies provide the papers. But back then, we were working there illegally and didn't even know it.

"I remember the end of one show when someone said that the police were coming. Half dressed, we grabbed our stuff and tried to get out. But there was a partition at the Fiera where they have the shows, and we all said, 'How are we going to get over the wall?' Well, Gloria Burgess had this metal makeup kit, and she said, 'Put my bag there.' So we used it as a stepping stone, and then somebody at the end threw the kit over, and we were gone. It was wild, having to jump over a wall to escape, but we had some fun. A couple of the Girls walked off the runway with garments still on and just kept going because the police were backstage and they didn't want to be taken to jail. I know a few who got outfits like that."

If the racial pendulum could swing from one extreme to the other, it could never stay there. At collection time Black models had become mandatory for a great show. And by the mid-'80s conditions had stabilized so that designers were hiring Black models again according to their individual aesthetic needs.

Warren Jackson, a journalist and close observer of the show seasons in Rome and Milan, explained that Italians "refer to Black Girls as showgirls, and they are. What little Black girl never liked getting

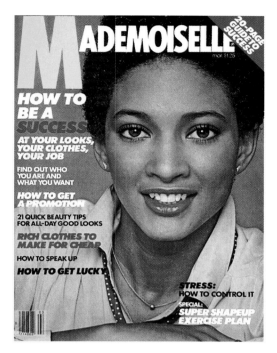

A wide range of expression on the covers of diverse magazines helped lay the groundwork for **Peggy Dillard**'s fabulous career around the world. *Mademoiselle*, March, 1978.

dressed up? Show me one. They never had much of anything anyway, so the first chance they get to put on something shiny…. Of course, they love getting up there, putting on their stuff, getting dressed up in high heels, with makeup and hair, getting all that attention. And when they get out there, they work. They sell those clothes. That's what they do that the White Girls didn't know how to do. That is why you have the shows, to try to sell this stuff. You can't just walk out there, turn around, and come back and talk people into buying something. I never would have looked twice. It's a fantasy thing. The consumers are all White. And they all sit and talk about how beautiful the models are, how fabulous they are, the way they walk."

Selling on stage and selling in print were two vastly different markets, however. When the time came to document the show-stopping style of Black models, photographs may suddenly become scarce, especially if the outfit was a guaranteed scene-stealer and was given to a Black model to present it most effectively on stage. Warren Jackson explained, "If you don't have your own photographer for the shows, journalists go to the P.R. office of each designer afterwards, and they'll give you pictures. Ninety-nine times out of

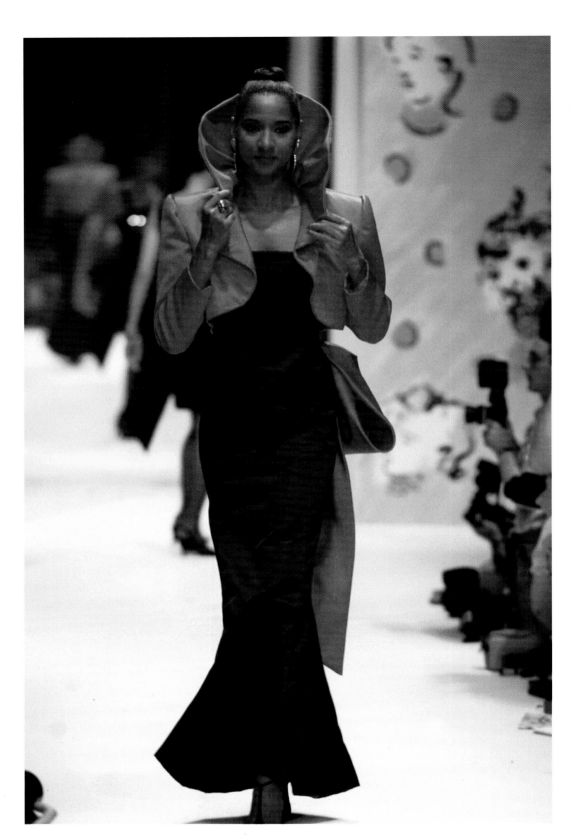

Trained in dance, D.C. native **Gloria Burgess** worked in Japan before moving to Paris, where her frenzied pace prompted *People* magazine to subtitle their '83 profile of her: "Showing the collections is trial by fatigue." Always a vision of grace, she never let the stress show.

one hundred you get pictures of White Girls. Now, you can't tell me that I could get just one shot with a Black Girl when the Black Girls are among the top there are and get the best clothes in the show. Once I went back to a designer asking for a shot of a particular yellow dress which was really fantastic. He said, 'Well, I don't know if we still have it.' And I said, 'Could you please check because it was spectacular and indicative of the whole collection.' When he came back, he claimed that he didn't have it. The dress was hot, but Katoucha wore it, and I couldn't get the shot.

"There was a very interesting incident in '89 at the Versace show. He had booked about forty Girls, about thirty of them

Black. This was in and of itself scandalous. Then the show was divided into two parts: one was couture and the other was prêt-à-porter. For the haute couture part, which is custom-made dresses, it just turned out that all the models were Black Girls. All Black Girls! This made it even more scandalous. Apparently somebody protested, and he wound up having to put in one Asian Girl. He had picked his best dresses to put on the Girls he thought could sell them the best. Obviously. And they were all Black Girls."

Paulette James

No one in fashion Stateside had told Paulette James that she was beautiful. After working in Chicago for Time-Life as a marketing analyst, it did not take long for her to see that a model could make the same money in three months that a working woman on a regular job could make in a year. She headed for New York, where she did not stay long because there was too much competition for too few jobs for a dark Black Girl like herself. In 1977 she went to Paris. Although she stayed only a few months on her first trip, she decided to return and pursue modeling further.

When she returned she landed a job in the Paris showroom of Italian designer Giorgio Armani. On the strength of recommendations she went to Milan where she worked as Armani's fit model for seven years. "I thank God and my mother for my shoulders," she said, "because Armani's work is jackets," and shoulders are the key to their proper fit. "I think it's good to start in the showroom. You can learn and get confidence in your moves, in your walk and turning."

Paulette was often called upon to teach, especially with more print Girls—with less experience on the runway—working in shows. "It takes a mannequin to sell clothes. They say I have a good personality. I must, to sell clothes."

After more than a decade in Milan, she knew everyone, and had seen people come and go. "Black models were used a lot more before," she said. "Today, out of twenty-five models in a show, maybe five will be Black. I would never say it was

racism. That would be too easy. I remember when Armani said he didn't want any Black Girls in his show. And me? He said he didn't see me as Black!"

Anna Fiona

At the other end of the color spectrum was Anna Fiona, who was half-Scottish, half-Kenyan, and a full-fledged star on the European circuit. Born in Nairobi, raised in convents and boarding schools, she lived in Kenya until her family moved to Switzerland when she was seventeen. A friend wanted to introduce her to a Swiss model agent but the agent was reluctant because, said Anna, "they'd had a few experiences with Black American Girls that drove them crazy." After the agent was reassured that she was not from America but from Africa, Anna finally got an appointment.

"I went there in the latest fashion from Africa, dressed up with every mixture of clothes, outdated '70s high heels, and all this curly hair." To her surprise, the agent signed her to a contract the same day. "The first job that really got me started was a fifteen-day booking with *Harper's Bazaar* in New York. They were really lovely with me."

When Anna returned to Switzerland, she gradually began to do shows in nearby Milan, and eventually also in Paris and Tokyo. "I decided that I'd rather be a runway model than a photographic model. It was more exciting, much more interesting. There was much more going on. You got to meet the designer instead of being in the studio just wearing someone's clothes. Being in contact with the designers allowed me to find out what they're all about. And, in fact, many of them are the sweetest people you could imagine.

"You're still a Black Girl, though, whether you're from the Caribbean, Africa or the States. And in the fashion business Black Girls have to work twice as hard, prove themselves more, and be more special. The doors were never really going to open after a certain point, whereas if you're not Black the doors were more open. It could be frustrating, but I've been very lucky and very protected. My instincts have always kept me clear-headed. There's more to life than just being a model. There'll come a point when you'll need to have something more, and sometimes models forget that."

Japan

The spirit of our clothes was free.

Yohji Yamamoto

If Paris has been the traditional center of European fashion with Milan a stiff competitor, Tokyo has emerged not only as a required stop on the style circuit, but also as a major launching pad of its own. Tokyo gave notice to the fashion firmament in the mid-'70s when Kenzo, Issey Miyake, and Kansai Yamamoto started to go international. In the early '80s when designers Rei Kawakubo and Yohji Yamamoto received unexpected accolades for their collections shown during the Paris prêt season, Japanese names were no longer tongue twisters. They were part of the accepted vocabulary. When ever-curious Western buyers traveled to investigate the source of the Japanese boom, they discovered a Tokyo as intoxicated with traditionally chic foreign labels as it was, at least theoretically, emboldened by its own black-swathed avant-garde. Although the cliché persisted that the Japanese had no desire to look different from their peers, as clients they were still perceived to be tasteful and rich enough to buy—if not wear—it all.

Expanded fashion markets created more job opportunities for models. In Japan the relatively prosperous economy and creative atmosphere allowed foreigners combined to establish regularly scheduled show seasons and lucrative off-seasons, which have become a work staple for many successful Girls. For these jobs numbers of non-Asian models were imported. Improbable as it may seem, several Black women have started their careers in Tokyo.

A native of Ethiopia, Tara said, "In London, where I was a student, I was working in a Japanese restaurant. Some Japanese people had come to town to do a show, and they were looking for people who were not models. They wanted characters. I never knew people in the fashion business or anything about it except for Iman. I never thought that I would get involved in this business at all. But I went to Tokyo, and I did just one show there. Six months later I joined an agency in Paris, and that's when I really started to work.

"My mother was so upset with me, because I had dropped out of school, that she didn't talk to me for two and a half years. Where I come from education is very important. But her reaction didn't really bother me because she hadn't lived abroad to know what my life was like. I can take care of myself. I'm happy. Now she understands. I knew that she would."

Some models actually have extended careers in Japan. From Chicago, Gamiliana worked briefly in New York before she "fell into a contract for Japan. I was stressed out to the point where the offer was just like a holiday. Tokyo was a long way to go, but it was just what I needed. When the first two months were over, I got a contract for another two months to do a tour for Chanel. I liked it a lot, and they seemed in no hurry for me to leave, so I stayed a year.

"I never thought I'd stay in Japan as long as I did. Looking at the business, I can see how it's changed in just the short time I've been moving around in it. When I was working in the States, and I wasn't there too terribly long before I left, even then mobility seemed to be the thing that was happening. It is up to you to create the demand and do it on your own."

Although it was the mad money models were reputed to earn which drew them to Tokyo, it was not easily made. Jade Brown explained, "You could only be in Japan if the Japanese wanted you to be there. Apparently not that long ago not many Girls wanted to go to Japan because it was like being in the middle of nowhere. But now Tokyo is becoming almost as crowded as Milan. There're about 3,000 Girls in Milan, and they're having only 40 shows. Well, Tokyo is not that bad. Not yet."

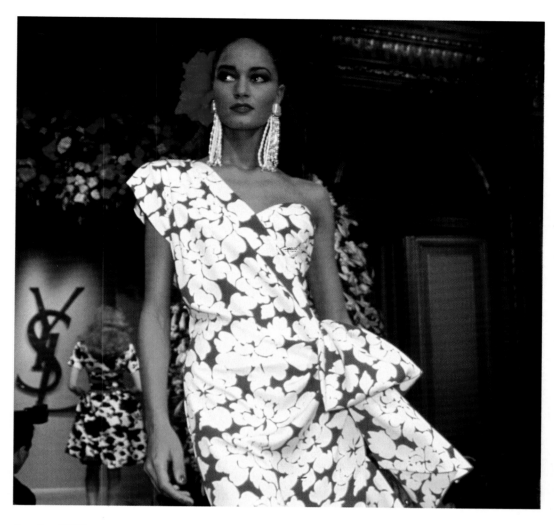

Anna Fiona, born and raised in Kenya, chose shows over print because they were more exciting.

Judy Gillett

Judy Gillett, who was born in Chicago and raised in L.A., told her own dramatic story. She said, "I tried out for that Elite contest, you know, the Look of the Year. There was a load of talent scouts out there, and they asked me to go to Japan for about two months. I stayed there for, like, two years. I had to pay my dues. They had to get used to me. In Japan they always consider that a Black model should do only shows. It took them a while, but then they started to let me do print.

"This is how it started. They have entertainment at nightclubs, right? Instead of someone on stage singing or dancing, in this one club they decided to have a fashion show, every night, six nights a week. You wore the same outfit each night. It wasn't really for people to buy the clothes. It was just to display the Girls from California walking around the stage. They got a kick out of that, you know what I mean?

"After our two-month contract was up, a couple of us decided to stay in Japan. No one would take me on because it was

after the show season. I was struggling. I went on castings but no one wanted me. After a while, though, they got to know me, and they got used to me. I have a certain style. I'm not trying to be Miss Diva. I'm not trying to be a perfect walker. I might do a little bit, but I'm not trying to be perfect.

"They had off-season shows, and once in a while I'd do a little print in a little magazine. They would put a wig on me to make it look like I was not Black. But I was Black, you could tell.

"There's another story behind it, though: who my boyfriend was. He was part of the Japanese Mafia. I had suspicions. I knew it, but then again, I didn't want to know. I stayed in this really rich hotel for six months, and he just took care of me. He was older, thirty-eight, and I was twenty-one. He wasn't hard Mafia. All he dealt with was loan-sharking and gambling; that's not too bad. And he wasn't your typical Japanese Mafia-looking guy with the permed hair and the white shoes. He wasn't like that.

"But when everybody found out, nobody wanted to use me. Then things

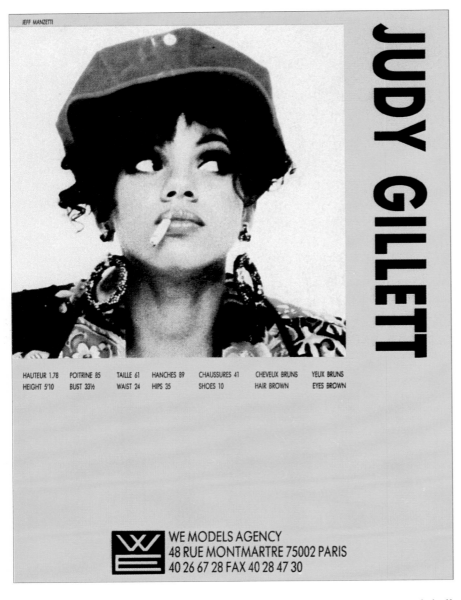

JUDY GILLETT

HAUTEUR 1.78	POITRINE 85	TAILLE 61	HANCHES 89	CHAUSSURES 41	CHEVEUX BRUNS	YEUX BRUNS
HEIGHT 5'10	BUST 33½	WAIST 24	HIPS 35	SHOES 10	HAIR BROWN	EYES BROWN

WE MODELS AGENCY
48 RUE MONTMARTRE 75002 PARIS
40 26 67 28 FAX 40 28 47 30

Judy Gillett's career in Japan was influenced by her Mafia boyfriend.

changed, and it kind of helped me. I did all the shows I could do, all the print, all the ads, posters, and commercials. I was making a lot of money. My boyfriend never let me see all the money I was making. He just wanted me to save it.

"Part of the Japanese mentality is to give you a lot of presents. I had jewels, diamonds, furs. But I had to leave, because all my life I wanted to be a model. I wanted to do well. I wanted to see myself in *Vogue*. And nobody knew what I was doing over in Japan. No one knew I was doing well. People from Europe would come over and say, 'Why is she the star of the show? Who is she?' I wanted to grow. So I decided to

go to Paris. I went and paid my dues there. The French don't pay you any money. I'm doing well, but it's not like Japan.

"Now, I also have a taste for New York once I found out how much more money you can make. I never worked in America, so I never knew what it had to offer. But I feel like I haven't finished paying my dues in Europe yet. I don't want to go to New York just yet. The timing has to be right."

If Tokyo seemed an unlikely launching pad for beginning Black models, it was even more unusual for it to be a nesting ground where an accidental start could develop into a full-fledged career. There were no Black models permanently based in Tokyo when Terri Coleman arrived in 1980. Yet she lived and worked in Japan for over a decade.

Terri Coleman

Terri first went to Tokyo for a week's vacation from her job as a flight attendant in the States. The day before she was due to leave, a Japanese modeling agency contacted her and asked if she could stay for a month to develop a modeling portfolio and meet potential clients. Her good luck continued when, through that agency, she was hired by fashion show director Kohei Katsura.

"Kohei gave me one outfit, because he wasn't sure what I could do. I used to walk with my shoulders hunched up from fear and insecurity. I had no experience. I'd never been on a stage before but I knew that I could do it, that I had what it took to do it. That whole month, I would put on my Walkman and just strut. All I knew was that you had to walk with the rhythm and the music. At that time, 1980, we didn't have so many fashion videos. You didn't see it on television. You just had to imagine what was expected of you.

"Fortunately, for that first job I wasn't to be just a fashion model. I was to be Josephine Baker. So Kohei built this grand stairway. It cost him 300,000 yen, or something like that, to build this stage for me to make my one entrance. He gave me a cassette of her songs in French, a language I had no experience in at the time, and I had to pantomime the song while I came down the steps as Josephine Baker. It was the funniest thing I've ever done. No, I take that back. I've done funnier. It was the scariest thing I've ever done, because I was so terrified.

"Then Hanae Mori saw me at this show, and she asked Kohei who I was, because she likes Girls with thin legs. That's one of my biggest assets; my legs are long and thin. She started booking me, and I've been working with her ever since."

Contrary to some expectations, Terri found the working conditions in Japan agreeable. "In Japan your agency takes you everywhere. Either they have a car or they take you by taxi, and they pay for that. They even provide housing for you. It's a service to the models. During that extra month I stayed, I left the hotel which I could no longer afford, and they put me up in one of the agency's apartments, so I didn't have to put out any money up front. Naturally, when I started to work, they gradually deducted this from my pay.

"The agency also provides you with interpreters who go everywhere with you. Most of the staff in the fashion business speak English anyway. It was never necessary to speak Japanese for work, and it still isn't. The Girls coming from Europe for the collections don't speak Japanese, and it's never been a handicap for them."

Terri, however, did learn to speak the language. It was important for her on a personal level to be able to have private conversations and to travel around the city and later, the country. In her early days she experienced a generosity from strangers that made a lasting impression. "I've had incidents where I stopped people on the street and asked directions. And they would take me in a taxi take me where I wanted to go and pay for it. This can happen nowhere else in the world. Especially in America, to bring up a racial issue, I don't think a White person will ever go out of his way like that. So this gave me more of a special feeling. Because I *am* a Black woman, and I *was* lost in their country, and they *did* take the time to go out of their way to help. And it happened more than once. Their hospitality enveloped me so that I didn't feel alienated."

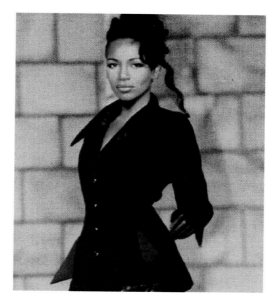

A native of St. Kitts, **Terri Coleman** was an airline hostess in the United States before she landed on the runway in Japan.

When she started out, however, life in the dressing room was another story. "The older Japanese Girls were bitches. They gave me a hard time. They also used to be that way with each other because they have a system of seniority in Japan, for modeling and for any business. The young Girls would come in, bow down, and make tea for the senior Girls. They gave seniority a lot of respect.

"I got caught up in that because I stayed. During the '80s all that broke down because the Japanese started having to deal with us foreigners. The younger Girls began to develop a different attitude, but still when they talk to each other they use certain expressions to show respect. It's the only city in the world where they cared about a Girl's experience."

Terri felt that it took time for a model to develop, to build up her self-esteem and confidence, to learn the skills and tricks of the trade. "I think a model's at her best when she's had five or six years in the business. But by that time most people are finished with her. They don't want to see her anymore. She becomes an Old Girl.

"I thought I would only stay one year in Japan, but three years passed before I left and actually started to go to Europe. My reception in Japan ruined my European experience. My quest was to go to Paris and work with French designers, but I never really broke in. I made a dent, but I didn't open the door. The bulk of my work in Europe was with the Japanese designers who knew me from here: Hanae Mori, Comme des Garçons, Junko Shimada, the Koshino sisters. Then, too, the problem was that the collections in Europe overlap with the busy off-season here. Twice a year—in February and

March and then in September and October—you travel around the country showing the things that were just shown in Europe. They're like trunk shows but they're treated like full-scale press shows. The Japanese buyers go. They book all the good foreign models, and the money is excellent.

"The work is harder here. The Girls are in the dressing room six or seven hours in advance of a show. Often we do three shows a day. We used to do four. But you make a lot of money, much more than in Paris.

"At one point in my career, I asked myself what was important to me: Did I want to be famous or did I want to make money? Because in order to break into Paris, you had to be there. I don't have fame and notoriety. I've dug out my niche here. And I feel I made the best decision, to go for the money."

While some star models were flown in—and quickly out—for direct bookings to work with only one designer or to do only one production, Terri found a philosophical middle ground in the stability of her work. "When I look at the Girls who started at the same time I did, only one or two made it. But then you have the hundreds who're still in there trying to beat down those doors. If you're not a print star, you don't make it. And only a few of the top show Girls do the big-name designers. I don't know if the market is expanding for us. We're more visible but there're not more of us. That string of top Black show Girls from the '70s and '80s has shrunk.

"Still, my advice to any Girl who wants to work in Japan is: Go to Europe. Just as the agents do in New York, the agents here will tell you to go to Europe and work there first. For the Japanese, the few designers I did do in Paris meant a big deal to them. And that helped sustain me here."

Terri's presence has helped to establish new ground for Black models. Her work in Japan also had a direct benefit on her family. Her younger sister, Greta, came and modeled in Japan for three years. "When she came, I was already established. So she came in making big

guarantees, fees that I had worked long and hard to earn," Terri said with a laugh that did not completely conceal a touch of envy. "I was really glad that I could do that for her." And perhaps for other, unknown Sisters as well.

Down Under

I used to sit out on the stoop
and dream of a larger world.
Barbara Bennett

Although Black models have long been known to travel the traditional fashion circuit, some of their more surprising moves took place far off the beaten track, in countries where fashion was not a big, highly organized and popularized business. Not surprisingly, they managed to make names for themselves there also.

Barbara Bennett

The first Black model to have a successful career in Australia, Barbara Bennett said, "When I was a little girl living in Harlem, I used to sit out on the stoop and dream of a larger world, another world out there. I knew people spoke other languages, and I always told my family and my teachers that when I grew up I was going to live in Europe. I knew that. By the time I decided to be a model, and it wasn't happening for me yet in New York, I figured the world was my oyster and I could go anywhere. So I made the decision to go, just go, just like that."

Barbara left her accounting job and her studio apartment in the '70s and went first to Paris and then to Rome. "That's how I met photographer Carlo Scimone, who said, 'If you're not a model, then you should be.' And that's how it started." Barbara worked out of his studio for a number of different magazines.

"I stayed in Rome for two years working, doing photography with Carlo. Then I went to Australia." In the interim, she met a member of the Packer family, which was highly influential in Australian publishing. Although there were no Black models in Australia, he encouraged her

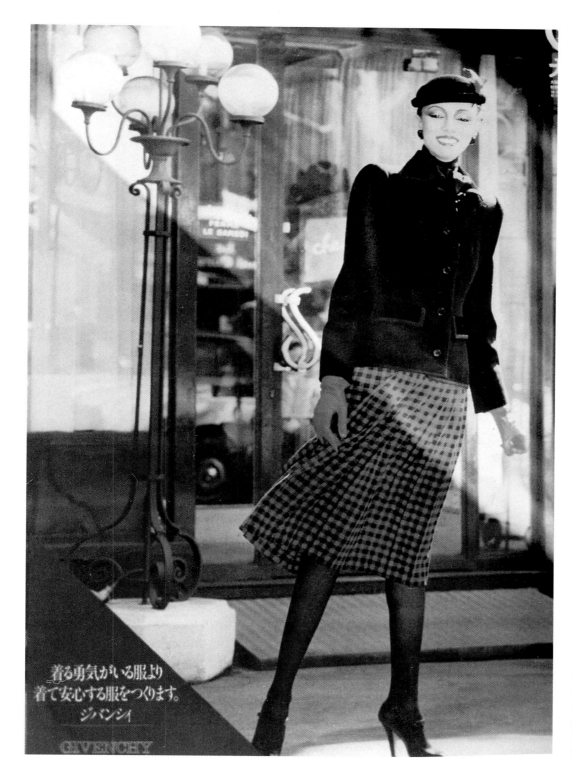

着る勇気がいる服より
着て安心する服をつくります。
ジバンシイ

GIVENCHY

A member of Givenchy's original Black *cabine*, **Sandi Bass** lived with her family for many years in France, Italy, and Japan, before returning to the States to work as an international model scout.

"to relocate, saying 'If you come to Australia, I'll open the door, but I'll only open the door.' So, I decided to give it a shot. I figured, what do I have to lose?

"I was in Sydney, and for the first month, I did nothing. It was just too wonderful to do anything. Then my friend called me up and said, 'So, are you going to sit around and do nothing, or are you going to become this famous Black model from Australia?' I said that I was going to become a famous Black model from Australia. He said, 'Good! Because you have a job on Thursday, and afterward Vivian—a big modeling agency—would like to see you.' And that's how I started.

"It was very rough in the beginning, though, very rough. Some clients and some people in the audience would say, 'She's wearing that outfit, and it looks great, but how will it look on our White skin?' They were ignorant to the fact that blonds and Black people can wear the same thing.

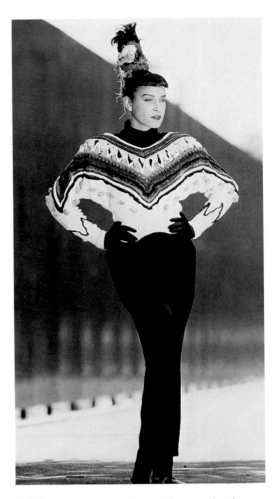

"In my life, in some way, I've always been politically involved. So when this happened, I began to think to myself, This is my politics. This is my battle. I can do this, and I can do this for Black women all over the world. It became my mission. What was I really doing? I was convincing people that no matter the color of your skin, no matter what race you are, you can survive. You can get along in this world, and you can be a success.

"I never, ever forgot that I was from Harlem. As I became famous in Australia, I would be invited on TV talk shows, and they would ask me where I was from. I would never say New York. I would always say Harlem. I was very proud of it. I grew up in Adam Clayton Powell's church, and I don't think you come out of Abyssinian without some pride. So, with that background, I figured I could live and work in Australia without having to give up anything. I could still be me. And I could make them see that they could open the doors for other Blacks, which they did, eventually. Now there are a lot of Black models who not only go to Australia on a special promotion but they also live there.

"I was never treated as well in my life as I was treated in Australia. As for work, I did everything. I did print. I did commercials. I did runway—for Australian designers and for European designers who came and showed their wares. I went to Japan and worked there. We went to Manila, took Australian designs and worked there. They had staging, lighting, and choreography for fashion shows that were almost like Broadway shows.

"Then I started to choreograph and style fashion shows for my clients. I knew that I wanted to move from modeling into that area. Although a very popular prop stylist was already working, there was no such thing in Australia as a fashion stylist. Working with these designers, I got to be in their shows for many years. Adele Weiss and I knew each other before she became so popular. When she wanted to have a show for the press and all the big fashion wheels of Australia in her showroom, she called me, and we worked together on ideas for it. The show was so successful that we got a standing ovation. When Adele came out and we all came back out on the runway, she said that she wanted to introduce the person who had coordinated the show and choreographed the Girls. Then she said, 'Barbara, would you step forward?' People couldn't believe it. When my other clients heard of this, they asked me if I did that for Adele, why didn't I do it for them.

"The eight years I lived there, it was really home. In Sydney it was almost like a family atmosphere. Everybody knew you. They knew what you could do, and you didn't have to call around. They called you.

"I felt really good about that part of my life. I had maintained whatever dignity I took from my Abyssinian beginnings to Australia, and it helped. Whatever I'd done, I had done it right."

Sandra Stevens

Sandra Stevens was the first Black cover Girl in New Zealand. The road that led her there had more twists and turns and strokes of good luck and bad than any one young woman should experience without a breakdown. But she seemed to have an actual talent for living life on the edge.

She grew up in Detroit and spent her

summers in Alabama as part of a large, proud family whose ancestor, Thomas Ruffin "was a slave who came to inherit not just the house but the entire plantation he'd been a slave on. My grandmother had fourteen brothers and sisters, and they lived across the street from Alabama State University. So with all that in my blood, I just never thought about working for anybody else."

After attending Phillips Academy, where she "got to see how the other half really lives," she attended Pomona College in California, "because Angela Davis had taught there the year before," and finished her undergraduate education at the University of Pennsylvania. Then she went to Berkeley Law School. "Being a lawyer was prestigious, but actually studying the documents and reading the Constitution and studying property law and seeing how the rich get richer and everybody else keeps struggling….I just had this gut feeling that it wasn't for me to be a lawyer." Approaching the third and final year of law school, she wondered, "What are the bounds of being outrageous?" She was angry, rebellious, and frustrated. The law school sent her to talk with a psychologist, who made the improbable suggestion that she try fashion modeling.

She became a house model for Miss O, a branch of the Oscar de la Renta empire. She admitted that she had no patience with the job, which required that she "sit there in a room with no windows, wait to put on a dress, order lunch, and just sit there some more. So I was very happy, actually, when Oscar let me go.

"I wanted to do photography, but I was suffering from age paranoia. I was twenty-seven, and when I would talk to agents I just hated having to say I'm twenty-one. I didn't want to not tell the truth. I wanted to be who I was. You can't hide your age. The camera picks it all up."

Sandra wound up going to Australia with a group of wealthy African Americans who were headed for the America's Cup race. At a party she met an agent who asked her if she was interested in working as a model. She worked in Perth very briefly before moving on to New Zealand. There she met the agency manager for the oldest and best agency who promptly told her, "We've never had a Black model. It could be tough, but I'm ready to go for it if you've got strong nerves. When you walk in to auditions, people might drop their jaws, because I'm not going to tell them that I'm sending a Black Girl. I'm just going to send you, and somebody's going to give you work."

Eventually, Sandra met the top photographers and worked with the leading designers there. "I was *it* in New Zealand for Black models. They liked my attitude because I didn't come in really pushy. But I would go routinely to the top magazines and say, 'Hi, How're you doing today?' No appointment, you know. 'I'm still here. When you're ready to give me a job, call me.' Eventually, I told one editor, 'Look, I've been here three times. You know me. Just tell me straight up: Would you ever use a Black model in your magazine? If you're prejudiced, then let's get it on the table right now.' She started stammering, 'Oh God, Sandra, I'm going to book you. I'm just trying to find the right thing.' I said, 'Forget the right thing. Anything is right if I put it on. It'll work.' And she wound up giving me the cover, the first Black face on the cover of *More* magazine.

"There're more Girls coming through now. My friends used to call me from New Zealand whenever a Black model was on TV or in a magazine, and they'd say, 'That would have been your job if you'd been here.' They're mostly experienced Black American models who come down or Girls who're just beginning and want to model. They go into the agency, and the agency feels, if you're there, fine, work. It's a nice, new attitude. I definitely broke the ice. I took the blows. Definitely.

"Everyone projects fantasies of what models are doing and what it's about. They don't see the hard work or the suffering. They think it's all glamour and one big party and one nice dress after another. I thought, I have to at least let my parents know that I didn't turn my back on what they prepared me to do, because, of course, they were in shock from me leaving law school to now, she's what? A fashion model?!"

CHAPTER
6

Sirens
Desire and Danger

*You set me up
to fall into yr
dreams*

Ntozake Shange

ust as the Homeric Greeks were lured by the sweet songs of the Sirens to danger and destruction, many adventuresome young women—and men, too, naturally—were enticed by the enchantments of the modeling profession. To be one of the Beautiful People wearing the most beautiful clothes and jetting off to unbelievably beautiful places was more than a tantalizing notion. Especially if you already had the face, figure, and desire, or if people in the know suggested that you could do it. Modeling was tremendous fun. You got paid for playing around. What few people talked about was the price you must pay to play.

Unlike the mythological Sirens whom no one could describe—for no one who saw them ever returned to tell the tale—the Sirens of the modeling world were the star models themselves. Not that they actively recruited newcomers to the business. They didn't have to. Their work—the fabulous fees they earned and all the auxiliary perks—was enticement enough. Average good Girls made more than the President. Entry-level supermodel status was reserved for Girls posting minimal annual earnings of $1,000,000. They appeared on the financial page, the society page, and the ad page. They passed from hard-working anonymity to instant recognition and were called by their first name alone. They were surrounded by other creative types—designers, photographers, and star-dusted

companions—with nearly household names. They had the public's attention without any accountability, freedom without responsibility. They were not in charge, let alone in power. They were, simply, in.

"To be in your early twenties and have this kind of opportunity is amazing," said Tanya Eggers. The best part of modeling, for her and many others, was "definitely the financial freedom, being able to travel, and becoming professional at a young age. You can handle modeling any way you want to. You can show up late for work and give people a hard time about bookings. Or you can be really professional and take care of your money, be diplomatic with your agent and your clients, things like that. I like that a lot. It's like having your own business, but *you* are your business."

The stress of running a business which consisted of oneself and one's body was tremendous. The pressure to be perfect in the midst of hundreds of other women trying to do the same was constant. Not everyone—even among the chosen few—could handle it. Normal concerns about body weight and shape, complexion, hair, nails, hygiene, and wardrobe could escalate into anxieties and neuroses. The ordinary tasks of arriving for a job on time and in a cheerful mood often induced tensions resulting in sleepless nights and edgy tempers. When common expectations became uncommon fears, a model was in danger of losing her original

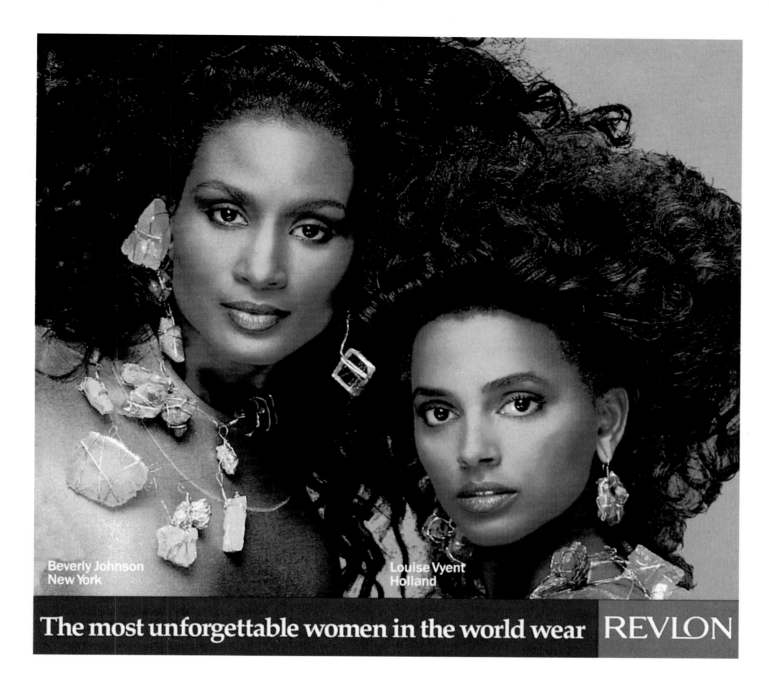

motivation. The money was no longer enough, the travel became exhausting, and the fun boring. After the energizing high of work, the letdown and loneliness afterward were even more palpable. The Sirens' song was no longer so enticing.

Dangerous undercurrents began to exert their pull. When a model found little stimulus on the job, she might reach for stimulants afterward. Misuse of alcohol and drugs, abusive relationships, and confused priorities were the rocky shores on which careers and lives could be wrecked. Factor in extreme youth and big money and the results, as dramatic as they could be, were not unexpected.

"We have more losers than winners. Being a success you don't see too often. Being not a success you see a lot of," said agent Bethann Hardison. But she was speaking strictly from the inside. The business was based solely on successful models. As far as the public could see, they were the only ones who existed. Beyond the public's eye, however, was a murkier reality, a complex world where winning was never unqualified. For Black models, in particular, the business was rarely evaluated in the mutually exclusive terms of success versus failure. They soon came to realize that success often *included* failure.

Bethann insisted that "even the star models have been had by the system. They go out there and smile and be nice. Or they look like they have attitude. But deep down inside it's lonely out there. The higher they climb, the more the system will tempt them.

Beverly Johnson and **Louise Vyent.** Beauty campaigns such as Revlon's Unforgettable Women reflected—and respected—the increased purchasing power of women. To appear in these flawless ads was every model's dream.

We're so unprepared to resist." And other sirens, those sounding shrill alarms, go unheeded as they speed by.

Money Magic

What I learned about money, I learned the hard way—by having had it.

Margaret Halsey

Models made money, the Sirens sang. Models got rich quick. Women who modeled ranked among the highest paid workers in the world. With today's minimum hourly fee of $200, show fees ranging from $2,000 to $10,000, and daily fees from $2,500 to astronomical—and often unreported sums—it was no wonder that so many tall, thin Girls flooded the modeling agencies looking for acceptance, work, and a financial return on their biological good luck. Since the agencies' foundation in the '40s and expansion throughout the '80s, the beauty rush to the capitals of fashion has only continued to swell.

Black models—and those who want to be—continued to arrive in ever-increasing numbers as well. Every decade since the '60s has counted at least one Black model among the top-earning Black women in the country. Or so it seemed. It was difficult to know the actual figures for few Girls talked candidly about money. There was a natural, to-be-respected desire for privacy, especially with the dread Internal Revenue Service always lurking in the background. And then there were the inflated egos—of the Girls, their agents, and the press—eagerly pumping the celebrity smoke machines to maintain the illusion of solid success. As with blondes and their hairdressers, so with models and their money. Only their bankers knew for sure.

One of the significant turning points in the professionalization of modeling came when Girls were finally financially self-supporting from their work. Before the '60s most models indulged their dreams as they kept a close hold on the steady paycheck provided by less glorified jobs.

While Ruth King made headlines as a Sepia pin-up Girl in the '40s, she maintained a much lower profile as a secretary in the court system. "I wasn't happy there," she admitted. "I loved modeling. But my job was a means to an end. That was where my financial benefits lay. I'm very happy that I stayed as long as I did, over forty years. I imagine the Girls who are hungry or the ones who really want to model badly will resort to anything. It's very sad because people are just playing, making fools out of them. But I was not hungry to that extent."

Dorothea Towles claimed that it was American assertiveness—and the need to pay her bills on her own—that forced the designers she worked for in Paris to increase her rate during the late '40s. Working for Elsa Schiaparelli, she earned what sounded like the enormous sum of 30,000F a month. Translated into American money, however, her salary shrunk to less than $100. French models, who were paid even less, later organized marches to demand better wages.

When Helen Williams, one of the star models of her era, first started in 1954, she earned $35 an hour, an honorable sum—outside of the modeling business—even today. Forty years ago, she said, it definitely reflected the upper-scale standard of living of the times. Even "with earnings of $8-9,000 a year, which was a lot of money in those days, I couldn't live on a model's salary alone. I had a very comfortable lifestyle, a nice apartment, a car. I loved to travel. I went to art school." Like many other models far less successful, Helen kept her day job. She worked with the Pagano studio, a major catalog house where she had gotten her start, as a stylist, a position which she held proudly for over thirty-five years.

Black models in the '60s wanted their notoriety translated into cash, but few achieved the financial success that their glamorous images indicated. The '70s would start to see that change.

Joyce Walker's cherubic face and angelic Afro were a bankable combination during the days when Black was beautiful and more than a mere slogan. "When I was a senior in college, I was also going to the Negro Ensemble Company twenty-five hours a day every day and making $37.50 every two weeks. I got an apartment for $75 a month. So I had the rent, but I had no money for food. My mother would bring me care packages, and the first time she saw the apartment she cried. As a matter of fact, the ceiling actually fell in, and I got $600 from the landlord later on. I loved it.

"I went from working at NEC making $37.50 every two weeks to *Hair*, where I made $150 a week, which was the minimum contract back then, and from there to modeling, where on my first job I made $400 each day! I was working on the beach, and it was so much fun. When I got that check, I just looked at my boyfriend like, We're stealing something. We had so much money we had three different bank accounts. We really did not know how to handle it. I never expected it, and I was not prepared."

Marketed primarily as a junior model, Joyce Walker worked steadily for over a decade for most of the major magazines, as well as for commercial catalogs, and beauty clients. She estimated that she was "making a good penny and a half," averaging about $100,000 yearly. "I must have made at least a million in the business."

Smart models invested. They put their money into real estate, investment portfolios, and small businesses. Lu Sierra profited from another model's advice. "Billie Blair taught me that all this beauty doesn't mean anything if you can't take what you earn and invest it. I have a certain image to uphold, but I don't spend a lot. After I've worked for the money, I put my money to use by having it work for me."

But if a model's money did not last, no one knew. Her image did, and it was her image that drew other women to seek their fortune in this world of mirrors.

Ming

Ming Smith was running away from a broken marriage when she ran into modeling in the early '70s. A graduate of Howard University with a B.S. in microbiology and a minor in chemistry,

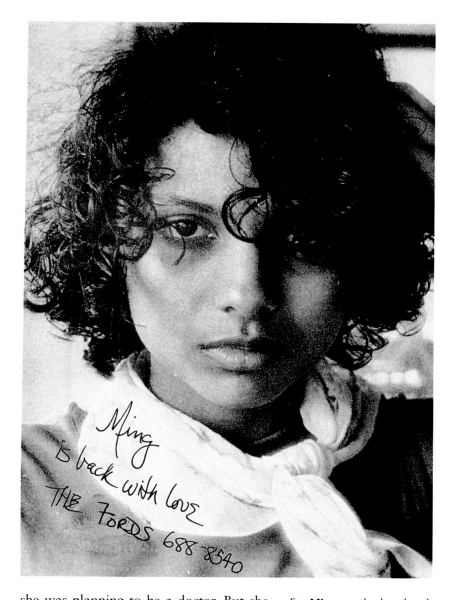

she was planning to be a doctor. But she had a child with her, and she had to put her medical studies on hold.

"My head was not into being a model. I was always more political, into Black consciousness and Malcolm. Modeling was capitalist; it was like everything I was against. But because I could make money and make it fast, I hoped to bring my son, Kahil, from my parents' home in Ohio to live with me in New York City.

"Now, all of my friends who were really into the Black Power thing, I couldn't tell them that I was a model, because I was ashamed. Nor could I tell my parents and grandparents. They were the type of people who thought that being a model or an actress or anything like that was like being a whore. They thought New York meant the fast life. So no one knew I was a model. It was just that serious to me. I was only twenty. But I knew what I had to do for my own sanity as a whole person. Modeling was a secret for a long time until

For **Ming**, motherhood and modeling posed a prolonged conflict.

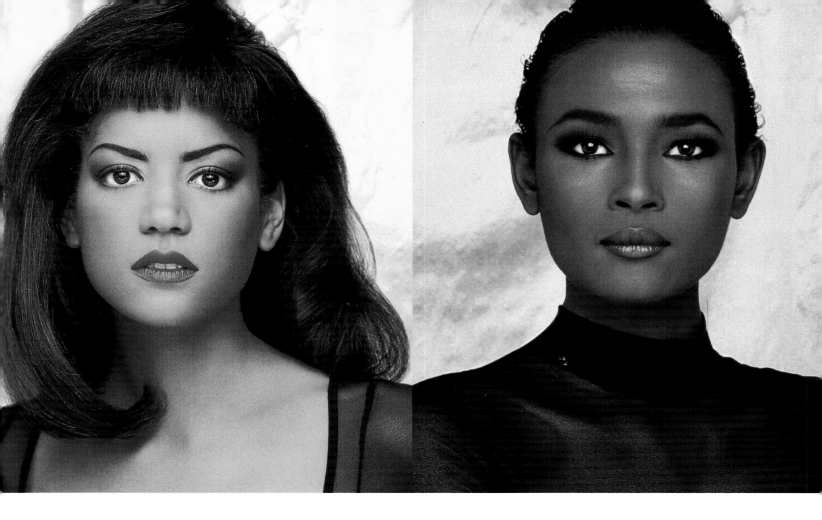

Veronica Webb (left) was signed to a major contract with Revlon's ColorStyle line in 1992. Other Black models used in the campaign's ads— **Waris**, **Gail O'Neill**, and **Aya**—represented a rainbow of shades.

someone told my parents that they saw me in a magazine. Then after I started working well, people would say that they saw me, and it became OK to model.

"I must be 5'4" or 5'5". That was short, but most of the things that I did were beauty. I also did a lot of fashion for juniors.

"There were a lot of little catalogs I used to work for. But I used to get frustrated because the White models would be booked all day, and I would come in and do my little one hour or two hours and say to myself, 'Think of how much more money I could make.'

"When I was working at my peak, I opened up one issue of *Essence*, and I had every ad in there. I had catalog work, all-day bookings, five days a week with overtime, and I couldn't book anymore. Then I read that one of the top Girls was making over $100,000. When I put it on a computer and figured it all up, I saw that she couldn't be making that much money. That's when I realized that a lot of modeling was all show, a real hype.

"At my strongest, maybe 1976, I would say I made $30,000, at the most. I had these illusions that I was going to have my son with me and do the whole thing

right. There was always this fallacy in modeling. I thought that if I got with another agency, I would make more money, as if someone else was going to do it for me. There might be a little truth to that, but for the majority of Black models, I don't think so. When Beverly Johnson left Ford and I was still there, I got all kinds of bookings that I had never done before. I didn't have any interviews or go-sees. I was just booked. So there is some truth to the idea that there may be one that they push, but that's it."

On her own initiative, Ming went to Europe. Her first day in Paris she started doing print work, earning "outrageous money." Time was a factor, however. "You had to wait for the money to come. I didn't know how to tell my agency, 'I need money to stay here.' I didn't understand being social and laid-back. I was there strictly for business. The French say, Get to work at noon. You get there at noon, but they don't start working until seven, and they're drinking wine all day until they start. To be relaxed is fine, but I couldn't be loose that way coming from New York, having to pay bills, having a son and all these other responsibilities. I was too insecure." And she returned to the States.

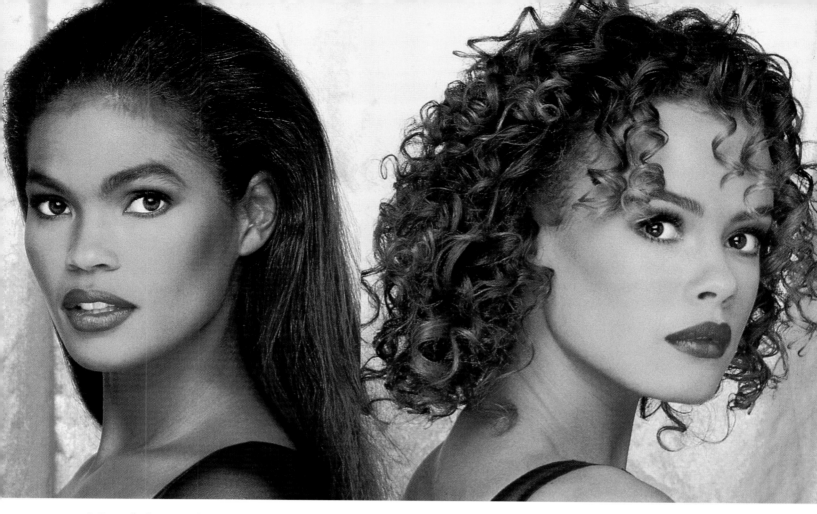

Ming's light complexion and straight hair did not make it easy for clients to place her in a secure racial niche. "I always had a problem with people saying that I was too exotic and that I didn't look like the average Black model. When I was modeling early, they never said anything about my hair. I have three ads with an Afro wig on. I didn't care. I'd put on an Afro or anything else, because they were paying me $100 an hour at that point. And that money was too important.

"Times have really changed, though. Models make $250 an hour now. And on a job I did not long ago for Ivory soap, they were complaining, 'Oh, you're so dark.' They were trying to make me up lighter. I was too dark. It was so funny. The times have changed, and I have completely missed out. I felt like I never fit in."

Like many Black models, Ming made a place—and a name—for herself. But throughout her career, she said, "I was really searching, wondering if I should have my son with me and do the single-parent struggle. I had all this guilt. We were separated almost all of his formative years. He came to New York during the summer, and I would visit in Ohio. But I was in so much pain, I felt as if I had disgraced my family. Most of all,

though, it was the pain of not being with my son. Was it worth it? I don't know, but I think so."

Modeling did not operate on a level accounting field. Many Black models testified to the insult, humiliation, and smaller paychecks of double-standard bookings. Yet they had little recourse. Most working Black people—who earned far less—could sympathize with their plight only in theory. If models complained to their agents or clients, they risked being accused of ingratitude and subsequently punished by fewer and smaller bookings. Jobs for Black clients alone were hardly regular or lucrative enough to sustain a career. Part of the pride Black models took in their achievements had to be swallowed on their way to the bank.

"It's very subtle," said Jane Hoffman Davenport, who continued to work as a stylist after retiring from modeling. "It's about how much time people will spend on a shoot. I would see them do two versions of the same shoot, the White ad, then the Black. There was a big difference. They would take more time with the White shoot, and consequently, the White models would end up getting more money even if the rates were the same. They would

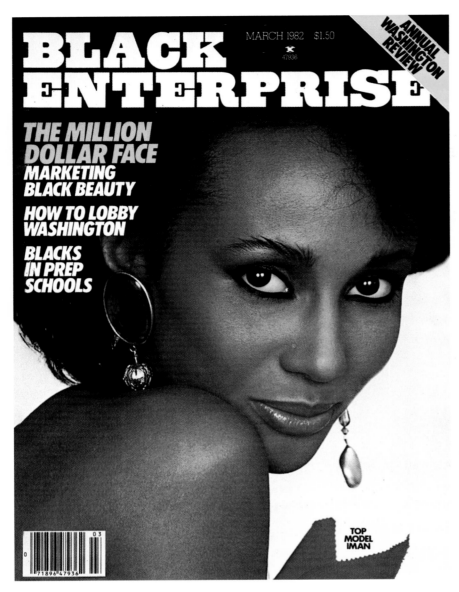

BLACK ENTERPRISE

MARCH 1982 $1.50

ANNUAL WASHINGTON REVIEW

THE MILLION DOLLAR FACE
MARKETING BLACK BEAUTY

HOW TO LOBBY WASHINGTON

BLACKS IN PREP SCHOOLS

TOP MODEL IMAN

When **Iman** became the first Black contract model in 1979, the role of Black models in the business of beauty made headlines.

always book the White models longer than they booked the Black models. You always knew when you were being shuffled along as opposed to being nurtured.

"So much of this comes down to economics. When it comes to infringing on White people's economic development, that's when the ax falls. I don't care what business we're talking about. The ax falls. It all comes down to numbers. In modeling, the social aspect is about the visual, and the work aspect is about the numbers. Black models are caught in between the two. Still, there's no reason for us to quit. If we like what we do, we keep doing it. That's the bottom line.

"There's a certain amount of teaching that we have to do. Whenever I can, whether it's in humor and jest or in a flat-out statement, I will teach something to somebody. You have to constantly be educating." Especially when it comes to White ignorance of Black culture.

"I remember going into Wilhemina's

office one day. We were just having a discussion about my work. You know how they tear out all your sheets from magazines and keep them on file? She asked me something, and my response was, 'Well, I had two ads in *Ebony* this month, and something else coming up in *Ebony*.' And she turned to me and said, 'What is *Ebony*?' I almost fell to the floor. She did not know what *Ebony* magazine was. And this is my agent? Now, there weren't that many places for our photographs to appear at that time, and she was totally oblivious.

"It really gave me a clue to what being a Black model in this business was really about. It amounted to the fact that you have to constantly fight for yourself. Nobody's going to fight for you. If you happen to go out and get the job on your own, fine. They'll take their little commission. If there was one Girl they could do a star trip on, fine. But they couldn't understand the regular Girl who was simply working."

In the '70s and '80s, Barbara Smith had six covers of Black magazines, for which she said, "Thank God for Black publications and ads." She continued, "It's glamorous to see yourself on the cover of a magazine, but the feeling only lasts, at best, thirty days. I got over feeling grand immediately. I thought there would be a dramatic increase in work after a cover came out. For a White model on a White magazine she might see as much as a 90% increase. For a Black model on a Black magazine, maybe 50%. You're only as hot as your latest cover."

If all Girls worked hard for their money, it seemed that Black Girls worked even harder. Jackie Booker Reeves, who worked on the staff of several prominent fashion magazines, told the story of one promising Black model from the '70s. "Shari Hilton got a job doing the Dark and Lovely relaxer box. P.S., she got $1700 for the job, that's all. As time passed, when Shari had been on the box maybe three years, she called her agent, because she had been at a shooting where some White Girl was talking about how she was getting, you know, a bazillion dollars for some product that was sold only on the west side of North Dakota. Her agent told Shari that she should be grateful, that that was the best she could do for her, and that she wasn't going to go back and renegotiate.

"Fortunately, Shari found some savage lawyer who went to the advertising agency of record and not only made them pay her retroactively, but also made them pay every time the box was in an ad or a commercial and her face was shown. And this lawyer made them give her a contract where she got money for the next five years."

In 1975, it was estimated that "Black models average $30,000 per year, while White models average $50,000." Just seven years later *Black Enterprise* magazine, reporting on "The Earning Power of Black Beauty," charted an elite group of models whose "estimated income" ranged from $50,000 to $350,000. At the top of that list was Iman, whose unprecedented contract for Polished Ambers in 1979 guaranteed her "an estimated $150,000 a year" from Revlon.

If the word "estimated" kept popping up with unusual frequency, it was because financial figures were the most closely guarded secret in the business. Anyone could get access to a model's bust size. No one knew when it came to money. And that made the Sirens' song even more alluring.

The deepest significance of the Polished Ambers contract lay not in the actual numbers, anyway. Rather, it had to do with a major cosmetics company recognizing and respecting the consumer clout of Black women, and for the first time, signing a Black model to represent it. Sixty years after the death of Madam C.J. Walker, her preachings were still being practiced. Looking one's best to succeed had become even more important as better educated and increasingly mobile Black women competed no longer only among themselves but with Whites and men for better jobs. The number of hair products and cosmetics targeted specifically for Black women increased significantly during the early '80s. And although the Polished Ambers campaign lasted for only a couple of years, the fact that it existed at

all led Black models to believe that it could happen again.

If there was one Girl in the '90s voted most likely to win a contract, it was Naomi Campbell, the one Black model most often linked on a first-name basis with the White superstars and contract queens of the period. By the age of nineteen, Naomi had already done the covers of British, Italian and French *Vogue*, as well as the September '89 issue of American *Vogue*, traditionally the literal heavyweight of the year.

With her proven selling power even *Cosmopolitan*, always reluctant to use a Black model on its cover, put Naomi on the front of its Valentine issue in February, 1990. The last Black *Cosmo* cover had featured Khadija, a Kenyan beauty, over three years before. "That's too long a time," said Naomi. "There are sexy Black women out there, and plenty of Black women buy *Cosmopolitan*. Why shouldn't a Black woman be on the cover, too? Such a long time is awful."

Despite the publicity about the five-figure sums she earned by the hour and the breathless coverage of her every change of hairstyle, Naomi felt there was still a disparity between her and her so-called peers. Although she claimed not to feel "a big difference" between her work and that of her good friends Linda Evangelista and Christy Turlington, she did make an exception for beauty contracts. "There're loads of contracts out there for White models, but I think there should be more for Black ones," she insisted.

In 1992 came the long-awaited announcement that two cosmetics contracts had been signed with Black models: Lana Ogilvie for Cover Girl and Veronica Webb for ColorStyle, a division of Revlon. While both Lana and Veronica were highly regarded for their print and runway work, their selection came as something of a surprise. Lana's hazel green eyes and Veronica's ivory complexion sent mixed and potentially confusing signals to the very market they were chosen to represent. While fashion observers had to agree that the contracts were proof of progress being made, they also had to acknowledge that this one financial step forward was accompanied by at least one cultural step backward.

And the lyrics to this dance music? That musty antique: If you're light, you're all right. Naomi Campbell, the brown-skinned Girl with full lips, was neither mentioned nor featured in any supporting role. In the biological sweepstakes, of course, the Girls had nothing to do with it. In an odd way, it was nothing personal. It was strictly business.

The actual business was less than crystal clear, though. As usual, press accounts made no mention of the factual dollars involved in the contracts. Other terms also seemed unclear. Would Black Girls get the lavish treatment and exposure that the White Girls did? Would the public see Lana doing more than the mascara and fingernail polish ads that Sheila Johnson had done in the '80s? Would Veronica and other ColorStyle models be seen outside of Black publications? Or would they be useful, hopefully high-priced tokens restricted '90s-style to a gold-plated ghetto?

Lana Ogilvie

After starring in a high school fashion show in her hometown of Toronto, Lana Ogilvie was courted by top New York City agents. Although her parents agreed to let her model for a year before she started college, when she returned to Canada to study fine arts in Montreal, it was only a matter of time—another year—before she chose to devote herself full-time to fashion, living in Paris and working throughout Europe before settling in New York.

"A lot had changed by the time I came into the business in 1989. There were so many different types of beauty being shown. There was already that openness to using Girls who were not typical blue-eyed blondes. *Elle* magazine used every kind of model regularly. Bennetton had the United Colors campaign, and Revlon, the Most Beautiful Women in the World. People were looking for something different."

Lana's Cover Girl contract was doubly unprecedented: she was the first Black Girl for that company, and she did not advertise

Lana Ogilvie, a native of Canada, was Cover Girl's first Black contract model.

a separate line. "It was still Cover Girl, just with more colors." She was discreetly proud of what she had achieved. "I didn't come into the job with the attitude that I was going to use it as a stepping stone or make myself a star." Such modesty made it no less difficult to reconcile her newly-minted star status with the stubborn realities of racial imbalance.

"The contract did not necessarily guarantee fair treatment," Lana stated bluntly. Although she acknowledged earning "a lot of money," she also recognized that a Black model—unlike her White counterpart—was not in the best bargaining position financially. She took what she was offered. Minor money irritations involving working extra days beyond contract terms and upgrading travel arrangements to first class were automatically resolved for White models. In Lana's case they caused unexpected problems. The major discrepancy, however, sounded an all-too-familiar note. "They will not put an ad of a Black Girl by herself in a mainstream magazine. They'll use her in a double with a White model or in a group, but a Black Girl's singles will appear only in Black magazines."

Despite increased ads, personal appearances, and P.R. exposure, Lana was

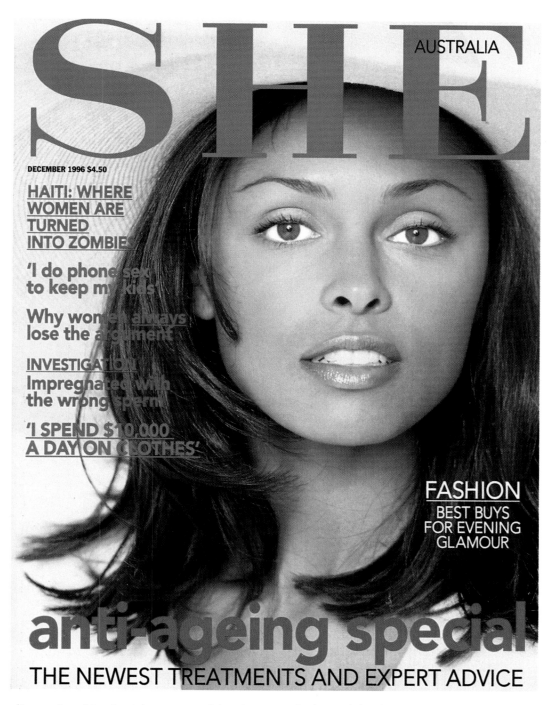

SHE AUSTRALIA

DECEMBER 1996 $4.50

HAITI: WHERE
WOMEN ARE
TURNED
INTO ZOMBIES

'I do phone sex
to keep my kids'

Why women always
lose the argument

INVESTIGATION
Impregnated with
the wrong sperm

'I SPEND $10,000
A DAY ON CLOTHES'

FASHION
BEST BUYS
FOR EVENING
GLAMOUR

anti-ageing special
THE NEWEST TREATMENTS AND EXPERT ADVICE

Lana Ogilvie appealed to women around the world.

disappointed in the job opportunities that followed. "In public I always praised them, but Cover Girl was not behind me as I was behind them. I didn't feel a push. Cover Girl didn't use their clout as much as other companies to insist on magazine covers."

While she felt "the positives did outweigh the negatives," she admitted, "some days I'm still struggling despite major successes. And it's because I'm a Black model. There is still a huge way to go to make this business equal. I hope a lot of things that I was able to accomplish continue. But I also hope that a lot of old issues regarding Black models will change."

In the mid-'90s, model-actress Tyra Banks and actress-model Halle Berry replaced the Black women at Cover Girl and Revlon, respectively.

As long as the unsuspecting public was appeased with the new, beautiful, and still fair-skinned faces, the cosmetics companies who sponsored them could breathe an uneasy sigh of relief. Pressure from Black consumers and Black models was off, at least until the next push for financial parity reached a critical stage.

Then in 1997, Cover Girl expanded its traditional fresh-faced campaign with a new crop of models, including Jua Perez and Christine Thé representing women of Latino and Asian heritage. Lana welcomed the newcomers. "It is so refreshing to see more ethnic diversity."

Flying High

I was doing more than I could handle.
Jolie Jones

Donyale Luna in Federico Fellini's *Satyricon*. Supernova Donyale died of a drug overdose in Rome in 1979. She was 33.

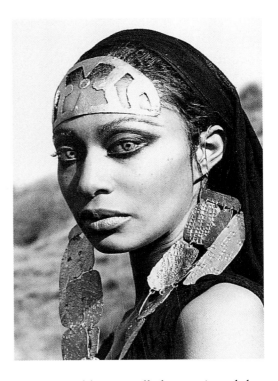

Nicotine, caffeine, and alcohol saturated the modeling profession while raising nary a plucked and penciled eyebrow. The insiders' tip sheet said that cigarettes kept you thin, coffee kept you awake, and champagne kept you happy. Although serious health dangers became more widely publicized in recent years, the public image of a chic mannequin remained what it was in the '50s, when, according to Helen Williams, "people thought that models lived only on coffee and cigarettes." Such legal drugs, however deadly, were still not considered "real" drugs. It was the abuse of illegal substances—marijuana, cocaine, and heroin—and prescription medications which came to be so closely associated with models that outsiders could self-righteously consider the entire fashion industry a den of vice and debauchery.

No one would deny that the recreational drugs of the '60s which expanded consciousness and creativity were commonly found within the fashion establishment. When agents, photographers, and designers—let alone models—did not themselves indulge, they often politely disregarded others who did. As long as the job got done, censure was rarely heard. When the job was over, there were no rules. A model was on her own.

"I would go to all the parties, clubs, and discos, but I would be on the fringe of things," said Rene Hunter who started on Seventh Avenue in the '60s. "I would not be in the center. I always extracted myself and watched what was going on. I saw a lot of people get really screwed up, eaten alive, people who were fragile. They got hurt in this business. I guess in any business there's the potential that you can be eaten by it. There were always drugs, but I was terrified of them, so I went through the '60s never having even a joint.

"They had after-hours clubs in those days. My one fear was that the police would bust the joint, I'd be in the lineup in the morning, and then I'd have to meet my stepmother, who was a corrections officer. So when they started passing stuff around, I got my coat and went home. I was proud of being a model. I wanted to prove to my family that I wasn't doing anything sleazy or immoral. I was lucky and had the background—or whatever it was—that I didn't get hurt."

Each era would see new drugs, new social attitudes toward them, and new models having to deal with them. Unlike money, drugs were never a lure as much as they were a crutch, an occupational or environmental hazard of the profession.

But like money, drugs could be mesmerizing, and if used unwisely, addictive and destructive. The combination of the two would create a vivid backdrop for the tales told by and about many models, some of whom were the best the business had ever seen. The formula for disaster was easy to imagine. What was more surprising was the rate of success and survival.

Jolie Jones

I started modeling when I was twelve or thirteen," said Jolie Jones, the daughter of music mogul, Quincy Jones, "in 1965.

"There were no Black models whatsoever at the magazines or in the catalogs or pattern companies. You couldn't find one.

When I started they were trying to introduce Black models, and they would put me in a double or a triple with White Girls. I was really the first one. My first job was at *Seventeen*, I was so lucky. I started working right away. I thought it was fun, like heaven. The work was not that strenuous. Then there was the travel, the flash, and the cash. My whole career happened between thirteen and twenty.

"I worked every day and went to the Professional Children's School and Lincoln Square Academy. If you were working you did your school work at home, and you came in once or twice a month to do all your tests on that one day. It was a bitch. I did all my work in the

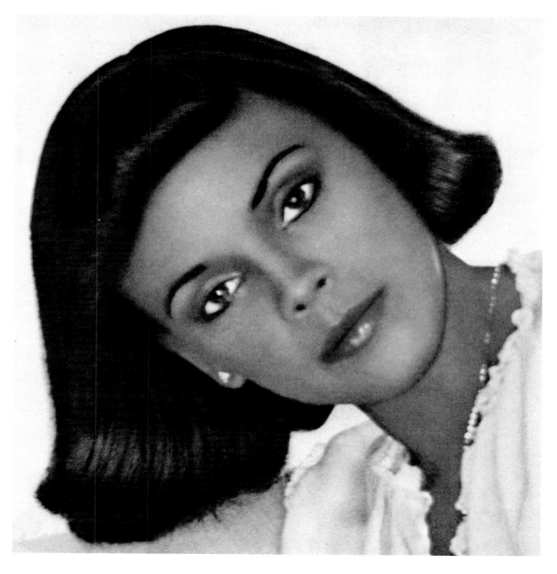

The innocent image of
Jolie Jones.

middle of the night. I went to work at seven in the morning and came home at seven at night. I was pretty responsible. I took care of all my own bookings, work, clothes, getting there. Not that I managed my money that well.

"I was doing more than I could handle. I was living two lives, as a model and a teenager. I took speed to be able to stay up and do it. It becomes a problem because you crash so heavy. You have heavy depressions, and you have to sleep for twenty-four hours. It catches up with you.

"I looked like the most innocent thing. I had pictures in *Glamour*—head shots, beauty shots—that were the softest, most romantic, sweetest-looking pictures in the dead heat of when I was taking the most speed. But when you're young your body has all this extra stuff to fight back. It didn't show. If I were doing that now, I'd look like death warmed over, but I was only fifteen. Nobody I worked with knew, but I did talk with my mother about it.

"I was so insecure and nervous. I was years younger than my co-workers, so I was pretending to be older than I was, but inside I was trembling half the time. I lived a whole lifetime before people even begin to go out and see anything. I realized that I couldn't go on. I saw a therapist for a while. I moved to L.A. when I was seventeen to get off that track and to change pace.

"I wouldn't want to go back for a minute. Growing up was hard, painful. But I wouldn't change it at all. I'm glad for the experiences. It gives me something to tap into. Although I got a lot of things from modeling, I missed a lot as well. I had to work very hard to get reinterested in reading and educating myself. I had to do all those disciplinary development stages later when I was on my own and after I had picked up some bad habits. You don't get a free lunch."

Anna Fiona believed that she began modeling in the '80s at too young an age with too little exposure to the sophisticated ways of the fashion world. While still a teenager she ventured out into European couture from an insulated upbringing in Kenya and Switzerland.

"I came across difficulties where I had

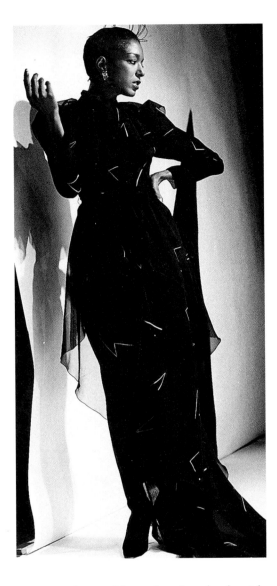

In repose and on the move, **Billie Blair** was one of the most dramatic models ever.

to strongly avoid getting involved with people who had drug problems and becoming a drug addict myself, to the point where I didn't want to associate with them or have anything to do with them. Even if it meant staying locked up in my room just to keep away from them. You still have a few people who think that it's fun to do. But once you get deep into alcohol or any sort of drugs, it's difficult to come back. You don't know the limits anymore."

One African-American model whose success came to her surprisingly quickly during the radicalized '60s lost not only much of the money she made but also her self-esteem in a harrowing relationship complicated by cocaine.

"I said that I would never touch drugs. But there was a well-known actor that I went with, and I looked up to him. He told me we couldn't make love unless we had this stuff. He was twelve years older than I was. Everybody looked up to him, and he looked down on me like I was such a little girl. I was twenty-four years old. To me, I was a woman, liberated. So what happened was that I started doing it. But every time I would go on a location trip, clean up from the stuff and go to work, he'd have a bouquet of roses with a packet of cocaine in it waiting for me when I got back. He wanted to control me. That was really the ruining point. I looked terrible. I messed up all my money on drugs, in bad investments in stock and real estate, and just giving it away. I didn't see my family for years. They thought I was in some sort of cult. I just worshipped this man. He had so much to say about life and the streets that I believed him. I didn't know. I thought that everything was so hip. Even though he practically destroyed my life, there were some good things that happened. It got me into writing. And it got me more serious about life."

What happened when drugs were not merely a private option in a personal relationship, but an unwritten job requirement "where people in the business are very happy to put a cocaine spoon under your nose," according to another cover Girl? One of the unarticulated attractions of cocaine was that it inhibited the appetite for food while it created a general feeling of euphoria. Thus, models could fulfill two basic conditions of employment: be thin and look happy. That coke was illegal and addictive mattered little. Where there was a will and a wallet, there was sure to be a way.

Magic Jordan, a print and show Girl, explained, "It was just like playing a game of chess. You had to go by the rules, especially on the show people side. It was very political, dealing with who's in power and the nightclub owners and the drug dealers. If you didn't fall in with who was supposed to be the In Crowd of kids, you weren't happening. I didn't want it that badly. I'd rather love myself in the morning, because I could see those Girls coming home with no money after some fabulous night out. They had to sleep for dinners. And they used to tell me that I was old-fashioned."

Journalist Carol Mongo observed the scene in Paris. "Back in '82, I was doing a story on the modeling profession. There was one Girl in Givenchy's *cabine* who was a dealer. Everybody knew that. But, of course, when I went to Givenchy, they adamantly denied it. However, we all knew who the Girl was, by name and by face. When I did the research for that story, it was not only Black Girls, but White Girls as well doing drugs. If the first show started at ten-thirty a.m. there would be some models who were clearly drugged out already. The French looked at it as something brought in by Americans."

The geography of addiction, though, is not external, but internal. Katoucha, one of the runway divas of

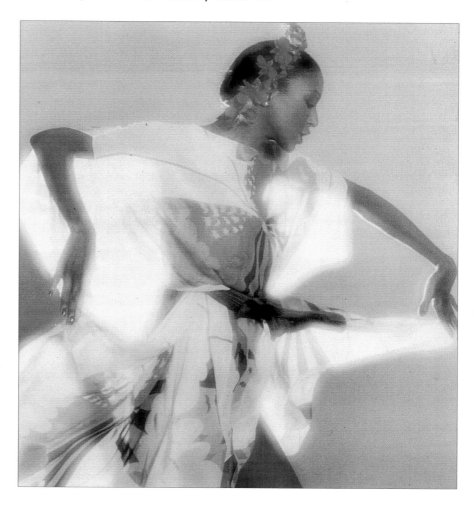

Paris during the last decade, admitted that she traveled infrequently to New York because the temptation to abuse drugs there was so strong. She had seen too many Girls personally and professionally destroyed. Early in 1995, on the verge of a new career as a designer, she came close to being one of them after a brush with the law.

Jane Hoffman Davenport agreed that drug abuse did not discriminate along racial, national or economic lines. "I think that drugs were a very important thing, very heavy with the models. And not just with Black Girls. This was very, very heavy throughout the business. I'd be curious to know how many people succumbed to that in order to keep moving on and moving up. I mean, nobody is going to admit that. We're talking about top Girls here. Models and photographers. It was part of their payoff."

One of the stars who acknowledged the pressure and refused to succumb was Sheila Johnson. She cited an explosive magazine article published in the '80s where her agent implied "that he would rather have the model who stayed out all night and got drunk and got a reputation for being late for work because that gave her stress and pizazz and sex appeal. I didn't want to be connected with the agency, that's how profoundly disgusted I was. That's not what I'm about at all." Although her agent later sent a letter of apology to his Girls, Sheila thought "this was a perfect exit moment. That's when I started auditioning and got *Coming to America*."

Billie Blair

For fourteen years Billie Blair was a powerful presence in the fashion world. From 1972 to 1986, her rich coloring, angular features, and faultless footwork earned her a lifestyle that she could never have envisioned as a nursing student in Flint, Michigan. After a three-day stint in New York shooting a fashion supplement for the *Detroit Free Press*, she began to make her move. *Essence* magazine and Halston's showroom provided her first Big City jobs. As she sprinted up the ladder of success accolades

rolled in from around the world. The Talk of the Town in *Women's Wear Daily*, Billie was also listed by *People* magazine as one of the Most Interesting People of 1974. She even became one of the very few Black models to be featured—and reproduced on a mass scale—as a department store mannequin.

Her public success, however, was accompanied by a shadowy partner, cocaine. Over time escalating drug abuse led to a life-or-death crisis. When she found herself wanting to jump from her twenty-seventh floor apartment, she knew she had to call on a higher power for help.

"I wanted to come home. The little bit of Baptist that I had in me from my mother and father sustained me when I was working. But I was headed toward total destruction. I'd do ungodly stuff. Whenever I got a good shipment, I shared with all my friends. A lot of them died. I wish I'd taken the time to help the needy. But then again, I guess we were needy."

She had looked for answers in many spiritual disciplines, but doubts persisted. She returned to Flint. "God knows what He's doing. I went to a pentecostal church and had an awakening. God gave me a vision of Jesus. Now I'm in fellowship with God. I'm ministering and preaching the Gospel." In seeking to help others, Minister Billie Blair was candid about her own experience. "My testimony includes a history of fame, fortune, substance abuse, low image of self, a lack of spiritual focus, spousal abuse, the occult and cults. Whatever Satan decided to give, I took!"

Taking the plunge as a born-again Christian did not mean renouncing fashion altogether. "I still model a little bit in church fashion shows. There're a lot of lethal big ol' hats," she added with a chuckle. One of her goals was to open a modeling school to teach young women the basics of grooming and style. "I'm not a prude. I remember wearing little short skirts with my butt hanging out. But I want to be a holy woman of God. So when I talk to girls today about the way they dress, I ask them, 'What are you trying to attract?' If we understood God, we wouldn't abuse ourselves. Modeling is a wonderful life, but I wish I knew then what I know now." She hoped that her primary goal—a tell-all biography—would help herself and others to heal.

If cocaine was part of the fashion currency in the money-hungry '80s, heroin seemed to be on the rise in the '90s, especially among those fashionalities promoting the wasted waif look. Commentators blasted the allure of "heroin chic" while heaping praise on films dealing with junkies. If society was so confused, it was no wonder that models were.

One Los Angeles booker told of receiving a call from a photographer's studio to cancel a Girl who had nodded out on the job. She insisted that the incident was not an unusually isolated one. But a conspiracy of silence—or, at least, stringent anonymity—prevented almost everyone from acknowledging the extent of the drug dilemma. The pressure to appear publicly flawless involved keeping a lid on private choices that could be criminal and, eventually, deadly. The complicity of those in the know must be seen as part of an irresponsibly dangerous deception about what it meant to be beautiful, happy, and healthy. The bare truth was that drugs demeaned women, distorted beauty, and debased the truly creative side of fashion.

Heart's Desire

O, beauty, are you not enough?
Why am I crying after love?

Sara Teasdale

The Sirens crooned, If you make it in modeling, you'll be loved not just by the adoring masses but also by that one person you've been longing for. You're up there on the runway; can't he see you? You're out there on the billboards; won't he find you? You've got looks, you've got a career, you've got money. All that remained to get was love. Surely he would come along and complete this almost perfect picture.

If Sleeping Beauty woke up to a Prince, many thought that models should, too. Expectations ran high. No woman—

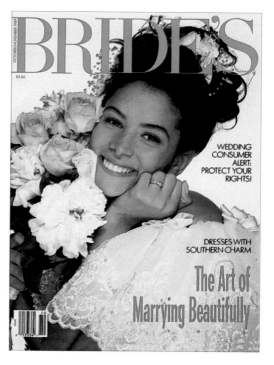

Lovely **Kara Young**.

Black models rarely appeared on the cover of bridal magazines.

especially a rich and beautiful one—deserved to be loveless and alone. On the contrary, one of the classic rewards for exceptional beauty was deemed to be an equally exceptional love. For every model, there should be a rock star, an actor, a director, a millionaire, a hero. Or maybe just an ordinary nice guy. Somebody.

Tanya Eggers met her boyfriend on a street in Paris. "I was going on castings for the collections, and that day alone I had seen about eleven or twelve different designers. My feet were hurting because I was wearing high heels, trying to look taller. It was at the end of the day, and I was really, really tired and totally lost, trying to make sense out of this little map book. I just couldn't take it anymore. Then I heard this wonderful English voice saying, 'Excuse me, do you need any help?' And he actually lived on the same street where my appointment was. So he took me in and waited for me while I tried on an outfit, an incredible dress. I got the job, and I got him." The fact that this boyfriend proved not to be her "one and only" simply proved that models lived in the real world.

There were many relationship stories with happy endings in which models had the leading role. The second time around, pioneer Dorothea Towles married Thomas Church, a Canadian-born lawyer from a historically well-connected Black family, which included famed activist, Mary Church Terrell. According to Dorothea, there was some resistance from his proper relatives who "considered modeling unsavory." There was also some resistance from him during their eight-year courtship when, Dorothea said in her typically candid fashion, "he didn't want to commit." They have been married for over thirty years.

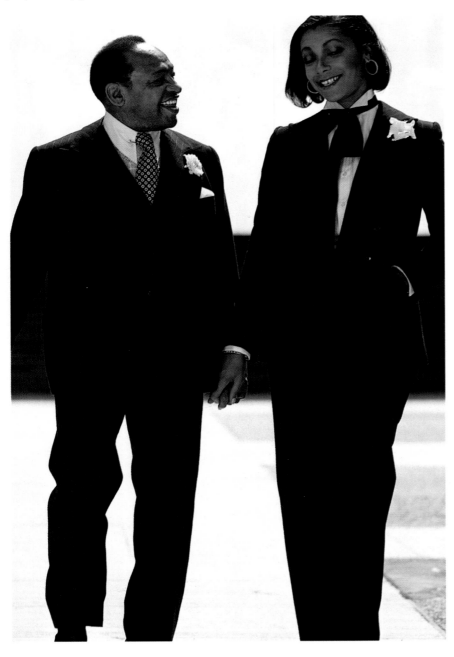

Audrey Smaltz with jazz maestro **Lionel Hampton**. They were a power couple in New York society and the Republican party for many years.

Elegant Sara Lou Harris eased out of her modeling career but still remained in the public eye—and ear—with her husband, Buddy Bowser. For four years during the '50s they hosted a daily radio program in New York City called "The Bowsers" where they interviewed local and national celebrities. That marriage lasted for a decade. In 1959, she married Guyanese attorney, John Carter, who was knighted by the Queen of England in 1966 before coming to the United States as ambassador from Guyana. "Thrown into the deep end" of society and the international diplomatic corps, Sara Lou, now Lady Carter, was the first African-American chatelaine of an embassy in Washington.

Because models were most often seen as images and not known as people, few knew what happened to them when the spotlight went off, the cameras were put away, and everyone went home. Dorothea Towles and Sara Lou Harris were two women who found happiness in successful partnerships, as did Helen Williams, Carol LaBrie, Sandi Bass, Peggy Dillard, and Pat Cleveland, among others. But many, if not most, models were not so lucky. Or whatever that elusive quality was. Their beauty exerted a contradictory force. As it seduced, it intimidated. As it attracted, it also repelled.

Pat Evans, the bald beauty of the late '60s, said that she always felt "it was either/or. Either I could work or I could have a boyfriend. It seemed that I could never have them together. I knew that I had to work. I dated some famous people, but I found that even when I did run off to be with someone, he would always end up with somebody else anyway."

Rene Hunter never married and claimed she never wanted to until a few years ago. "I wanted to do what I wanted to do when I wanted to do it. I wanted to be free, and I had it hooked up that you couldn't do that and be with someone. That's not necessarily true, but that's how I had it in my mind. I would like to have someone now to share a life with. But all in all, it's been fun. It's been good."

If love was hard to find, sex was ever present. At least, in theory. The models' market was one in which sex—however it was dressed or undressed—sells. Assumptions about models—and Black models in particular—have always included pre-judgments of their sexual activities. A few sensationalized accounts of ribald exhibitionism only seemed to confirm suspicions that all models were wanton nymphomaniacs. Scratch a model's makeup, and you'd find a prostitute's paint.

After ten years in Paris, Lynn Watts was adamant. "A lot of people think that for success, you have to sleep with people, show up at parties, dance on tabletops…. Not true. I may have gone to one or two parties that had to do with a design house or a photographer, but never—and I have to knock on this wood table—never one time have I had to sleep with anybody or lie or cheat or scheme to get any form of work. What people don't realize is that most of the people in the design houses are gay guys. They don't want us. To mostly all of the designers a woman is the image of fashion, really nothing more than that."

Warren Jackson had to change his opinion of models once he "got to know all the Girls in Milan. There's always this image of models making all the money and doing drugs and having parties all night. Once I got to meet the Girls, I saw that they weren't like that. They did their work, and they went home at night. They were married or they had steady relationships. They were religious, they believed in something. They worked hard, and they took their career seriously. That wasn't the image I had. And if I thought that, then certainly other people must have thought that, too.

"In Italy, in particular, the Black Girls have a terrible image. Black women are seen as sex objects. The things I heard men say in the audience. They're just sitting there, dying, waiting for the low-cut blazer to open up so they could see something. And it burned me up. I didn't like to see my people treated like this. Every last one of these Girls deserved everything she got. They worked hard, and their work was beautiful."

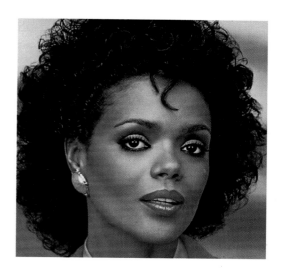

Sheila Anderson specialized in beauty ads.

Sheila Anderson

The search for security was the major theme of Sheila Anderson's story. The dually charged elements of the Sirens' songs—money and struggle, drugs and illness, love and cruelty—combined in a unique mix. She shared one fundamental trait with survivors of the Sirens. She, too, had lived to tell her story, but just barely.

Sheila Anderson used modeling to break free from an abusive husband and a stifling relationship. It hadn't started like that. Before they were married, she and her husband were "the Romeo and Juliet of high school." Vietnam and separation, early parenthood and maturity compelled them to grow in different directions. Eventually, there was no turning back to togetherness.

"I had a friend visiting me," Sheila said, "a really sassy Black model, and my husband went off on me a couple of times verbally in front of her. I'll never forget this as long as I live. She said, 'Honey, you are a descendant of African queens. You do not deserve to live like this.' And she convinced my husband that I needed a vacation. My husband had never let me out of his eyesight. But this Girl kind of mesmerized him and convinced him to let me go with her to Puerto Rico for two weeks.

"It was my first time away on my own in my life. When I walked out on the terrace overlooking the ocean, I just started crying. I used to really relate to Cinderella. I had gone straight from my mother's house to my marriage. My mother was always telling me what I could and couldn't do, and then my husband started telling me what I could and couldn't do. That trip was the first time in my life that I didn't have to cook or clean or take care of anybody, and I went hysterical. If you take a little slave off the plantation and give it a whiff of freedom, you've got a problem on your hands. This was a fool out of captivity. The woman who got on the plane to go to Puerto Rico and the woman who got off the plane were two different people."

Her self-esteem on the rise, Sheila took her young daughter, left her husband, and went out looking for work. Although she had signed on at the Stewart agency, her husband had never really agreed to her modeling. Without him and with another agency, Black Beauty, she started working immediately, doing "ads, ads, ads, and more ads. When I went out for my first commercial, I booked it, an Avon commercial. It was almost like God said, 'Don't be afraid, I will show you that you can make it out here.'" She became a very popular model, specializing in hair and cosmetics ads and commercials.

While Miss Sunshine was one of the images Sheila was good at projecting in her modeling work, she also had an appealingly sensual side. When she won a "Miss Sexy" contest at CBS, about a year into her career and separation from her husband, she was disappointed to find that part of the prize consisted of front-row seats at a Miles Davis concert and an opportunity to meet the musician himself after the show. Having been "a suburban housewife, this meant nothing to me. I was pissed off. They called this a prize? I went with an attitude. So I'm sitting there in the front, drinking champagne. And this man comes out and has the audacity to play with his back to the audience. Then, when the concert was over, people went crazy. The music was pretty, but I was ready to go home. So long, backstage."

The night was still young, though. Reluctantly, Miss Sexy met Master Miles, went to a party at his house later, and got better acquainted. "I can honestly say that

I came into Miles's life not as a woman who wanted to be with Miles Davis, the star, because I didn't have a clue. My naïveté was probably very charming to him, because I was legitimately square. I learned about him after the fact.

"Miles Davis got me unmarried. He simply went to the phone, called his lawyer, and told him, 'Don't ask for anything because she's not going to need it.' I waived everything. I got nothing from my ex-husband because Mr. Davis said I was going to be Mrs. Davis, and he had enough money that I didn't need to ask for child support. He said, 'You're going to be Mrs. Me.'"

When Miles's reputation for brutality penetrated the idyll, Sheila confronted him with it. "I said, 'Miles, people keep telling me that you beat women. Why do they say that?' And he said, 'Because it's true. I knock bitches out.' That's what he said. Then he proceeded to give me a list of women he had knocked out. I said, 'So, are you planning on knocking me out?' He said, 'No, because very few ladies have ever come through this doorway. You're one, and I'm going to treat you like one.' And he did for a long time.

"Miles taught me a lot. He gave me style." As Sheila's lifestyle changed, the career that had provided her with an independent income and a strong self-image faded in importance. "Miles called the agency and said that I would no longer be taking any bookings. I was hurt by his aggressiveness about my career, but I thought he was right. This little bit of money that I was earning, he called it annoying. I was making $75 an hour, and Miles would say, 'I'll give you $100 an hour to keep your ass at home.' When I said No, he let me out a couple of times. Then he just got pissed. So eventually, I stopped. Meanwhile, I had made a lot of enemies in the business, because I did not show up for bookings. They would call my house—I gave everybody Miles's number—and Miles would get the call, take the message, and never give it to me.

"I wanted Mrs. Miles Davis, modeling, and all the rest. I was feeling very secure because I was getting ready to marry the Black prince. And then I found

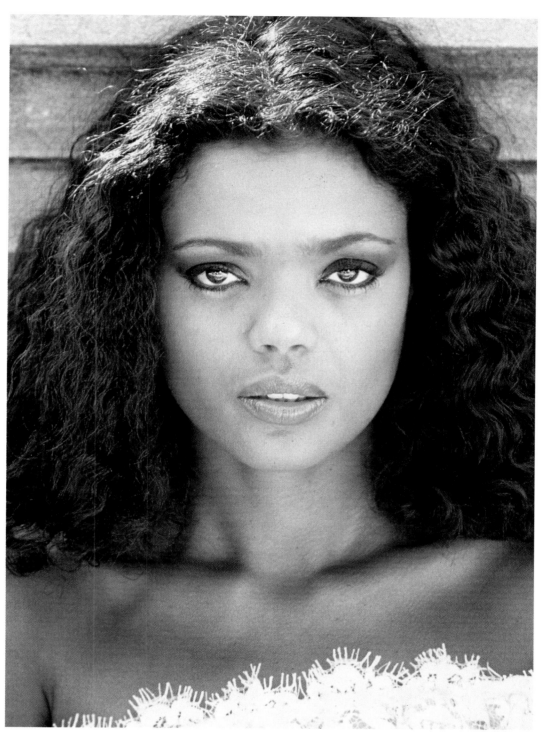

Sheila Anderson. The end of a fairy-tale romance propelled her career toward independence and the double-edged sword of success.

out that I had jumped from the frying pan into the fire.

"It's no secret that Miles had a tremendous drug problem. That cocaine personality couldn't care less about me being a lady or anything else. It got abusive. He was on a lot of painkillers for an injury to his hip as a result of a car accident. The combination of cocaine and painkillers produced a personality that would make Satan back up. One day I told him, 'You have really confirmed my faith in God, because you have to be the Devil, the way you are acting.' He had the nerve to tell me that that was one of the nastiest things anyone had ever said to him.

"When Miles's personality changed, his face changed. It was amazing. In the beginning of our relationship I thought he was the most beautiful looking man I had ever seen, the most gorgeous thing God had ever created. Now, he looked like the prince of darkness. I had to leave him. One of the hardest things I have ever done in my life was leave Miles. I almost lost my mind, because it was something I knew I had to do. Yet he had won over a part of me that was unbelievable.

"I became physically sick from leaving Miles. My mother"—'40s actress and singer, Sheila Guyse—"had been diagnosed with cancer, and I just crawled into bed with her. We were two deteriorating, pathetic patients. I had left a man that I knew was detrimental to my existence, but it was killing me to leave him. It was a macabre love story.

"My private life has been always so outrageous that all the billboards and all the fanfare of the business could never touch what was going on in my personal life. My career really started again after Miles. Once he stopped asking me to be Mrs. Him, and once I realized that wasn't going to happen, I worked for about ten years straight."

Modeling was not a natural profession for Sheila's physique. "I was not a naturally thin person. I went through the trauma of having one of your most major agencies send me to a diet doctor who constantly gave me injections to keep my weight down. If you had to go on location, the doctor gave you a note saying that you were diabetic so you could explain to customs why you were traveling with a sack of needles. After I had taken the injections for so long, I built up a resistance, and they stopped working. What the medication did was reverse itself, and I blew up. If I ate celery, I gained weight. So when people see all these models, they're either naturally thin or they're on a discipline."

That discipline included drugs and eating disorders that have made modeling infamous. "When I did designer shows, there were Girls snorting cocaine in the bathroom before a show. I did it one time, and my body freaked out. I said this is not the way to stay thin. Then one of your very famous runway models taught me about throwing up. I was bulimic a large part of my career. I was killing my body."

Her body retaliated to the point where it started killing her. She underwent a radical mastectomy. "No wonder I got breast cancer. I totally screwed up my body. The injections possibly helped my liver to deteriorate. Maybe even before the cancer, the decline in my career had started. That might have had a lot to do with my illness, you know, the disappointment of the decline.

"I think cancer is despair and anger. I think they're synonymous. Often people who are very wonderful get cancer because they internalize their hurt. I was a professional at internalizing hurt. So, in retrospect, it was almost inevitable that someone like myself would have gotten this particular disease, which is very oriented to hidden despair.

"I was trained to be happy. As a model, your clients don't care about your personal life. I have been trained to show something other than what I really feel, to be happy and wonderful and twirl and smile, regardless of what is eating me up inside.

"I'm not Miss Sunshine anymore. I'll be Miss Sunshine if I'm happy. But if I'm not happy, I'm not going to pretend. It was very important to me that people thought I was wonderful and nice. Now I don't care what you think of me. It took me a long time. And it took threatening my life."

Her early experience of "being the practical suburban housewife" never left her. Sheila said, "When I did make money I did not buy furs or jewels or move into a larger apartment. I invested. I have enough to make sure that my rent will be paid, and I can cover the basics every month whether I work or not."

Two years before Miles Davis died in 1991, Sheila had a poignant reconciliation with him in the south of France. "I collapsed into his arms like the years we hadn't seen each other just evaporated. I fell right into the rhythm of the relationship again." A few more

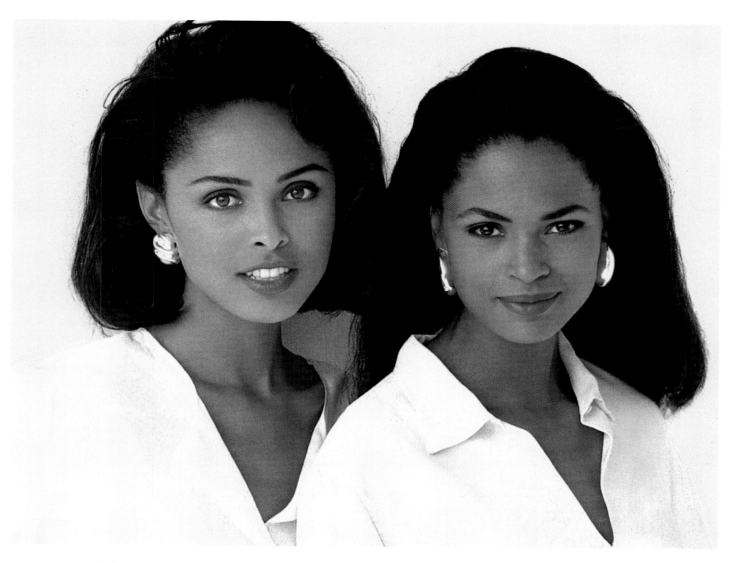

encounters with him in New York made her feel as if she was "reliving the best part, the beginning of the relationship when it was magic." It was clear that despite time, distance, other relationships, and major life-altering events, "this relationship didn't end. There's a part of me that will love Miles Davis for the rest of my life."

Sheila did not deny having regrets about the choices she had made. She was still a caretaker, but now she included herself on the list of those who needed nurturing. After twenty-five years "in the same apartment Miles used to send champagne to," she moved into spacious and serene quarters with her family. "I had seen my mother, the diva, be dethroned, so I said No, No, No. Making that home base became more important than being in

the lights. Sometimes I wish that making that base hadn't been so important. Now, I would put more attention on my career. If I had done that before I might have had a few more dollars to hold onto. Money gives you freedom. But I only have to look back in retrospect and say, What have I done for this money? And I can smile and say I've done nothing against my integrity for a dime. Nothing. There's been no drugs here. There's been no denigration of my morality here. If I had been more aggressive I probably would have had more time to buy, so to speak. But most of my attention was on the family. To be treated like a queen, like someone treasures you, I know it's possible. And I think that inside of every woman there's a hankering to be treated like that."

Lana Ogilvie (left) with **Karen Alexander**. Unlike many models, both Lana and Karen were able to balance demanding careers with successful home lives, marriage, and motherhood.

Being and Meaning
Identity

odels may be manne-quins. Dummies they are not. Yet the image of the bimbo starlet relaxing at home in leopard tights with a tome by Sartre, Shakespeare or Schopenhauer open on her lap, was a familiar Hollywood parody that was transposed to models as well. Beauty and brains could not possibly coexist, according to the stunted logic of certain image controllers. Fortunately, the evolution of women and the feminist movement of the last three decades have thrown that notion on the growing trash heap of anachronistic stupidities. Beautiful women could be and often were educated, experienced, intelligent, perceptive, crea-tive, and articulate. In the fashion busi-ness, especially, brains and beauty were a common combination.

Of all the high-earning professions, modeling has been the least examined, models the least analyzed. First-hand stories from the front lines were extremely rare. Second-hand stories were often second-rate. With their penchant for disaster and blood-stained tragedy, news media hardly took notice of models unless they could sensationalize some torrid combination of sex, drugs, money or death. And serious social scientists were only beginning to evaluate the results of long-range developmental studies of girls and women that would help to educate people out of corrosive stereotypes based on gender.

Meanwhile, pictures of models sur-rounded us. They populated our public spaces on billboards and bus stands. They appeared in the magazines we subscribed to, the catalogs we didn't, and the television commercials we couldn't avoid. We carried on wordless dialogues with them, asking them for beauty tips while blaming them for the epidemic of self-loathing, eating disorders, and promis-cuity among young women. Inevitably, we came to feel as if we knew these Girls. And without hearing from them, we assumed we had the right to judge them.

But nowhere was confusion between the real and the role more likely to exist than in the silent world of modeling. And it was likely to be even more exaggerated when the models were Black, the opportunities fewer, and the spotlight, however brief, more intense. Black models were neither paragons of instinctive virtue or paradigms of unbridled vanity. They were distinctive individuals grouped together for one reason only: their racial identity. This single physical factor, however, encompassed a range of diversity that would be stunningly contradictory in any but the most racialized societies.

All models, however, had a decisive advantage over most other professional women for whom gender was still a serious handicap. Models were valued precisely because they were female. They were among the rare women who automatically earned much more than

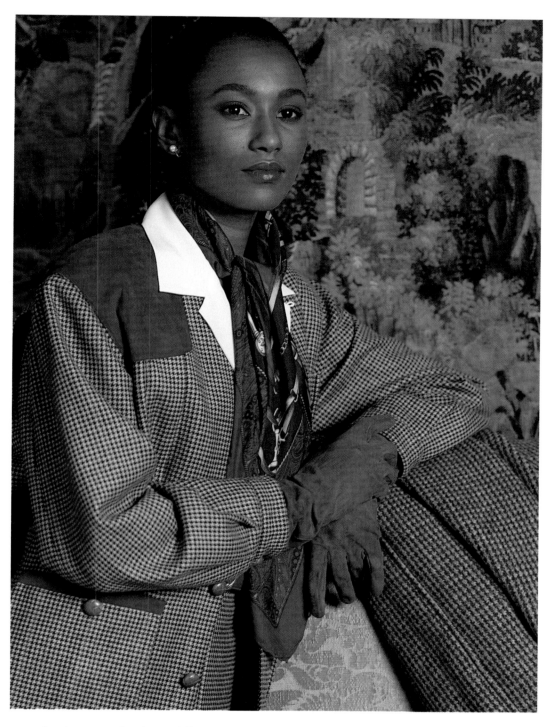

Aria. Her image of the aristocratic Afro-Saxon was a perfect fit for **Ralph Lauren's** first Black ad in 1989.

men in the same business. Their success was often directly linked to the unlimited expressions of femininity they were able to embody. If there was tension between these various images, in no case was a model required to act more like a man in order to succeed.

Intelligent models were intelligent people. They constantly analyzed the requirements of the profession and weighed them against their own needs. Balance was key, and often between surprising polarities. Between self and image, and then between old image and new image or new and next. Between essence and appearance, and also between appearance and disappearance. Reinvention was the middle name of this game of identity. Models were who they were, but they were also whomever the client wanted them to be or, at least, appear to be. Beyond gender, race, profession, and individual booking, models wanted to know who they were as people. It was not just enough to *be* a model; they wanted to know what it *meant* to be a model.

Contrary to what people outside the business might think, models worked hard. Such passive attributes as patience,

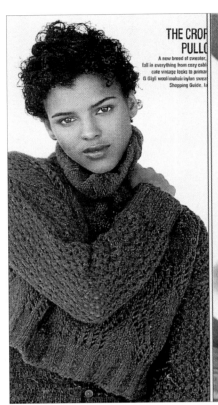

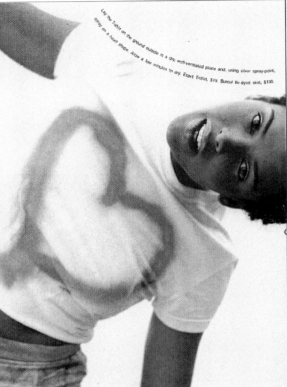

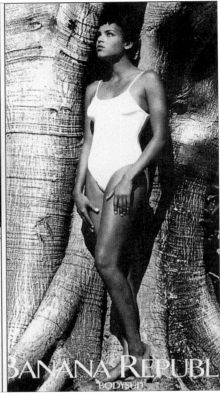

Tanya Eggers's composite. Part of a model's success depended on the variety of attitudes she could portray without losing her core sense of self.

endurance, stillness, humor, subtlety, flexibility, and receptivity did not rate highly on a performance scale geared to men and machines in constant motion. However, these same qualities, combined with the immeasurable attributes of a beautiful face and a graceful body, were essential elements in the making of a good model. Although she stood on her own, a model did not stand alone. Something within her had to inspire something in others. It often took some time—and a few mistaken detours—before a model learned these nuances.

Nineties newcomer, Tanya Eggers said that when she started to work she "made good money right away doing catalogs and everything. And I thought that's what modeling was. But then I met some people who told me, 'You can do catalog until you turn blue in the face, and sure, you make a good day rate, but that's basically the nine-to-five of this business. You can make a lot more money if you get more editorial exposure.'

"I had no idea what editorial was really about. If you can break into that magazine market, that's going to make

more money for you in the long run. I've learned a lot more about how to work this business. And one of the important things is, the more exposure you have and the more people you know, the more money you get. It's more than just calling up the agency and getting your bookings for the day. It's a business, too.

"I worked with just about every magazine in America. But to actually get the pages is another story. I've had one foot in *Vogue*, then I had a shot where I'm dancing, and you can't really see my face, and there're a couple of other pictures where I'm cut off from the eyes down. But I was in there," she said with a laugh.

Disappointed with her pictures in American *Vogue*, she pointed with pride to an Australian *Vogue* cover, the first to feature a Black model.

"I've done shows, too, and I was really excited. The adrenaline is just pumping. It's absolutely fabulous, but it's really stressful. After a week of shows, everybody has to take a break. It takes so much out of you."

To be able to replenish their strength and vitality, models had to understand who they were at their core, regardless of the challenges, on the job and off, that were putting them to the test. Youth and inexperience, money and freedom, beauty and brains, all made for a heady combination. To negotiate in the fashion business and to retain a healthy degree of personal sanity, Black models had to be smart. Few others expected them, encouraged them or taught them to be.

Divas and Social Lights

I carry myself the way I do because
I am royalty within myself.

Imam

By the late '80s a new wave of sophistication—borne on the success of internationalized style—had swept through the modeling profession. Designer labels corresponded to one's spending power and aspirations, if not necessarily to one's actual achievements. Out of the closet, fashion developed into a new entertainment industry generating its own celebrity directors, actors, and newsmakers. And as the influence of traditional movie stars faded, models vied with each other to become the new glamour girls.

Having staked their claim to beauty, Black models now intensified their claim to individuality. They insisted on roles as varied and nuanced as their features, and on personalities as unique as they could invent and maintain. When the work lights went off, the social lights came on. In such an incubator, Girls with the looks, temperaments, and P.R. machines to match, became fashion divas.

Among the early show stoppers this was not an entirely new phenomenon. Rene Hunter, a Seventh Avenue star during the '60s, said, "Your social life expanded because you were the girl of the hour, however long that hour was. Maybe it was only fifteen minutes, as Andy Warhol said, but you went a lot of places in that time. I was a privileged person."

The price of that privilege was always open to negotiation. While past stars Donyale Luna, Naomi Sims, and Pat Cleveland were treated as larger-than-life figures, pampered, indulged, and regarded with awe and admiration, most models were not. Many, however, wanted the special attention and tried what they could to get it. The concept of Black models as part-time mannequins and full-time divas was further enhanced by their experiences in the gilded couture houses of Europe. As early as 1973, acting outrageous was considered—by some clients and models alike—to be part of the job.

Whereas the image of the cool sophisticate or the likable neighbor had been the safest one to project on the job in the '60s and '70s, some models soon learned that socializing after hours was increasingly important in order to secure the job in the first place. Barbara Smith, claimed that "it was important to go out. Being social helped. But I had to be the life of the party to keep people off my back. I was moving fast, keeping the jokes going. It was work keeping myself out there in order to work."

June Murphy, who started modeling with the Ebony Fashion Fair, knew that she had personal style to burn but she had to learn how to make it work for her as a model. "I decided that if I was going to be in this business, I was going to have to be social. I went out five nights out of seven going to dinner parties or having dinner parties, running around in the dead of winter with these low-cut dresses on. My signature at the time was a white gardenia. I always had a cold in the winter because I never had enough clothes on, and I didn't have a proper coat. But that's when I started to really work, and it was because I was social."

Being social should not be confused with being sexual, however. "Everybody I was hanging out with was gay," June insisted. "I took my straight boyfriend to one party just so he would know what was going on. He thought it was like a circus, that everybody was so weird. I thought everybody was really normal, because that was the world I worked in. So from then on, whenever there was a party and I asked him if he wanted to go, he'd say, 'You go and have a good time.'"

Nevertheless, the diva attitude was not based purely on social activities,

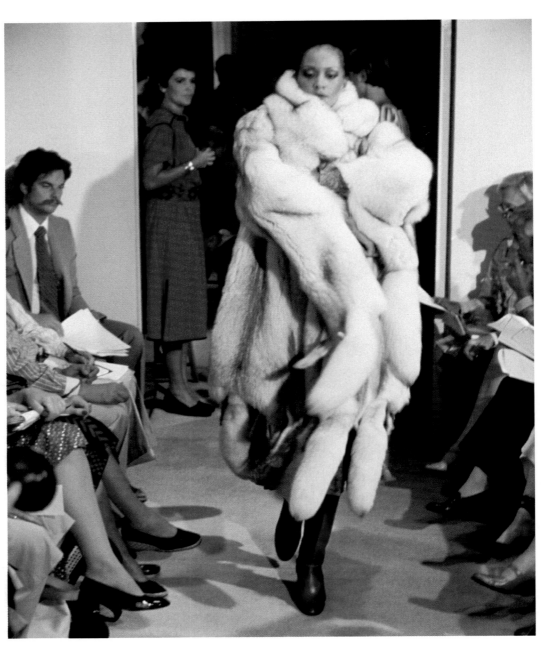

parties, and posturing. It originated in the work itself. In studios and on runways, Girls were studiously defining and redefining themselves. June continued, "There were Girls who looked like nothing but they had stamina and flair, and they believed in themselves. I'd see these Girls making up before a job, looking in the mirror thinking how gorgeous they were, and they were because they *thought* they were."

They were also gorgeous because they learned how to be. Interactions with photographers and designers made for a vital symbiosis, and thus an immediate sense of just how indispensable a model was. Nagging questions did surface. Was she aspiring to a status—educational, social, or financial—that she could never truly achieve? With every click of the camera, she was told that she was beautiful, perfect. With every turn in a dress, she was told that she was fabulous, to die for. Being called divine made her feel—and act like she was—divine.

With a change of cultural context, however, fashion models could easily become the negative role models people loved to hate, and with good reason. Esther Kamatari, a princess from Burundi, was one of twelve Black models invited from Paris to Kinshasa, the capital of what was called Zaire, to celebrate the fifteenth anniversary of the presidency of Mobutu Sese Seko. Mobutu had come to power after the 1961 CIA-backed assassination of Patrice Lumumba, a charismatic revolutionary elected to office during the early days of the country's independence. The sinister details of how Mobutu had maintained his position for so long was of little importance to the group of models, most of whom were African Americans, "whose dream," Esther said, "was to go to Africa to discover their roots. It was not *Roots* they found, but the reality of African life. Chris Seydou, an important African designer, organized everything. We wore his clothes which were based on African styles, and we put on shows for Madame la Présidente. The Zairians made a tremendous effort to welcome the Black models from the United States."

But this desire to understand another culture was not always reciprocated. Esther recalled, "One of the Girls had brought her toy poodle on the trip. You have to remember that in Zaire people eat dogs. Can you imagine a Black woman in Africa carrying her dog around in a pocketbook? This model's fingernail polish even matched the polish on the dog's nails. How can you go to Africa like that? Some of the Girls didn't act right. You don't go to the market in a miniskirt. You don't just flash your money around. There is a lot of poverty, and you must respect the laws of society and the way people do things."

The fun-loving party girl had always been a fixture on the fashion scene. But the '80s and '90s brought larger fees, higher expenses, and a more serious financial awareness into the business that directly affected models. If they appeared carefree on the set, they were hardly that way in the offices of their agents and accountants. Power suits and deep pockets took their place in the new vocabulary. Economic success, like the social revolution twenty years earlier, was to be attained by any means necessary. The Girls who could were getting away with—and getting paid more for—being haughty, naughty, and openly ambitious.

The past few decades have proven the truth of Mae West's maxim: "When women go wrong, men go right after them." Models did not have to go—or do—wrong to exert the allure that they might. Smoke and mirrors were considered ordinary tools of the divas' trade, just as powder and paint were for merely mortal models.

In the case of Iman, a patently false biography spiced up the news coverage of her unprecedented Revlon campaign. The multi-lingual daughter of Somalian professionals, she was hardly the barefoot shepherdess portrayed in the media. Neither was she the African queen so idealized by Black poets and romantic revolutionaries. But she looked the part, fitting her time and place so precisely that she became one of the most highly paid and recognizable women in the world. "It's like being an actor," she said. "If you have a great agent, he can get you through the door to meet the producers and directors, but after that you're on your own." If, after two decades, she was still a first-name fashionality, it was partly because once she grabbed the spotlight, she learned how to stay in it.

Parading around on the arm of a celebrity who was already in the public eye was part of an age-old tradition. Ambitious Black Girls of the '90s put a novel spin on it by romancing an exciting new generation of Black movie directors, actors, and entertainers. The sum of shared fame was greater than two individual names, especially to the Black public avid for success in its own skin tones.

Mounia

One striking model had only her unflagging ambition to guide her. In 1987 when she published her story—the first autobiography of a Black model—she did not hesitate to crown herself Princess Mounia.

She was born on the island of Martinique, a *département* of France with a personality split between its Afro-Caribbean heritage and its European governance. Baptized with the gender-spliced first name Monique-Antoine, she felt that the unusual combination had power, granting her a special connection to both female and male qualities. When her father nicknamed her Mounia, she considered that equally unusual abbreviation an omen of good luck which would help her forge a distinctive career.

Breaking out of the proper convent school-nursing school pattern imposed by her family took courage. She knew

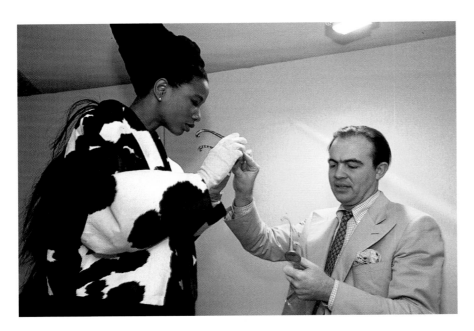

Mounia with **Christian Lacroix**.
Ambition compelled her to leave
Martinique.

what she did not want to be. A certain pragmatic realization that she was not the only sixteen-year-old to dream of becoming an actress or a singer also shortened the wish list. When she readjusted her dream to the more realistic one of becoming an airline stewardess, her friends laughed at her. Didn't she know that the French airline would never compromise its elite status by hiring a Black woman in that position?

Mounia did not let what she did not know stop her. From announcer at the airport in Fort-de-France to on-ground hostess at Orly airport in Paris, she moved steadily closer to her goal of doing something different with her life. As she wrote in *Princesse Mounia*, "Don't believe that once I landed at Orly I stayed put like a mango fallen from a tree. I told myself that the airport was a crossroads where powerful people passed, well-known people, people who could change my destiny. I had renounced childish dreams and the idea of becoming a stewardess. And in the classic fashion of the young girl who is pretty and not too stupid, I started to look toward the modeling profession.... It's true that at that time [Black Girls] were not at all in style. But there was something in the air, at least, that's what I felt."

Eyes and ears on the alert, she made her first contact with Hubert de Givenchy, who, after one fitting, decided to hire her

for a season. Unexpectedly, she collapsed at work, stricken with viral hepatitis. Hospitalized for months, she was reassured that her future in fashion was not lost when Givenchy vowed to use her for the following season.

It was not until 1976, when an important American client withdrew her patronage from Givenchy after Mounia had modeled a suit before her, that Mounia was slapped in the face by the ugly realities of racism. She wrote, "I had had problems with my identity like any adolescent of any color, and people had often alluded to the difficulties of Black people in general. But since I considered myself privileged and excluded from these difficulties by my destiny, all these depressing 'ancestor stories' seemed to me to date from another century."

Suddenly she was forced to see that history was not separable from the present, and that she was a part of them both. She confronted herself, saying, "You are Mounia and you are Black. It was new and revolting. And dynamizing. There were some victories that needed to be won. I had to be beautiful, very beautiful. Today, I would be the exception, but tomorrow it would be all the rage to be Black, to have Black beauty acknowledged, applauded, preferred. And then after tomorrow, the real victory: there would be White beauty and Black beauty, and the color wouldn't matter, as long as it was beauty."

As she developed her career, Mounia began to work with designers other than Givenchy. They included Emanuel Ungaro and Karl Lagerfeld. Lagerfeld, an iconoclast who did "not detest provocation" hired her to do Chloé and his own line. When he took over the design responsibilities at Chanel, he hired Mounia for that house as well. She became the first Black model to present the Chanel collection.

It was her connection with Yves Saint Laurent, however, which was to prove the most fruitful and long-lasting of her career. Not only was Mounia his star runway model for almost a decade, she was also propelled by Saint Laurent's fame onto the pages of fashion magazines around the world.

She assumed the gloss of her surroundings. She acted, spoke, and wrote with the suavely narcissistic attitude of one who expected her excesses to be forgiven because she had, at least, the honesty to call them excesses.

Mounia admitted that affairs of the heart were never as successful as her business involvements. Men were prey. Whenever she set out to attract attention and love, she could. But once the chase was over, she was gone. Seduction was a role requirement, part of being a public princess. Humility, sincerity, and vulnerability were not. One could almost picture her, resplendent, seated in front of a sparkling vanity, asking herself the words she wrote in 1987: "By being so preoccupied with me, me, me, can I ever really love?" Perhaps no one other than herself.

It was well known that some models could be as susceptible to their own myths of beauty and success as the unsuspecting public. Less known was the fact that some seasoned fashion professionals were not immune to diva fever. Black models had often experienced a subtly competitive hostility from White editors or advertising clients, who found it difficult to keep their egos in the background. To the classic wannabe come-on, "Be a model—or look just like one", another phrase was added: or act just like one.

Diva Fever

Jackie Booker Reeves, a native New Yorker, had a résumé rare for an African American because it listed some of the top fashion publications in the country. Within these hallowed precincts she learned the practicalities of organizing models and styling fashion merchandise for shootings. When she got to *Essence*, "that is when I ran into racism. White people didn't know what *Essence* was. It was very hard to get clothes and shoes and things necessary for a shoot. It was not the easy path that I had had working at *Bazaar* and *Women's Wear* and *Mademoiselle*. Also, that's when I began to have a great deal of empathy for Black models.

"At *Essence* Friday was model day, and since *Essence* was the first Black

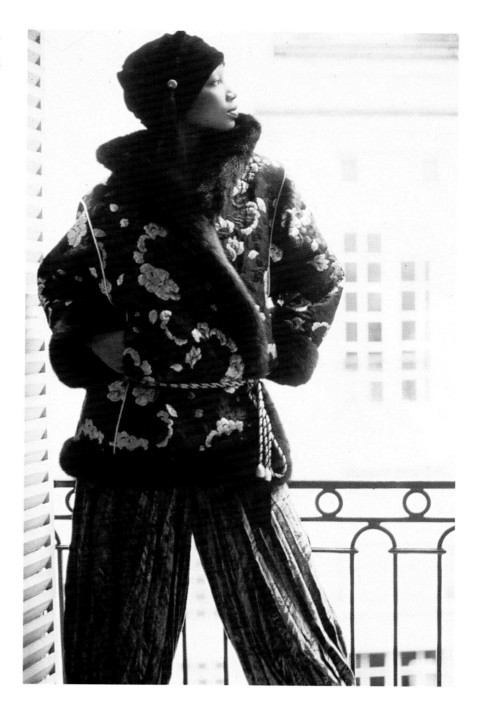

fashion magazine and still in its infancy, women would fly in to make this Friday model day. I cannot even begin to count how many women would just sit there and cry after I spoke with them. All this was during the height of that period when there were fabulous Girls: Naomi Sims, who was the superstar, and Charlene Dash, Beverly Johnson, Norma Jean Darden, Patty Cleveland, and Carol

Mounia wearing **Yves Saint Laurent**. She was one of his star models for over a decade.

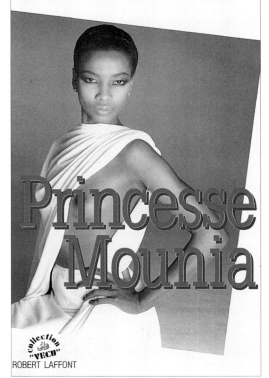

MOUNIA et DENISE DUBOIS-JALLAIS

Princesse Mounia

Collection "VÉCU"
ROBERT LAFFONT

The first autobiography of a Black model provided a perversely honest look in the vanity mirror of a diva.

LaBrie. I think that Black women have just been so downtrodden that their idea of beauty or being accepted as being beautiful is to be a model. Women would come in expecting *Essence* to photograph them even if it was only once, because they felt it would change their lives.

"I always had every fashion magazine of that month on my desk, and I would say, 'I want you to look through these. How many Black women do you see in here?' I'd say, 'Do you see anyone who even vaguely looks like she's your height? Do you see any Black women on any of these covers?' I told them, '*Essence* is only one magazine, and because we're young, we must use the best of what's there.' And then I would send them to Ford or Wilhemina where they would get the truth.

"Years later when I was in Jackson, Mississippi, I saw a girl whom I had rejected, and she thanked me because she understood that modeling wasn't the life for her. But that desire to model is so entrenched that I have my own story about succumbing to it. I got into the styling end of the fashion business as an aside because I wanted to be attractive. I grew up with my father continually telling me that I was too dark, not attractive, and so was not going to be worth two spits in hell. I wanted to know how to dress well and how to fix myself up. It took me ten

years to learn how. I spent all of that time developing a skill to be pretty.

"So, not listening to the lecture that I'd given everyone in the past that because you're pretty in person doesn't mean you're going to photograph well, I went out, hired makeup and hair, got a stylist, hired a photographer, and sat myself down in front of the camera—where I was immensely uncomfortable. I was just a wreck. It was so nerve-wracking to have all these people tugging on me. What if this had been a real shoot where there would be two or three editors, the hairdresser, his assistant, and all? Now I understand better what it is like to be in front of that camera. I mean, it was good for me to see first-hand that I had tortured so many Girls. 'More light! Put another fur coat on her!' You know?

"Now, I understand that. But the whole point is that I was not any less susceptible to wanting to be a model than anyone else. I assumed I was smarter than that, and that's the part that chilled me a little. Then I got rejected. Thank God. So I wound up saying to myself, Wake up. Again, you're looking for that quick, easy fix, which I really thought I was above — not better than, just more intelligent than."

Color Cast

Our faces are the
light & dark window panes
we paint our smiles on.

Carolyn Rodgers

Professional chameleons, models could change almost everything about themselves except their skin color. Although photographic lighting and processing techniques, such as airbrushing and retouching, could indeed change skin color—always to lighten darker eyes and complexions—many Black models were more concerned with changing the meaning of color, rather than color itself.

They wanted to discard the tired notion that dark brown skin connoted danger, fear, and poverty, and, at the same time, sexual power and primitive authenticity. They wanted to dispel as well the antiquated conceit that lighter brown skin signified safety, success, and intelligence, but also instability and aspirations to be—or, at least, pass for—White. Whatever their philosophical intentions, however, models did not make the casting decisions. When it came time to decide who would wear what outfit in a show, a shot or a commercial, designers, editors, and ad execs had final say. Those were simply the rules of the game. And rare was the conscience that could afford to reject a paycheck.

Television became a prime outlet for models who moved from fashion or print advertising to commercials. The increased number of Black sit-coms—aired after Bill Cosby's unprecedented '80s success—generated an increase in the number of commercials with Black talent paired with those air times. Yet, for Black women, the roles were, in general, as predictable—the housewife, the overweight cleaning expert, sweet Grandma, soda-drinking teenagers—as they were few. No one denied that things had changed. No one disputed the fact that there were some Black faces in TV land where there had once been none. What remained were the old questions: who and why?

The Generic Black Girl

One model-turned-actress, described a situation satirized by Robert Townsend's hilariously on-target film, *Hollywood Shuffle*. It could be sub-titled "How White People Define Blackness." Connie Fredericks said, "I walked into a commercial casting session where they wanted a nurse or somebody like that. I wore a string of pearls, a soft blouse, and a jacket and skirt. The casting director said, and I've been told this many times, 'Look, this is a mama. She's got three kids. She's a single parent. We want you to get away from the pearls. We want you to get down, honey.' When they are looking for that clean, basic, here-I-am personality, America is still filtering that personality through their perception of what a Black person is supposed to be.

"There are lines that are drawn within the advertising industry. I have a girlfriend

who's extremely fair-skinned, and she had a wonderful Lysol commercial that ran for a long time. Then I have another friend, a very brown-skinned sister, and she just did a roach commercial. There are associations with certain kinds of Black people and certain kinds of products that advertisers simply will not shake.

"I had a Charmin commercial that ran for four years. In it I was just this happy mom with a little girl. But I was very happy in that particular commercial because I was also in there with White mom and her daughter. That's one of the reasons that the spot ran as long as it did and I got those residuals."

Connie's background in the

Of Dutch and Surinamese parentage, **Louise Vyent** brought a fresh spin to the international identity of Black print Girls.

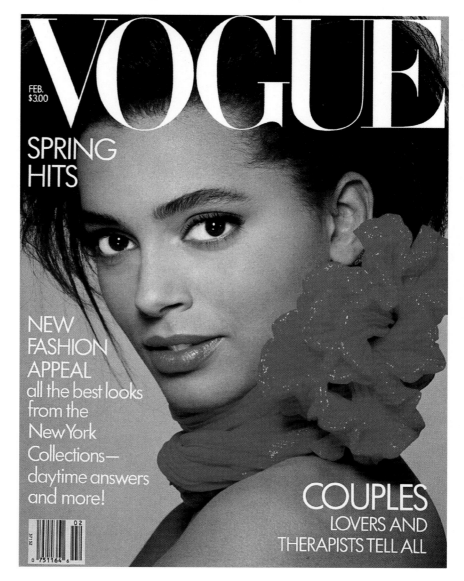

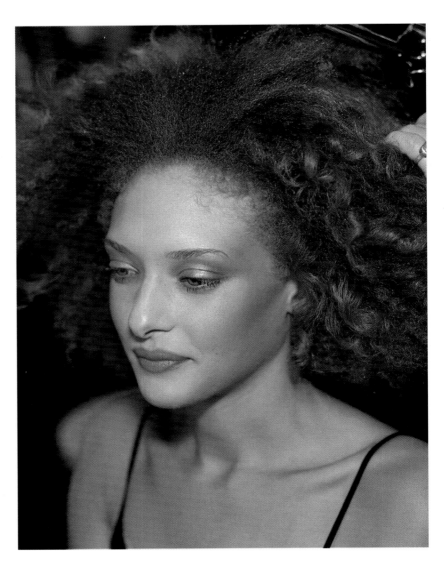

Chrystèle. Beauty beyond word barriers.

production end of commercial and industrial television had provided invaluable experience and substantial financial security. But her childhood dreams of becoming an actress kept surfacing until she could no longer suppress them. Once she made the leap in the '80s, starting as a model and moving quickly to work as an actress, she worked for ten years on stage, in commercials, soap operas, and prime-time television. The change came "from a very spiritual place," from believing "that there is a God, and that God is guiding your soul.

"I used to call myself the generic Black Girl. You could see twenty of us in a room, and we all had these prim little wigs, and we all had our Peter Pan collars with our little soft, flouncy bows. Non-threatening, very simple, very plain. If you could be the generic Black Girl and you had a little personality, too, then you could work. Then again, maybe you would book a job because you were browner than another woman, and they

wanted you to definitely read Black to the audience. So it depended on camera angles, it depended on what the advertiser and the client wanted to say about their particular product. My type was very generic. It was when I started to stretch out and be more of an individual that I felt it was harder to book me. Because I was saying, 'This is who I am, not who you want.' In the commercial market you are putting yourself on the line. You are selling your very self.

"Clients are just beginning to allow, at least as far as I've seen, Black women to show off the range of their personality. We were still fitting into the niche that was comfortable for the advertisers.

"If you take a look at the number of commercials out there that have minorities in them, there are more but they're still very few. In the children's market they may be more aware of multi-ethnic casting. Thank God for Bill Cosby and the sports stars. Advertisers have to believe that if you cast a Black person in a key position, that person can sell their product not only to a Black market but also to a White market. Bill Cosby is one Black man who represents a personality in commercials, and he can sell to the world. The same with Michael Jordan. It's all based on dollars and cents. They've got to know that you can bring in millions of dollars.

"That's where it's like a Catch-22. As I've said, I've been on too many calls where they've told me, 'Get away from the pearls. We want you to be a tough chick.' And I've said, 'Well, this is *my* tough.' It might not be the way they perceived tough to be, because they'd already decided their character was going to be this kind of tough. They already knew the kind of Black person they wanted to sell their product. And that's how they were going to go ahead and sell it.

"That's why after you've been in it for ten years, and you've done all the things you thought you could do, the best thing is to evaluate whether you can put in another ten years. And if you don't think you can stomach another ten years of either the rejection or the almost getting it or the big check coming in after which you've got to wait months before the next one.... If you can't handle that anymore, if you can parlay your skills into something else, maybe behind the scenes where you can influence those decisions, that's what you should do. And not feel ashamed of that."

The Invisible Princess

Never a bona fide model in the fashion sense, Carole Cole, the daughter of Nat "King" Cole and the sister of music diva Natalie Cole, was nevertheless part of a family that was held in high esteem as role models. She wrote, "I never had a desire to be a model, but I admired most of them as much as every other female. My first theatrical venture was *The Owl and the Pussycat*. I was the first actor to play the role that Diana Sands originated on Broadway. Interestingly enough, the role of Doris was a hooker trying to pass herself off as a model.

"At twenty-two, I screen-tested for a gig as a contract player with Columbia Studios. My screen test was a passionate scene from *A Taste of Honey*, a raw, quasi-avant garde Brit film import from the '60s, focusing on interracial romance, unwed motherhood, parental neglect, homosexuality, and poverty. I received a lot of press on two counts: I was the daughter of a famous celeb, following in his celebrated footsteps, and I was the first Black thespian to become a contract player. What did this mean? Basically, I was one of a small, hand-picked group that would be given a weekly salary, 'groomed' by the studio, 'trained' for film, and hired when the studio was producing an appropriate property.

"My first publicity stunt for Columbia was to reign as 'Princess of Hollywood' for the month of October. I was supposed to be flattered by all the attention. It was great P.R. for the studio and the Hollywood Chamber of Commerce to put this particular Colored Girl on display at ribbon cuttings, openings, premieres, etc. My presence authenticated their claim to liberalism."

That claim was, at least in one dramatic instance, a sham. "I was in attendance at some big board of directors meet—tiara and all—presided over by an old guard Hollywood star. The Watts riots had just been 'contained'." And this star, who owned a TV station, boasted that his helicopters were shooting not only news footage but people, "helping the LAPD do their job." The actor "forgot that the Princess of Hollywood was sitting on the dais and that she was as Black as the folks he authorized his snipers to shoot at."

One of the recurrent weaknesses of authority was to insulate itself in a delusional world above and beyond the purview of others. So it was not unusual that Black people have seen so much in situations where White people did not consider them capable of seeing, let alone understanding anything. Unfortunately, Black people have not told more of what they have seen. Perhaps the personal prestige and financial profit associated with being one of the privileged few silenced them. Perhaps their own confusion and insecurity left them unwilling. With more talented Black people moving into view as fashion and role models however, the public expected them to take more responsibility for their image and their essence. After decades of silence and sacrifice, it was the least they could do.

Hair Apparent

strange hair/ entangle/ my touch,
that i may/ fingerstand/ a way to life/
that is not/ smooth.

Lucy Cooper Summers

As representatives of a race, Black models have always had to answer—by their presence alone—loaded social questions. None carried more weight than an age-old issue that mixed the personal, the political, and the paycheck: What to do about their hair? The simplistic rhetoric of the '60s equating processed hair with processed minds had left a bitter feeling behind. Personal integrity and cultural brainwashing could never be reduced to cut-and-dried issues of nappy vs. straight or Black vs. White. The complexities surrounding hair were no less entangled at the end of the 20th century than at the beginning when Madam C.J. Walker and her colleagues opened for business.

Since their first appearance Black models had made their own aesthetic choices and established their own pragmatic priorities. A generation of models who had worked hard to get their foot in the door was followed by another generation of models who worked hard to get through the door. Once through, they were followed by Girls working their way into good and then even better jobs. Progress itself was a process. Since straightened hair was—and still is—very much the norm in African American communities, most Black American models conformed. Only a few were willing to wage the struggle to get White agencies and commercial clients to accept their natural hair.

As the more relaxed mood of the '70s encouraged everybody "do their own thing," not all Black models would be able to. While Girls with straighter hair appeared to be confronted with fewer negative reactions from clients than Girls with kinkier hair, the operative word was appeared. Jany Tomba's wavy hair was judged still not smooth enough for some clients and often had to be straightened. Ming's straight hair was sometimes covered with an Afro wig. One cover Girl remembered an ambivalent attitude prevalent during that period. "When your hair was short, the clients wanted it long. And when it was long, they wanted a wig. It was ridiculous. The fact that you even had to wear a wig to get a job was ridiculous. I lost one account because I didn't bring the wig. I had hair. Why couldn't I use my own hair?"

But attitudes among models also varied widely. Wigs could be used as back-up, as problem solvers for bad-hair days or as stylistic alternatives that increased one's versatility. While some models resented them, many others loved them and carried several in their work bags.

It took the stress-for-success '80s to bring about the most energetic innovations in Black women's hairstyles. Wigs lost their appeal as improved permanents, chemical curls, and no-lye relaxers became the order of the day. At home Black women were freed from their fear of water and from twice-monthly wrestling matches with the hot comb. In dressing rooms, Black models were liberated from the public stigma of problem hair. Their crowning glory could be styled, just like that of White models, to blow in the breeze. And just as in the '40s and '50s, Black models were hired to advertise the new formulas to the market of Black women that awaited them.

As Black and White manufacturing firms rushed to develop products to retexturize Black hair, and as Black women of all occupations—and mind-sets—rushed to purchase them, one area of potential concern went unnoticed: medical side effects. Elaine Evans, an African American hairdresser who worked in the States, Africa, and Europe, was hired by Gazelle, a Black beauty firm based in France in the mid-'80s. "For two years, we did only research and product development. I worked in the best laboratories—in Switzerland, Italy, France,

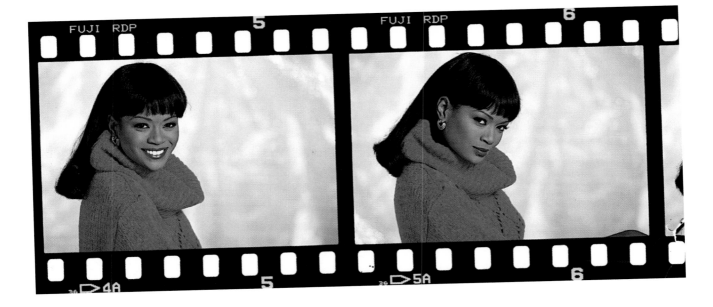

America—developing the products. And from working with Gazelle, I found out that nobody's really doing any research on Black products, especially for the hair, to see if they're going to be damaging us in the future. A few years ago in the United States there was a big scandal about hair coloring causing cancer in women. Well, we put perm on our hair every six or eight weeks, and this is really acid. So we're getting an injection of some very strong chemicals every six to eight weeks."

Elaine, who wore her own hair natural, believed that the majority of women who straightened their hair did so for two reasons. "Most people feel that they can't be sophisticated or well-dressed without having straight hair. Then those who would wear their hair natural won't because it's unmanageable. There are only a few products to make your life easier with your hair natural or to give you a variety of styles and textures. Most of the product marketing is geared to working with permed hair.

"The bottom line is that many Black women conformed to society's idea of beauty. We were willing to conform. We don't fight it. We didn't think that our identity could be accepted. If you don't give much thought to your identity, you didn't wear it right. You don't wear it with confidence. *You* have to feel and accept it first, and then the world will have to accept it. But most of us don't have that type of strength. We just go with the flow."

And the flow was toward straighter and longer hair. While natural hair could be seen in the '80s and '90s in a variety of cropped curly cuts, braids, twists, knots, and locks, the most radical and popular creations were the result of fusing the old-fashioned removable wig with the new-fashioned permanent: hair extensions and weaves. Fashioned from real or artificial hair which was braided, glued, sewn or woven into one's own, weaves and extensions provided the texture, body, length, and, most of all, psychological security that had eluded many Black women. If skillfully done, the labor-intensive process produced a seamless flow of luxurious tresses which looked so…natural.

Models were quick to popularize the innovation. Divas with weaves were generally—and not surprisingly—the highest-earning Girls. Naomi Campbell, a well-documented fan of wigs and changeable do's, continued to make her impressive mark with perfectly straight, exaggeratedly long hair. Pictured on the 100th anniversary cover of American *Vogue* in April, 1992, Naomi was the only Black model among a group of Girls considered the top ten in the business. She also sported the straightest and longest hair, a Rapunzel-like fall which brushed over the backside of her white jeans. She had what everybody else had, and even more of it.

But for some Black models extensions were a mixed blessing. If improperly attached or treated, the additional hair could injure their original but perm-weakened hair, causing it to break. Beside the potential for physical wear-and-tear, however, there was also the deeper issue of identity. If style says, I am, then what do store-bought hairstyles say about *who* I am? Although, as hairdresser Elaine Evans said, "the Black woman can now sling her hair back with some poise and feel some hair bouncing," whose hair was it? And who was the Black woman wearing it?

Cover Girl and runway star, Stephanie Roberts admitted, "What irritates me sometimes is that I feel almost obligated to have extensions in my hair because the hair people in the business—I'm not saying all of them, but the majority of them—don't know how to deal with Black hair. Some of them don't know how to deal with extensions, or they get an attitude with me because I have extensions. But if the business weren't so geared toward being White basically, then it wouldn't be such a necessity to have this kind of hair."

More than most people in the public eye models had to work out who they were and be able to separate that from—or integrate that with—what they looked like. Twenty years after appearing as *Vogue*'s first Black cover Girl, pioneering superstar Beverly Johnson was pictured as a blonde on the cover of her 1994 book, *True Beauty*. In it she insisted on the freedom to choose for oneself. "If you prefer to relax or straighten your hair, don't let anyone else's preconceived ideas about what ethnic women should or shouldn't do, or should or shouldn't look like, limit your style."

Excellent advice. However, the fully equal counterpart—to *not* straighten—did not yet apply to the beauty business. Despite the fact that Whoopi Goldberg, who wrote the forward to Beverly's book, was one of the highest paid Black women in the world, models with locks similar to hers were rare to non-existent.

While Black models—and women in general—in the developed world blithely conducted experiments on themselves, they were being observed and imitated by Black women in less developed countries. During the three years Elaine Evans spent in Abidjan, capital of the Ivory Coast, she began to understand some of the less positive ramifications of international cultural exchange. "Black people in Africa look up to African Americans for beauty in hair and skin. For fashion? No, because they think we dress terribly. But for hair and makeup, they know that we're the most advanced, so they're following us. We're setting the pace for all people of color, but we might not really understand what we're doing."

She injected that cautionary note because she has seen imitation lead to exaggeration and distorted values, sometimes with disastrous results. "Some African women have taken skin whitening creams to the limit. I've seen them mix those creams with Clorox, and paint it all over their body. They burn all their skin off, peel it off, then put oil on it, suffering all that pain just to become light. But they're following us. It's the same thing with hair straightening. In Africa they don't have the racial pressure, but they have the social pressure. You're not considered cultured, sophisticated, and educated if you run around and your hair is kinky. It can get to be a sick thing."

Roshumba

Roshumba stood out as a symbol of unadorned, authentic African-American beauty. Her head-hugging natural was her trademark since she first started modeling in the late '80s. "I took a two-week vacation from my job as a medical technician in Chicago to go to Paris," she said. "And I stayed five months. When I first got there, I went around to see the agencies one day, got an agent the next day, and the day after that I was working. I was lucky. It was weird but it was fun. It didn't hit me until a year after I had been working that I was actually working. I said, My God, they don't pay us to do this. But they do."

She considered her hairstyle "less of a look and more of a statement. I find that I'm representing something: the woman who is more natural. I can get a hair weave, I can get a this or a that, because you just buy it. I know that beauty and strength are seen outside, but they really come from inside. Being able to draw from inside yourself, that's true beauty, and I've been appreciated for that. Look at all the bald heads," a group in which she joyfully claimed membership, "so happy. There goes another one!

"I don't think I'll mess with it. We did go through that period where it was all about big hair, and in some ways it still is. But women now are focusing more on inner values than external ones. It's about time, too. The thing I like so much about

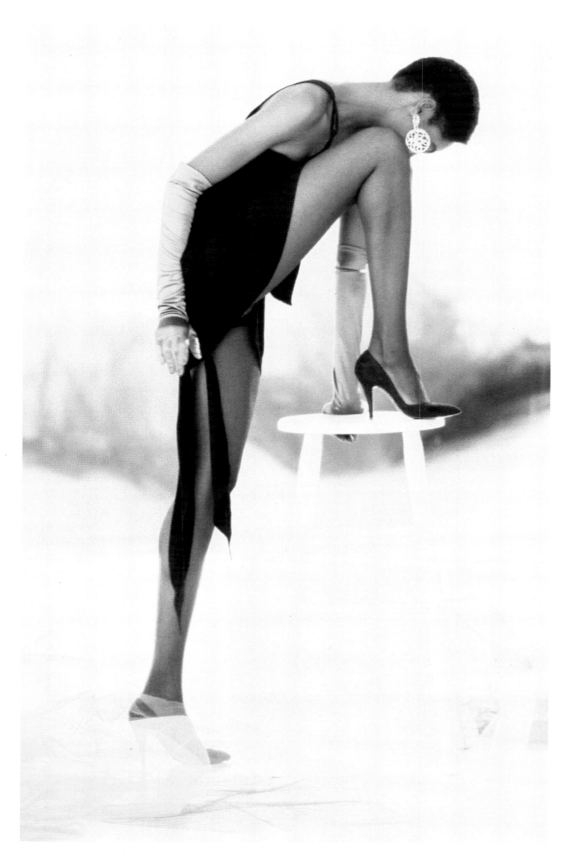

Roshumba's head-hugging natural and gorgeous legs became her trademarks.

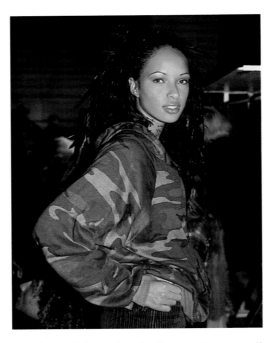

Exciting natural permutations were also bound to appear. One of the most intriguing additions to the mid-'90s ranks of Black cover Girls was French model, Chrystèle, whose porcelain complexion and ice-blue eyes were crowned by the striking aureole of a sand-blond Afro. Present and future generations would no doubt continue to branch out from the creative streams explored in the past. And if Black hair, as a cultural indicator, was about any kind of process at all, it would be a learning process.

Growing

To expect yourself not to change
is not doing yourself any favor.

Peggy Dillard

Brandi prepping for a **Chanel** show. When she started modeling at 15, she was a year too young to work in the Paris collections.

Black models today is that we're not all the same. You can't put us all in the same category. I think it's because the Girls know more about who they really are. Also, the market is opening up. There's more interest now in what you have to give, rather than how to make you fit in. I think that's the best thing that could have happened in fashion, ever."

More than many others, Black models knew that truth and illusion were partners in the beauty business. How much personal responsibility they assumed in retaining some core truth of their appearance varied from generation to generation and from Girl to Girl. The search for self within style was continuous, the quest for truth in beauty, perpetual. These transformative issues gave weight to what could become just another routine job.

If the past gave any indication of future possibilities, it was clear that Black models would never be completely satisfied by wigs, straighteners, weaves, or bleach, as popular as they might be at one time. Like everyone else in the business, they were always on the lookout for something new, some way to keep themselves fresh and appealing. Changing hairstyles was easy and dramatic. Length, color, and texture were only a matter of their hairdressers' time.

As the profession of modeling matured, Girls entered the beauty business at increasingly younger ages. Earlier generations started after college; succeeding generations, after—or during—high school. At eighteen, some were told that they were already too old to begin a career. The '90s only reinforced the unwritten law; the younger the Girls, the better.

Many Girls who started early were, in fact, just girls, very young women who were still growing physically, mentally, and experientially. They were prized precisely for what was most fleeting: their youth. Their fresh complexions were innocent of makeup. With their slim bodies and carefree attitudes they were willing to wear any outfit and try any pose. Their very inexperience was marketed to a jaded public as the dream of purity it could never recover.

But after about a year of steady work in the business, even very young models began to worry about time: booking time, vacation time, show season, catalog season, off season, and cut-off time. Time passed in tangible increments measured by agency vouchers, tear sheets, and repeat bookings. Personal development time, for which there was no yardstick, also passed. Slowly but surely, the fear of aging and younger competition would begin to creep in as well. How models dealt with time, change, and growth was a crucial part of how they defined themselves.

Peggy Dillard

Peggy Dillard was sixteen years old when she moved from Greenville, South Carolina to New York City to attend Pratt Institute. She had known since age fourteen that she wanted to model after she spent a summer in the city with her brother and his friend, designer Lester Hayatt. She also knew that as much as she wanted to model, she did not want to spend her life being subject to others' whims. Modeling was not a secure profession. Not that security was her major preoccupation at age sixteen. Her first priority was to complete her education in a field that combined her artistic talents and interests with marketable skills.

The youngest of thirteen children of whom eight survived, Peggy said, "I always felt like I was bridging generation gaps. When you have all these people around you there was always this extra need, I guess, for everyone to express themselves or identify their individuality. We were very supportive of each other, and no matter what you did, you always had your own team rooting for you. Even after I started modeling, I used to kid the magazines and say, 'Well, you know, this cover is going to sell out if my family alone buys it.' And sure enough Vogue used to say my covers sold more issues than any other. My own family as a P.R. agency definitely helped."

At Pratt she chose to major in merchandising management because "that meant you could merchandise any art, whether it be architecture or fashion or fine art or whatever." Peggy started modeling during her junior year, working not through agencies—which had refused her—but through contacts of Lester Hayatt and Scott Barrie. Eventually, she signed with Ellen Harth, a major runway agency. Then, the magazines started calling. Very early in her career in the late '70s she had two *Mademoiselle* covers and three *Vogue* covers. People in the fashion business were advising her to drop out of

school once she started making money, but she refused. "I was such a student in my mind. I had gotten full scholarships to college, so it did not make sense for me to drop out just because Ralph Lauren was hiring me for one day. The main thing on my mind was trying to get term papers in and keeping my grade average.

"Then there was a moment when I was doing so much work modeling that I didn't know which way I was turning. The only time that it became a serious problem with me was when, unfortunately, a rumor went around Europe that I was pregnant when I wasn't. When you're lined up to do twenty shows in a season and one week before you're ready to go off, all of a sudden your living is canceled, it's a very strange feeling. Physically and mentally, I didn't feel like I had any control. More than anything, spiritually, all I felt was a sense of betrayal by fellow models. And on top of that experience, I had the IRS come back and say, 'I know you filed your taxes, and I know you did your books, but, little girl, you don't realize that you're such a big business to us.'

"I had to grow up very fast and realize that accountants and agents and all these people aren't always the nice people that they seem to be. You realize that you're a major commodity and that you're supporting more people than you know in more ways than you know. Models make a lot of money but people never look at our expense side. To make a lot of money, you must spend money. And as I really started paying attention, I realized that the reason some Girls didn't work as much was because they didn't take good care of themselves. I was very religious about all that.

"You must continue to grow. You must continue to search out all the different things in life that you were meant to do. I think this is one of the most important aspects of being a successful model. I've come to the realization that in spite of all the *Vogue* covers, at a certain point you reach your quota. This is the way it is. So you go on, you do other things. You don't get stuck in the feeling that I have to be making a certain amount of money per hour to feel that I am

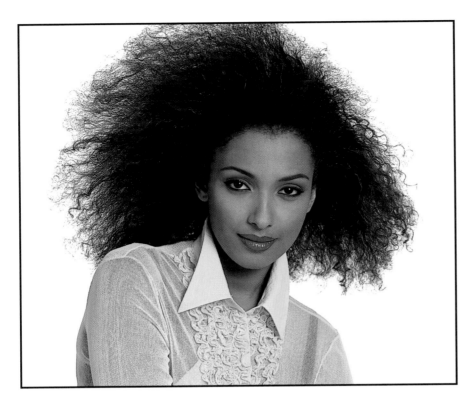

Anika Poitier. Free hair, free spirit.

worthy of being who I am. To expect yourself not to change is not doing yourself any favor.

"The whole time you're modeling you see older Girls going in and out of the business, having babies, coming back. This was always positive to me. The industry became multi-faceted, so it wasn't like those old clichés: you modeled for three or four years, then you'd better marry a rich man and give up the business. All the people I looked up to, I saw them going through transitions in their life. Taking it another step further and living their life, going through their relationships, their marriages, their pregnancies, the whole thing. It was a profession that you lived.

"I've been called by a lot of community groups. These people pay me my day rate to come in and give seminars and lectures. The least thing you ever think people will remember or see may have a lifetime effect on another individual. This is one reason why I don't promote cigarettes. And for that same reason, I won't do nudes. You have to remember that the world is not always full of sunshine, that you've got pornography. Sometimes we take pictures

for clients, and they come back two years later and use it to advertise some other product. Any time you make your living off of public appeal, whether you're a politician, a musician, a singer, an actor or actress, you take on that responsibility. That's the obligation we have.

"To young people coming into the business, I say, Look at yourself as a client might look at you. Learn how to work with yourself. Know how to do your own makeup, know how to do your own hair. Learn to do for self, more than anything. Not to depend upon your agent to manage your career or your life.

"Learn about your body, the changes that you are going through as a woman. This has a lot to do with your longevity and your potential for being successful in this business, knowing how to feed yourself, nourish your skin and hair. Internally, externally. These are the things that are even more important than learning your makeup.

"Sometimes I call the American way of life the unconscious way of life, the unconscious existence, because of the combinations of things we put into our bodies without thinking about the actual chemistry. You have to sit down and evaluate your environment, your diet, and your lifestyle. And if you don't do this at some point, you're not growing wiser, you're just growing older. You're killing yourself, and you're not really learning from your mistakes. You have to know what you want in life, not just in terms of a modeling career, but your overall life, and then put modeling in perspective. If it becomes your whole life, then you're going to have problems, because as a model you're a commodity, and your life can go up and down with your career.

"I'm very basic about survival. I'm not one who survives on people giving me handouts. I want to pay my own rent and make my own dress if I have to. Success to me is being able to go to bed at night and get up in the morning and not feel a sense of anxiety or insecurity because I don't know if I'm going to be able to impress someone or get what I want or what I think I need out of a certain situation on a certain day. If I had to do something that I did not like just for the money, or if I had to keep working to feel that I had to make a certain amount of money to be successful, then I would be miserable. It's not so much the money aspect of it. It's having a sense of peace, a sense of spiritual evolution, and the privilege of knowing that you're spiritually free.

"We have to start realizing that everyone has their own beauty. If you get up and have to be at work by nine o'clock and you put on your makeup at the same time every day, you get into this routine of seeing yourself the same way. But you don't really see yourself. All you see is this illusion that you keep creating every day. You don't leave yourself much room to grow. It's boring if you have to play that same role all the time. And I think you're really missing out on the other part of being a woman, understanding the real, diversified human being that you can be."

For the past several years Peggy has been one of the busiest full-figured models in that newly expanding side of the modeling business. And she has successfully operated a hair salon, Turning Heads, in Harlem. Her long, unprocessed hair came to be part of her signature look as a model.

"I never really made a point of it, but it's been a point in the industry that I've kept it natural," she said. "It has brought me certain jobs, and, for sure, I lost work, but I just feel that it wasn't for me anyway. Some people feel that in order to be a sophisticated, educated, intelligent Black woman, you must have straight hair. Some of the models are into that look, yet there're a lot who would prefer not to straighten their hair, but because of the money they do.

"I always go back to the very beginning when I thought about modeling. I said, OK, are you going to be dancing to everybody else's music or are you going to listen to the music in your own head? And my music always tells me that I like myself as I am. It helps me to enjoy my success, seeing the influence it has on my younger nieces and nephews coming up saying, 'I like my hair just like it is, 'cause Aunt Peggy wears her hair like this, and it looks good.'

"If you ever forget that you're Black in this industry, you're making a major mistake. It's like being in the middle of West Palm Beach where I was shooting with *Vogue*. I'm the only Black person in the whole room. What do I do? Disappear? No, I can't avoid being there, you know. And I can't ignore it, because you have to remember that if Naomi Sims and Beverly Johnson and other women had not at some point made some statement, whether they did it visually or orally, we might not even be here. So I think we just have to get past withering in the face of danger, because as long as we don't, we will not be free."

Peggy has been married to artist and art teacher Lloyd Toone since 1980. Maintaining a solid relationship while working in an insecure and stressful profession is one of the most profound successes a model can point to. There are not many who can. The myth of the beautiful woman with the exciting and fulfilling love life is often just that, a myth.

"He's a terribly secure, rounded person, and he puts a lot of emphasis on being secure as a Black man in America and just as a person, period. I love that, because for me, I wouldn't say that I was flighty, but I didn't feel that I was bound by time and space and distance at all. And I still don't feel like I am. I really don't.

"Whenever we were together a certain magic would just happen. We're good business partners as well as good lovers. Everything we do is joint. In spite of all my ups and downs, Lloyd has always been very spiritually supportive. I never look for anybody, man, woman, child, whoever to work for me. But it sure helps when there's someone there who says, 'You can do it.'"

Stephanie Roberts

Stephanie Roberts has had the cover of *Vogue* and the *Fashions of the Times* as well as the spotlight at the European shows. At twenty-two, she seemed already to have lived a long time.

Born in Mississippi, raised in Ohio and California, as a teenager she "used to come home fighting the air," frustrated by her inability to fit into the Black community. When Stephanie moved to

Oakland at age thirteen, she said, "I used to get harassed all the time by the kids because of the way I spoke. I didn't have the Black way of speaking and Black identification. And I kind of went to the other side. I used to hang out with all White people.

"I started smoking pot when I was fourteen. I said I was going to quit within my twenty-first year. It was a goal of mine, to quit. I actually went over to the twenty-second, but it was in the right vicinity.

"It's a thing that I know a lot of Girls went through. Especially when you come to New York, because you just basically go wild. My first two years here were wild and wonderful. I don't regret the drugs that I did. I am proud of it, because I did it and I lived it and I know. I don't have any judgment against anybody who does it, because I know what it's like. I'll tell anybody, yes, I did that, and I got out of it. That takes a certain amount of power."

When Stephanie came to New York, she had just turned eighteen. "I wrote in my journal that August when I first joined the agency that I was going to become one of the top models in the world. When I told people that, they thought I was being cocky. But I wasn't being cocky. It's just that, for me, no goal was too high. I learned I can get anything I want out there. The thing that's harder to conquer is what's on the inside.

"I'm getting a lot of good lessons. I'm getting what I wanted, what I asked for. Then you have to work for it, you have to deal with it, and you have to drop your ego in order to be receptive to things. I like to think that I know everything, that I got a grip on life and a hold on everything. And I don't. Some things came that I really needed to learn. So I needed to humble myself to take it in. The teachers say, 'When you ask a question, your answer's already in the question.' You just have to be open to see the answers. And to deal with the things that you don't necessarily want to see about who you are.

"I had to see who I was. I had to see me being a total party animal. I had to own that and accept that and accept that I created it, in order to get out of it. Instead of saying, Well, all my friends do drugs and in the business you have to drink when you go out because everybody else is doing it, I had to say that I was *choosing* to do it. And that's when it stops.

"I don't want to walk around lost. I don't want to be unhappy. True happiness isn't being on the cover of a magazine. True happiness is loving yourself and knowing yourself, even if you're something that's not so great. My family is very supportive. But if all of a sudden I were to say, 'OK, I'm not doing this anymore,' they would say, 'Allright, so what are you going to do now?'

"With your mentality, you can create things. When I first started modeling, people used to tell me things like, 'It's going to be harder for you because you're Black.' Or, 'The market's not so big for Black models, so it's going to be easier if you do things this way.' And I decided not to take that in. I didn't want to accept that mentality that said it was going to be harder for me because I'm Black. But when you hear that certain people don't use Black models, it pushes your buttons. Like, what's wrong with Black models, you know? There's nothing wrong with us. It's what's wrong with them and their mentality.

"It's a constant test, because I am human, and I feel everything that's human. I feel jealousy, you know, I feel envy and irritation, aggravation. I feel all that stuff. But I don't want it to own me. I don't want to end up being an angry, jealous, pissed-off person all the time. Anything that comes my way may be a blessing in disguise. I've had jobs cancel, but then I got a great job or maybe I got to do something that I really wanted to do instead. So it worked out fine. I'm testing myself in the world.

"At first, in the business, I kind of gave into that whole 'You have to be smiley and ditsy and not really say what you feel' kind of attitude. When you look good and you're pretty, a lot of people don't want to know that you have a brain. That would be too much for them. It starts to reflect on them, and they start to feel really inferior. I realized that if that's how they feel, that's them feeling it. It's not me making them feel that, you know? I'm not

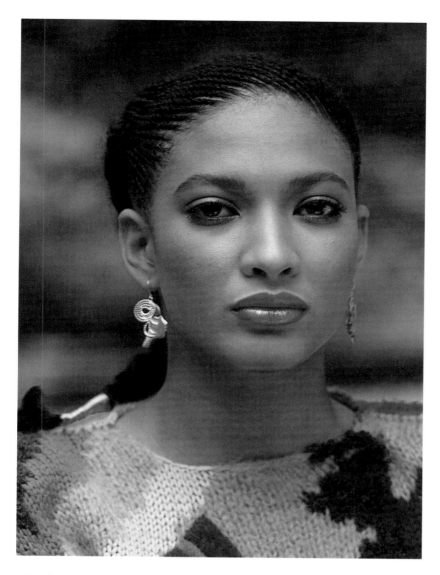

stupid. I'm far from being stupid. So from now on I'm not going to act like it.

"People just want you to nod and say Yeah. Certain people, even big models who are really doing well, don't want you to go up against them. People don't want any opposition. And for me, I found that I'm sort of asking for it. I *want* some opposition. Go up against me, challenge me, tell me something. I like that, because it tests me. It's up to us to bring forth our power from within to push us.

"It's hard. I can't teach somebody something. They have to find it themselves. They have to fall on their face. I've fallen on my face many, many times, made a fool of myself and felt so stupid. But when I felt stupid, that's when I was most open. I was so humbled, because all of a sudden I thought I had it, and all of a sudden I realized I didn't. When it's time to cry, I let it out. It's like something within you saying, 'Release this. You're holding back all this junk. Let it go.' So I'm just learning, living and learning. I get

what I need, you know. I own the good life. I can't complain about it at all."

The kind of crazy, confrontational courage, which can be an asset for a model like Stephanie Roberts, can be a parent's worst nightmare, especially for the mother of a very young girl who won her first modeling school scholarship at age eleven.

A Mother's Story

Dr. Lucia Beverly Peele, an educator and the mother of three children including young superstar Beverly Peele, wanted her only daughter "to feel good about herself, carry herself well, be a lady, and have confidence in herself." And so she enrolled Beverly in an etiquette course at Bullock's, a leading California department store. She was preparing her daughter to enter junior high school "where blue eyes and blond hair were predominant." The goal to help Beverly build self-esteem was enhanced by her own ability, "a knack for putting herself together," as her mother described it.

Peggy Dillard, a balanced beauty.

Two years of amateur fashion competitions and shows in Los Angeles led to Beverly being invited to spend a summer working in New York. She was all of thirteen. Under the supervision of family and friends, she made the trip. "Her father and I talked about it a lot. But it wasn't presented to her until we were comfortable with it, because it wasn't an option for her unless we were comfortable." Jobs in New York and job offers in Europe soon followed. Protected living arrangements away from home seemed to satisfy the stringent parental requirements of "the ebony bambino." Organized independent study courses kept her academically on track. And mother Lucia often traveled with daughter Beverly to see first-hand what this new life entailed.

She admitted, "It frightens me. It does. And I know that there are people in the business who don't particularly like me hovering so close. But I feel that I have to. Still, I cannot be every place with her, and I can only give her direction on what to do. She's creative. And I think that's something that we as parents have allowed her the opportunity to do.

"A Black school superintendent whom I admire once said, 'Do you know how you can tell when we as a people have arrived? It's when we are not pushing our kids to be only doctors, lawyers, and Indian chiefs. When they can go the way of the arts if they want to.' And I think he's probably right.

"As a young woman I wanted to dance, and I did dance a little bit. But I thought, nice girls don't do this. You go to school, and then you become a secretary or a teacher or a nurse. Those were the things that we had to do, and you didn't question it. At least, I did not question my parents, and most of my friends didn't. You did what they said. It was a very conservative, much stricter upbringing. Even though Beverly thinks we're strict, she doesn't know what strict is. We made her a very special child."

A child in the modeling business is, however, even more confounded by the contradictions of the business. No longer a child and not yet a woman, she lives in a strangely uncertain world. Her body assumes a pose for experiences it has not undergone. Her eyes reflect but cannot yet project. She must cope with loneliness and insecurity at the same time that she is being pampered and flattered. She yearns for independence and impetuosity at the same time she must stick to a schedule and follow directions. Changeable personnel and locations uproot her sense of stability. And a girl who only last year played with dolls can this year be playing with men.

How does a mother deal with her own conflicting need to both protect and let go? The best way she can.

Lucia Peele spoke with the resigned optimism that many parents of ambitious teenagers must feel. "She met a young man in Paris. Could be worse. I was talking to a teacher who really takes charge of Beverly when she's home, and she said, 'Don't worry, she's always in love, in love with a different person every two weeks. And this, too, shall pass.'

"It's been difficult as a mother. I'm the Wicked Witch of the West because I say No. When I asked Beverly about this boyfriend that she had in Paris, she said, 'Why do you want to know about his mother and his father?' And my answer was, 'It worked for me. And we don't always have to tell you why. This is the way it's going to be because we are your parents, and we're responsible for you if you get in trouble.'

"You can only give them so much, and you can only watch them so much. You pray a lot that what you do is the right thing for them and that you have given them a good basis."

In 1993, at the age of eighteen, Beverly Peele gave birth to a daughter, Cairo. At first, reports in society columns and eager fashion spreads indicated that grandmother, mother, and daughter appeared to be doing fine. But the star that had risen so fast at such a tender age might have paid—or still be paying—dues that were better handled away from the public's prying eyes. By the time Beverly was twenty-one, photo and runway bookings were declining. And, of course, there was no shortage of other, even younger Girls ready to take her place.

Next
Afterlife

Is there life after modeling? To those on the outside looking back, the answer was an emphatic yes. To those on the inside still looking around, the answer was not so clear. What other work could provide the lights, attention, glamour, and money? How could a model leave all this behind?

The truth was that the model most often did not leave the work. Instead, the work left her.

Staring that fact in the face was one of the most difficult tasks of a model's career. Throughout she had to cope with the seasonal changes of catalog bookings and designer collections. She dealt with fluctuating trends in trivia—hair style and brow shape—that could mean the difference of thousands or even hundreds of thousands of dollars. She confronted the daily unpredictability of bookings, income, competition, and status with a sense of persistence and panache. She disagreed with agents who wanted to use her more—or less—than was good for her overall exposure. After facing down so many challenges—which created its own kind of routine—many a model found it difficult to accept that work was no longer slow, but simply over.

The attachment to modeling was not only to a paycheck or to a profession but to a sense of self-worth. Years of affirmation and special acclaim were not easily relinquished, especially since society often relegated Black women to the ranks of the invisible and the powerless. Anonymity had a particularly bitter taste after such public visibility.

In addition, few models retired at the peak of youth, as Naomi Sims did at twenty-three. Most confronted this job change at the same time they faced a major life change, the onset of middle age with all of its attendant doubts and necessary re-evaluations. Fading beauty was only one of their fears, perhaps the least. Exercising long-unused skills and taking complete responsibility for one's future were even scarier. Although only a few hundred women per decade—and even fewer Black women—truly succeeded as models, billions of women succeeded daily in less exalted roles as human beings. Models desired to be both exceptional and ordinary, to achieve in a tiny, exclusive world as well as to flourish in the largest one. Recreating themselves as real people was their greatest challenge.

If the stories of transition out of modeling were not as eye-catching as the stories beginning the adventure, they were, nevertheless, perhaps more instructive. Lucky circumstances beyond their control helped many Girls achieve at the start. But it took smart, informed choices—and often painful sacrifice and solitude—to shift into the next phase of life. There were as many roads leading out of the business as there were roads leading in, and many ways to travel those roads.

> *Use what Mother Nature gave you till Father Time takes it away.*
>
> *Aunt's advice to Lu Sierra*

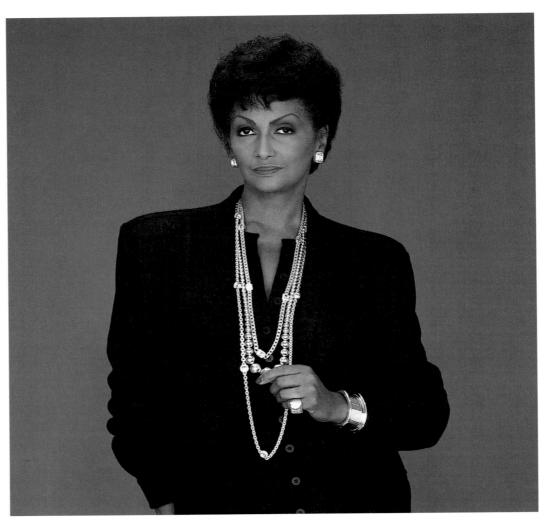

Quitting Time

Models are not like goldfish—you flush them away and who cares?
Alessandra Donghi

Although a few new facial lines, a couple of stubborn pounds, and an occasional gray hair could be overlooked in the mirror, others saw what a model wished she could deny. She was aging. A print Girl might be slightly more anxious because she knew a photographer could examine her pores through the camera lens even more closely than she could in the makeup mirror. While a show Girl often benefited from a designer's loyalty over several seasons and was not subject to the same scrutiny—as long as she fit the clothes—

she, too, could begin to feel the pressure to make way for a new Girl.

Rene Hunter remembered some of the tension she felt before deciding to "hang her leotard up" in the late '60s. She had to deal not only with her own body changing, but also with a taller, leaner body type beginning to enter and dominate the profession. "One day you're the toast of the town, the hottest thing since sliced bread, and the next day you could be the char lady. That's a big ego-kicker. But I knew I couldn't compete with new people like Pat Cleveland, Naomi Sims, and Alva Chinn. I wasn't as tall, and I was never as thin. I'd had a nice run, five years. So I got out while they still wanted me."

Alessandra Donghi, a booker for the Milanese agency Stage/Riccardo Gay, spoke for many agency workers when she said that most models sensed when it was

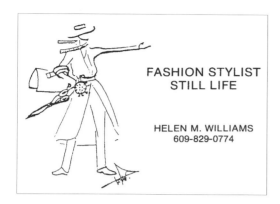
time to retire. The difficulty lay in actually making the move.

"From doing twenty shows, a model goes down to ten, and then the next season she goes to eight. The season afterward she goes up to twelve, and then down to two. She knows. But if she considers herself The Model of the World, she blames it on the agency. Normally, models change agencies when they start being pushed just a little bit by the new Girls, the young ones. Maybe the first season they do a little something more, but then it's no, N-O.

"There comes a day when you have to tell them, and so you do. You say, 'Maybe you can stop for six months and come back with a new look.' Or 'Listen, I think it's really time for you to quit the business before it gets too depressing and humiliating for you.' I guess modeling is like getting old. When you get old, some women don't accept it. Models think, It's not all over. You're still beautiful, you're still looking young. It's sad. Models are not like goldfish—you flush them away and who cares?"

For many models, however, quitting time was a decision reached by both the body and the mind. The intellectual curiosity and creative restlessness that models often brought into the business were no longer adequately stimulated after a few years. Paradoxically, the longer the time in, the harder it was to get out even though the thrill was long gone.

After ten years with the biggest agencies in New York, Jordan decided to quit, because she wanted to do other things. And, she added, "I wanted to know *how* to do other things. In this

business if you're just occupied with modeling you could lose your perspective about life. You lose your identity, you forget about who you are.

"There're periods when you work all the time, and then, all of a sudden, you don't work as much. And you think, What happened? What do I do now? If you don't have any background and you don't have any training, you're going, oh well, this is it. There's nothing else for me to do. Your mind is going crazy waiting for the bookings to come in, but they're not coming in. And the more anxious you are, the worse it seems to be."

Branching Out

Sometimes you're lucky that you
get displaced.

Pat Cleveland

As they moved out of active modeling, some women retained close ties to the modeling business. Several models retired from their own careers to handle the careers of other models. Ophelia DeVore and Pat Evans opened agencies in New York dealing specifically with women of color. Bethann Hardison in New York and Pat Cleveland in Milan handled models of all types, the majority of whom were White.

Pat said, "To get a career is very difficult, so once you get it you have to hold onto it a bit. But you have to control your life. I try to teach each individual Girl to take pride in her career, to keep it dignified and strong, but also to push her own career. You are your own best agent, I always tell them. You have to have respect for people. You don't want to hurt them. On your way up is on your way down, too.

"I do the best I can. I watch, and then I tell the Girls little things that I've learned that maybe nobody else will tell them. A lot of the Girls are much smarter in business today because they watched other models over time.

"The Black Girls who come here, especially those from the States, had to go a long way. To work here, they had to be stars there first. Then some, like Paulette

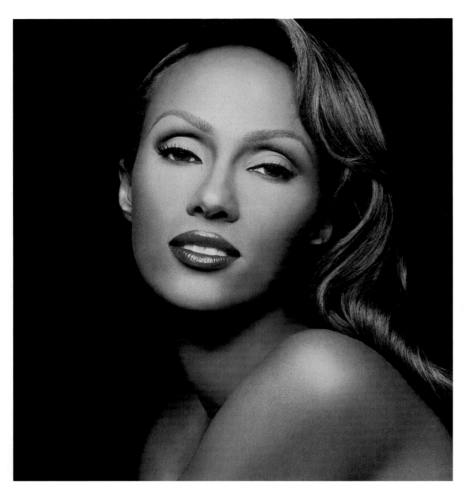

honesty, I have to say that I only think about using a Black stylist or a Black makeup or hair person when I'm doing a Black book or a Black campaign or a Black shoot of some kind.' So, it hasn't changed.

"I don't mean to be a pessimist, but as long as we have racism anywhere in the world, we're going to have that attitude. And it isn't that the people in the business are really racists; it's just that they don't take the time to think about it. They don't make an effort. I think the only way it can really change is if Black people become such an integral part of life and living to everyone that they don't have to think about it."

Rene Hunter used her experience with designers and fine clothing when she made the transition from modeling to working in department stores. "The knowledge I had about fashion I took into retailing. Eventually, I became a buyer at Saks Fifth Avenue. Then I helped to run a dress company. I took my fashion background being a model and my retail experience being a buyer, and applied it to the other side. I liked it. It was very rewarding and creative."

Audrey Smaltz

Audrey Smaltz also went into retailing when she left modeling, but she added a few twists of her own before re-entering the fashion fray. "From Bloomingdale's I went to Lane Bryant, where I started modeling again, modeling and buying clothes. All the clothes were made on me. By that time I was a size fourteen tall. I stayed there until I got married and moved to Chicago. I married a physician but that didn't last. So then I decided I would try out for the Ebony Fashion Fair.

"The Ebony Fashion Fair started in 1958. When I had gone to see Freda DeKnight in the late '50s about being in the show, Freda said No, that I was too tall and that they wouldn't have any clothes to fit me. The Girls that they were hiring were 5'4" or 5'6". So it took me thirteen years to get into the Ebony Fashion Fair, and when I did get in, I didn't get in as a model, I got in as the commentator, coordinator, and fashion editor for *Ebony* magazine. I

James, really didn't get their chance in America. Paulette is lucky that it happened here. Sometimes you're lucky that you get displaced. I'm a little displaced, but maybe it's for a good reason. Maybe I'm that one person to tell these Girls something. And maybe I have to be here to say that."

Many women separated from modeling but branched out into some allied area of the fashion business. Helen Williams worked as a catalog stylist for over three decades. Sharon "Magic" Jordan became a designer. Jane Hoffman Davenport worked as a consultant and stylist for special projects. Her continued exposure to all sides of a shoot confirmed some of her experience as a model. Jane found that racially restricted thinking was still, unfortunately alive and well. Talking with a photographer not long ago, she said, "I was asking him about some styling work, and he admitted to me, 'Jane, in all

worked for Mrs. Johnson. My first trip with her to Europe was in 1971, and I made thirteen trips altogether. She bought all the top designer clothes. You name it, she bought it. It was wonderful. Eunice Johnson with the Ebony Fashion Fair exposed the Black community all over the United States, the Bahamas, and Canada to high fashion from Europe, to the high fashion designers in New York, and then, of course, to Black designers. She tried to make some Black designers famous by being in the Ebony Fashion Fair, and she would give them good exposure.

"I remember when I went to see my first Valentino fashion show, couture, in July, 1971. He had twenty-two models and not one Black model. Not one. That year Mrs. Johnson spent $50,000 with Valentino. Anyway, I had a big mouth, and I complained about the lack of Black models. I had taken Alva Chinn to Oscar de la Renta's showroom, because in those days they wouldn't allow me to take the clothes out of the showroom to shoot. They were afraid. So I was shooting in Oscar's showroom, and here comes Oscar. Looking at Alva, he thought she was the finest thing. He used her, and then he told Valentino about her. So Alva Chinn was the first Black model that Valentino used. He flew her over in July, 1972. Then in January '73, he used Pat Cleveland.

"Then the Black models took over when Eleanor Lambert, the head of Fashion Group, organized Versailles in the fall of '73. America met Europe. And when those Black Girls hit that stage, Europe went bananas. When Europe accepted the Black Girl, the American designers had to accept her."

For fifteen years prior to Versailles, the Ebony Fashion Fair had been showcasing the style and personality of a wide variety of Black models. A major part of the show's success, however, depended on the style and personality of its commentator. "No one had ever done commentary the way I did commentary," Audrey declared, "and no one really does it now. I did all the writing for my script, and I wrote some funny scripts. I read a lot, I traveled a lot. I put commentary on the map. I sat on a high stool, and I didn't use cards. I just called them as I saw them, and made fun. If the Girl had a fabulous body and the dress was sensational, then I would say, 'And Mama may have and Papa may have, but God bless....' You finish the sentence, 'cause there she was. The Girl would be in a wonderful suit with the fox, and it'd be just perfect. And I'd say, 'You don't have to have an attitude to be rich, but it helps.' Then I would say, 'Valentino' or 'André Laug.' That was it. Or I might say, 'What to wear on Sunday when you won't get home till Monday.' Or 'When the invitation reads, Don't dress, consider this.' And here comes this drop-dead outfit. Or it would be an Emilio Pucci dress, and I would say that he signs Emilio all through the design. So I would try to tell people something that they didn't know or couldn't see. I would never say, 'The dress is red.'

"I worked for the Ebony Fashion Fair for seven years. But when I turned forty, I wanted to go into business for myself. When I first came to New York I found this space. Lucky me, 55th Street right off Fifth Avenue. Donald Trump moved into *my* neighborhood. My business has changed in many ways because life changes, fashion changes. When I started out we called this place the Atelier. Because of *Ebony* I knew all the designers, and I could get the clothes that they had in the back room very inexpensively. But I was too far ahead of my time. I had a discount couture operation catering to Blacks, which was a total mistake. The women I was going after had the money, but they didn't want to spend it because they thought it was ridiculous. I was in and out of that business in a year because I wasn't making any money.

"After that I did some consulting, and then I started doing fashion shows for charities where you charge a lot of money. I got my name out there, and I got to be very good at organizing and presenting fashion shows. So that's what we do. We are the Ground Crew. We do fashion shows, videos, and shoots. We work for magazines, manufacturers, and designers.

"We're a service company. I try to service my clients as much as I can, as well as I can. We can do whatever it is that you

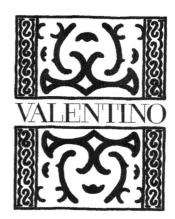

Valentino was one of the first Italian designers to use Black models.

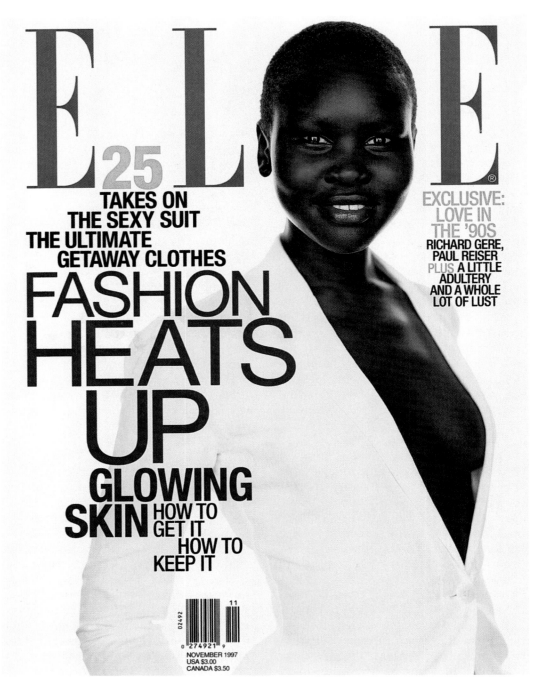

ELLE
25

EXCLUSIVE:
LOVE IN
THE '90S
RICHARD GERE,
PAUL REISER
PLUS A LITTLE
ADULTERY
AND A WHOLE
LOT OF LUST

TAKES ON
THE SEXY SUIT
THE ULTIMATE
GETAWAY CLOTHES

FASHION
HEATS
UP
GLOWING
SKIN HOW TO
GET IT
HOW TO
KEEP IT

NOVEMBER 1997
USA $3.00
CANADA $3.50

Alek Wek. One of fashion's newest stars came from Sudan. *Elle*, November, 1997.

need done. When I have big jobs, like the shows I'm booking now, I need seventeen people here, twelve there, twenty-three here, and thirty-five there. I have my Girls that I call on. I have my people, hairdressers, stylists, whatever you want. We do a lot of things, and we have a lot of fun. Fashion is in a spin. Whether you're selling it, buying it, servicing it, making it, sewing it, whatever you're doing in fashion is crazy.

"Black models have come a long way, but I still do a lot of shows where they have only one Black model. There are all kinds of beautiful Black women. But if there's nobody hollering and screaming and demanding, then they won't use you.

When they do use us, it's as a token. Their conscience beats them, 'Oooh, I'd better give them one little job.' That's the way it is. That's the way it's going to be.

"So we always have to have somebody hollering and screaming, because they forget about you. You're invisible. Do you know how much is going on in this world where you don't see one Black person at all? Where there are *no* Blacks, period? Millions of things. We have to be loud, it's unfortunate. As Black as we are, they don't see us. If we would stop being the consumer, and say, 'No, I'm not going to buy that unless you do so-and-so,' but, generally, we don't. We Black people have so little self-esteem. We're so scared. We're afraid of the White man, and we don't like each other. We don't uplift each other.

"Sometimes I think I'd like to travel more, take off for a whole year, just travel and let someone else run the business. I've been in fashion since I was sixteen years old. Over forty years, that should be enough. I'm a happy person, positive, very spiritual. I like reading the Bible. I like gardening, and I have a beautiful garden out there on my terrace. I'd love to read all the books I've always wanted to read. I also want to do my own book. I can't tell it all, though. Certain people couldn't handle that."

Cosmetics was another natural outlet that Black women who wished to expand into the beauty business often explored. Arlene Hawkins and Marcia Turnier became professional consultants.

In the '70s Beverly Johnson had plans to market a line of cosmetics named after her partner, makeup artist James Farrabee. In the '80s popular cover Girl and celebrity daughter Shari Belafonte also tried to launch a product line. In the '90s Naomi Sims Beauty Products Ltd. struggled to maintain its position as one of the half-dozen Black-owned cosmetics firms based in the United States.

With the battle of the beauty counter waged by huge conglomerates eager to cash in on the Black consumer market, new entrepreneurs in this field—with or without modeling experience—were expected to be scarce. But Black women were used to defying expectations. In the summer of 1994, Iman announced the debut of her cosmetics and skin-care line targeted for all women of color—African, Asian, Latin, and Native American. With the huge American chain JC Penney distributing products in 180 stores nation-wide, Iman was off to a spectacular start. And with seasoned makeup artist Byron Barnes at the helm as creative director, Iman Cosmetics was determined to make good on its promise to give customers "All You Want. All You Need."

Into the field of Black hair care—another specialized industry saturated with products—came Wanakee, a particularly creative and enduring beauty whose modeling work was a staple of quality catalogs in the late '80s and '90s. Defying the cliché that genetic programming prevented Black women's hair from growing, she created a collection of hair care products, Wanakee Verifen Complex, for which her own waist-length hair was the best advertisement. Wanakee's products have found enthusiastic fans among some of the most discriminating customers in the marketplace—other models.

Fran Cooper

In the mid-'70s, a palm reader in London told aspiring model Fran Cooper that she would make her money not from her looks but from her hands. The prediction was accurate and timely. During the next two decades Fran Cooper became the most successful Black woman makeup artist the business has ever known.

As a high school student studying drawing and fashion illustration in Los Angeles, she was mesmerized by models and makeup. Inspired by a Japanese classmate "who was already a phenomenal illustrator," she spent hours in libraries and shops scrutinizing fashion magazines. "I was tall and thin and always wanted to model a little bit myself," she said. "I knew all the names of the Girls in the '60s—Donyale Luna and Naomi Sims, Lauren Hutton and Astrid—and I got interested in all those different little makeup tips in *Glamour* and *Vogue*. I'd save my lunch money and buy cosmetics—the Revlon Meringues and Dewberry contour kits and eye pencils—and practice on myself and my friends."

A chance encounter with *Jet* photographer Howard Morehead led to her first portfolio. "I loved his pictures and the centerfolds from the late '40s and '50s. All the celebrities in L.A. wanted to be photographed by Howard because he specialized in making people look sexy and glamorous." After a stint with the Ebony Fashion Fair in the early '70s, Fran thought she had settled on her future.

When she went to Europe, though, she "was too busy going out with friends, dancing at the Club Sept in Paris, and having a good time with the playboys in Italy, to concentrate on being a good model." The excitement did not stop after she returned to New York. With model friends, Geneva Hutton and Romney Williams, "we were three Black hot mamas, traipsing around wearing Lester Hayatt's clothes, being the wild girls, dancing the night away at Studio 54. It was high time in New York." But soon it was also time to figure out what she was going to do besides party.

Fashion colleagues encouraged Fran to do makeup. After a stint at the Georgette Klinger skin care salon, she started to freelance. Photographer and ex-model Phyllis Cuington, "with her incredible eye for fashion," guided her in tests with Girls of all colors. *Essence* editors Sandra Martin and Susan Taylor gave her consistent nationwide exposure in the African-American market. "Basically, I began with the Black Girls who were starting to do print in New York. Those were the glory days of Alva Chinn and Pat Cleveland, Billie Blair and Jan Maiden, Sterling St. Jacques and all those spectacular people. Because of *Essence* there wasn't a Black model I didn't do." Then, in the '80s, her agent Elizabeth Watson, the wife of star photographer Albert Watson, opened the doors worldwide to the most prestigious magazines, cosmetic campaigns, and celebrity bookings.

Fran had no regrets about leaving modeling behind. "Sure, who wouldn't like to have had the cover of this or that? But makeup was my niche. It's where I started out. The elements I took from drawing I applied to the face. And nothing brought me the kind of gratification that doing makeup brought me. I came into fashion at a pivotal time. Joey Mills was *the* makeup artist in America, maybe the world at the time, and he was a Black man. The business wasn't saturated like it is now. It was open for more female makeup artists."

She credited the models themselves for helping her, recommending her to other Girls. "I was into beautifying women. If you're good, people see that. I was always nice to the Girls because at first, they were my peers, my sisters. Then, I became more like the older sister, and now, they're like my daughters, my babies. Like most

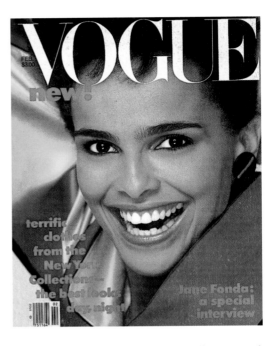

people, models are needy, but I don't mind them needing me because I like to be needed. I don't have any children. I don't mind mothering them. These are young girls; they're fragile. They have all the insecurities of normal women. They just have a *je ne sais quoi*, a chemistry that works, a magic that happens in a show or a shot or a commercial.

"I baby all the Girls because this business makes them insecure enough. You need a little love and attention to make you feel good when you stand in front of a camera and thirteen people are judging you in the tiniest detail for the way you look. You have to be confident. And it all starts in the dressing room in that chair: making those Girls feel great, secure about themselves.

"I love the Girls so much. There are so many special women in this business. I love the creativity, the actual hands-on application of makeup—the way you stroke and comfort—and then watching the change, the excitement it brings to the models when all these things come together. By the time you've gotten them through hair and makeup for two hours, you make them feel like, Hey, I can conquer the world."

Fran's dedication to beautifying women for two decades required that she change with the times. She found the

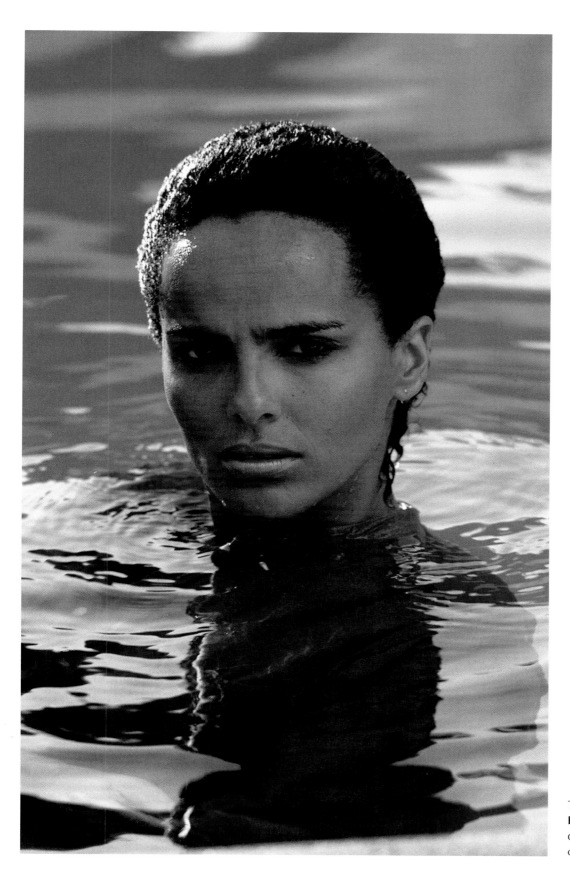

Two moods of **Shari Belafonte**. This celebrity daughter developed her own charm and appeal as a model.

transitions exciting. "You're around these young Girls, and that makes you want to be experimental. You want to be racier, edgier. In the '80s you had the sexy super Sirens. In the '90s the style has gone back to what it was when I started in the '70s: the stick figured, firagile bodies with an easiness and a little quirkiness in their personalities.

"Also, a lot of young Girls are doing heavy drugs again. Just a few years ago the Girls were into eating healthier and being more athletic. Now, they're into being bone-thin and waif-y, smoking cigarettes and drinking coffee. It's a cycle. Even makeup has gone back to the shiny, shimmery colors of the disco days, just revamped. But even if I'm doing something that's a little edgy, I still like the Girls to be a little bit pretty. It's very hard for me to make somebody look ugly. I appreciate beauty."

And beauty that is not limited to one standard. "Beauty comes in all shades from snow white to ebony black. Black models run the gamut these days from Chrystèle to Alek Wek. But I think the business is tighter again for Black Girls. You're not seeing that many in the magazines and the shows. Maybe that's a cycle, too. But that's why I have to respect someone like Naomi Campbell. She always reinvents herself. You have to be so exceptional or you will fall by the wayside. And you have to be willing to bare your fangs to get to the peak and stay there. It's the only way models survive."

Fran gave herself a few more years in the business. "I'll probably be here mothering one more batch before I go: chasing around fifteen-year-olds with my powder puff, saying, 'Stay out of the sun. Girl, you know that guy's not good for you anymore. You'd better take care of yourself. You know you shouldn't be smoking those cigarettes. You'd better save your money!'

"I don't know what tomorrow may bring. But the time that I've had in this business—the incredible people I've come in contact with—it's been extraordinary for me. I've been very fortunate. I always help and share. You have to leave your hands open to keep the energy flowing in and out. Give and take, that's the way the world flows."

Independents

I understood that I had to own something.

Barbara Smith

Ambitious and adventurous as people, some models became artists, writers, and creative businesswomen when they retired.

Apart from the time-consuming involvement in her wig and cosmetics businesses, the prolific Naomi Sims has authored four books: *All About Health and Beauty for the Black Woman* (reissued in 1989 and still considered a valuable resource), *All About Success for the Black Woman*, *All About Hair Care for the Black Woman*, and *How to Be a Top Model*.

In 1994, two world-famous models published books. *True Beauty: Secrets of Radiant Beauty for Women of Every Age and Color*, by Beverly Johnson, was a timely guidebook to self-worth as much as a cosmetics primer.

The story of Naomi Campbell's novel, *Swan*, took place in the fashion world. The book itself, a misguided product of marketing hype, took a quick dive after publication and quietly disappeared. Naomi herself was her best creation. This fact became even more evident with the publication in 1996 of *Naomi*, a splashy hard-cover catalog devoted to photographs of the young diva.

Norma Jean Darden

Norma Darden became a writer and subsequently, a caterer. In 1978, she and her sister Carol published a hugely successful cookbook based on traditional Southern Black recipes. *Spoonbread and Strawberry Wine* sold over 40,000 hard covers in its first year and 200,000 paperbacks and continued to be in print two decades later. The book led to a catering company, Spoonbread, that Norma never advertised but which provided her with both a comfortable income and a fertile outlet for her creativity. Recently Norma has adapted *Spoonbread and Strawberry Wine* for the stage. Combining writing, cooking, and acting, she has presented her one-woman show, complete with tasty samples, in New York City theatres.

"After the book came out," Norma said, "we spent about a year promoting it, doing television shows and writing food articles. Then I got very, very ill. Just as I was going to shoot the cover of *Essence*, I went into the hospital with acute peritonitis. I never modeled after that. I had been in the business about seven years. Models seem to change every seven years. At that time people just didn't model past thirty, and I was already past thirty.

"I felt that if I had died I would have been totally disappointed to have on my tombstone, Norma Darden, model. That would not have encompassed enough of me. I was ready to move on. If I had to put on one more dress and walk down one more runway, I would have freaked out. But at the time, I didn't know where I was moving on to.

"Having a family and an education helped me keep perspective. My advice to new Girls is to be grounded. Modeling is a career that doesn't last forever. I came into it knowing that age is always a factor. Some of these Girls have nowhere to go. Do you know how desperate that makes you feel?

"I do films from time to time. I will always maintain my ties with film and food, if not with fashion. I continue to lecture to women's groups and colleges on career transitions, family life, and food.

"So there *is* life after modeling. You don't have to know that when you're in the process of doing it. Why should you? I think it's wonderful that models now have the option to continue. It shows that the country is maturing, that people are feeling better about women. I love the fact that you can be a model at any age. I just wouldn't have the interest in it.

"When I was a child, there were no Black models in *Seventeen* and *Mademoiselle*. There were no people for us to look up to. Not necessarily to look up to, but just to look *at*, to see ourselves. People don't know what a fight it was to get us recognized. We were not represented, so just the fact that I could be out there, that I could bring the excitement of the Black creative experience into fashion was the highlight of that era for me."

Barbara Smith

After she had worked in other restaurants learning the business, Barbara Smith opened her own, B. Smith's, in New York City's theatre district in 1986. The big, subtly decorated room—with a separate roof-top café specializing in live jazz—became such a success that she opened a sister restaurant in 1994 in Washington, D.C.'s impeccably renovated Union Station. In 1995, she published a cookbook, *Entertaining and Cooking for Friends*, based on her restaurants' recipes.

For Barbara the transition from being a model to becoming a restaurateur had specific advantages and disadvantages. "When I first wanted to open up the restaurant, people were very skeptical. They were looking for who was really behind this. They thought it couldn't be me. It couldn't be my idea. Somebody else was really running it, right? That's the mentality that people have. They were saying that beautiful women didn't want to work as hard as I was working. Much of the concept of beauty is connected to the notion that you don't work hard. For most Black women, you have to be really, really, really strong, because you are fighting the odds. I mean, it's bad enough being a woman, and then being a Black woman, and being a pretty Black woman. You're considered just a doll, a Barbie doll.

"I was very happy with my career. And I knew when I was modeling that I was going to be able to parlay my career into much more because of being a model. To do a *Mademoiselle* cover, to do *Essence* covers, to do *Ebony* covers meant that I could sell myself so much easier than somebody else. Marketing is my big thing, whether I would have ever known it or not. I had to market myself as a model, and I continue to have to market this restaurant and myself. I don't think that you can be successful and just be stupid in the modeling business, because it will eat you

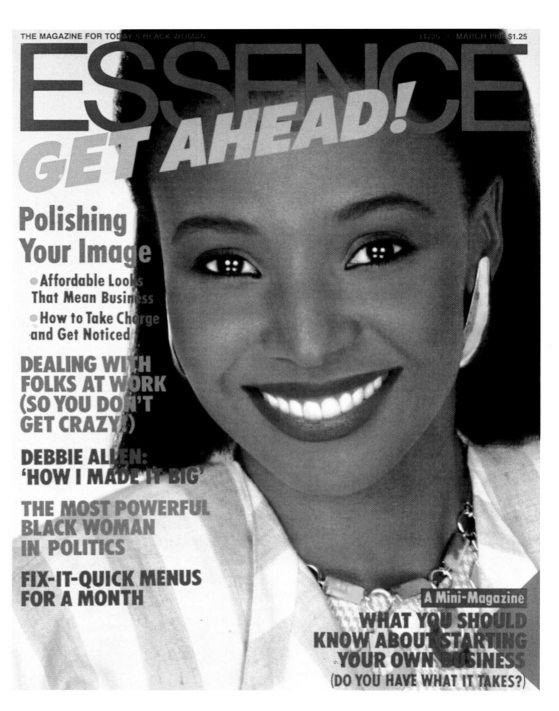

THE MAGAZINE FOR TODAY'S BLACK WOMAN   11725 · MARCH 199_ $1.25

ESSENCE
GET AHEAD!

Polishing Your Image
- Affordable Looks That Mean Business
- How to Take Charge and Get Noticed

DEALING WITH FOLKS AT WORK (SO YOU DON'T GET CRAZY!)

DEBBIE ALLEN: 'HOW I MADE IT BIG'

THE MOST POWERFUL BLACK WOMAN IN POLITICS

FIX-IT-QUICK MENUS FOR A MONTH

A Mini-Magazine
WHAT YOU SHOULD KNOW ABOUT STARTING YOUR OWN BUSINESS (DO YOU HAVE WHAT IT TAKES?)

Barbara Smith brought her savvy style to restaurants and television.

up. There has to be something else there, a resilience. There has to be something that allows you to be in a business where people are looking at every inch of you and wanting something from you.

"And when you put your name on a business, it's the same thing. Part of selling the restaurant is selling me with it. I didn't know what I was creating in creating a business like this. The learning process

never stops. I do believe that if you do everything you possibly can, all the right things, that the business will work.

"What was missing when I was modeling was really getting involved and making something work. I didn't have enough to do. Now I have too much to do, but I've also learned to delegate. Running the restaurants means that I'm the producer, the director, and the casting agent. I think that the most successful transition from modeling comes with developing who you are. It's something you really have to work at. I require most of my employees to have at least two years of college, even though I haven't had it. It's the discipline.

"You see, I had it in my years of modeling. To be a model for more than ten years, you had to have been disciplined somewhere. Professionally, I knew exactly what I was doing. I was on time to my jobs. I understood that it was a business and I was a product. Something in me knew that I had things to learn and that I wasn't gong to learn them just by myself but that I had to learn them from other people, whether I was in a formal school situation or whether I found mentors. And I understood that I had to own something, that I couldn't just spend everything, that I had to look towards the future, and that modeling wasn't going to last forever.

"Although I was happy with my career, there were lots of periods of intense insecurity and unhappiness during my years as a model. Part of it was due to the nature of the business and always being focused on yourself, with no guarantee where the next job was coming from. It was so frustrating, and then at the same time, it was very rewarding. You were always on the edge. I'm lucky I made it, because I don't think everyone does.

"I made it with therapy, and I'm not ashamed to admit it. I recommend it for most people, because sometimes it takes listening to yourself talk to hear what you are saying. I feel that Black women may need therapy even more because of the problems we often face in this culture. I've shed a lot of tears. I've felt a lot of pain. So to get to where I am today, I'm very happy.

"Sometimes people abuse you because of your spirit. It's almost like they want to suck out the spirit that you have. I don't know why. It's their weakness usually. But during the process, that's not what you know it to be. Whether it's family, friends or lover, you know that this is someone you love, and you ask yourself, Why is this person doing this to me? You have to go much further past that to understand that you shouldn't be there and that you're not going to let yourself be there.

"I learned a lot through reading, even if it was only *Cosmopolitan*, that a smart girl does not put all her eggs in one basket. A *Cosmopolitan* woman is a smart woman. All you have to do is read. *Essence*, *Working Woman*, *Ms.*, it's really all out there.

"Modeling was my first career. Running restaurants is my second career. I'm not quite sure what the next career will be, but there will be another career."

Barbara's next career entailed a logical move to television in 1997. *B. Smith with Style* presented a vision of gracious living incorporating her experiences in fashion, food, and family life. With a potential audience of millions, she was on her way to even wider success.

Darnella Thomas

After modeling Darnella Thomas moved into another kind of business entirely. "I was shooting catalog for Montgomery Ward, standing in front of the camera, and I said to myself, This is boring. I need something else, something that's really stimulating. I thought that there must be another life.

"A friend of mine had a company on Wall Street. He was into real estate tax shelters and coal tax shelters, and he had coal mines in Kentucky. He said that if I was looking to get out of modeling he could set me up in a business brokering coal and some of his real estate deals. We basically started with the coal business.

"It was great. I got a chance to go into some coal mines. One time we went in to see what they call the continuous miner. It extracts the coal from the walls of the mine shaft, so we wanted to see that in operation. It was the type of mine where you couldn't stand up. You go in flat on a scoop. You had to crawl down there. Some people went in and got scared, and they had to be taken out, but I was fine.

"Meanwhile, I went in chic. I was still thinking with a model's mentality. The guys were laughing at me because I'm kind of a clean, clean person. I wore a beautiful yellow sweater with this jumpsuit they give you, a jumpsuit with short sleeves. And I was down there crawling on my hands and knees cleaning out the mine,

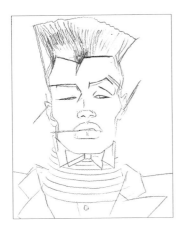

Grace Jones, interpreted by **Antonio**.

because they eat down there. When I came up, my sweater was destroyed. I just said to myself, How stupid can you be?

"It was real exciting, because we got to do things and meet people and travel in different circumstances. We were trying to get contracts, so we had to visit the Department of Defense, the Tennessee Valley Authority, and procurement agents. We got our first contract through the Southern Alabama Power and Light Company for 25,000 tons of coal. We had to monitor it to be sure that it was shipped according to spec. It was a great learning experience.

"Then I started working in the personnel business. I worked as an account executive with a personnel agency. Do you know why I liked it? It's a form of sales. It's something I know, because as a model, you sell, you're selling yourself. Here you're selling other people. Brokering coal is selling. I was traveling all over the country but I was still selling a service. What I'm doing now is still selling.

"I never thought of myself as a competitive person. But looking back, I see that all of my life I've chosen professions that were very difficult and very competitive. All of my life, it seems I've been fighting against the normal thing to do, fighting against the establishment. I don't think I'll ever stop. I'm always doing something, not only in the professional world but also in my personal life. I'm teaching myself how to play chess. I play tennis. I belong to a club that is dedicated to serious body-building. I went to the French Institute to take French lessons. I'm the kind of person who will always be doing."

Drama Queens

Do you know where you're going to?
Do you like the things that life
is showing you?

Sung by Diana Ross

Acting was, incontestably, the field that attracted the most models. There were so many obvious parallels with modeling that insiders and outsiders alike tended to consider the transition a natural one. A model was considered to be a kind of silent actress, a drama queen who wrote her own unspoken lines.

The physical and emotional requirements were, however, quite different, and may be partially responsible for the lack of success models have had in the past. Models were taller than most actors—female and male—and their beauty often verged on the unique, not to say eccentric. If acting involved becoming a character, it was no wonder that Grace Jones had been one of the most visible ex-model actresses on the big screen. Her roles in *Conan the Destroyer*, the James Bond film, *View to a Kill*, and *Boomerang* were basically kitschy extensions of the Afro-Amazon persona she had created for herself. Models playing real people—even real models—were much more scarce. In the process, bad acting and bad modeling became confused. As Diana Ross's portrayal of a star model in *Mahogany* clearly proved, actresses generally made unconvincing models. Likewise, models possessed all the emotional realism of cardboard cut-outs. Intensified study and increased opportunities would go a long way in changing the quality of crossover performance of both groups.

Sheila Johnson

"You'd be surprised at the subtleties involved in acting and how deep they run," said Sheila Johnson in Los Angeles. "To become somebody else, to allow that other person to live inside of you, you have to be pretty clean and humble. If you've got Paris on your mind, and you've got those $2500 booking days cushioning you, then you're not available. It's a big step to say to yourself, If I'm going to be an actress, my *life* has to be an instrument."

Sheila had wanted to be an actress before she became a model. When she won a highly visible part in Eddie Murphy's film, *Coming to America*, she was even more determined to pursue her old dream. Although Shari Headley, a finalist in Ford's '84 model contest, won the plum romantic role, Sheila found auditioning for that film was an experience in itself.

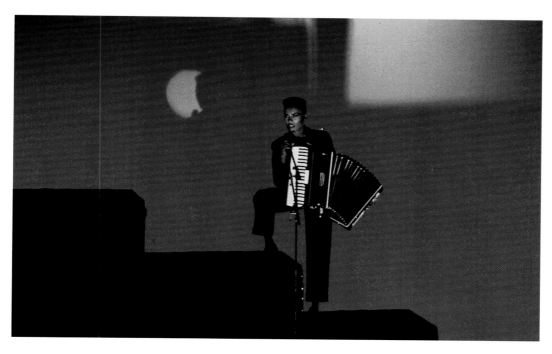

Grace Jones fashioned a visually extravagant persona: part disco diva, part she-man, all entertainer.

"The director, John Landis asked me, 'How much are you willing to show of your body?' I thought, Here we go again. I'm still being confronted with the same issue: What am I willing to do to get in? Landis offered me the role of the flower girl and then the role of a nude girl coming out of the water. And I said, 'Thank you anyway. It's really nice that you thought to offer me something.' Then I went home. Later my agent called me saying Landis decided that the king and queen needed a lady-in-waiting, and would I do it. My agent said, 'If you really want to break into the field, do this film.' I said I'd love to be the lady-in-waiting, even if she didn't speak a line. So it worked. Saying no for what you feel is OK. I'm proud to be a part of that. I felt really good.

"While we were shooting *Coming to America*, I wasn't just there on the set looking beautiful. Believe it or not, the pressure of being there and not saying anything, but being 100% present so that you're not a distraction, meant you still had to be in character. You had to create your own, because if you're not focused, if you're not with it, you're a total distraction. You're either blinking off or you're moving or fidgeting or something. I had to get that straight right away. That was hard to do, to be totally present without saying anything. It was all projection. For all the years I modeled I had the best experience in being totally present and saying nothing but saying everything.

"After seeing the movie I decided I really needed to commit myself. It was modeling that took me away from acting, so modeling had to be the thing that suffered now for me to do this. I decided I was just going to have to study, and I did. I was in a two-year program, heavy-duty theatrics, a serious commitment for two years.

"My acting teacher did something I really resented, and she did it because she saw something in me that I had not confronted. She said, 'No Black people have ever graduated from this school. They always cop out. They don't have the confidence level. You've got to get in touch with your Black anger. There's so much anger and rage there.' I thought, Why? Why did that have to be? It made me so angry. But it was cool. She saw that in me, the recognition of something that might not have been a part of my life. Making me question all this stuff in my head was the most fabulous thing."

Alva Chinn also wanted to pursue acting, although she candidly admitted that it was difficult for models to make the transition to full-blooded characters. Her explanation? "They're too busy looking at themselves. I hated looking at myself after I stopped modeling. I made sure I didn't look at myself for a long time.

"I've had actors who say to me that they don't see why I put myself through acting class. I really believe that without that pain there truly is no gain. Without delving deep into yourself, finding out what touches you, what affects you, what you can use from yourself, from your imagination.... If you don't know that,

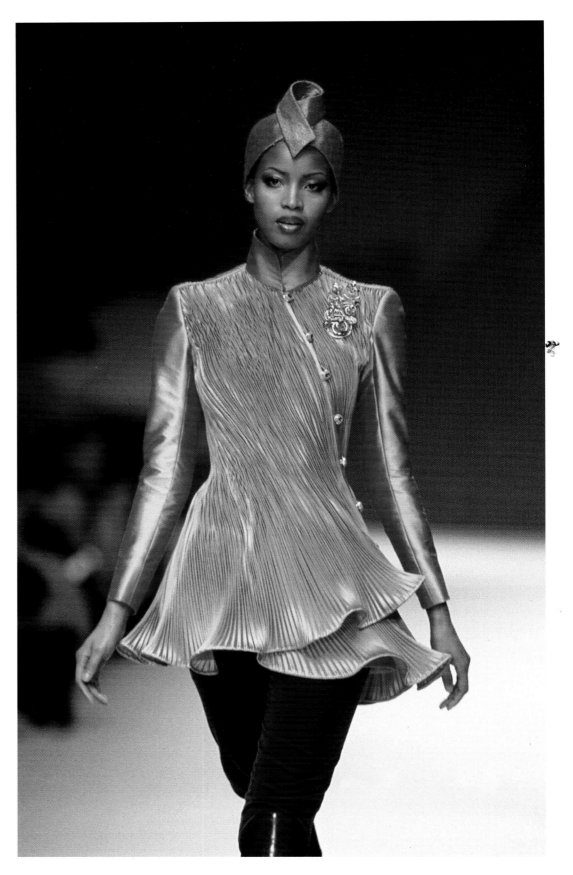

Georgiana played a leading role as a model in the 1994 comedy *Ready-to-Wear*.

what can you give to somebody else? Superficial stuff. Who needs that? It's all over the TV already. We don't need anymore of that. We need some substance. And in order to get to that you have to delve deep. The problem with modeling is that you don't use your mind. It needs stimulation, and if you haven't been stimulating it, it shows.

"Before I started modeling my interests were in theatre and poetry. Then I got caught up in modeling and my family. When I got divorced, I said if I don't go back to what I want to do, I'm going to regret this for the rest of my life. So I started with a coach in a small environment, and I saw not only did I have a facility for it, but I had a love, a passion. And I let my passion go. There are times when it's trying. I may not be where I want to be yet, but when I'm doing what I'm doing and it's working right, I am in my bliss."

A model's need to act, however, rarely coincided with opportunities to express this need. Feature films featuring Black women actors were not nearly numerous enough to make fullest use of the talents already available. Black models wanting to compete on Black actresses' turf found the going extra-rough. Their own brand of beauty was never enough. They had to bring something extra-special to the table. When singer Whitney Houston, who had enjoyed a brief career as model in the '80s, wanted to extend her chart-topping success to movies, she chose a musical vehicle originally designed for Diana Ross over a decade before. *The Bodyguard* resulted in another mediocre film—like Ross's *Mahogany*—with surprisingly spectacular box-office receipts.

The '90s had not changed one tradition much. A strategic link to influential men did not seem to hurt a Girl's career. Veronica Webb appeared in Spike Lee's 1991 move *Jungle Fever* at the same time that rumor mills pegged them as a social item. In 1995, Tyra Banks displayed her acting potential in a more full-bodied role in then-boyfriend John Singleton's *Higher Learning*. When TV stars Will Smith and Martin Lawrence made their leap into the Hollywood fast lane later that year with *Bad Boys*, they took Karen Alexander along for at least part of the ride.

One of the most opportune castings of Black models involved Robert Altman's comic muddle of fashion maniacs, *Ready-to-Wear* (*Prêt-à-Porter*). For the first time authentic Black models were playing themselves, or at least, a light-hearted parody thereof. And while the movie itself could be easily dismissed as superficial, it did provide an opportunity for fashion and models to be seen in the larger context of big-screen entertainment.

While the explosion of music videos gave some models an outlet on the small screen, television comedies and dramas also provided a hospitable environment for acting. Beverly Johnson co-starred in a number of TV movies. Shari Belafonte appeared for several seasons in the series *Hotel*. Toukie Smith did a stint on *227*, and the hit '80s classic, *The Cosby Show* afforded quite a few models the experience of walk-on parts. More recently, on the short-lived series *Models Inc.* Garcelle Beauvais stood out as the only real model in a cast of too-short California blondes. And Naomi Campbell, with sultry voice and attitude to match, had a repeat role on the mid-'90s urban drama, *New York Undercover*. In the future, television will undoubtedly become the major next-move medium for models evolving into actors.

Daphne Maxwell Reid

Daphne Maxwell Reid was one of the most visible examples of a model who made a successful transition into acting. She appeared for several years on the hit sit-com *The Fresh Prince of Bel-Air*, whose prime audience was certainly too young to know that she had been a pioneer during her generation of models. In fact, her career was studded with highlights for twenty-five years. In 1969, she was the first African American pictured on the cover of *Glamour* magazine. During the '70s she was one of many who suffered peaks and valleys in work due to wavering racial criteria. "One day in 1975," Daphne recalled, "I auditioned for two commercials: Johnson's floor wax and

Coke. As a result, I got two calls from my agency. One: 'They loved you, but they went ahead with a White model.' Two: 'They loved you, but you're not Black enough.' All this in one day! None of it affected me internally. It was no rejection of me. I was still the same person I was when I walked in there.

"I was self-supporting doing TV commercials, and I could help to support my family. But I was never one of the real money-making models. If you were not a star, modeling got boring. You'd put on Smiling Pose #14. I was just part of the utilitarian team.

"But then I went into radio. I was the first female rock jock on a 50,000 watt radio station in Chicago. I also did voice overs, so that the majority of my money was made off-camera. In 1978, I started in industrial films, and in 1979, I started acting.

"I auditioned for a TV show for Robert Conrad. He was also an alumnus of Northwestern, and he would call me 'Queenie' since I had been Homecoming Queen there. I got the part but it was just for the pilot. I thought I would try Hollywood. In L.A. I phoned Conrad again. This was late '79. I played a villain, an eighty-year-old woman, and I shot a couple of commercials. I thought I was in Hollywood heaven. I met Tim Reid that February. It was a re-introduction. We were supposed to have a five-minute date, but we ended up talking for five hours. We've been together ever since.

"Work started coming then. They were all small roles, but I worked more than most Black women. I haven't pursued feature films very hard because the TV field is much bigger. There are one hundred times the roles available. Still, there is a lot of political and racial stuff. You try to deal with it and fight it as much as you can."

When Daphne and the multi-talented Tim Reid debuted on *Frank's Place*, they caused a sensation among Black TV viewers. Set in a restaurant in New Orleans, the program was stylish in a non-stereotypical way, literate, witty, and populated by enjoyable characters who had not just stepped out of a cartoon. It was innovative television that did not tie a neat knot around the end of every half-hour segment. And it proved too good to last.

Daphne was undecided about her next move until *The Fresh Prince* came along to rescue her. Not that she needed to be rescued. "We had moved to a farm in Virginia where we were taking a year off from L.A. Tim allowed me that year to figure out what to do with the rest of my life. It was hard to decide what to do when you've been blessed with a gift all your life.

"What you see on the screen is pretty much who I am in reality. I enjoy show business tremendously, but I don't like its invasion into my real life. I'm passionate about my relationship, not about acting. I like to do too many different things to focus on one. I call it a blessed handicap."

Home Base

More of us want to be models and actresses than we want to be mothers.

Carol LaBrie

The transition made by most models and witnessed by the fewest outsiders was the move into family life. They became homemakers, wives, mothers, and all-purpose doers with little of the fanfare that accompanied their fashion careers but with a profound sense of personal satisfaction. Often they retained special, creative qualities. Their artistic side, perhaps somewhat neglected during their heyday, could resurface with mature vigor, as the paintings of Helen Williams and Jany Tomba attested. Their competitive drive might shift location from go-sees and auditions to horseback riding tournaments, as shown by Kari Page Selenow's trophies and blue ribbons. Their love of performance may be focused on an intimate family audience instead of mobs of fashion fans. Many models insisted that time spent with their spouse, children, and family was the most precious.

Speaking of her husband and daughter, Kari said, "I feel very blessed. I never took

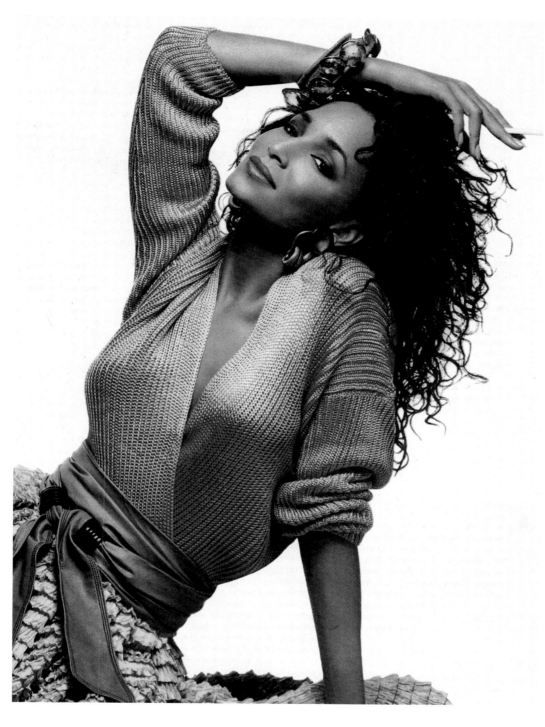

Sheila Johnson. Totally present, quietly expressive, subtly seductive.

my family for granted. Life, especially life in New York, has become too uncertain to take anything for granted."

"To me," said Carol LaBrie, "modeling was not that important. After I had my children, they were my main concern. I was very happy and am still very happy to be a housewife." Married to photographer Uli Rose for over twenty-five years, Carol enjoyed an open relationship with her five children. "I stay forever young because my children keep me young. The high living with the Rolls and the penthouse didn't do anything for me. Modeling was not my greatest joy. The things you have to put up with: other models, the long hours, the trips

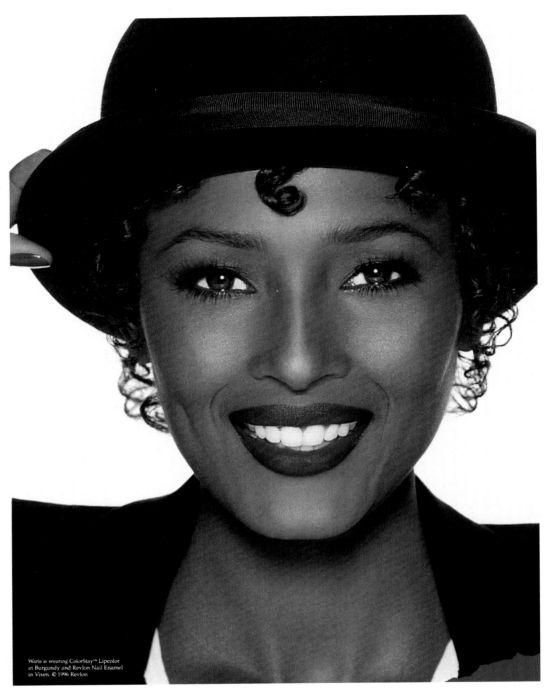

The triumphant smile of **Waris**. Brutally circumcised at age five in her native Somalia, she turned personal tragedy into a life-saving crusade, becoming the first Special Ambassador for the Elimination of Female Genital Mutilation for the United Nations Population Fund. In 1997, she gave birth to a son.

Waris is wearing ColorStay™ Lipcolor in Burgundy and Revlon Nail Enamel in Vixen. © 1996 Revlon

where you're lonely, all of the phoniness in people around you…. At the end of the day, you don't feel like you've done anything or accomplished anything. You looked beautiful for the person who hired you for that job, but you didn't do anything. You didn't help anyone. You helped yourself, and maybe not even that. All you've become is a vacuous, vain person who lives from one day to the next just to be pretty.

And when you're not, your life falls apart, and you fall apart. It happens to a lot of models unless you can do something else with yourself and go on to other things.

"As far as I'm concerned, being an actress is not going on to other things. It's the same thing, only on a different level. Many Girls who want to be actresses still want to be star models. They're addicted to stardom. And it seems that more of us want to be models and actresses than we want to be mothers.

"When you are a mother or if you work in a job, you can say, I've done something. Models have to have other goals and ideals, to do something and help other people. Be a role model. Be beautiful, be Black, but be what you are because you're beautiful as you are. Material things don't make you happy. I found my happiness. I'm living it now."

That serenity was not voiced by successful models only. Angela Baptiste, whose early attempts to become the model she had always wanted to be led to frustration and disappointment, echoed the same sentiments. After a stint teaching English in Japan, she returned to New York, where she settled down into a happy marriage, motherhood, and rewarding work as a fourth-grade teacher. "I love my life now," she said.

In the midst of a fast-paced career that combined dancing, acting, and modeling, Sherry Brewer married Edgar Bronfman, Jr., scion of the billionaire family that controlled Seagram's. At the time she wasn't looking to be rescued by wealth and romance. In fact, she said, "I think if I had been looking for it, it wouldn't have happened." Against his family's wishes they married, and Sherry retired from the business. Three children, several cities, and thirteen years later, they divorced. But she had no regrets about the choices she made regarding her family and career. "My life condition has been richer for all of that, the ups and downs, the pain and the goodness, the places that I have traveled to, the people that I've met.

"Modeling is one of the few industries where you can be a star whether you're qualified or not. I saw beautiful women used up and misused. I saw very painful things happen to beautiful, innocent, well-meaning dreams. With models, it's the drugs. With dancers, nervous breakdowns pursuing perfection in their craft. With actresses, the need to be with a certain type of man. I've seen all of that.

"I didn't buy into a lot of nonsense. I've always had normal friends. That keeps the balance. My children are fabulous. I like them in addition to loving them. I want them to know who they are and really embrace all that they are. I want them to have a good education so that they can appreciate their intelligence. I want them to know that beauty is not just an outside, visual appeal, that it comes from a very deep place inside."

One of the wealthiest Black women in America, Sherry Brewer Bronfman has been actively involved in the cultural life of New York City. A member of the board of the National Urban League and a conservator for the New York City Public Library, she was particularly effective in raising funds for the Dance Theatre of Harlem and the Schomburg Center for Research in Black Culture "My whole thing is to give something back to the community. If you're fortunate enough to have, then you have a responsibility to give back.

"At the end of the journey, I want to know who I am. I want to have some of myself left. There's a price to pay for everything, and the whole point is to hold on to those things that are important to you, to make sure that you maintain your substance. It's not about being perfect. We all make mistakes and wrong choices. But out of that has to come growth and depth, and also the ability to not be so judgmental and to be more compassionate. All the things that have happened that I find painful will make me a better woman, a stronger woman. And rather than become bitter about it, it's much more important for me to act in a positive manner, to be part of positive changes.

"There's an abundance of ignorance as to what Black people are about, who we are and what our capabilities are. The sooner we realize that our riches exist on many, many levels, the better off we are going to be. The thing is to set your own agenda and move forward no matter what, without limitations. I don't want anybody to put my children through any emotional blackmail because of who they are. I don't like people trying to put me into a category. Or making decisions about who I am or what my lifestyle or life conditions should be. Or what my opportunities should be or what I'm able to do or give. How dare they!"

Epilogue
Vision

Black beauty is the most inclusive on the planet. The extraordinary mixtures that have produced humankind though the centuries were nowhere more apparent than in the rich and unpredictable variety of women identified as Black models. Just as Black models helped expand the definition of beauty, they also helped explode the definition of race to the point of biological absurdity. For the growing number of people confronted by the limited choice to be either/or, race has become a more complex matter of cultural identification. Bloodlines flowed into newly-created territory, extending fertile deltas of experience and potential into old seas. And just as more kinds of Black women worked as models, more kinds of White, Asian, and Latin women did also. Yet to be seen, however, were the beautiful women of Native American heritage and other ethnic groups whose very existence often slipped beyond the margins of Western consciousness.

Against the persistent evil of racism and its shape-shifting subtleties, Black models have protested and prevailed for the past six decades. Through the '90s and into the next millennium they would continue to do so taking giant, newsworthy leaps as well as smaller, quieter steps. Though their complaints could seem to sound repetitive or unoriginal, models were never crossing the same river twice. The roster of women—their voices, accents, and experience—constantly changed, as did the circumstances in which they worked. But while statistical reports such as *Invisible People: The Depiction of Minorities in Magazine Ads and Catalogs* (1991) and its follow-up, *Still Invisible* (1992) showed pitifully small percentages of other-than-White models at work, optimism has proved to be a difficult disorder to cure.

The fact remained that racism was the disease, not optimism. And the inescapable fact was that by the turn of the century the American mainstream would include a greater percentage of people of color. Likewise, many European metropoles would host—willingly or not—more citizens of color from formerly colonized countries. The long view of history has shown us that even reluctant advertisers would eventually expand their marketing to include these majority minorities, and in the process employ an increased number of representative models.

In the face of resistance Black models offered their own tradition of polished defiance. "You've got to stand up," insisted Lu Sierra. "It's not going to get any better if you just keep quiet. Why should they change if everybody just takes it? There's no reason for them to change."

An example of this resistance was *Sports Illustrated* magazine, which for

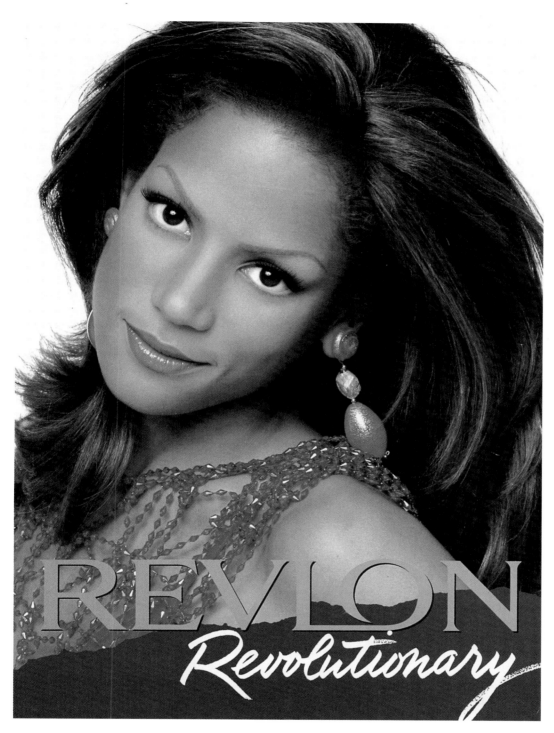

REVLON
Revolutionary

Veronica Webb, the first African American to sign a beauty contract, included a revealing account of her modeling career in her 1998 essay collection, *Veronica Webb Sight: Adventures in the Big City.*

thirty years published an annual swimsuit issue featuring models shot in provocative poses in exotic locales. Distributed during the colorless month of February, the scintillating special became one of this country's most popular sporting events with an estimated viewing audience of thirty million people. While *SI* regularly featured star athletes who were Black on its cover, it had never promoted a Black model to the cover of the swimsuit issue. In fact, Black models began to appear inside only in 1986.

The 1994 issue called its trio of White cover Girls "The Dream Team," which prompted Roshumba—one Black model used more often than any other in recent swimsuit issues—to ask the obvious: "Whose dream?" Presumably, Black people would have no dream in their own coloring. And apparently, Black, White, and Other men could not envision a Black woman beautiful enough to represent all women. Perhaps, though, this particular arena of sex and race was still so mined with fears and fantasies that it was deemed too dangerous to explore. After all, it took sixty-two years—from the first contest in 1921 to 1983—for a Black woman, albeit one with blue eyes and blond hair, to be crowned Miss America.

It takes time, say the old folks who have lived long enough to know. It also takes more than time; it takes pressure. On *Shades: The Dark Side of the Runway*, a 1993 cable documentary shown on BET and hosted by Roshumba, Gail O'Neill—another *SI* alumna—suggested that the athletes themselves could play a significant role in lobbying the magazine for a Black cover Girl. "We are a sleeping giant," said Gail, "if we don't make our voices heard."

Fortunately, voices were heard, and long-awaited changes were made. In 1997, Tyra Banks became the first Black model to appear on *SI*'s Cover. It was a landmark victory which signified an irreversible step in the right direction.

Tyra Banks

After Golden Girl Tyra Banks graduated from Immaculate Heart High School in Los Angeles, instead of proceeding directly to college to study film and television production as she had planned, she decided to see some of the world beyond the privileged enclave in which she was raised. She landed in hellfire. The Paris runways, always mined by competition, were particularly precarious in the early '90s, especially for the spotlight reserved for the One—and still only—Top Black Girl. Twenty-five shows during her premiere season proved she had not only style but stamina. A contract from Cover Girl soon afterward, a recurring role on a TV sitcom, and a starring role in a feature film soon after that proved that she could take care of serious business on more than one front.

By her own example, Tyra was determined to redefine the nature of a model's career. A Girl no longer simply modeled and then, in linear sequence, moved on to another life. As her movie character Deja declared in *Higher Learning*, "Use what you have to get what you want." Tyra had the tawny coloring, curvaceous sexuality, and hip, humorous attitude that put her in demand by designers, photographers, and directors. But what she wanted most was to be in command of her own professional future.

Having suffered the capriciousness of the catwalk early on, she said, "What I tell

Sebastian. She brought a daringly ambisextrous identity to fashion.

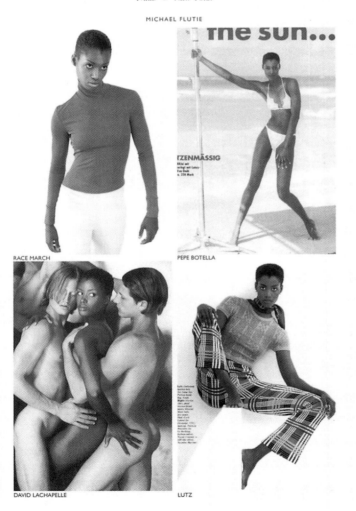

COMPANY

PARIS + NEW YORK

MICHAEL FLUTIE

RACE MARCH

DAVID LACHAPELLE

PEPE BOTELLA

LUTZ

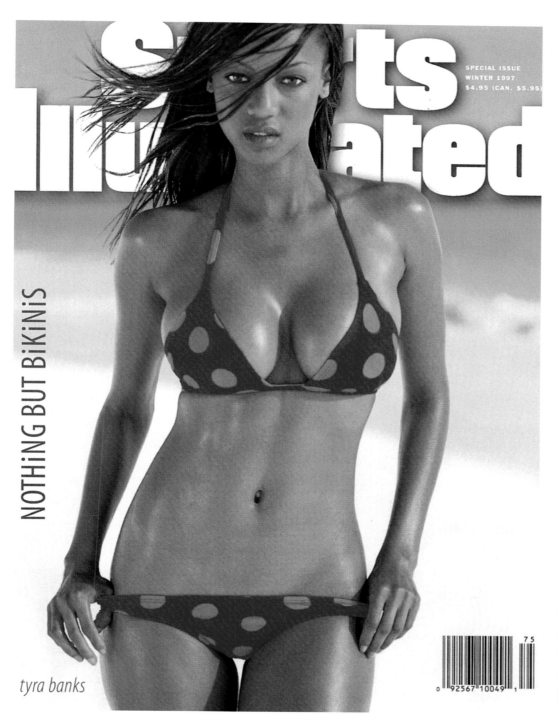

SPECIAL ISSUE
WINTER 1997
$4.95 (CAN. $5.95)

NOTHiNG BUT BiKiNiS

tyra banks

Tyra Banks made history as the first Black model on the cover of *Sports Illustrated*'s swimsuit issue. February, 1997. In 1998, she published a snappy guidebook, *Tyra's Beauty: Inside & Out.*

the other models is, Don't believe the hype. You'll be gone in a minute." Although she had broken editorial and commercial barriers—including the first cover of a Victoria's Secret catalog featuring a woman of color—in spectacular fashion within just a few short years, she, for one, did not intend to rest on her laurels or disappear when the Next New Girl arrived on the scene. She hired her mother, Carolyn London-Johnson, away from her job as a medical photographer for NASA to be her manager. She set up her own corporation, Ty Girl, to handle her business affairs. Rumors of romantic affairs, on the other hand, never seemed to tarnish her

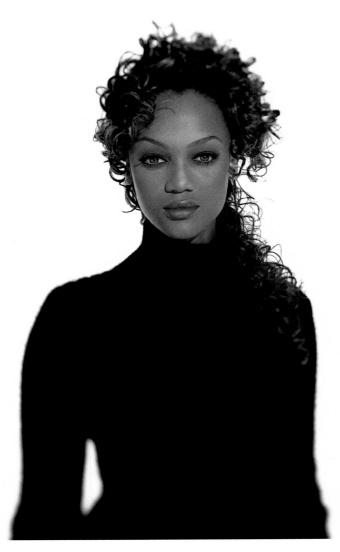

Tyra Banks. The simmering sensuality of the '90s Golden Girl.

the first Black model signed exclusively to the prestigious Ralph Lauren empire. His clean, dark, and distinctively African-Asian features, the perfect foil for the ultra-WASP casting of Polo productions, were shockingly beautiful in their appeal. "Tyson has an all-American look with a dramatic edge," said Lauren in the press announcement. "He conveys power, style and intelligence in a very exciting way."

Although Black male models have always been part of the business, even the most successful—including such durable stars as Mike Fields, Renauld White, and Rashid Silvera—earned far less in terms of income and prestige than their female counterparts. Certainly, no one group in American society was more deserving of an image overhaul. After being mired in decades of aberrant stereotypes—from Uncle Ben to the gangsta rapper and the glam drag queen—healthy Black men were slowly being pictured and appreciated in the fullest variety of their presence. It was a re-vision long overdue.

It was also a vision that sold. Daring casting earned increased dollars. One needed only to happen upon a Benetton ad to appreciate the original world-view that some advertisers were proud to sponsor. Other youth-oriented sportswear labels soon flaunted their carefully mixed crews across double-page spreads. They did so out of commitment to artistic invention and a democratic racial ideal. In this increasingly competitive market, however, they also did so out of commitment to a profitable bottom line.

The job of Black models, however, was not merely to sell products. They had a much higher calling. Ultimately, beautiful Black women and men became significant advertisers of the modern self. They sold the paramount fantasy: freedom. Fearless, questing, and self-defining, they embodied the modern spirit of challenge and survival. In their features, we read their ancestry; in their gestures, their aspirations. Every appearance before the camera or on the runway reinforced a personal pledge to confront the world on their own terms. Whatever their diverse and daily tactics, their strategy was to embrace defiance, even to delight in it in the most subtle

reputation. Not content to wait for calls, she wanted to call the shots herself, aiming to fulfill her pre-modeling dreams of writing, producing, and directing her own films while still at the height of a rewarding modeling career. It was a challenge others had attempted but few had realized. With a list of notable successes already behind her, however, she was poised to transform the future as she had the past.

Change could be torturously slow and awkward, or it could be breathtakingly sudden and graceful. Decades of hard-earned success for the Girls culminated in an unexpected breakthrough in 1995—for the Guys. Along came Tyson Beckford. Tyson became the first Black male model ever signed to a significant contract and

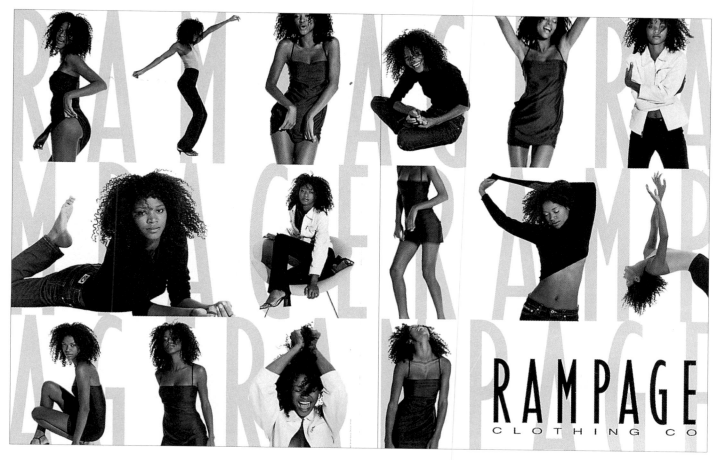

RAMPAGE

CLOTHING CO

ways, knowing that it was the only attitude which could not know defeat.

Naomi Campbell

When Naomi Campbell, wearing an outrageous pair of purple twelve-inch platforms, fell onto the runway during a Vivienne Westwood show, some spitefully eager tongues wagged that the fall was symbolic. Having been at the top of her profession for almost ten years, Naomi, they speculated, was long overdue for a crash. She had had a legendary beginning—discovered in London's Covent Garden at fifteen on her way to buy tap shoes—and seemed destined for a legendary end. But it would take more than a fashion show misstep to derail the most successful Black model of the decade.

In the pose of a guileless ingenue, she admitted that when she started she "didn't really know how to move like a model. I was just dancing around with the photographer Bill King," who booked her to shoot the Saint Laurent couture collection in Paris for French *Vogue*. Ads for Saint Laurent perfumes and clothes soon followed, as well as a resident apprenticeship chez Azzedine Alaïa. Trained in dance and drama, she loved to perform, and it showed in the expressiveness of her work. At the age of nineteen she became the first Black model to appear on the cover of American and French *Vogue* simultaneously.

Working primarily in the States and Europe, she eventually seduced the planet with an appealingly shy sexuality. She became an icon of the '90s, a brown-skinned, full-lipped, British-accented Black Girl accorded megamodel status at a time when fashion was at its finest. If she was living proof that modeling was integrated—at least visually—at the highest level, much of it was due to her own soft-spoken tenacity.

The secret of her longevity was, ironically, visible to all. Relentlessly, competitively fashionable, she reveled in contrasts. She was the acknowledged

Laura Bailey. Black models sold the paramount fantasy: freedom.

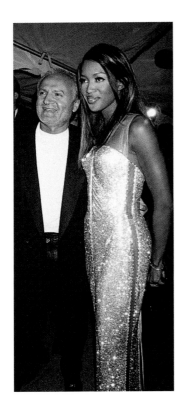

champion of reinvention in a business whose short-form vocabulary consisted of two words: new and next. What showed even more than the quantity of her work was its quality: the unexpected variety, spontaneity, and sheer fun of her many looks. Without any complicated, race-based apology, she seemed to change hair styles by the hour. She wore long, straight weaves, short, flippy wigs, blonde streaks, red streaks, and an attitude that declared, Accept me all the ways I am. She even wore blue and hazel contact lenses, shocking people with her untroubled ease in breaking convention. Perhaps her generation—she was born in 1970—had something to do with the freedom she insisted on. Perhaps the mix of African, European, and Asian in her Jamaican family was a factor. Perhaps overcoming childhood inferiorities influenced her also.

"I was chubby when I was younger. And I thought that models had to have thin lips. Sometimes I think I'm pretty now, but I don't think that I'm beautiful. I don't mind my lips, but the part that I like best about me is my shoulders. I think I have good bones. I like myself better now, but early on when I worked in London there were some jobs that would make me look stereotypically Black. One photographer actually put me in a maid's outfit. I didn't like it, and my mother was so mad. In London, they're not into making you beautiful. It's more about being trendy. It's in Paris and New York that they make you more beautiful and glamorous."

New York was a challenge for the teenaged newcomer. "In general, people in London get the wrong concept. They all think that if you walk down the street, you're going to be mugged. They all think it's too dangerous, and when I first came that's what I thought, too. But I loved it." After living under the protective eye of Eileen and Jerry Ford for a short while, she moved in with another model and then out on her own.

With experience and success came the inevitability of change. As a sought-after working girl intent on "becoming more ladylike" in her private life, she also began to move into the arena of public personalities. Famous boyfriends drew her

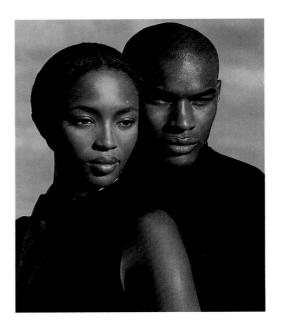

into their spotlight where, nearly always silent, she seemed to shine even more brightly than on the catwalk. She knew her P.R. value. "If I walk into a restaurant and I'm the only Black woman there, I take advantage of it," she insisted, "by dressing up and walking tall and acting snobbish and putting on my British accent, very strong."

Not everyone was charmed, however. She was the subject of an industry brouhaha when her elite agency announced in a press release that it refused to represent her any longer because of "abuse...imposed on our staff and clients." Whether factual or invented, gossipy news stories kept her name on the A list. When a big media splash showed her opening the Fashion Cafe in Rockefeller Center with superstars Elle Macpherson and Claudia Schiffer, no one was misled into thinking she was an actual owner. It was the concept of models as savvy businesswomen, expanding beyond fashion into the wider world of entertainment, that caught one's attention.

Naomi respected the lineage of great models who preceded her and was determined to leave her own legacy. "When I look at Iman and Beverly Johnson and Naomi Sims and Peggy Dillard, and all the others, I appreciate the fact that they opened the door for me. If they had not come before, I would never be as far along as I am now. And I hope that I'm opening the door for people who're behind me. It's gotten better. It's getting better. People take note of what you've done and give you that courage to go on. You have to show that we have the quality, too, that we can be out there as much as the White model can. And you have to let Black people see that, because a lot of them think it's impossible."

Undeniably ambitious for a performing career, Naomi claimed that she also hoped to make marriage and children a part of her life. As yet, acting and recording have not come close to competing with fashion for her time, and no one man has monopolized her affections to the point of marriage. "I want to be a big star. I'm not scared. And I don't want to rush it."

Those who want to rush her off the runway might just have to settle back and wait a while longer.

Whether models knew it or not, the vision they presented us with was complex and far-reaching. There was a wonderful variation on an old theme that said, When the going gets tough, the tough go shopping. Shopping was doing what war, politics, religion, and all the best intentions in the world could not do: bring people together. In our march toward the global mall, toward a truly interactive world culture, people all over the planet were destroying tired, artificial barriers and outdated, unrealistic images. At the same time they were replacing them with images, ideas, and attitudes more consistent with a multi-racial, freedom-loving, and economically egalitarian world.

In their own way, Black models were major agents of this change. It was understood that Black women as a group have been oppressed for so long that if they could achieve something seemingly impossible, then anyone anywhere could. Their presence was fortifying, their beauty, inspirational. They were proud of themselves, their bodies and spirits. Loving the freedom to choose, their hair was often the head's testing ground, and their bodies, likewise, a proving ground where clothing cultures could mix, clash, and mate. They were a sight, some of the ancestors might say, but they were also a vision.

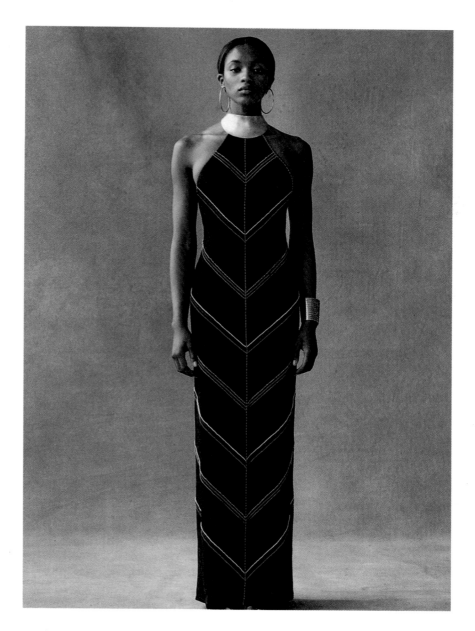

In the old age, black was not counted fair
Or if it were, it bore not beauty's name;
But now is black beauty's successful heir.
William Shakespeare

When William Shakespeare wrote these lines in "Sonnet to a Dark Lady" at the end of the 16th century, he was being idealistic. Four hundred years later, the Black woman, the Dark Lady, still struggled for her rightful inheritance, to bear beauty's name. It was in this struggle that Black models developed the qualities that made beauty so much more than skin deep.

Naomi Campbell. The Masai theme of **Ralph Lauren**'s 1997 collection brought African styling to fashion's forefront once again.

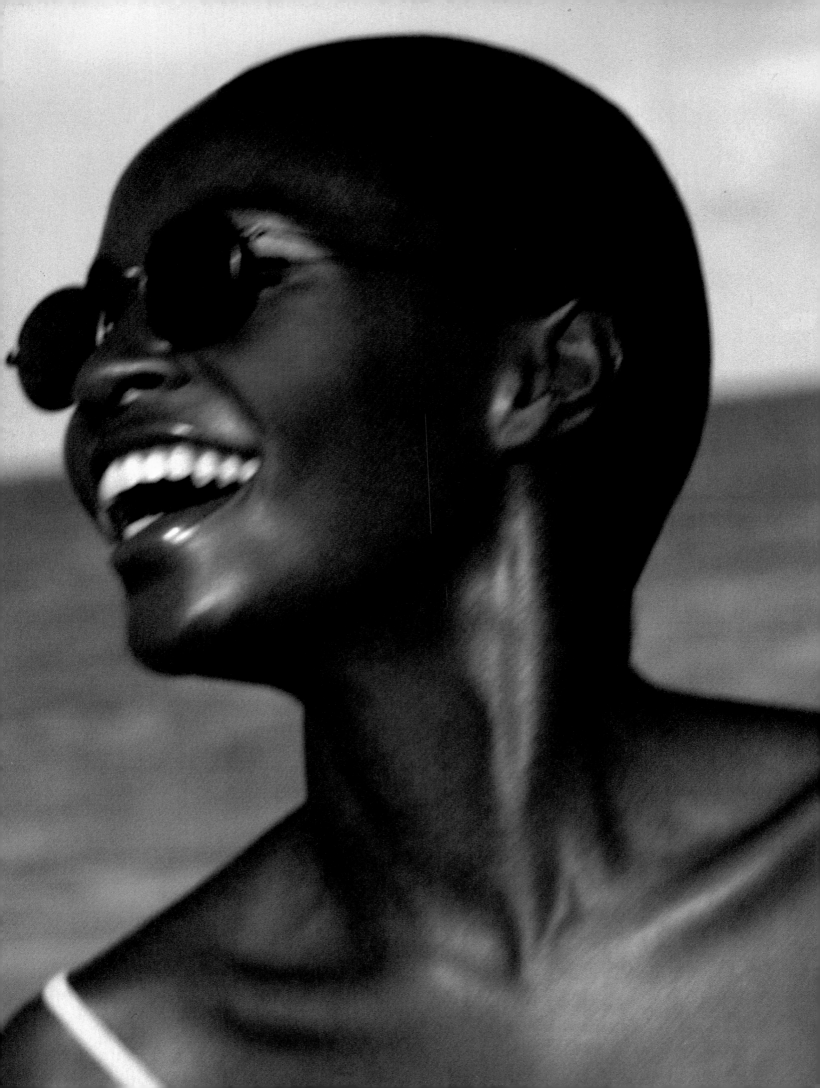

PORTFOLIO

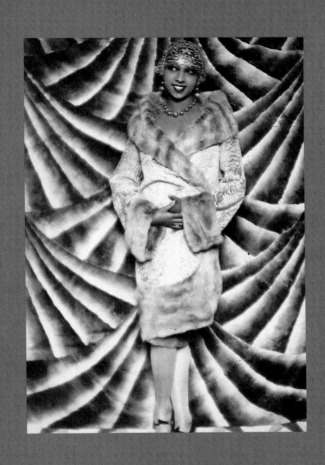

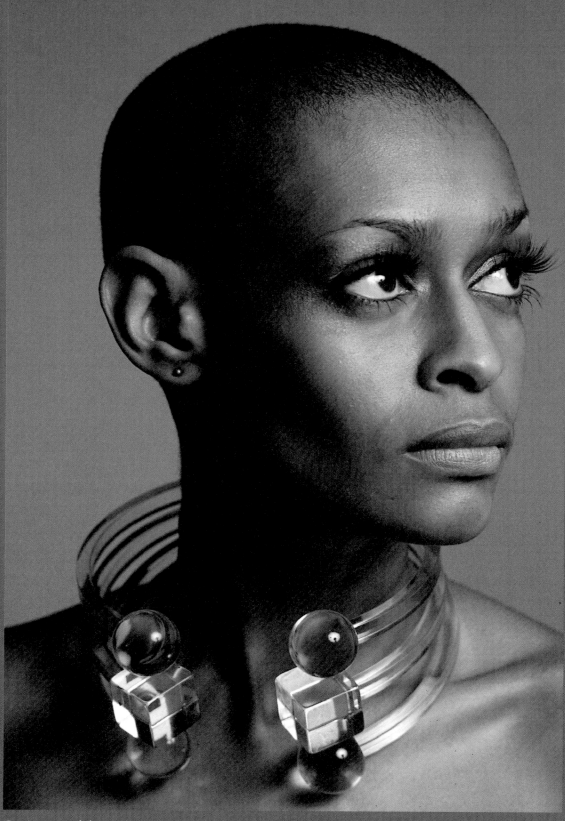

Previous page left: **Kiara**;
right: **Josephine Baker**
above: **Pat Evans**; right:
Georgiana.

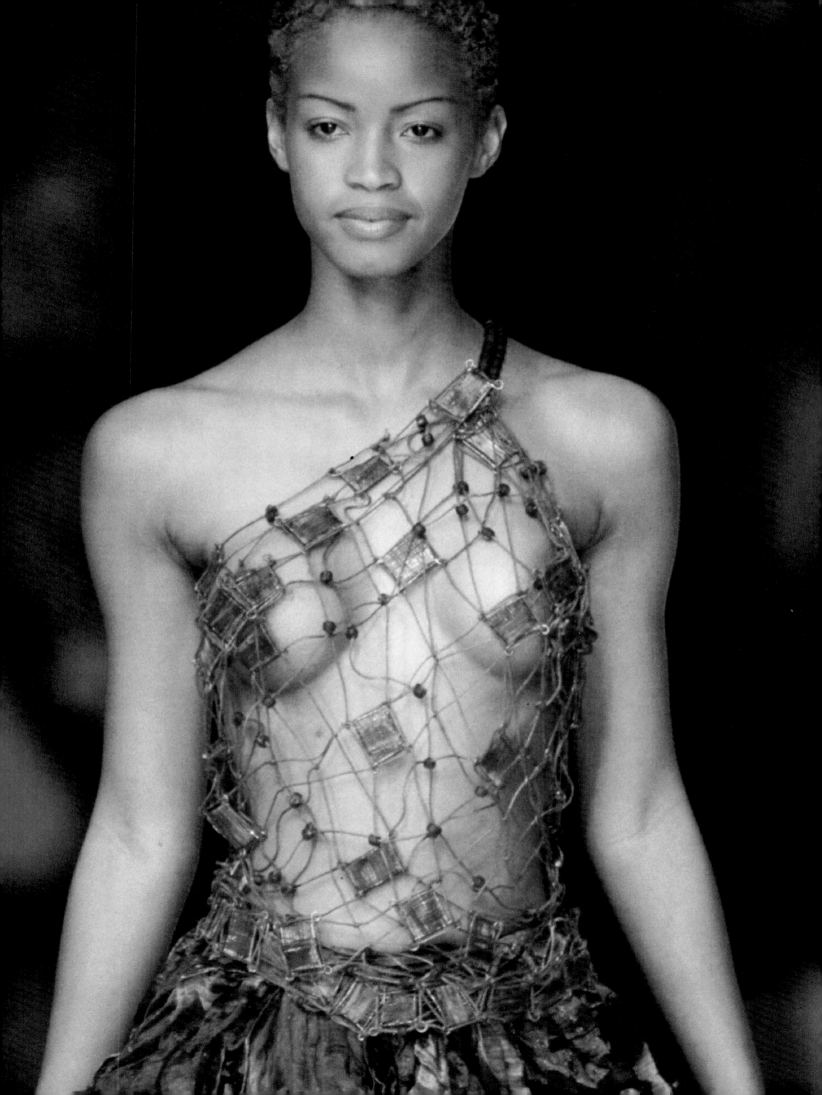

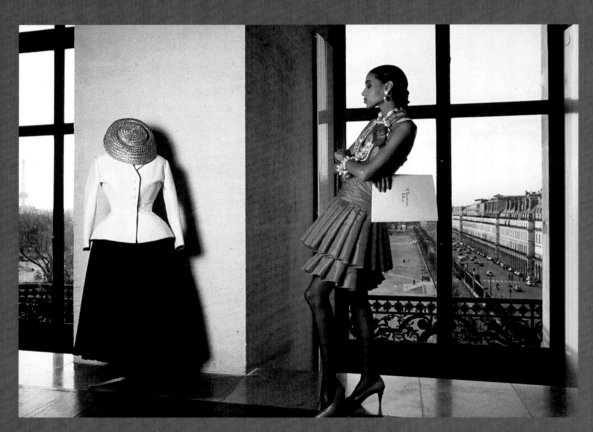

Above: **Sonia Cole** on the
40th anniversary of **Dior**'s
New Look of 1947; right:
Khadija for **Yves Saint
Laurent** Beauté.

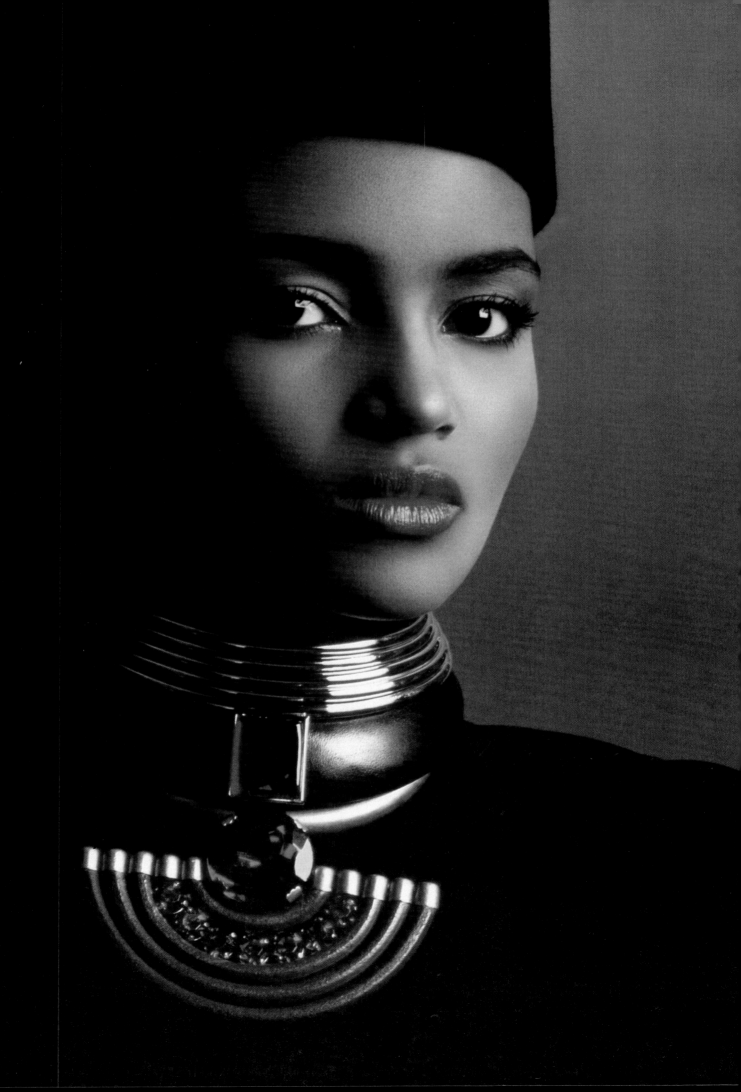

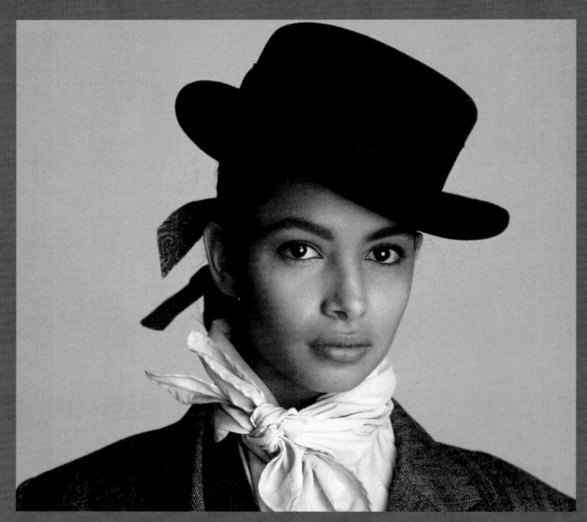

Above: **Kara Young**;
right: **Naomi Campbell**;
following page: **Waris**.

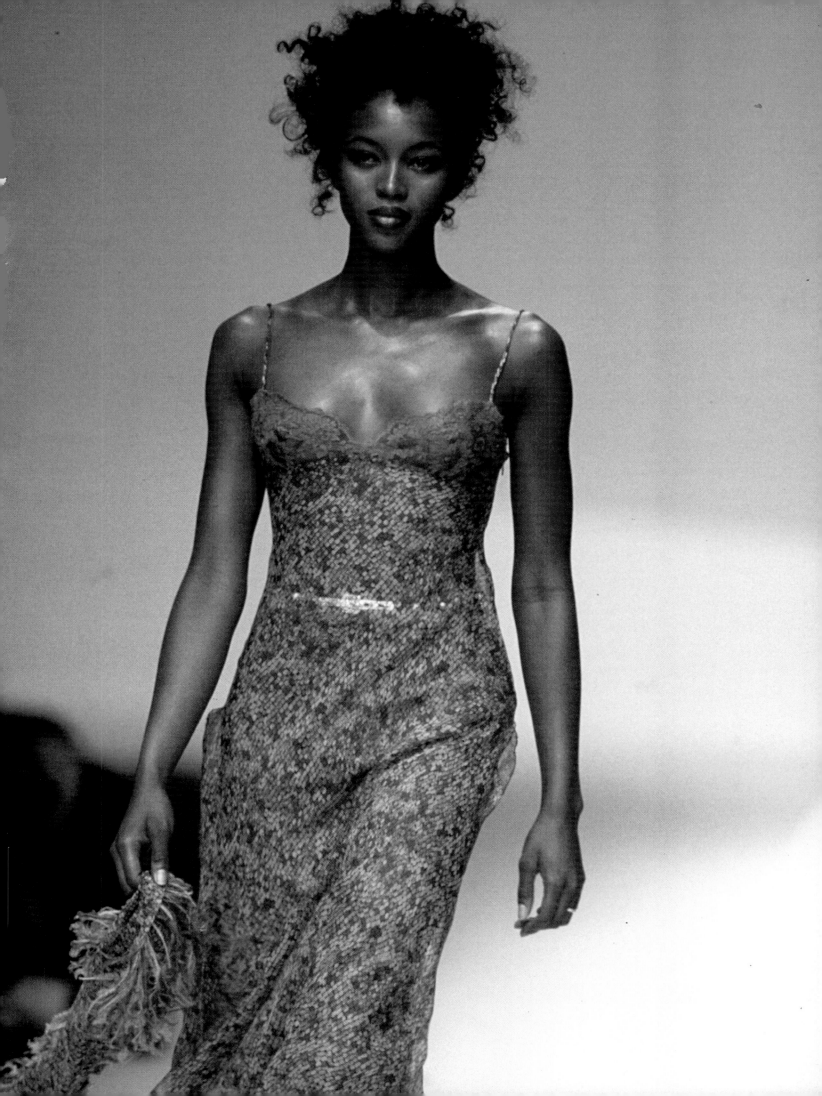

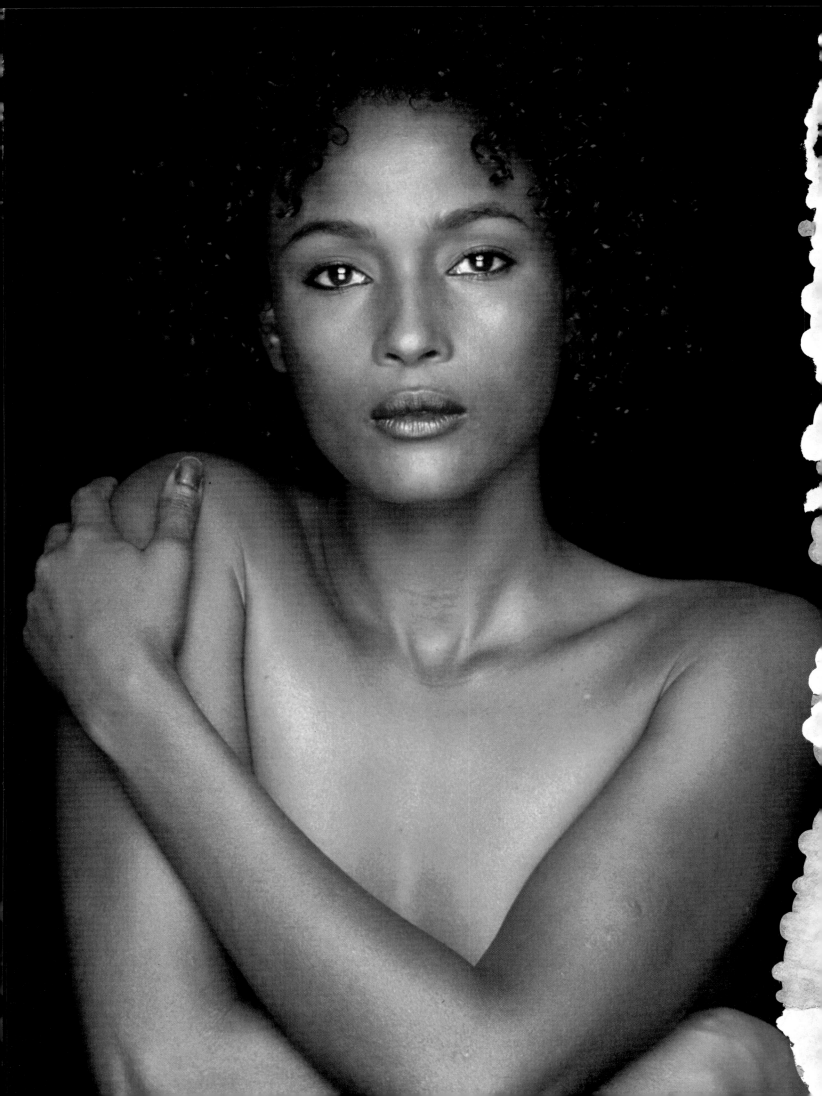

Book

2

CLOSE-UPS

I still look at a sheet of contacts for
the unplanned, unpremeditated revelation.

Alexander Liberman

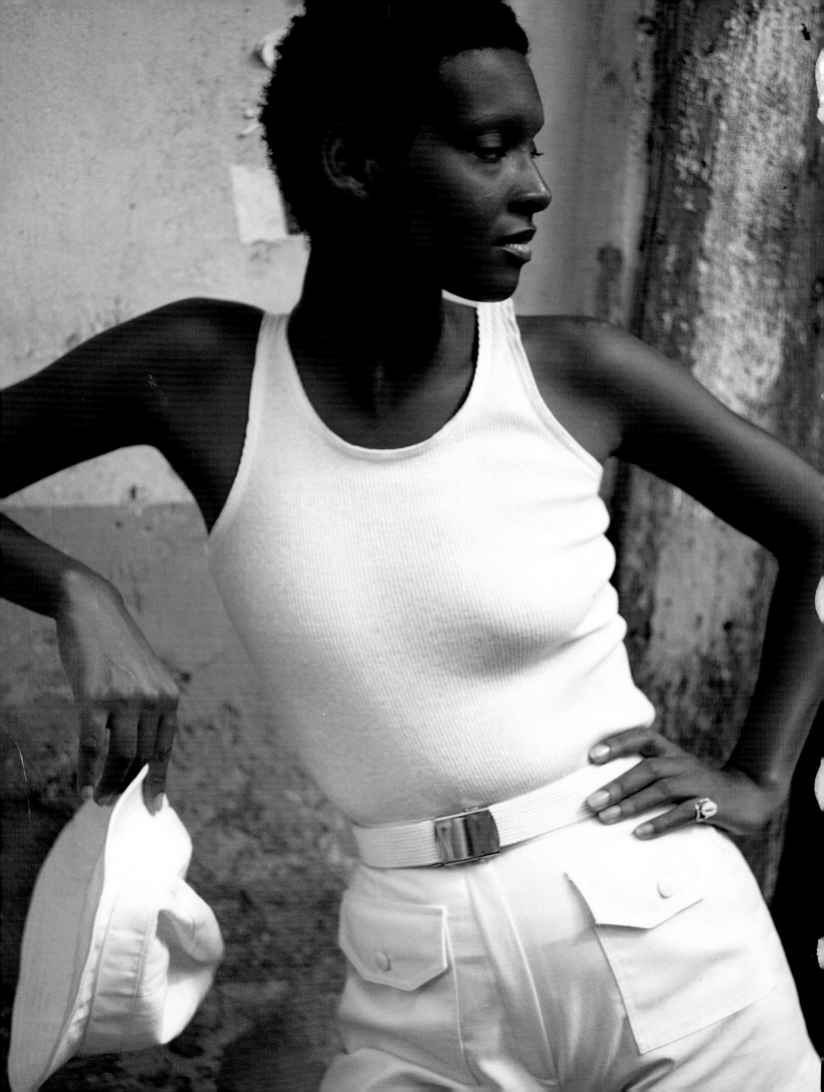

Self-Portrait

Everybody wants to model. At some time, at some secretly vain moment, we all sneak a peek at the thought: I could do that. I could look like that, or wear that, or be that. We try to convince the mirror: Why not me? In our hyper-visual society it seems as if the desire to be *seen* as beautiful is stronger than the desire to *be* beautiful. Magazines, television, and movies show not only that the camera can lie, but also that we expect it to. Art improves on Nature, and in our vanity, Smart improves on Art.

The worldwide cosmetics industry and the dramatic upsurge in plastic surgery, diets, and exercise programs are only the tip-of-the-iceberg evidence of our intense desire to change, to refashion our face and reshape our body. If we can look like the women in the fashion magazines whose personal gloss seems to come through even on the paper, if we can look like those women smiling, strolling, lounging, and owning—but rarely working in—the world, we can be those women. And sometimes, if we are young enough to dream and strong enough to act on the dream, we actually try to become that dream image, a model.

Of the many called few are chosen. I was one of the few, and my career took me by surprise as much as it did everyone else.

Born and raised in New England, I was a Black woman with an upper-middle-class education, lower-class bank book, and artistically vague pretensions. My father, a native of Charleston, South Carolina, was a graduate of Palmer Memorial Institute and Morehouse College, bastions of proper Southern Negro society. His well-exercised sense of humor invented romantic origins for his forename Don Alphonso, claiming descent from a Spanish grandee. My mother, Lucy Cooper, a graduate of New York City's Hunter College, when it was a prestigious all-women's school, met my father in the early '40s while doing graduate study at the Atlanta University School of Social Work. As young people, my parents made a charming, handsome couple. He teased her mercilessly about being born in Greenville, Mississippi, where, supposedly, people didn't have shoes or know how to wear them even if they did. And she eased him out of zoot suits and conked hair into respectable domesticity. In my parents' four daughters and the at-last-but-not-least son, they instilled the time-proven concepts of pride, progress, and twice-as-good-as.

Although they were both pioneering professionals, my parents were also the first artists I knew. My father was a musician and my mother, a poet. From them I assumed a hands-on right to art, truth, and beauty, although not to personal beauty because I was born with an embarrassing birthmark on my face. Attitude was also something of an obstacle. I was too impertiment to ever be considered cute.

After undergraduate studies at the University of Pennsylvania and graduate work at

My first location trip, to Puerto Rico for *Mademoiselle.* Modeling—and my own wanderlust—took me aound the world.

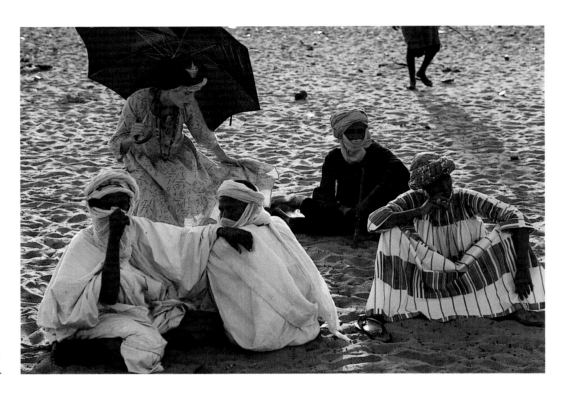

Abidjan, Ivory Coast. Identity issues: The cattlemen wanted to know who I was, where I was from, and what language I spoke—what African language.

Yale, and after a few years spent wandering through the '60s — in Paris, Puerto Rico, and Haiti—I was back in the U.S. teaching French and bunking with my young son Kimson on my sister Dona's couch in her apartment on the campus of Columbia University. Another sister, Sandy Head, was an associate fashion editor at *Mademoiselle* magazine and one of the very few Black people on the editorial staff of the many Condé Nast publications, which were, with the exception of *Harper's Bazaar*, the best of the fashion press: *Vogue, Glamour, Mademoiselle, Bride's,* and later, *Self.* In the fall of 1972, *Mademoiselle* was doing a story—a photographic spread—on clothes for working women. As a French teacher at Medgar Evers College, I certainly qualified as a working woman, but just as certainly, I wasn't a model and had no aspirations to be one. Sandy convinced me out of my doubts and into the world of fashion.

My first job with *Mademoiselle* was with photographer Gösta Peterson. The setting: a walking tour of the newly developing art/loft community in lower Manhattan called SoHo. Gus was a handsome, craggy-faced Swede with a crusty sense of humor who liked his fashion shots to have graphic, almost architectural elements to them. I did not know a fashion shot from a snap shot, and I knew nothing about modeling. Why should I? How could I? Even though I had lived in the fashion capital of the world, Paris, for three years, my budget nixed extravagant clothes, costly cosmetics, complicated hairstyles, and sophisticated attitudes. My privileged income from a John Hay Whitney Opportunity (how I hated that condescending term) Fellowship was all of $200 a month. My wardrobe consisted of jeans, my social life cafés and smoky jazz clubs. I'd lived through the strikes, marches, and all-night barricades of the May Revolution in '68. I had seen Paris burning and Panthers preaching at the Sorbonne. I wrote and lived on fried potatoes, fried bread, and two-franc (40¢) meals at the university restaurants. Models were as alien as Martians to me.

On my first job—in New York as a working woman—all I could do was wear the clothes and smile. Walk through the grimy but high-priced streets, look natural, and smile. A smile was my facial camouflage. Fear, doubt, and other unnamable internal dramas disappeared behind a wide, white shine of teeth.

Somehow I got through that drizzly, hectic day and was invited to do a second job with *Mademoiselle* on location in Puerto Rico. I hesitated, nervous about wearing bathing suits. I had stretch marks from my pregnancy, so bikinis were out. My hair was very short and very curly, so I didn't have the dread of water that plagues many Black women. But I barely wore makeup—even after that first shoot—and I still had that birthmark on my face. I did wear glasses, and I still didn't know how to pose. Near-sighted and natural were my middle names. Again, Sandy persuaded me to go. Once there I felt lucky. I was having fun and getting paid.

When my first pictures came out in the magazine a few months later, it was time to get serious. Fashion editor Nonnie Moore and one of her chief associates, Harriet Cain, encouraged me to consider modeling for a year or two. They made an appointment for me to see Eileen Ford, the head of the biggest and best model agency in New York — and thus, the world. Nothing, or perhaps, everything had prepared me for the day I first met Eileen.

In the most quotable and least libelous term, Eileen Ford was said to be "a character" by those in the business. It was instructive to see how dragons—and dragon ladies—were not as frightening in person as they were in the imagination. Eileen was of medium height, with short sandy hair and a quick no-nonsense tongue. I was 5'8½" tall, vegetarian thin, my hair boyishly short. I was new, and I looked it. But I had two sets of tear sheets—pages torn—from *Mademoiselle*. Somebody had shown that they liked me. Eileen sat me down, looked at my pictures, and asked my age. I shaved four years off and said I was twenty-four. We talked about my background. Paris piqued her curiosity, and immediately she began speaking to me in French. Never before had I experienced the instantaneous and intense snob appeal associated with speaking French. She spoke well. Certainly her experiences recruiting Girls in Europe had helped. But I, even caught by surprise, spoke much better. It seemed that whatever doubts she had about who and what I was began to fade.

I began to relax. Yet after a few more minutes of strategic chitchat, she shook her head and announced she was sorry but there was no work for Black models. I started for the door, my senses numb. I thought to myself, What else was new? I was asking, not begging. I was already working. I did not need a job. I was quietly on my way out. But before I left, she said to wait; she'd see what she could do. Still too numb to feel, I could see that my foot was in the door. On the other side lay a world I knew next to nothing about.

The people, the attitudes, even the language were strange. Girls went on go-sees. I understood about "Girls", but "go-sees"? I quickly learned that when your booker—in effect, your secretary, the person who arranges a model's schedule—called you at eightthirty in the morning or five-thirty in the evening, it was to give you different kinds of appointments. The most basic were go-sees where you literally had to go to see photographers in their studios, model editors at magazine offices, casting directors at advertising agencies, stylists at catalogue studios: any of the hundreds of people who needed to know your face, body, and personality, the better to consider you for potential jobs. Sometimes the go-sees were requests for you as an individual. Other times they were "cattle calls" where masses of models showed up at the same time for one, two or a mere handful of jobs.

Magazines, like pattern companies, department stores, and catalogs, "booked bodies for fittings in the closet." Translated, that meant that in a sizable, mirrored wardrobe room Girls undressed and tried on clothes being considered for photography. The creative core of magazines was each issue's portfolio of fashion stories—what's new, seasonable, catchy, necessary—called "editorials." Editorials had nothing to do with expressing intellectual opinion and everything to do with selecting the right designer's or manufacturer's garment for that month's fashion statement.

But, no jumping to conclusions. I quickly learned that magazines were in a different class from commercial jobs. Bookings at fashion magazines, often exciting and time-consuming, did not pay the regular big-buck commercial rates. An all-day booking at editorial rate often amounted to less than $200. (Less exalted, so-called family or shelter magazines paid close to full commercial rate, however.) Compensation was valued on a less strictly material level. Magazine tear sheets gave you national and international exposure, the kind of insider positioning that provided better access to the most prestigious and the most lucrative, full-rate-plus-bonus jobs. If a magazine showed that it liked you as a model by spreading your pictures over several pages and through several issues, other professionals got the message that you were interesting, new, hot—the one to hire. Photographers, hairdressers, and makeup artists who worked editorial shoots also wanted to—or did—work the real-money jobs. As you began to know people, you began to be known. And if you were lucky, you began to work a lot. I was lucky.

In my day—starting in the mid-'70s—the model look was clean, simple, and quietly rich. This was the period after girdles, false lashes, and white gloves, but before shoulder pads, Lycra, and ubiquitous designer labels. The Girls wore jeans to work, big diamonds in their ears and sometimes on their fingers, carried real Vuitton bags, and liked their job. What was there not to like? You could make in one day what most people—let alone working women—did not earn in a week. Whether it was $60 an hour/$400 a day when I started, or $250 an hour/$2,500 a day many average Girls earned twenty years later, the money was sweet. And it was extra-sweet to me. I needed it. I saved it, found an apartment for myself and my son, and started living the life of a progressive, culturally conscious New Yorker. I left teaching with few regrets.

Although there were a number of Black models when I started, it was nothing like the numbers today. As a matter of casting survival you had to know what category you fit in. I was the average, pretty, caramel-colored Black woman, intelligent looking, daring enough to wear my hair short and natural, tending toward the ethnic or untraditional mix in style, who happened to live well, but unpretentiously, next door. And I was a print Girl.

Many of the Black models of this period were outstanding on the runway, and this made for another division—and unspoken class distinction—in the profession. There were the slightly higher-class print Girls for photography and the slightly lower-class runway Girls for fashion shows. Few models were equally successful in both fields, and since designers had not exploded into the phenomenon they are today, few models aspired to succeed in both. Black Girls, however, tended to be shunted to the show side of the fashion business.

I did only a few shows. I did not consider myself glamorous or dramatic enough for the exuberant elegance of the runway. You had to have charisma combined with sure-footed improvisational techniques in order to present designers' creations at their best. On the runway I felt exposed and insecure before a lively critical audience expecting some kind of performance. I was more at home one-on-one, with the emotional subtleties of the camera.

My favorite work experiences were on location. Trips to Guatemala, Ireland, Jamaica, and Japan were especially enriching and personally rewarding. I went with high hopes to the Ivory Coast—my first trip to Black Africa—with *Mademoiselle*. It was not easy. I felt torn between my desire to do a good job for the American White people—now my friends—I was working with and my idealized need to feel some kind of connection with the African Black people—my people but strangers—there.

I remember one shot in which I wore a big cotton dress, printed in the colorful geometrics of Marimekko design. My head was wrapped in some similar fabric. I was to sit among a group of herdsmen in a huge stockyard at the edge of Abidjan. Gus Peterson, by now my guru, was setting up an island of fashionable tranquillity in a dust-driven sea of braying cattle and curious, photogenic African men. Where did I come from, they wanted to know. Was I Gus's wife? If not, where was my husband? They wanted to know what language I spoke. Was I not conversing with them in French? Didn't they know that Americans spoke English and that it was already unusual enough for me to speak French? I was laughing. They were laughing. But not at the same things. By language, they meant African language. They meant identity, family, history, culture. They said I looked Peul or Fulani or as if I could belong to several other ethnic groups. I was glad I could "belong"

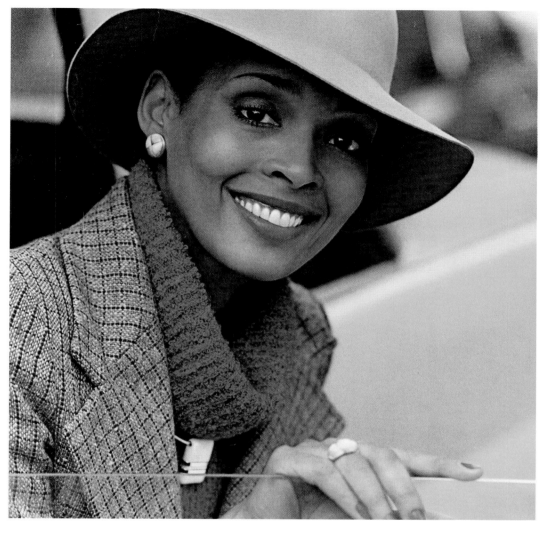

Shooting beauty ads—like this one for Avon—was great fun, especially since I never looked like that in real life.

and also relieved that I did not have to choose.

Modeling took me regularly to less foreign, but no less exotic places: Florida, California, Puerto Rico, and the Virgin Islands. Magazines, department stores, and mail-order catalog all loved the clear, sunny weather and easy lifestyle that made shooting outdoors in these locations less problematic than New York City. Those were the best of times.

The worst of times involved the monotony of catalog work shot in the studio. Poses became routine, nearly robotic. Smiles became phony and careless; other expressions, vacant and unconvincing. Boredom crept in with the bucks, and before you realized it, bright and easy-going young women became egocentric prima donnas, arriving late or unprepared, disrupting the precarious equilibrium of spontaneity and discipline necessary for a good shoot. The wise Girls simply shut up.

I tried to be wise. I had more education and life experience than many people I met and worked with in the business. But I wasn't hired for what I knew in my head. I was hired for what showed on my face. I could let none of my personal anxieties surface, and yet there were times when it was unavoidable. After all, I was a woman who was proud to be a parent in a business where being a real-life mother still clashed with the fantasy image of being a model.

One winter morning Kim woke up with a cold and a nasty nosebleed. The more I cleaned away scarifying clots of blood and mucus, the more blood gushed over his face. I

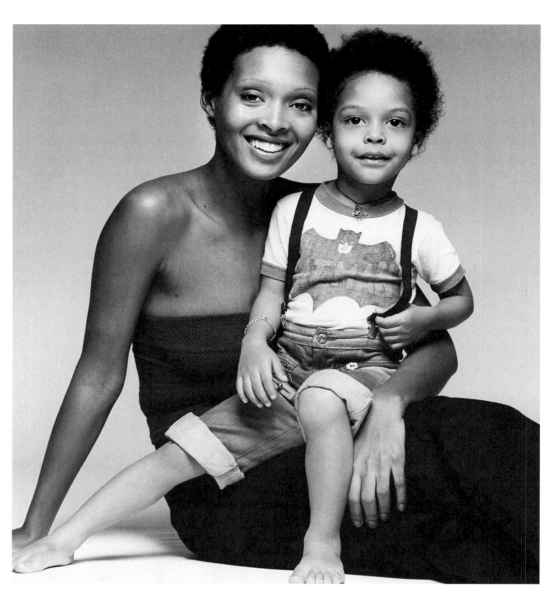

Shot for a Christmas special honoring models and their children, this portrait of **Kimson** and me was displayed in the window of Charles of the Ritz on Park Avenue.

was terrified that my baby was bleeding to death before my very eyes. At the same time, I knew I had to be at work shortly—on location, away from a studio and phone—and my sitter was late.

On the verge of panic, I bundled Kim up in a quilt, left a note for Lucetta, grabbed my purse, ran out onto West End Avenue carrying my child, snatched a business-suited White woman out of the cab she had just entered, and ordered the driver to St. Luke's Emergency Room. He made a screeching U-turn, and we arrived in a flash. Minutes later, a doctor cleaned Kim up and calmly diagnosed the effects of bad cold. "Nothing serious," he kept repeating while Kim seemed to recover instantly. "We see it all the time."

But I had never seen so much blood and felt such terror before. By the time I arrived at my booking my nerves were frazzled, and my eyes were puffy and bloodshot. The photographer was understanding, and we did get the job done, but I'm sure the retouchers had a lot of work to do on that picture.

Black models, like most ambitious Black people in White America, had to prove themselves to be twice as good as their professional peers in order to be treated half as well. The proof was in the paycheck. The top-quality Girls, regardless of color, all had the same hourly or daily rate. What varied was how many hours or days you were booked. I went often on location for one-day bookings, leaving New York in the late afternoon, arriving in Miami, Los Angeles or St. Thomas at night, ready to start shooting early the next morning, and wrapping up at four or five in the afternoon, just in time for me to catch a flight back to New York. The White Girls on the job were booked perhaps six or seven days to my one or two. It was humiliating to see such a disparity and annoying to have to do three times as many garments as the other models because I was there only a fraction of the time.

To add insult to injury, catalogs often used smaller pictures of Black models in the least appealing outfits or placed them strategically in the "gutter," that evocative place name for the center crease that separates one page from another. It was always the least interesting—and least influential—page position because the reader, the potential customer, rarely got a total, undistorted view simply by nature of the binding process. It was surprising to see how often pictures of Black models fell into the gutter—and still do.

Nevertheless, being a Black woman in the modeling profession was far from being a constant tale of misery and woe. The truth is that modeling was tremendous fun. It took me some time to learn to accept that, and more importantly, to enjoy it. Smiling, even as a pose, had a curious effect. The body began to relax. The spirit began to lighten. As the photographer sent a constant stream of "beautiful...fabulous...perfect...yes..." to the model, a kind of dual hypnosis sets in. Both aspired to that moment when—"yes, yes"— the body was moving gracefully, the face was divinely alive, the camera was clicking, and the potential for perfection reached its climax with: "We got the shot." It was an inspired synergy that gave me a valued sense of accomplishment and empowerment, which kept real smiles on my face. I was having fun. I was happy.

One of the most contradictory experiences of my career centered around a ten-day location job in Ireland for a respected department store in Washington, D.C. This took place in the late '70s. We were a rather large crew doing a harried cross-country tour, shooting in historic castles and manor houses and also in picturesque outdoor settings. Alongside the highway in one lush spot I saw a huge billboard picturing a row of tall brown bottles of Guinness Stout, the strong dark beer that was the national drink and a nationalized industry. Its advertising slogan was a three-word knockout: "Black is beautiful." I had to laugh. A political slogan that had terrorized White America only ten years earlier with its threat of revolution had immigrated to the Emerald Isle disguised as peaceful, commercial publicity. Irony had come full circle. It was obvious that Black people's struggle for civil rights within the United States had made an impact world-wide.

The trip was a good one even though we were rushed and tired, and our faces in the resulting catalog showed it. Its epilogue, however, left a bitter aftertaste. Upon our return from Ireland a few interior shots still remained to be done. A suite was booked at the Plaza Hotel in New York where the shooting continued. After my job was finished, I received a phone call at home from the account exec—a highly unusual occurrence. She asked if by any chance I had mistakenly, accidentally, just somehow walked off the shoot with a necklace—amethysts and diamonds—I had worn with one outfit.

I was flabbergasted before I was outraged. Basically, I was being accused of stealing. While it was not uncommon to forget to remove pierced earrings after a shot, almost all professional models were scrupulous about returning any and every thing worn for a job. Naturally, most jewelry used in photography was not the real thing, and most successful models could well afford any item they desired. But this was different; this *was* the real thing. Being Black, I was always doubly aware of the scrutiny I was under, representing as I did a challenge to the stereotype of the thieving darky. I felt that as the only Black person on the job I was immediately suspected of a crime when someone else had probably slipped up on the job. I never heard from the woman again, but that singularly sour episode helped me realize how fragile was the image of the sophisticated modern Black woman I was trying to portray and how tenacious the negative cliché.

The highlight of my career came in January, 1976 and helped establish a standard not just for me but for all Black fashion models. This was Issey Miyake's glorious and grinding two-week tour of Japan with twelve Black Girls. Everybody wanted to go. Not for the money, but because it was Japan: when would we ever go there? Because it was Issey, the most artistic of the new fashion designers, and because it was a chance to make history. We could already read the headlines in our mind's eye: "Black Beauties Invade Land of the Rising Sun."

The auditions in New York were crowded, noisy, and hot. The selection process, suspenseful. Print Girls like me didn't have much chance because we often did not project

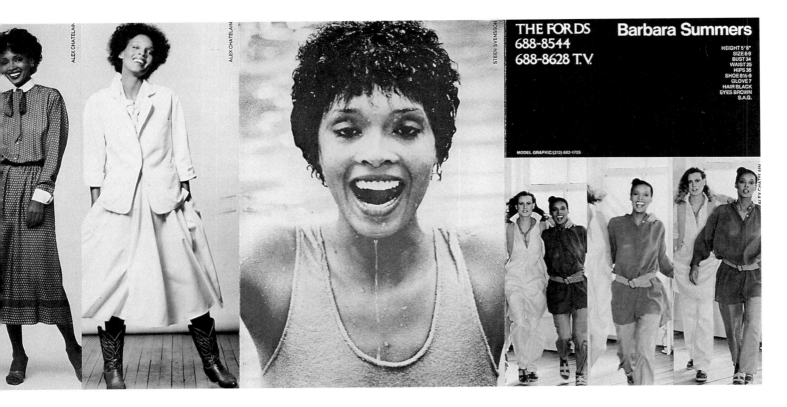

One of my numerous composites. Unlike many models, I stayed with the same agency for my 17-year career.

the larger-than-life personalities needed for stage productions. On the other hand, strictly runway Girls sometimes got locked into a stale presentation routine that became repetitive and boring. Tension was high. When I found out that I was one of the chosen, I was thrilled. And when I returned home after the trip I was delighted to be back. In between were long days of hard work. Issey's production was no walk-and-turn fashion show. It was a theatrical performance where actors and costumes—in this case, models and clothes—took second place to the real star of the show: Issey's wearable concepts of freedom, movement, and color. We were the hot ticket in town playing at least two shows a day to sold-out theatres in Tokyo, Kyoto, and Osaka. But we were also underfed and overworked. So when it came time to shoot a series of TV spots and magazine layouts which had not been mentioned in our original contract, we organized and went on strike—successfully—for an increase in pay.

Much has been written about the rigidity of Japanese society, about the racism, classism, and materialism that structured its daily life. Our experience as stars exempted us from the negativities, allowing us to appreciate the elegantly refined aesthetic which prevailed. I began to understand why we were there. Not only our color and height distinguished us. Our sheer emotional expressiveness set us apart from the Japanese. We laughed and cried and cussed and fussed—out loud.

While we were getting to know the Japanese, we were also getting to know each other. Before the trip I knew only a few of the Girls. My roommate, Toukie Smith was a bald, bodacious pixie whom I had met once before and now liked immediately. I knew June Murphy and Barbara Jackson slightly, and knew of Ramona Saunders and Grace Jones. Although tensions and misunderstandings were bound to arise, they were quickly dissipated because of our fundamental desire to do something that had never been done before and to do it spectacularly well.

While I was relieved to be out of the Western harness of Black-and-White and curious about this third way of being and doing, I came to learn that it, too, was imperfect, even to insiders. Riding the bullet train to Kyoto, Issey told us about living in Hiroshima as a youngster and surviving The Bomb. As a child, he said, he had been teased for having wavy hair, evidence to the pure-blood, straight-haired Japanese of some inferior racial strain. Though he spoke in a light, almost impervious tone, I could not help wondering where his rage and anger were, and what had happened to the pain.

Our director, Minoru Terada, who was half German, had lived in Europe. It was through him that we learned how essential it was for creative Japanese to escape the confines of the fatherland in order to develop their personal style and understand their worth as unique individuals. Our set designer and art director, Eiko Ishioka, was the only Japanese woman in authority close to us. She was a petite dynamo who showed tremendous wit, originality, and flair in her work. The way she wore Issey's clothes with completely casual confidence helped us to see that we were not gallivanting onstage in mere theatrical costumes. We were showcasing the clothes of the future which some folks were forward-thinking enough to be wearing already.

Less than three years after my first pictures appeared in *Mademoiselle*, I was part of the elite being toasted in Tokyo. My professional life looked promising. My personal life at that time was more confused. Still, in most of my work I felt no serious discrepancy between who I was on the page and who I was at home. Yes, I was a divorced single parent, disappointed in love, lonely, and struggling. But, I was also curious, courageous, creative, and optimistic. Modeling taught me about shaping reality: accepting rejection, uncertainty, and change, while continuing to focus on endurance, sincerity, and beauty. To have been chosen and to have worked in the business for seventeen years is a gift for which I will always be grateful. To have been tested for so long made me a stronger person, but not as strong as I needed to be when the time came to leave.

In a business defined by short careers I worked for a long time. Too long. One summer, broke, alone, and underemployed, I began to do what I had always done in private: write. By the time I retired from modeling in 1990, I had published several short stories and dozens of book reviews. I had also edited *I Dream a World: Portraits of Black Women Who Changed America* by Brian Lanker, a magnificent portfolio of photographs, short biographies, and personal statements of outstanding women, some well-known, many silently heroic. My first book, a collection of short stories entitled *Nouvelle Soul*, was close to completion, and I was under contract for *Skin Deep*.

Skin Deep had germinated for a couple of years. Two articles I authored were published in *Essence* magazine in 1987, profiling Black model pioneers, Dorothea Towles, Helen Williams, and Naomi Sims, and also giving an overview of Black models in the present-day business. There was much more to the subject than an article would allow, I knew. But I also knew an illustrated book on the history of Black models would require extensive travel and research, which required the support of a perceptive publisher. Just as Black models had had to fight to get into magazines, we had to fight to get into books. My agent, Marie D. Brown helped forge a fortuitous alliance with Charles F. Harris of Amistad Press, a man who understood my dreams.

I wanted to show what I thought I knew about us. But what the models revealed to me was much more than even I had expected. They opened up their lives with a generosity and candor that were at times overwhelming. I am profoundly thankful to everyone who shared their experience and insight with me. Although I did not talk to everyone I wanted to, parts of their story are here somewhere, too.

I also wanted to situate these women in a context larger than the exclusive world of fashion. For their stories were not simply personal accounts confined to photographic shoots and designer défilés. While the models were busy looking in the mirror, a growing and increasingly curious public was busy watching them, identifying across color and age lines, borrowing styles, and imitating attitudes.

It is not surprising that *Skin Deep* is one of the first fashion and beauty books devoted—not to photographers, designers or publications but—to the most obvious and most often unidentified participants: the models. Although many have tried to make us so, Black models have never been anonymous. In *Skin Deep* I am proud to name names and to include my own among them.

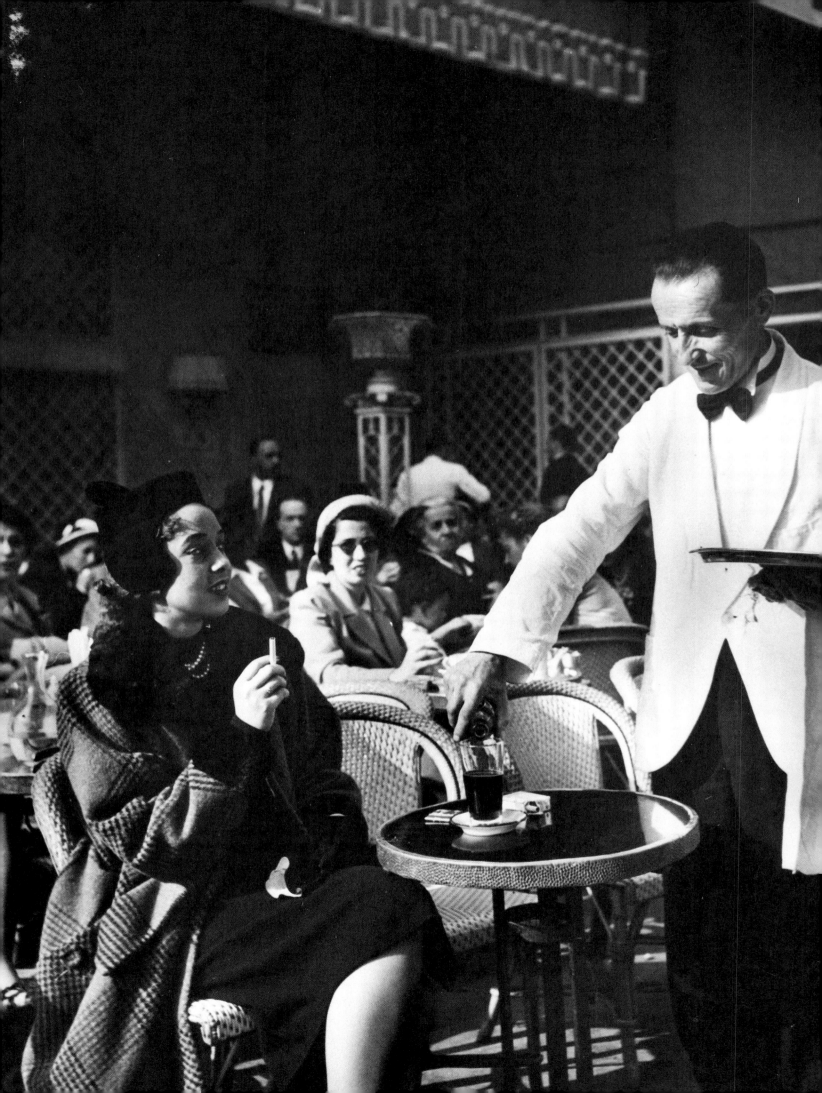

Dorothea Towles

forgot that margaritas knocked me out. One would do it, especially the big frozen kind they served at ¡Caramba! where I met Dorothea Towles for the first time. The smile in her eyes said she'd seen a lot of life. And maybe the crowded café was a familiar sight or had a familiar feel to it, like some place she'd known before in Paris, Rome or Algiers. Or maybe she was simply being—by heritage and by choice—the gracious Southern belle, polite enough not to laugh at my crossed eyes. Maybe it just didn't matter. Once she started talking, she didn't stop.

And, fact is, I didn't want her to. The tropical turquoise smear of her eyeshadow showed me she still believed in the power of makeup and thus, the dream of paradise and perfection. Margaritas weren't the only thing that had me mesmerized. Her voice was textured and energetic, her language vivid, and her story extraordinary.

Dorothea was the first identifiable woman of color to make her living as a professional model. She was also the first international star model of color. She landed in Paris in 1949, only a few years after its liberation from Nazi occupation and racist ideology. Forty years later, when she spoke about her experiences there, it was with an exuberant sense of personal liberation, certainly not an unusual feeling but also certainly one due to singular historical conditions.

Born in the late 1920s in Texarkana, Texas, the seventh of eight children in a highly motivated, well-educated family, she was raised in the schools of the segregated South. "Segregation," she said, "worked to your advantage. With students jumping up and down about Black Studies today, I say, Big deal. I had Black teachers back then who taught Black history with the curriculum. We grew up knowing all this. It's hard to envision now just how segregated things could be. There were separate rest rooms and water fountains, separate basic things like that. And you grew up programmed that way. But you also grew up knowing that if your family was one of the Black leaders in town, you could be anything that you wanted. I knew I could go all the way to the top.

"I found out later in the integrated world, Black people didn't always believe you can be all you want to be. Even with integration—maybe especially so—you really need to know who you are first. Then you can go out and mix all you want. But first, you need to know who you are."

A graduate of Wiley College in Marshall, Texas, Dorothea readily admitted, "I'm rare for the era, because even today a lot of models don't go to college. But being from the South, you had to have a college education unless you wanted to do some junky, nondescript job. Either you were a servant or you ran the whole damn thing. You became the principal of the school, the mortician, the doctor, the dentist, and the lawyer, because you couldn't go across town to the other professionals.

Dorothea Towles, the first high-fashion model of color, started her career in Paris with **Christian Dior** in 1949. Coat by **Robert Piguet**, 1950.

"I majored in biology and took a minor in chemistry, math, and physics because I wanted to go into medicine. Then, when my mother passed, I went to the West coast to live with my uncle. I earned my master's in education from the University of Southern California in Los Angeles. That's when I saw that there were so many other things, job opportunities, that weren't available in Texas at that time. When I left Texas, I decided to be free.

"I wanted to do something like Mary Church Terrell or Mary McLeod Bethune, but I didn't know how. I didn't have their kind of skills, but I grew up reading about them and knowing about them. I knew about Josephine Baker, too, but to me she was like a myth. So I used to think, What can I do? This was the late '40s.

"Everybody in L.A. kept saying, 'Oh, you should be in the movies.' But when I was growing up nothing was happening with Black actors in the movies. I was always commercial-minded, thinking, if I've got all this, how can I use it to make money? So I looked around. I liked clothes. I looked in a fashion magazine and said, Why can't I be one of these, you know, models? Because of being well-trained, analytical, and majoring in science, I said, OK, there must be somewhere you can learn these techniques.

"So I went to a school called the Dorothy Farrier Charm and Modeling School in L.A. I was the first Black student there. Now there was some segregation in L.A., too, at that time, but since I was light-skinned and in Southern California where you have a lot of dark-skinned people, a lot of Mexicans, I didn't have any problems. I mean, I just went right on into the school.

"I did my first national publications from L.A. They were Black publications like *Our World*, which was published in New York. And whenever fashion shows came up, I would do them. You have to start where you are. We weren't organized like an agency. You did all the shows on weekends, in churches or with sororities where you would use your own clothes. We were so heavy into buying clothes. I had a Black dressmaker. So did lot of the girls my age. That's all we did with our money, just buy clothes. And not the laid-back stuff you wear going to the beach.

"That's where the Black influence came in. In L.A. Black people always had more money than people in most parts of the country. And they had one damn party after another in these big old estates they had bought from Whites. A lot of them were professional people—doctors, lawyers, dentists—who came from down South, from Texas and Mississippi, sick of the prejudice. They had made a lot of money during segregation, so they came out there loaded, and they bought these big show places. Some of them even had projection rooms in their houses where they would screen movies like people do now.

"There were other Blacks earlier on who made money in show business. Eddie 'Rochester' Anderson, who has been touted as the first Black millionaire. Hattie McDaniel, the first Black person to win the Academy award, had a big show place. Louise Beavers, another actress whose career was based on playing maids. They did some roles that I found embarrassing. But later I learned to expand my mind, and I no longer feel that way now. The entertainers mixed in with Black society, but Black society was not only about the movies. They were people just living the grand life.

"Shortly after I went out to L.A., I married a man who was old enough to be my father. My husband was a dentist,

Black magazines helped **Dorothea** become a celebrity, encouraging women to experiment with style and dress with panache.

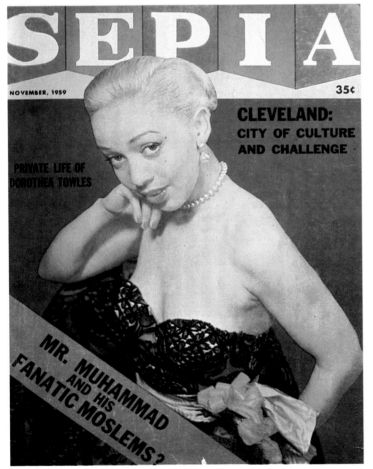

very well off. He spoiled me to death, bought me everything I could think I wanted. But I didn't want somebody giving me everything. I wanted to do it on my own. I soon got disgusted, and I wanted to do my own thing.

"I had an older sister Lois Towles whom I worshipped. She was a classical pianist, and she was going to Paris to study. When I got into fashion and saw that I liked it, I wanted to go to the center of the fashion world. Even out on the West coast I knew that Paris was where it was happening. So I decided to go over for a two-month vacation. But when I got over there I said, This is it. I'm not going back.

"I didn't speak French or anything, so I learned French after I arrived in Paris, after I stayed awhile. It was hard for me. I don't get languages easily. I really had to dig for it. There I was, six thousand miles away from home, just everything to learn. But I had the luxury of not being alone. Although I didn't live with my sister, she was there studying.

"I had enough money to last me about three months, but to stay any longer I knew I had to work. Then I said, If you're going to get a job, go to the biggest and the best because the little person is not going to have much. So, who was the biggest and the best? In that era it was Christian Dior.

"It must have been about August, right after the collection had opened, when I went to meet Monsieur Dior. He was very mild-mannered, shy. You never would have thought he was a great man. Of course, Dior, like all designers, had to look at every model because you're the one projecting their ideas. I didn't get a regular assignment, but I was hired at Dior as an interim model while one of his regular models was on vacation. When the Girl came back, they sent me over to Madame Schiaparelli, who had peaked in the '30s and was then nearing the end of her reign. I worked for her for about a year until I learned the ropes and could get in the swing of what was going down.

"I was a house model. The couturiers took the time to make the collection on you, stitch for stitch. You had to stand for hours for them to put the fabric against your face, and then they made a muslin up against your body. We didn't have stand-ins. We did our own standing until the collection was finished. Each model had about twenty outfits that they made up just for her. It was very expensive. The most expensive dress, an evening gown, ran into two or three thousand dollars. Now, some of them start there. But they were the most gorgeous clothes in the world. It hasn't changed. Just the costs are different. A model could be as poor as Job's turkey, but when she had on those expensive clothes, she was anyone she wanted to be. It was only the elite who could afford them.

"We did our own makeup and hair except when we were doing the couture collections twice a year. Then they would send you out to a hair dresser and a makeup artist, whom they called a *visagiste*. And you'd go for other things, too. Your bras and girdles would come from a certain place, your hose from a certain place, your shoes, jewelry, hats, all from the most famous places in Paris. Buyers would come and ask you everything: Whose girdle are you wearing, whose hose, whose shoes? The wanted to know everything that you had on, inside and out."

Poignant stories about getting her hair straightened—and her scalp burned—left her laughing and me cringing. "I thought, Here I'm ready for the chance of a lifetime,

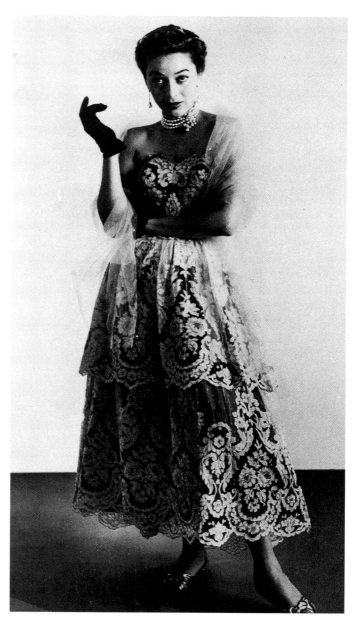

Timeless chic. **Dorothea** in **Balmain**.

and my hair is going to hold me back. But once I learned how to do it for myself, it worked out fine.

"The people I worked with did not seem to care that I was American and looked different. I had the bone structure they were looking for at the time. They only wanted to see how you looked in the clothes and how you showed in the showroom. Anywhere you go, though, you've got to learn your value, what to charge. I was paid unbelievably little, peanuts.

"Being a fashion model is like being an actress. You have to be frivolous, you have to add a little frou-frou. It was all an act for me. I knew there was a serious side, but nobody wanted to see that. You have something they want. And I had something as an American Black that those girls from Africa and from the West Indies didn't have at that time. I came with a drive and a push and a *savoir faire*. One day Madame Schiaparelli called me in and told me to sit down and show her the whole breakdown of how I spent my money. She paid me so little, she didn't know how I was living. That's when I realized my value. The American Girls were the ones who came in and made them up their price because we were accustomed to living better. We weren't at home, and we had to pay our own way for everything.

"We had a lot to do with raising the class of the French model. I read about the history of models, going all the way back to Charles Worth in the 19th century. They were almost like mistresses or call girls. When we came in, we brought freshness and the work ethic. The French Girls would get paid a lump sum and go off for a long weekend or simply wouldn't return. But we took care of business. The designers could count on us because to us modeling was a job. We elevated the status of the profession by demanding more money and by being more aggressive.

"And as far as the social life, it was dynamite. You were treated like a move star. Everything opened up to you. I had a ball. I got invited out all the time. I was the only Black model in Europe, and I just thought I was an international person.

"I was so liberated by then, I didn't realize how much I wasn't before. I was having such a ball, but I was still married and terrified of my husband. I would come home from work thinking I was going to open the door and find him hiding in the closet. He never did show up. He wrote me and even called me, but I told him I wasn't coming back. He finally got tired, and then he got a lawyer and sued for divorce.

"This was in the early '50s. I was pre-Women's Lib, experimenting with sex and everything else, which I'd not had the liberty to do in the States because Blacks who were raised properly are worse than anybody else. We're so damn proper, so careful of our status and so forth. And the French are open about love and sex and all that. So I took an attitude like a guy. I didn't want to get tied down. I wanted to hit and run, you know, have an affair and move on. I didn't want anything permanent because I'd just been in a marriage. I was very immature, and then I grew up.

"I never had an agency in Paris. It was like networking. You met people you didn't know, and they liked your style. I left Schiaparelli through the recommendation of a saleslady, and I went to Robert Piguet, which was a big couture house then and now exists only in perfume. I went there as a *vedette*, a star model. They were lovely to me, and I stayed there for about a year.

"The head of sales there told me that if a model was too dark people would pay more attention to the Girl than to the clothes. They wanted you to blend in with the clothes. I even heard myself described as Tahitian. Still, at that time it was easier to get recognition abroad than it was in the States because the Europeans were more open-minded. They had so few Blacks, you really had to take a magnifying glass to find them, especially American Blacks. Historically, we had had slavery and a long history of resentment. They didn't have that. And the French are more *bons vivants*, more open-minded. If you're beautiful, they don't care what color you are.

"When I was working at Pierre Balmain, *Ebony* magazine wanted to take pictures of the clothes. The public relations woman said No. She said that she was not prejudiced but

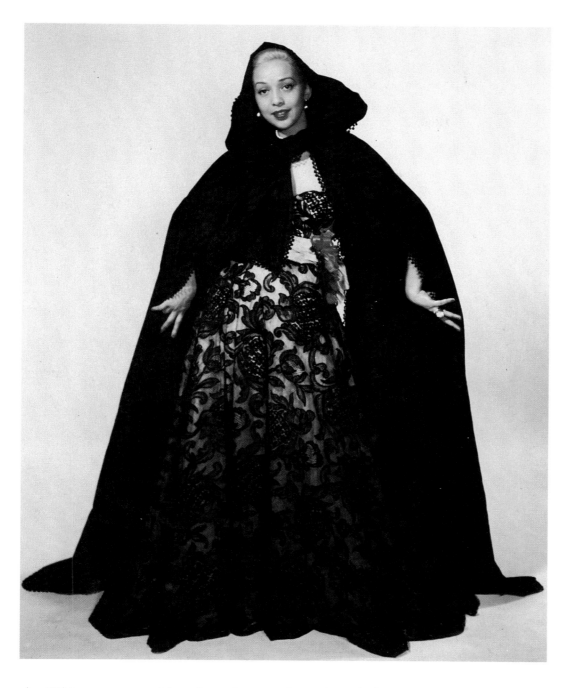

The modern romantic.
Dorothea in Balmain again.

that White women would not buy what was shown in a Black magazine and that it would hurt their American sales. So I just smiled and said to myself, If this door doesn't open, I'll go in the window, I'll go in the back door or the side. In those days models were allowed to check clothes out for the weekend. It was good P.R. So I borrowed six outfits, and we shot the pictures anyway. They didn't think that Black women would buy the clothes, that they *could* buy the clothes. But that's where my education and my experience came in. I knew there was more to me than bone structure. I knew about Black history and Black society. I knew who I was and where I came from.

"I was getting all this mail from the States asking me to come back. I had gotten a lot of publicity while I was in Europe, mostly in the Black press. My family was very proud of me. People were curious. What I was doing had never been done before. With the money I made I bought a wardrobe which I could never have afforded. Models could buy clothes that were reduced in price: *soldes*, sales. I would go through and pick out the things that were in better condition and get them cleaned. I knew there were certain groups that were interested in fashion shows as fund raisers. And I set up a whole itinerary to travel from the East coast to the West coast doing shows for the two-hundred-plus branches of the Alpha Kappa Alpha sorority and for Black colleges. They had a natural built-in system called Fashionetta, and my sister had a lot of contacts from her

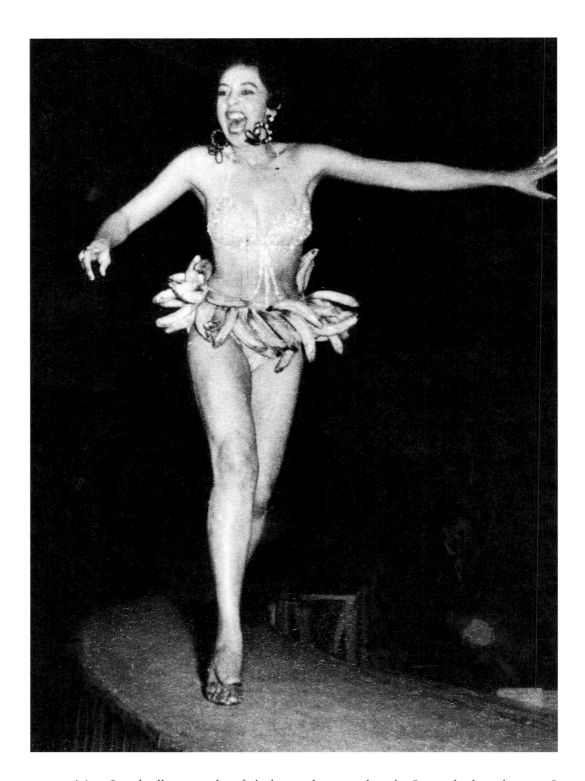

In an update of **Josephine Baker**'s banana skirt, an exuberant **Dorothea** took to the stage in a Milanese production, *Bianco e Nero*.

concertizing. I took all my trunks of clothes and returned to the States, by boat because I had so much luggage.

"I had left for only two months and stayed away for almost three years. During the first two years I was back in the States I was on the road a lot. It was hard. When you go abroad, at first you work so hard to learn another language. Although I had spoken English all my life, when I came back I was almost like a foreigner trying to say, What's the word for this, you know, thinking in French.

"I went on tour with my collection of clothes, like a trunk show. I got tremendous press. They said I had a $75,000 or $100,000 collection—which was a lot of money then. People couldn't believe it. They didn't know I bought the clothes on sale because they were so avant garde, from the latest collections.

"I'd go maybe four or five days before the show, and I would work with the local models in each town, rehearsing them for the show. On college campuses I would teach the girls social graces in an abbreviated culture and charm course. How to walk, how to talk, how to make friends, basic things. There were sessions in grooming, makeup, hairstyles, exercise. The body beautiful: I'd start at the feet and go all the way up to the top telling them what they could do.

"When I first came back, my dream was to live six months in Europe and six months in the States. But if you're going to be in fashion New York is the place. This was where the garment industry was, so New York was the logical place to be, and I used it as my headquarters.

"I tried to do some photographic work as a model, again with the same idea: Go to the best. I signed up with Ophelia DeVore at the Grace del Marco agency and also with a White agency that did shows in the garment district. DeVore would get jobs for the Black market, and they were often to shoot the same picture the White Girls had done. But the timing was not right.

"Rejection did not bother me, though. I had had so much success. Modeling is such an ego trip. You really need something else to put it in perspective. Some of us will be frivolous, which I consider myself to be, but I had to be in order to go into modeling. It's a vanity trip, and I see nothing wrong with being vain. I had my serious side, too, but must we always be serious? You have to take things on the lighter side sometimes.

"I knew I was a token, but I would not have been able to do what I did if I had not gone to Europe and come back with such momentum. I'd come out like a bullet at the shows because the idea at that time was that the clothes were so expensive, they didn't want people to have the time to draw and copy them. Then, back in the States, I outshot all the Blacks, put them away in the shade, because I'd gotten all this fantastic experience. I feel that my going all over America with my show had a great influence on American Black women dressing differently and feeling good about themselves. I saw them dressing more creatively, more internationally. They could say, If she can do it, I can do it, too.

"I've never had a last job. If I were one hundred and two I'd still be doing something in fashion. I always had this great love for clothes. It's just a part of me. You cannot separate fashion from history, from what's happening in the world. Designers get a lot of ideas right out of the street. Fashion is a politically international language, a language of liberation.

"When I first got back to the States I found prejudice. But then times and political activities changed in the '50s and '60s, and Blacks gained more purchasing power. This country's about power and money. That overcomes color and any other hardship. In Europe I got away from Blackness. If you're seething, fighting, and angry, sometimes you need to get away. When I came back, I could see things more clearly. I even toyed with the idea of running for public office because I'd had so much press. But politicians are too deceptive, and I am too candid. So I try to fight in ways that I know how, by using my experience, my looks, my contacts.

"People used to tout me as the first Black model. I consider myself the first Black international model."

The increasing numbers of women who have made successful careers in international fashion during the last five decades owe a debt of gratitude to a free spirit who refused to be bound by the limits of race, class, gender or nationality. And who always knew who she was. Dorothea Towles was the first to say how frivolous and unevolved she was, how flighty and unserious. But she was also the last to say how important her career was in opening up a path for future models and other creative spirits who loved fashion.

Older models have a lot in common with old soldiers. Their pictures may fade but they never die. Even without the help of a few margaritas, they made you wish you had been there with them on the firing line, in those opulent showrooms wearing gorgeous gowns, freshly pressed marcels, and victorious attitudes. In the case of Dorothea Towles, it was almost enough to sit and listen, and in your mind, to watch.

Joey Mills

The interview was going well. Joey had talked about his experiences in the beauty business over the past twenty years. After spritzing his face several times with Evian—"I don't see how anybody can live without this," he declared—he was now making up Tanya's face so I could record step by step just how he did what he was so famous for.

Then Glenn, a hairdresser from the other side of the busy salon, said something about the makeup, something nice, actually. "This looks good, Joey, very natural. Sometimes you make her look, you know, so dead...."

Faster than a spin in a salon chair, Joey whipped a hot curling iron off the stand and slapped Glenn on the arm with it. Glenn froze, reset his jaw, and managed to hiss that one of these days he was going to set Joey straight. It was a cliché, but close to the problem between them, very close.

Grace Jones was on the sound system singing "Love on top of love." Joey kept waving the curling iron in one hand, a powder puff in the other, waving and ranting and raving that there was no such thing as a good straight hairdresser. And everybody knew it. He insisted, "Anybody can learn to be a hairdresser, but makeup is an art."

"So is hair," protested Tanya from her chair. She was a hairdresser herself, and an acting student.

"Only for a few." Joey refused to relent. Glenn stayed frozen, a hairclip's aluminum claw in his hand. When Joey's diatribe became much too much, Glenn's lips cracked open, and out of the fissure came "One of these days, one of these days...."

As Joey flung the tails of his long purple cardigan behind his black suede trousers, he pirouetted in the middle of the salon to make a point. Queen of a much-reduced court— no slight to the primo John Atchison establishment—Joey was no less a certain kind of royalty. A solid six-footer with a wide smile—and what would have been a nose to match were it not for a surgical pinch years ago—Joey was one of those fashionalities whose every step took place on the Great Runway of Life, whose mere seat was a throne in front of the Grand—and Aren't you Gorgeous?—Mirror. Flip hand on his slugger's hip, chin down, as Scavullo would say, he fixed his audience, which by now included the entire salon, until the darts, disguised as undebatable truisms, started to fly again.

During the pause for a pose I eased the curling iron out of Joey's hand and laid it back on the rack, safely holstered with six or eight other magic wands. Only then could I start to breathe again.

It was a typical beauty parlor showdown, a Black East side throwdown, the kind of drama that made you want to pun around with language: the frivolous curlicues of salon mixed with the duel-to-the-death of saloon.

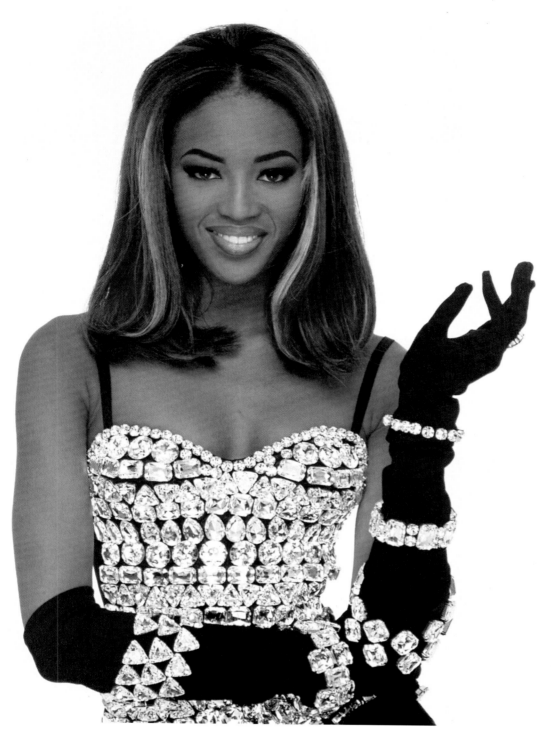

Naomi Campbell, daring and dazzling.

Joey was, of course, Joey Mills the makeup maestro, the designer of beautiful faces gracing over 625 magazine covers, the first Black person to have his cosmetic artistry appear on *Vogue* and Condé Nast covers.

"This goes on every day?" I asked John Atchison, the silver-haired Aquarian owner of the N.Y.C./L.A.'s hair salons. Joey and John and I had worked together during my own career, but I'd never witnessed such theatrics before. "I'm surprised there's only hair on the floor, no blood."

John smiled, amber-eyed and confident. "We're like the airports with their metal detectors. We check for guns and knives at the door." Stiletto scissors in hand, he continued to clip a fine straight line across the bottom of his client's freshly-dried hair.

I was reminded of the Raelettes humming "Yes, indeed," behind Ray Charles. Only now the salon's background chorus, multiplied by mirrors, mumbled with irony and relief, "Every day, every day...."

"I was never a kid. I was always like this," Joey explained.

I repeated, "Always like this? I wonder how you survived."

Joey's reply was instantaneous. "I tend to have carried a pocket full of confidence."

Always. From when he was young—albeit never a kid—in Philadelphia. "My mother was a department store model. I used to do her makeup before I went to school. When I first started, I fell madly in love with *High Society* and Grace Kelly. I wanted my mother to be a star. My brother said, 'You can't do Mom like that. She isn't blonde.' But is blond in the hair or is it inside here?" he asked, pointing to his brain. "It's psychological."

No Black person in makeup has made a more successful career of thinking blond than Joey. In his concept, blond has nothing to do with yellow hair coloring and everything to do with looking rich, gorgeous, healthy, and privileged. In another color-based word, golden. He is unique in the business: the first makeup artist who was Black to build a world-class career, and this on the faces of top Girls who were White.

Mills attended Temple University and modeled for the Mike Douglas television show in the summer, eventually becoming, he said, one of the top models in Philadelphia. But modeling was just a means, a point of entry into the business of beauty, not an end in itself. A successful job for Nice'n'Easy by Clairol led him to New York City.

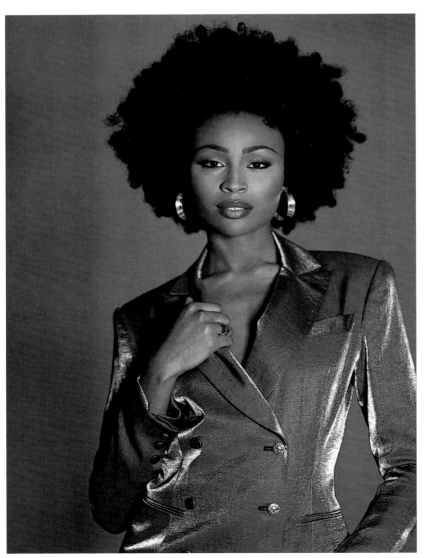

Bernadette Cusseau. Iridescent glow, nouveau '90s 'fro.

"My only goal when I came to New York was to work really fast so I could catch up to Way Bandy. I loved his *Cosmo* covers and the *Vogue* and *Bazaar* covers. Way was very content with *Vogue* and *Bazaar* and *Cosmo*. So I did those covers and *Glamour*, *Mademoiselle*, *Seventeen*, and *Self*. Way wouldn't do *Seventeen*. I did them all. Then I ran to London and Paris and did all of those *Cosmo* covers over there. In Europe they shoot something like three or four covers at a time. And I was smart enough to do French *Vogue* and Italian *Bazaar*, too. I was working seventeen hours a day."

His first breakthrough onto the cover of American *Vogue* was an adventure in itself. "I had already done about twenty-five *Mademoiselle* covers, twenty-five *Glamour* covers and twenty-five *Seventeen* covers. Until then I was averaging twenty pages of beauty a month, but I still had no *Vogue* cover. It was my birthday. My agent let slip that Way Bandy was doing a *Vogue* cover try the next morning, and Patrick Demarchelier was going to shoot it. I jumped up from my birthday cake, ran into the bathroom, and got myself in full drag, didn't I? I put on a Bill Kaiserman jumpsuit and scarf and jumped in a cab and ran into Patrick's studio. I did my cover try, and the next morning they did it again.

"Alexander Liberman, who was the editorial director of the Condé Nast magazines, picked the pictures. The secret is they put all the cover tries into a slide projector and flash them on the wall, and Liberman goes, 'That one!' Well, I got that one, and guess what? I got five in a row. After *Vogue*, the rest was history. All I was doing was covers and opening beauty shots. When you went to a newsstand, you'd see that I averaged eight to ten covers a month. I even did *Architectural Digest*!"

His signature style? It was more of an attitude than a formula. The psychological blonde could be drop-dead glamorous or deceptively natural. The results depended on the individual Girl and the particular magazine's desire. During the '70s and '80s Joey was one of the best interpreters of that subtly changing formula.

"You have to remember that everyone wants to look like a movie star for at least one day in her life. And everyone can. Whether it's a real person, a model or a celebrity, I make them look like a movie star. Don't forget, I've been reading *Vogue* and *Town & Country* since I was young. They love that no-makeup, rich-girl look. I said to myself if the Grace Kelly look got me to the ball, I might as well stay and continue that look."

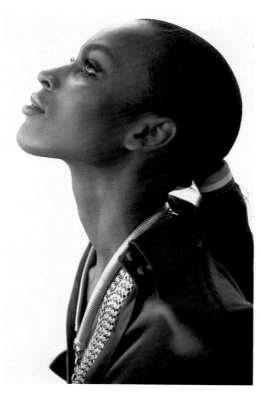

Naomi Sims. The lustre of polished mahogany.

So it came as no surprise that Joey would bristle when asked if he was considered the top Black makeup artist. "I don't *think* I am," he replied emphatically. "I doubt it. If there were a Black makeup artist he would have done more Black things than I did. I have always been available for the Black magazines. But they thought that since I did all the White Girls, I didn't really have to put makeup on them because they were already pretty. If I had waited for Black bookings I would have been standing on the corner with a cup."

Did that hurt? Did he feel left out? "Only when I went home to visit my family at Thanksgiving and Christmas. I was the second top makeup man in the country, and they thought I hadn't made it yet because I didn't do *Essence* or *Ebony* covers. I would have been happy to do them, but I never got the calls.

"I'm a Black person who does makeup. I resented the term Black makeup artist. That's why I wrote my book. I had done over four hundred covers and people—Black and White—were still surprised and said, 'You actually worked for *Glamour* and *Mademoiselle* and *Vogue*?' So I thought while I'm still interested I ought to do my career in a hardback book."

New Classic Beauty, published in 1987 by Random House and still around, is a big, pretty book full of color photographs of familiar cover Girls. "Kim Alexis—on the front and back covers—was my favorite." Reminiscing, he continued, "One of my best covers was with Isabella Rossellini for *Elle* in Paris, before she started modeling here. I first worked with Brooke Shields when she was eleven. Later on I designed all fifteen Calvin Klein commercials with her.

"I do the Girls like the classics. And that's exactly how the fashion industry looks at models, by category. The Girls loved being part of tradition. Beverly Johnson is like Dorothy Dandridge, forever young. Iman, like Naomi Sims. She was fabulous. Mounia is also from Naomi Sims's school. I saw her in Saint Laurent turning in front of Catherine Deneuve. Fabulous. Darnella did the Charlie campaign for five years, and she looked lady-like, elegant, like the girl next door. Karen Alexander is elegant and divine. She looks very rich, out of Beverly's tribe. Khadija is too pretty. But now, have you noticed? Some

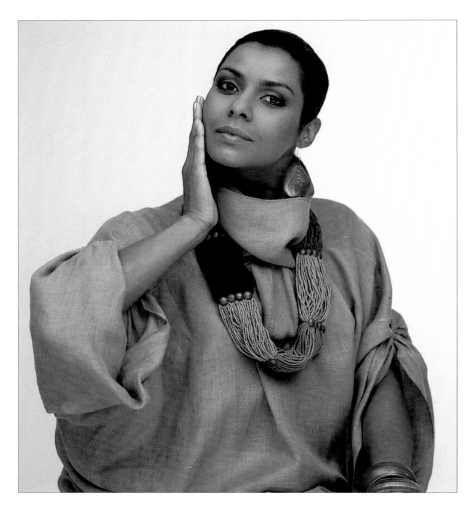

Marcia Turnier. The luxury of simplicity.

of the Girls today are cheaper copies of the originals. I asked Naomi Campbell, 'What are you?' She said, 'I'm English.' 'I mean before that,' I said."

"No one was difficult for me," he claimed. "The only one who could be difficult on my shooting was me. And nothing could make me difficult unless the photographer wasn't fabulous. I only worked with the best hairdressers."

I dared to mention the unmentionable: hair extensions. "Oh, please. I feel the same way about them as I do about colored contact lenses. They remind me of the girl in the projects hanging out the window saying, 'Make sure you bring me back a bag of potato chips.' You know that look. Always had to have some red somewhere, a blond streak. When I like any of that it's when it's on a movie star."

And what is the difference between a real person and a movie star? "The stars have more style. A movie star can crawl in here looking like the hunchback of Notre Dame, but once you finish beating her face, doesn't she jump up and start to pose like Michelle Pfeiffer?

"Real people haven't learned how to go through the change. It's more than the new dress, it's how you wear it. If you really have confidence, it shows in your walk and your stance. When you're *not* done, you tend to sit like this," he said, slumping and splaying his legs. "But when you're *done*, you tend to sit like this." He crossed his legs at a glamorous angle, put his hand to his hip and lowered his chin to his shoulder, Grade A glossy Hollywood-style. He knew exactly what he was doing, as befit a veteran of numerous television shows and seven films. He even appeared as Faye Dunaway's makeup artist in *The Eyes of Laura Mars*. "But certain things, certain people, you can't teach," he shrugged.

Joey has maintained a comfortable, active, and surprisingly discreet lifestyle. With his brother as his financial adviser, he has lived in a condominium in New York City's Lincoln Center area for many years. He admitted, "I always kept my boyfriends at a distance because I had so many other things to do." Was there any chance of getting lonely? "My apartment is 90% mirrors. I can always look at myself."

Recently Joey has started to market his own line of cosmetics for women of color in handy little compacts. "Why was it so difficult for companies to make the colors we need?" he asked. "Because they didn't use professional makeup artists. They always used somebody's boyfriend or girlfriend at the company."

But what was the real value of makeup? Psychological uplift? Physical but non-surgical face lift? "Makeup is really protecting your skin," said Joey. "Most people with bad skin, pimples and blemishes, are the ones who don't wear any makeup at all. If you're living in the city every piece of exhaust flies right into your face. Gorgeous girls wear makeup. The ugly ones wear nothing. It's true, isn't it?"

He rolled his voice with his shoulder, once again posing as the embodiment of his own unshakable opinion. And in that quietly hilarious moment, in that emphatic, ironic stance,

Joey Mills, makeup artist—long out of, if ever in, the closet—was no less a man: a Black man, a rebel, an unexpected survivor, and a magician. In America, regardless of personal or political persuasion, if you were gay and still alive past a certain age, you were an exceptional statistic. If you were alive and kicking, you were a phenomenon. Joey Mills was still with us. And for better or worse, still loud about it.

His was an attitude that would find quieter variants in many of the Black makeup artists whose numbers increased with the rise of Black models during the past three decades. One of them was Byron Barnes, who has said, "The trick to getting ahead is aligning yourself with the right people." Joey Mills would certainly agree with that. After years of print and show work, Byron became the creative director of Iman Cosmetics. Others included QuietFire, whose long-time client Whitney Houston elevated him to the status of an intimate of Hollywood royalty; Reggie Wells, who used his background in the fine arts—as a painter and art teacher—when he moved into fashion and TV; and Sam Fine, whose work with celebrities inspired his 1998 book, *Fine Beauty*.

One of the most respected and versatile makeup artists, beauty consultants, and all-around fashion authorities has been veteran Alfred Fornay. A graduate of FIT, Alfred's work first appeared in 1974 with a pioneering spread on Black beauty in the *New York Times Sunday Magazine*. He became creative director of Revlon's Polished Ambers collection in the late '70s. Since then, he has traveled around the world giving training seminars for Clairol and Revlon, as well as advising such firms as Cover Girl and Naomi Sims. He has also become closely identified with the Johnson Publishing Company, working as the beauty editor of *Ebony*, the editor in chief of *Ebony Man*, and the training director for Fashion Fair Cosmetics. In 1989, Fireside, a division of Simon & Schuster, published *Fornay's Guide to Skin Care and Makeup*, a comprehensive manual for women of color.

Alfred Fornay, as suave and refined in manner as Joey Mills was loud and rambunctious, was no less effective in his sphere. His makeup tactics and career strategy shared common traits: soothing persuasion, patient encouragement, and tasteful results. Although he has worked with many divas—and divos—he has managed to keep immune from celebrity posturing. Sophistication *sotto voce* was always the key to his success. After a quality career of over twenty years in the business, however, Alfred was hinting that Mr. Nice Guy himself was undergoing a makeover. "I've made everybody else rich," he said. "It's time for me to think about Alfred Fornay, now." Short-term plans involved a new book on grooming for men and women. Long-term plans were geared to owning and publishing an upscale lifestyle magazine reflecting contemporary African Americans as they dealt with the challenge to "assimilate more into mainstream society without the hang-up of sacrificing culture."

Whatever the volume of their individual presence, makeup artists—and their indispensable colleagues, hair stylists—have professionalized issues of potent secrecy for Black women. With their help we have been able to examine more closely and less fearfully our most intimate features in order to objectively assess ourselves. Many Black women had long been accustomed to paying scant attention to "fixing themselves up." The visibility of Black models helped change that. Wanting to look better—and thus, feel, do, and be better—ordinary women followed the professionals' guidelines and improvised their own.

But while the makeup artists were peering into us, models were also looking back at them. As they performed—some, like Joey, with a capital P—we wondered about their male insights into our female selves and that thorny terrain we both had to cross to understand the other. Makeup became more than a kit of brushes and paints. There was always an element of mystery in the transformation. Like Pandora's box, it released complex, unanticipated issues that could not be re-confined and, in the fashion business at least, masterful personalities to go along with them.

Patrick Kelly

I. Seine Scene

July 12, 1989: A brilliant summer day along the river Seine. ABC TV's *Good Morning America* is broadcasting live this afternoon—minus the six hour time leap—from Paris. From the Quai de la Tournelle to be exact, a broad, pleasantly cobblestoned walkway edging the Left Bank, directly across from the Ile St. Louis and directly behind the Cathedral of Notre Dame on the Ile de la Cité. *GMA* and its sibling rival, NBC's *Today Show*, are both set up in this picturesque location where I imagine the viewers back home will enjoy similar camera shots of the cathedral, the river, and its bridges.

For July 14th, the day after tomorrow, spectacular celebrations are planned in honor of the 200th anniversary of the storming of the Bastille. The Bicentennial of the French Revolution and the multinational economic summit are what brings the stateside productions here. Or so they say. As far as I'm concerned, any reason at any time is a good one for visiting Paris.

Patrick Kelly and a mini-défilé of his Autumn-Winter '89 collection are what brings me to the quai. They're scheduled to be the closing segment of *Good Morning America*. I'm a little nervous; I wasn't exactly invited. And I don't have much experience crashing national anniversary parties, live television programs or fashion shows, even open-air public ones. But I wear my notebook like an authentic press pass, and my timing is right enough to get through security. When I do, folks seem glad to see me.

Six models, tall, thin, with incredibly matte complexions in this midday heat, arrive in a van along with Miss Liz, Kelly's senior assistant; Pascale, his press attachée; and The Clothes. After rehearsing cues and camera positions along the water's edge, the fashion crew retires to the program's location tent for finishing touches to makeup and hair, and also to snack, smoke, and chat. This is the ordinary, unglamorous state of being known in all show businesses as Hurry Up and Wait.

I exchange double-cheek kisses with elegant Gloria Burgess, who has been a runway star in Paris for ten years; sleek Aria, who shuttles between work in the States and Europe often enough to keep an apartment near the Arc de Triomphe; and long-haired Emilia, whom I interviewed a few days ago. When I mistakenly identified her as a Black model, she smilingly explained that being Brazilian, she knew she had Spanish and Portugese ancestors. "But look at my skin color," she said, "I know there's some Black in there somewhere, too."

Coco Mitchell comes over to say hello. I know her face from New York and her fabulous TV commercial for AT&T, I think, where she was draped all over a motorcycle. I flag down Lu Sierra of the dramatic eyebrows, and silent, coppery Edia to introduce myself. Otherwise, I just watch and listen. No one would believe that these women, as thin as baguettes, are actually eating them, devouring the crusty sandwiches stuffed with ham and cheese and wishing for more. The models are relaxed, pros and perfectionists. Waiting time causes no sweat.

Three minutes to camera and the host, Charles Gibson, is hairsprayed once again, especially over his rear bald spot. His first guest is the Mayor of Paris, Jacques Chirac. Gloria's got to go but can't use the toilet because the prep crew is in there powdering Chirac. The Girls are tickled. The power of powder. Everyone wants to shine, but not on their nose or forehead.

Nearing one-thirty, Patrick, in his signature overalls and sneakers, arrives with his "sister" Rene Patterson, also in overalls, and Rudy Townsel, best friend and hairdresser, in grey-streaked braids and kente-accented overalls. They didn't know where this rendez-vous for "behind" Notre Dame was supposed to be. Funny how Paris is small enough to consider across the river and through the trees "behind" Notre Dame. Patrick tells the cab driver who brought them to stay for the duration of the show because he doesn't want to get stuck without a taxi when he leaves. The meter continues to tick as the driver leans back against his big Renault and smiles.

Patrick checks on accessories while Rudy finesses the Girls' hair. Miss Liz tries on the leopard-print sunglasses which Patrick thinks are still too big. He wants them to be made smaller. And a logo, a label? Miss Liz suggests his trademark, a smiling Black face. "Are you kidding?" he snorts. "You can't even put a Black face on a shopping bag." It is understood that he means, If you intend to sell in the States.

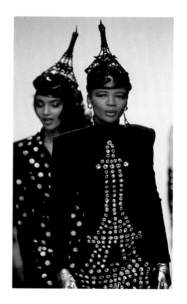

Rebecca Ayoko in **Kelly**'s Eiffel Tower dress.

The talk in the tent is that offhand mix of the personal and political, a swift, intense shorthand which all guild members share. Some of the Girls are more vocal than others. Edia, of Somalian and Italian descent, barely opens her mouth, the better, she tells me later, to follow everything. Gloria talks about how impressed she was with the way the late Guy Laroche showed his appreciation to the people who helped make his last collection such a success—by sending a case of fine wine to each one. Patrick sniffs that *le Dé d'or*—the prestigious Gold Thimble Award—should have been given to the best collection of the year, and not awarded out of sympathy to someone just because he was in misery or dying. He chuckles that his friend and ex-employer, Paco Rabanne, has been passed over so many times, but that he's sold so much perfume that he told the award jury, Let's talk, and they will. Many uh-hmms in response.

While Patrick is getting powdered, Emilia, in a short skirt with rows of silver leather fringe and tall red suede boots, needs to change her pantyhose which has just sprouted a hole and a highly visible run. No problem, no panic. She changes *al fresco*.

It's too hot for anyone to get completely dressed. Aria, who has a charcoal gray suit jacket to wear over her magenta dotted shirt, holds a stunning magenta fox jacket at arm's length. Same with Edia in a short leopard-print halter dress. She has a quilted jersey coat in a matching print to complete her outfit, just not right this minute. Same with Gloria in a double-breasted marigold suit with a reversible gold and black cape. Everyone agrees that this particular creation is spectacular. Björn Amelan, Patrick's partner, says they were not allowed by their parent company to make more than this sample outfit. He states dryly, "We changed opinion-makers. That was the last thing she said." I hear a falling guillotine in his voice.

Coco, the chocolate color of her name, waves to the surprised passengers of a passing *bateau mouche* in her red jodhpurs and black jacket buttoned with several rows of golden fleurs de lys. She looks like a cavalry officer who would have reported only to Napoleon himself.

Six-feet one-and-a-half inches tall in her stockinged feet, Lu sashays as much as she can—and she can—in a long, body-hugging black dress decorated with a torso attention-getter: an Eiffel Tower in big rhinestone buttons. She didn't always have this body, she admits, and she shows it off with flair. She also wears a miniature velvet-wrapped version of the 100-year-old monument on her head. On her feet, sinfully serious spikes. How will the Girls walk in these shoes on the big, uneven stones of this outdoor runway?

"Cobblestones is a blessing," says Patrick, "compared to a gravel road in Mississippi." Rene amens to that.

Two-thirty in the afternoon here, eight-thirty in the morning in New York. The models line up off-camera waiting for their cue to perform. Patrick is smooth and chatty on the air, but he also projects a solid sense of humor about himself. He confesses that when he first landed in Paris he spoke no French and pretty bad English. (Coco says later that when she first met him in a club in Paris, he told her that he'd like her to work for him some day. She answered, Sure, the same way you shrug off someone with leaping dandruff.) He must have told his rags-to-riches story hundreds of times but it still manages to ring true. As a part of the fashion establishment now, he wants the other designers to stay the way they are, sophisticated and polished. He says, "I'm polished in my own funny way."

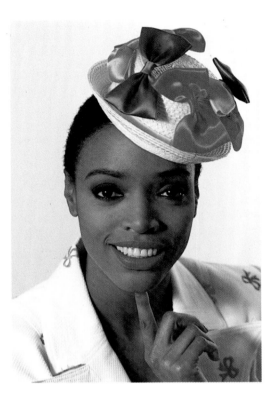

Finally, it's time for the fashion segment. The cathedral, the river, the boats and barges, the quai and the breezy blue day make a perfect backdrop. The Girls work their outfits. Two cameras, one on a cherry picker, work them over. Patrick says he's from the old school. He likes models who can turn it out, exaggerate the slink, the tongue-in-chic of his clothes. There is a ripple of applause when the show is over. For the models it's one job done, now on to the next. Or maybe to some other aspect of real life, like shopping. Coco says friends in the States are taping the spot for her. Lu called her mother to watch it; she knows she'll have something to say. Her mother is only thirty-eight and gorgeous. Gloria's mother, visiting from D.C., and her four-year-old daughter come strolling along the quai. They're too late for the show but right in time for group shots and a signature Patrick Kelly button. Everyone poses and gets in that last flash of a smile.

II. Tarbaby and Pink Tofu

A round Black smiling face is Patrick Kelly's logo. On his shopping bags, on the fashionably crumbling wall of his studio-boutique in the fashionably re-re-gentrified district of Le Marais. It's everywhere, itchingly provocative, stylistically retro/nouveau, disturbingly cute. That tarbaby black face, watermelon red smile, dandelion yellow ears. It's the first thing we talk about.

Well, not really the first thing. We talk about Josephine Baker first. Hard not to. She's all over the place, showroom and workroom, sequined and buttoned, idealized and idolized, bejeweled banana tutu over poked-out 'Bama butt. The first Black pin-up, from *les années folles*. La Baker and her two loves, Paris and the States. A shameless shaman and her Rainbow Tribe. Maybe in his next collection he will coif his models to look like her, as Coco Chanel once did the models in her *cabine*. Just a thought.

I'd like to really talk with him but right now he's too busy in the workroom. I take what I can get: the opportunity to hitch a ride with him when he goes to the dentist. But before he leaves, he's got to find something. The cab is ready and waiting while he lays out a selection of buttons on a fuschia fabric: self-covered, silver, pearl, rhinestone. "*Où sont les boutons en strass?*" he asks in energetic, self-assured French. His impatience is on the rise, along with his voice, until more rhinestones appear, more choices, but still

Coco Mitchell. Kelly lavished his designs with colorful buttons and bows.

not the right ones. The cab and the dentist can wait a bit longer. Patrick Kelly has serious work to do.

Once in the cab Kelly talks about women, the women who influenced him or those he simply likes: Josephine Baker, Lucille Ball, Lena Horne, Bette Davis, Gloria Steinem, Oprah Winfrey, his mother. His favorite person in the world is his grandmother. It was she who introduced him to fashion magazines as a child in Vicksburg, Mississippi. It was she who gently tried to explain that the reason there were no Black women pictured in them was due to designers not having the time to create for Black women. Neither "fashion" nor "racism" was a part of his vocabulary. Then.

He talks about the church fashion shows which he loves. He has said, "There are enough ideas in one church lady to do a whole couture collection."

And he talks about his models. "We fight down," he says, "but we take care of each other. Sometimes a Girl will get lonely, pregnant or drugged-out. I give them advice on their private lives." And perspective. "For me," he emphasizes, "the business has been a fairy tale come true." He has gone from hanging home-made clothes for sale on the fence outside the church at St. Germain des Prés to running a thriving multi-million dollar enterprise. But he is careful to point out to the new Girls that that kind of success is not for everyone. "Everybody is not going to be Mounia or Pat Cleveland," citing two of the profession's brightest stars, now eclipsed by time and newer faces, but still working, still special.

Later, I sit alone in the Marais showroom which faces an oasis of lush, emerald-green grass. A life-sized statue of a Black boy in striped pants and sneakers perches on a gilt chair in a corner not far from a large handsome canvas by Harvey Boyd, very Harlem Renaissance in feeling. The artwork is so intriguing that I could spend all my time on that. I have another assignment, however, one which is equally fascinating.

I watch videos of Patrick's last two collections and tapes of television interviews. Even with almost two decades' experience in the business, I ooh and aah at the clothes, the colors and poses. The flash, dash, and who-cares-about-cash. The sheer fun of fashion.

No wonder he has dressed bodies and personalities as diverse as Bette Davis, Grace Jones, and Princess Di. Add to that list Jessye Norman, prima diva of the Bastille Bicentenary, who thrilled all of France with her spectacular rendition of "La Marseillaise" from the hallowed ground of the Champs-Elysées. For Jessye's heroic proportions as well as Bette's iron waif, Patrick provides wearable, stretchable goodies possessing a surprisingly flattering fit. They give me a lot more to think about than the "amusingly sexy outfits" usually profiled in a somewhat disparaging press. There is more to this country boy than some care to admit.

"The people who complain about my Black face are the same people who haven't donated one dime—and probably won't, and probably can—to the Black medical schools in the States that they always say are so bad." *En garde.*

The Black dolls, collected by the dozen and displayed behind glass, the trademark, the Black baby pinned on an assistant's T-shirt are all, he insists, images from our past. They are at least as valid, if not more so, than other new-fangled icons of success that surround us. "Aunt Jemima represents what?" he asks. "A maid. In *all* of our families somebody we love has been a maid."

Kelly has been praised in the international media for his accomplishments as the first—and in 1989, only—American designer elected to the prestigious Chambre syndicale, the inner circle of French designers. He is also the first—and so far, only—Black person to be a member of this august group.

But he has also been criticized—less openly and perhaps more deeply—for hanging some of the Black community's dirty linen out in the open. How dare he expose our chronic color sickness and pickaninny phobia? He has made a lot of folks quietly uneasy if not overtly angry. "They don't want to admit to a blackamoor, to an Aunt Jemima. They want to put me down for having these Black dolls. They say the symbols are wrong. But I look at the Black church. I'm religious. I believe in God, I believe in Jesus. I also believe that the people who don't believe have the right to survive. For a long time the

> *"There are enough ideas in one church lady to do a whole couture collection."*
>
> Patrick Kelly

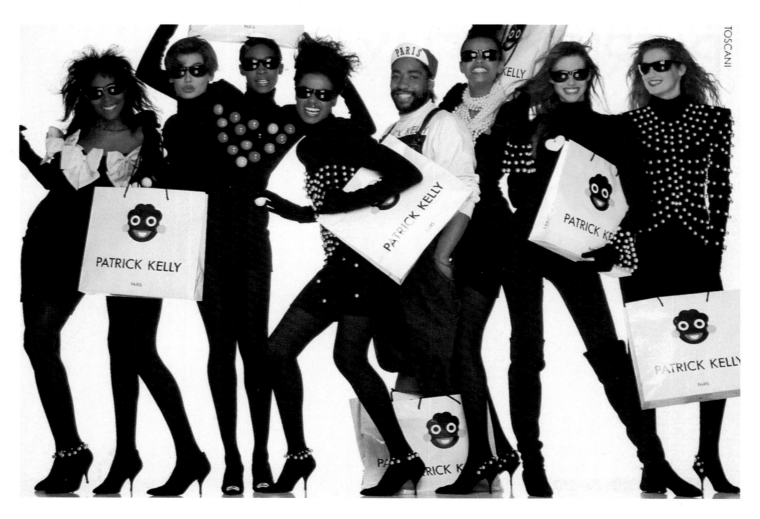

Kelly and crew.

Black church had us fooled, and at the same time it was the only foundation that had us truly united. But why don't they have a Black Jesus? A Black God? You can wear camouflage and a T-shirt with a machine gun that says 'shoot', but show a Black face, and people want to get crazy."

It is obvious that for Kelly Black faces are not mere cultural decor. He takes it all the way live, becoming a magnet for Black models who aspire to work in Paris. In his fashion shows, he admits, "I use too many Black Girls for the general public. I use White Girls too, a lot of ethnic Girls, character Girls. But Black Girls walk the best, they show the clothes the best." And yet he claims that if he did what his friend and supporter, designer Sonia Rykiel did, namely put 'Black is Beautiful' on a dress shown on a Black Girl, he'd be called a militant. He was, he won't deny it. He still is. And he doesn't back down from the present-day challenge. "Where," he asks, "are all the militant Black groups? Why have they been dissolved when the militant White groups are still around and on the rise?"

I feel as if I've stumbled on an underground bomb factory. This kind of talk from a fashion designer? From a man who likes to describe himself as a Black male Lucille Ball? No doubt about it, Patrick Kelly is funny ha-ha. Laughter constantly ripples around him. Feeling good and having fun are important to him. And this spirit is communicated in his clothes. Despite all the obstacles, though, he gets the job done and more.

He is serious, dedicated, consistent in philosophy and professionalism. He is no reverse plantation fluke. Warnaco, his corporate backers, and Pierre Bergé, president of Yves Saint Laurent and his sponsor to the Chambre syndicale, would not invest in a febrile fly-by-night no matter how colorful he was. Patrick Kelly, the business, has looked at a five-to-ten-million dollar bottom line and expects significant increases in the future with a new line of sunglasses, accessories, and the serious money-maker, a signature fragrance.

"I don't mind working hard. I just finished two collections, and it's time to finish another one. I'm gonna work like sin. But I've never really been on a vacation, so I'm going on one this year. Luxuries are important. Like M. Bergé says, they give you a goal to get to. Just don't die trying to get there, because in the end, all the money and all the luxuries, you leave them here.

"It's deep. The critics come at me, and I'm not as sharp as I would like to be. Like some of these learned Blacks, the BAPs, the Black American professionals. I would like to know as much as they know. Like Alice Walker. From what I hear, they say Madame's sharp. She don't miss a lick. And I heard that from the most diva White chick I know, Gloria Steinem." Steinem, who once called Kelly "the king of cling" told Kelly "and this is out of her own mouth, 'Alice is a heavy broad, heavy, heavy.' Rudy did her for the cover of *Essence* and said, 'Baby, she got a pink tofu for you that won't wait.' For us pink tofu is those people who have a spiritual thing, who believe it, who mean it. Who maybe don't eat pork, but don't give a damn if you got a pig in your pocket. I want to be like that, 'cause they come at me, and I want to be ready for them."

Kelly is adamant that we can—and must—learn. From the schools and from the street. "We can take the time to go and get a hair weave, and we can't take the time to find out who the hell we are? We can take the time to go get sculptured nails so long that they ain't even necessary.... We can look all over town till we find the place that sells Yves Saint Laurent men's suits cheap.... We can take the time to go jack up our Jeep/Range Rover so high to ride around in Manhattan.... You know, we can take the time for so many other things, but if we can't find out who we are, then we're in serious trouble."

He snaps at the accusation of running away to Paris to escape being Black. "People say, 'Did you make it here because you couldn't make it in America?' I don't know. I would like to think I would have made it in New York. But I didn't make it there. I came here, and I made it here, so I can only tell them about that experience."

A self-described "maniac for organization," he says one of the hardest things in growing a business is finding the right people to work with. "You start out with your best friends who helped you. Then, when you start to get big, the power people say, 'Oh, you don't need them. We have a person who's been trained at Yale, and he can help make your business better.' But you better keep your people as you go up. Miss Liz will be with me until she can't take my madness anymore, not because somebody in corporate life thinks she shouldn't be there. They try to dissolve the people around you. They do that to a lot of Blacks."

Friends are more important to him than bottom lines or headlines. But the media have pushed Kelly into a limelight he likes yet sometimes feels he doesn't quite deserve. "When we did *Lives of the Rich and Famous*, I kept saying, 'But I don't have any money, honey.' Every dime I have I put into the bank or the business. It's weird in this crazy world of fantasy and fashion and money and limousines and all of that. I mean, sometimes I have only $20 in my pocket, and I'm on my way to the Waldorf Astoria to some dinner that some corporate person paid $1,000 for. I don't want to eat nothing that costs $1,000, really, unless it's gonna last me for the month!"

How long can he stay that mentally healthy? "Oh, crazy? For a long time. I want to do a lot of madness. Maybe even open a restaurant. Do costumes for movies. There's no end to all of the stuff I want to do."

Then there's a genuine fuss in his voice when he says, "One thing I'm mad with myself about. Everybody's making clothes for little skinny girls. Which I love. But if I could come out with a line of fat ladies' clothes...." And his voice rises, sparkling with bubbles of possibility. "Eight-five percent of the women in this world are fat, 85%!" Frank? Yes. Impossible? Who's to say?

If Kelly can confront us with challenging images of Blackness, womanhood, and beauty, we likewise challenge him to give us something back, something witty and

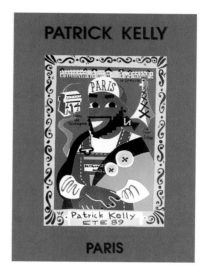

Folder for **Kelly**'s Summer '89 collection.

profound to wear, something accessible and affordable. He does his research. He has the unpredictable imagination of the true stylist. And he is, he appears, too modern, positive, and constructive to live an expatriate's bitter exile or to degenerate into simplistic folklore.

He says, "It's hard, but the only thing I have to do is stay Black and die. The one thing the whole world's afraid of—and the one thing we're sure of—is dying. Nobody has *not* died. We're told that when somebody dies, we're supposed to be miserable and suffer. Let's just hope that they're going on to something better than this. Because dying is the one thing you're gonna do, you have to do. I just wish that God could have hooked it up so that somebody could have gone over and come back.

"The dead don't die for the living to suffer, so why in the world is the funeral so important? Even that expression: 'to be put away good.' I don't think that's one of the luxuries I want. I want a party, child. When I'm gone, just give me a party, a shindig."

And maybe a fab fashion show.

III. Undressing

January 1, 1990. The new year opens with terrible news. On the first day of the first year of the last decade of the 20th century, Patrick Kelly died. In the Hotel Dieu, a hospital near the Cathedral of Notre Dame in Paris. Of bone marrow disease, a brain tumor, and complications from AIDS. He was buried in the historic cemetery of Père Lachaise.

It is all a little hard to handle. When I spoke with him in the summer, less than six months ago, he did not look sick. On the contrary, he looked round and robust, eagerly polishing ideas for a sparkling future. But soon afterwards in the fall of '89, rumors began to churn in the unlit side of the fashion world, like a mysterious undertow whose strength is unknown until someone actually gets carried away. Kelly was expected in New York in August for an event to honor Black models and designers. He did not show. In September, he was hospitalized. A nervous breakdown, some said. We breathed transatlantic sighs of relief. You can recover from a nervous breakdown. Hadn't most of us? But he did not present his Spring '90 collection in October during prêt-à-porter week in Paris. And if that was not enough of a red light flashing, the grapevine had it that clothes, accessories, everything in the boutique that could be sold was being sold. It was hard to believe the constant denials. A ringing cash register did not sound like the bang or whimper of the end. And then he was gone.

I feel haunted as I review the tape of my interview with him. It can't be coincidental that we actually end our conversation talking about what he wanted to happen when he died. All this cannot be a freak coincidence. But if it's not, what is it? The answer is too obvious, yet at the same time, too unbelievable. He knew. On some level, some part of him knew that he was dying. And he wanted to talk about it.

On a sunless January day in New York City I spoke with Liz Goodrum, aka Miss Liz, over lunch. According to her, Patrick's dying was not serene, not transcendent. Why, during those worrisome months, couldn't the truth about AIDS have been acknowledged? Liz could not answer a question that has challenged thousands of families in the last few years. I did not expect her to. She simply admitted, "I was lying until the bitter end." Had Patrick himself been any more honest? Not according to her. He did not prepare for the business to continue without him. And so there was none.

On the 28th of March, 1990, the Fashion Institute of Technology in New York City was the scene of a gala memorial for Patrick Kelly. In its Seventh Avenue windows his designs were displayed on mannequins arranged on intricate scaffolding. Little brown baby pins were given away at the door. Folks unlucky enough to not have an original outfit piled on their buttons, hearts, and other PK insignia. Videos of his shows and interviews were played as we took our seats in the carpeted amphitheatre. People hugged and kissed who had not seen each other in too long, and who would have thought like this?

Audrey Smaltz, who directed Patrick's défilés, mistressed the ceremonies with the polish of the fashion show pro. On stage were the things Patrick was never without.

PATRICK KELLY

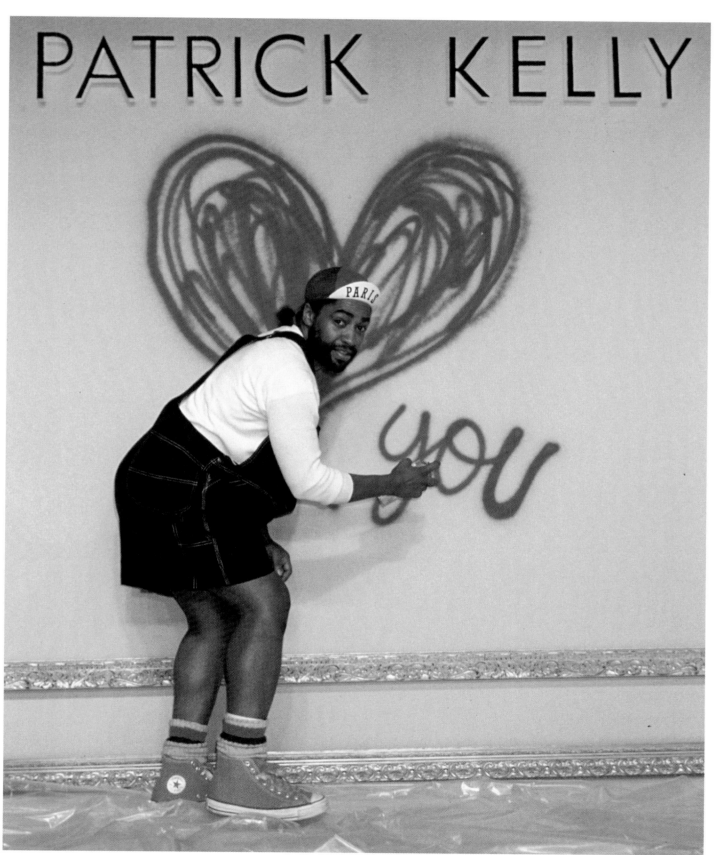

Signing off.

Art: Rudy Townsel spray-painted a big red heart in the middle of a huge gilt frame so that the whole picture read Patrick Kelly ❤ you. Music: Rene, in overalls, sang "My Soul's Desire (is to serve you, Lord)." Kevin Thompson, of the design team Kevin and Robert, (whose partner Robert Miller had died only a few days before—yes, the same old story…) sang "Don't Cry." Janice Pendarvis sang "You Are So Beautiful to Me." And young D'Atra Hicks from *Mama I Want To Sing, Part II* tore the roof off the house with "You'll Never Walk Alone."

And there were other things Patrick liked: good talk, laughter, and testimony. Rev. Dr. Eugene Callendar of Harlem's Church of the Master spoke about Patrick's "can-do consciousness." How "he never let society define for him who he was." How "he took stereotypes like watermelons and made exciting things that even White people wanted to wear." How his deep spirituality led him to join all his models in prayer before his shows. Rudy spoke of being more than friends and brothers. Of being roommates: "Before I knew it there were fabric, wigs, dresses, and drag in every corner of my life." And of being soul mates: "Patrick gave me the opportunity to make my dreams come true." More than one person amened to that.

Gloria Steinem eulogized him in elegant '90s terms: "He was totally himself. He was shit-free. He unified us with buttons and bows instead of dividing us with gold and jewels." And as "we mourn an unacceptable thing, the death of the future," she insisted that we must somehow recognize that "we are his future."

Toukie Smith thanked Patrick for understanding that "it didn't matter if I was a size six or an unfashionable size sixteen, I was still his brown Venus." She brought the whole design and business team up on stage: Björn, Liz, Rashida, Maryann, his lawyer Bob Levine, "who with all his lawyer realities made it work the right way so that Patrick owned his own name," and many others. The audience was happy to acknowledge them. And maybe Patrick's people were glad for a brief, last moment of recognition. He could not have done what he did without them. He knew it, he would have said so.

But it was all coming and going so quickly. The videos, so colorful and vivid, were not a memory; they were tangibly, confusingly real. The smiling man in the turned-up cap that read Paris was what? Both here and not here. And more somehow. There is talk of a Patrick Kelly Foundation dedicated to developing and promoting the talents of Black Americans. There is talk about how more needs to be said and done about AIDS. There are more people wearing shiny plastic buttons that shout Color and brown babies that say Grow. And there are more people who wish they had gotten on the bandwagon sooner, who had no idea that the joyride was going to be such a short one, who will have to make do with the spin-offs and imitations from less original minds.

If there were few obvious tears at the memorial, there was much interior sadness and silent regret. Black models will surely miss the home-away-from-home that he provided in Paris, the sense that there was a kindred soul willing to take a chance in a foreign land and succeeding.

Along with a line of clothes, Patrick Kelly initiated a new line of dialogue about culture, history, and aesthetics, one that needs to be consistently updated and reevaluated. So it's hard to speak of him in some kind of terminal past tense. It's hard to get happy when you're saying goodbye, when you're listening to Bebe and Cece Winans singing "Love said not so," when you know that's what Patrick was listening to as he was undressing, leaving his body. It's hard when you're sitting in a school that you know he never finished, and you know that school is just another corny metaphor for life. It's hard when the minister tells you to greet the strangers around you, because even though we may not know each other, we all knew and loved him. So the shindig that Patrick wanted is not exactly what he got. But it was the best that we could do.

It is obvious that Black designers—as a group and as individuals—deserve hard-cover recognition for their contributions to the fashion world and beyond. Still, some stories may be more aptly cut from the fabric of fiction. Patrick Kelly is one of those. It's not surprising. He always did like stretch.

Pat Cleveland

"*If you want to get famous, dress up!*"

Pat Cleveland

The British call it the catwalk. The French, *le podium*. The Americans, the runway. Wherever in the world Pat Cleveland has modeled during the last four decades, the stage belonged to her no matter what people called it. Flights of fantasy were her specialty. Airy, winged spins and long, liquid gestures were standards in her repertoire. Impossibly ethereal, she could, as model Rene Hunter said, "tell a story in a dress." And like a turbo-charged Tinkerbelle, she made you believe in another reality. She made you believe that you, too, could fly.

I waited for her after a Moschino show one fall. It was a late Milanese afternoon, and the shops and arcades behind the Duomo were filling up with people ending their work day. Surrounding the Società del Giardino where the show took place, the limousines of life were awaiting their passengers. Uniformed chauffeurs leaned against their Mercedeses, Maseratis, and Lancias as though cool and class did rub off. As the show ended, buyers and editors streamed through the archway with nods of 'Just what I expected' or shakes of 'Not what I expected at all.' Interestingly enough, they all had smiles on their faces.

The models were the last to exit. They were tired, soaring on their final energy until they could land peacefully or crash.

Pat was one of the last out. We walked across the street with her friend Maura to sit inside a café. Her face was scrubbed a clean, squeaky pink, and her finely plucked brows hovered over restless eyes. She talked fast, flipping her dark curly hair behind her shoulders. She had a train to catch back to her family and home in the countryside near Lake Como. In breathless Italian, she paid for and then ordered—that's how they do it there—our juice. Then, while we watched the oranges being squeezed, she started a rapid-fire recital in breathless English.

"I was born in New York City on the Golden Edge, in the 90s, East side, just before you go into the Spanish area. This area was called the Golden Edge because everybody was mixed: Irish, Black, German, and Spanish. On every corner you had a different nationality. Art was a world I had to enter because it took me away from what everything was about in the streets. It was color, it was fantasy. I wanted to be a painter because my mother, Ladybird Cleveland, was a painter, but I leave that to her. I can't compete with the dynamic forces. I started posing for her as a child. That's how I understood the art world was different from everything else."

Dressed with her usual flair, a teenaged Pat was on her way home from art school one day when an editor from *Vogue* stopped her and asked her to come to the office with some of her clothing designs. She did, and *Vogue* published a feature on her as a young designer.

"In the meantime, my mother sent some photographs of me to Mrs. Johnson at *Ebony*, and she asked me to come on a go-see for their Fashion Fair. I was fifteen, and I had never done anything like that before. But Mrs. Johnson accepted me in her show. I had to stop regular school and go into professional school so I could work. I did it not because I wanted to model. I did it because I wanted to explore.

"My aunt was a dancer with Katherine Dunham. When I was five years old I used to dance with her, too. My aunt used to travel in Europe and work in the opera houses. She inspired me. I would get postcards from her, and when she came back she'd dress up like Josephine Baker around the house. My great-aunt was Josephine Baker's Sunday school teacher. So I always heard these stories about this little girl who went away to Paris and never came back. And that's what my plan was.

"My plan really was to learn about the fashion business and become a designer, but I threw that out the window when I saw how hard they had to work. I used to stay home and sew all the time, but it was so exhausting. I wanted to go out at night. I didn't want to sit at home. I was only a teenager. It was too much, it came so fast, the business world. So I stuck to modeling after I had the opportunity.

"I was looking for fun. I used to go out dancing at Le Club and the Cheetah because I had the right clothes. If you want to get famous, dress up! Yes, fame was on my list. I had to get out and get famous because those people were the ones who were having all the fun.

"I started in photography because the shows weren't like they are now. You had to be different. You had to be real skinny for photos, and you had to be a little more full for the shows. And the shows were more serious. Nobody wanted to do shows, because in America they had them on Seventh Avenue, and nobody wanted to do that. But I didn't mind it, so I did it.

"Jacques Tiffeau gave me my first break. Then I started meeting all the designers. The first one who really took to me was Stephen Burrows. He was the master. He knew the bias cut and how to use jersey, and it fit my body perfectly. Stephen Burrows was the ultimate dancer, designer, and fashion innovator. With him dressing me I was able to attract other people: Andy Warhol, Halston, movie directors. Colors just kept flashing till I was like a big fireworks, and I had to leave America. I was like a bomb ready to explode.

"I was twenty-one years old when I had my first glass of champagne in Paris at La Coupole, dressed in a see-through negligée. When I entered the restaurant everyone stood up and applauded and threw flowers at me. I thought, Vive la France! I was ready to burst at the seams because I knew that was it. I met all the right people in the right place at the right time. And it was boom boom boom! From then on I was a free woman. A free Black woman.

"Do you know what that is, freedom? Do you know slavery? My grandmother was in slavery. Even my mother picked cotton. I was never going back to America. I'm not saying America's a bad place. If I wasn't from there I never would have had the career opportunities I had."

Had she not been from the United States, she may not have had certain traumatic experiences early in her life either. She recalled some of the more intense days spent traveling with Ebony Fashion Fair in the mid-'60s. "I was in a bus in Arkansas not long after those little girls got killed in the church. People were throwing bombs around our hotel. Disgusting things would happen. When we'd get off the bus, we'd all have to go to the bathroom, but my girlfriends weren't allowed to use the facilities. They'd let me go, though. Another time we were pulling out of Arkansas, and the Ku Klux Klan were coming, and they were throwing things at our bus with flames and fire, trying to kill us. I'll never forget that, because they didn't want to *hurt* us. They wanted to *kill* us because of our color. People threw rocks at us because we were Black. They tried to rape this one Girl. It's so awful to see what can happen.

"It's not so bad now, not like before, but I still feel it a little bit when I go back to America. I always thought about representing a whole group of people, Black women. I can see who's not being treated well. I left America the first time and said I wasn't coming back until I saw a Black model on the cover of *Vogue*. It took me a long time. In 1974, that's the year I went back. I stayed out until I saw that cover because I saw so much stuff

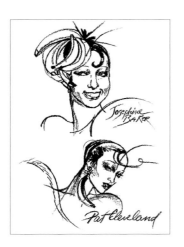

Stylistically, **Pat** was a direct descendant of **Josephine Baker**.

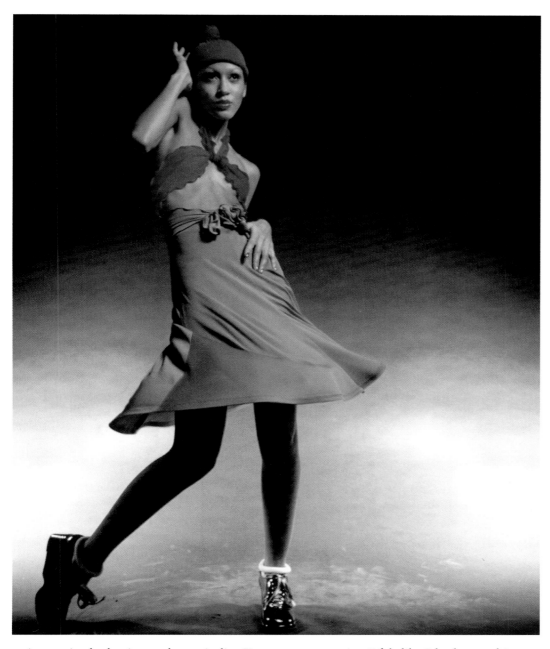

Adding her own ebullient swing, **Pat** delighted in **Stephen Burrows's** imaginative cuts and effervescent colors.

going on in the business, the prejudice I've seen at agencies. I felt like I had something to offer, and that's why I stayed over here in Europe, because they gave me a chance to express myself without boundaries.

"I worked with everybody, and I learned from all of them. You keep your eyes open, and you keep your mind open. There was so much to learn. I felt like a big sponge. There're many things that people taught me that are now surfacing in my life as a kind of wisdom. I remember Mrs. Vreeland always telling me, 'Stand like a tree with your feet rooted in the ground.' And Manin inspired me to walk a certain way. That's what we get out of this modeling profession, inspiration. It's like the arts. If you're in it just for the money, you're going to get the money, but you've got to find some other reason, some logic to all of this. Often there was nothing after you finished your job. You're like a Christmas tree. They put all the bulbs on you, and then when they take the bulbs off, you get all dried up. Nobody waters you with love or anything. You have to have something else going, too, a deep private life.

"You have to keep your fantasies alive. If you think you can be something, go for it. If you think you can go somewhere, try. You have to be a bit bold. A lot of my friends in this business have passed away. It's very strange. It makes you think. But before all of that happened, it was a lot of fun. Such parties. You could go on and on. Just living it up in the South of France or taking off with our little backpacks and going to Egypt. The opportunity to see the world is definitely there.

PAT CLEVELAND

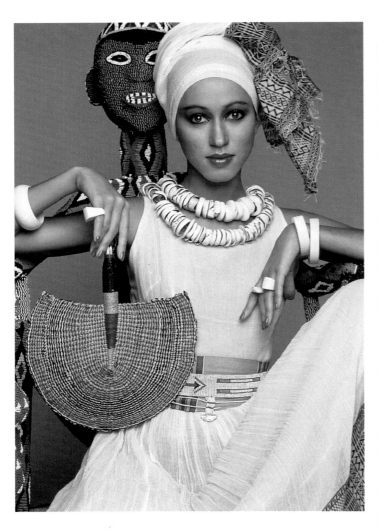

African styling, a reminder of heritage and responsibility.

"When I first came to Europe I traveled with three trunks. Not that I thought I'd ever get stranded in Germany in the middle of the night in a pair of wedgie high heels and a tiny leather skirt sitting with my three trunks. I had to have my clothes with me. I've had so many strange scenes. I've been on boats, you know, the only girl in the midst of ten men on a trip to Africa, decked out in pearls, with tons of Vuitton luggage following behind with your personal wardrobe."

Pat had a well-documented history of attention-getting hijinks on the runway. "Sometimes I did something outrageous, shocking," she admitted. "Not bad, just shocking." In one show she was reported to have fainted at the feet of a male model "causing 150 cameras to whir in her direction." In another Sterling St. Jacques, flamboyant fashionality, carried Pat on his shoulders downstage and "twirled her back upstage in a mad tango," as her top slipped down to reveal a bare breast. Her performances reached mythic proportions. Show-goers anticipated her theatrics as much as the designer's collection.

Pat got to know well a legendary character who was one of the first Black models to star in shows and high fashion editorials in the States, Donyale Luna. Before she died of an apparent drug overdose in Rome in 1979, she and Pat had been roommates there for a few months.

"Donyale Luna was the most exquisite creature you have ever seen. She was tall as a tree, had hair that was immensely thick, the longest arms and fingers, and green eyes. She was living in a fantasy of her own but she was so delicate in spirit that she was overtaken by this earthly thing. Sometimes you come into the business on such a level that it's all power and money and wealth. You get lost in this vein of people who live on that level, and you don't continue your own work.

"Donyale was a poet, a love child, one of those people who really lived in a dream world. She had a child named Dream who lives in Rome. She never wore shoes. Wherever we went she would arrive in her bare feet. She was so beautiful that people would stop eating if they were in a restaurant and they saw her walking by. An entourage of six boys followed her constantly like she was a queen. She always wore dresses with trains, and they would walk behind her and settle around her like she was a princess. She was really the princess of fashion. She was above everything, not of this earth. Then the drug world took her away. She let her real self be seen by me, but she never would come out of that other world. She's one of the beauties that got trapped in the world of pleasure and passed away.

"After you get to be known people start keeping their eye on you, especially guys. They stalk you, they want to meet you, they want to have affairs with you because you are a stepping stone. There's a lot of that going on in modeling. There are so many fantasies Girls have about meeting people and being with them. You have to look at the thing clearly and be careful. Just keep your eye on your work and keep marching.

"For a Girl it's not easy, because people in this business build you up and suddenly one day, maybe they'll pull the rug out from under you. You have to learn a lot about how to watch out for the future. It can be a lonely life. Experience being the lonely Girl, the lonely model. Without love, without a home, just hotels and backstage. What if you have to pay that hotel bill and you don't have the money? Then you're sitting in the café with a glass of wine and a piece of cheese, and you've got black eye makeup on, *alta moda* fashion victim, waiting for the next dinner party. It can be very terrible.

"But I'm a businesswoman. I've had many opportunities and dealt with many types of men. And I'll tell you something, I'm not stupid. There are powerful men in the business who want you, but they want everybody else, too. They can eat you up and spit you out. I've seen it happen, so beware. You can't be a shadow if you want to star.

"You learn about yourself, and what your priorities and morals are. A lot of that is preached into you when you're little, so you try to keep all of that together. From my Baptist upbringing in the church, God tells me when to do right. I don't take a step without talking to God first. But if I do, I get zam-pop-boom! on the back of my head, like a little child. People say, 'Well, how come you lasted so long?' And I say, 'I don't know, but I talk to God.' Every time I do something, I pray first and God says OK. That's basically where it's at.

"My husband is the saving grace of my life, but that didn't come till later, when it was the right time. Before that it was a long search to find someone. He's in the business. But a lot of my boyfriends had been in the business, and they were very competitive. They wanted to be in front of the camera, too. I didn't mind them being there, but I

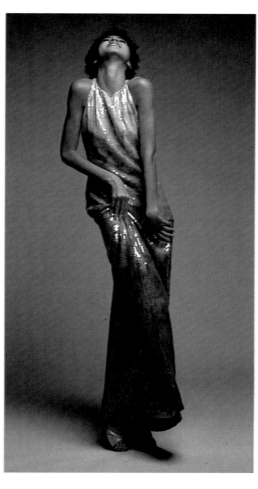

Pat wearing a **Halston** gown, the exquisite distillation of modern elegance.

didn't want to be pushed out of the way. Let's be together, but let me have some space, too. I had fun with all of those guys. You can have fun with people, but you know, Girls need security." Common-sense wisdom for an uncommon business.

Pat Cleveland was unique. Resisting the Sirens' song, she set the standard for both the dazzling party girl and the long-distance star model. But she packed away those roles easily as she prepared to head back to her husband and two children. It had been a long day. Night had come, darkening the sky and brightening the already spirited colors in shop windows. The arcade of La Rinascente, Milan's premier department store, was festooned with brilliant yarns and vivid weavings from Peru for a special promotion. Seen from the other side of the Duomo their color-saturated gaiety was muted by the wistful melodies of Andean flute players, performing like displaced spirits in front of the somber cathedral. As we walked to the subway station, Pat was still talking, unspooling bits of stories, linking the present with the past.

"Once I started traveling, the globe started opening. I worked for *Vogue* in Peru. In Africa, I went to the slave forts. Barry McKinley took me there by boat. Seven days across the ocean, and I was dressed to the nines with pearls up to the neck. Then we went to Kenya and on to Ethiopia and the Red Sea. I went with Toscani on the Red Sea on a boat. We had Italian food, and we ate barracuda. I almost got eaten by a barracuda. I didn't know. What did I know? When you're innocent, God watches over you."

There was still so much to say. She was telling a story about being in Africa and someone going to pee behind a bush. The lion was just about to leap out, and the Jeep was just getting ready to pull off when she stopped mid-sentence. We had arrived at the train station. "Back to reality," she said and laughed. Then she was on her way home.

Beverly Johnson

Up close Beverly Johnson looks as beautiful in real life as she does in photographs. The smooth complexion, lustrous hair, and trim figure seem to abide in some elevated dimension where pimples, naps, bulges, and wrinkles simply do not exist. She is flawless—that exhausted but apt term used to describe treasures from diamonds to divas. Until she opens her mouth. Then her voice, its timbre and energy, restores her to this planet.

It is not easy to describe. She speaks with the determined stride of the jockette she was in her teens, as if she puts her swimmer's shoulders behind every word, willing them to muscle past the blinders regular folk tend to wear around those who emit that exceptional glow. She is more real than royal, and while that may not be your first impression on meeting her, she doesn't mind helping you over that hump. She has been called everything from a goddess to the supergirl next door, with probably a few unprintables in between. After over twenty-five years in the business, it's no longer about good guys finishing last or first. It's about staying power.

The April afternoon that I spend with her is not the first time that I meet her. Our paths crossed occasionally during our working years at go-sees and auditions, although she headed the A team, and I was on the B+ squad. This time is the first that we talk about our lives in some depth.

We start at her apartment on Madison Avenue. Just out of the shower, she greets me at the door in a terry cloth robe with insignia from the Hard Rock Cafe. She's getting ready to tape a television interview, so she leaves me alone in her sprawling living room with its grand view of the Central Park reservoir from the 36th floor. Suede sofas and sectionals, a walnut baby grand piano, modern paintings and sculpture, all share the huge, open space with honorific plaques on the wall and busts of famous Black scientists.

A long mirrored wall enlarges the already uncrowded room. Books are stacked—and perhaps even staged—on the marble and glass coffee table: *Starring Mothers*, shot by fashion photographer Barbara Walz, a compilation of women celebrities with their children, among them Beverly with her daughter, Anansa; a hefty volume of *Paintings in the Louvre*; a copy of the *Black Voices* anthology, opened to a passage by James Baldwin: "If you don't know my name, you don't know your own." There is also a sumptuous edition of dramatic photographs by the French designer Thierry Mugler, who dressed his models in daring costumes and then placed them in epic contexts, on the edge of a sand dune, a skyscraper, a glacier or the tip of a red star on a giant Mao Zedong. Mugler has autographed the book "To Beverly! The Goddess! Bravo! Bravo!"

Beverly enters to less thunderous applause. She is simply but expertly made up, wearing a black unitard over which she has tied a big white shirt. A long, lipstick-red

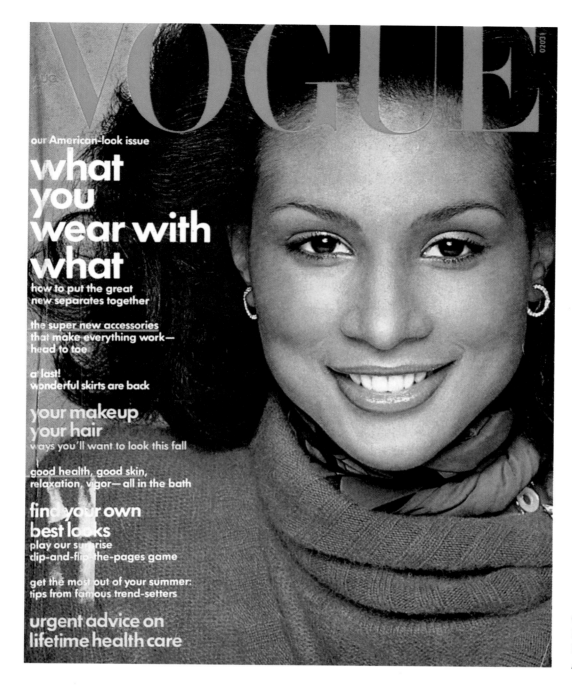

Changing the face of beauty.
Beverly Johnson was the first
Black model on the cover of
American *Vogue*. August, 1974.

jacket, flat black shoes, and a small leopard bag complete the ensemble. It reads confident simplicity, modern good taste. Her sizable diamond earrings sparkle. They read rich.

Beverly Johnson started her winning career by losing. "When I was thirteen I used to compete all over New York state in swimming. I wanted to make the Olympics. That was my goal. I remember getting up early in the mornings, practicing before school, and later practicing after school. Practicing all weekend long. I loved it. I was a fish. But I missed qualifying for the Olympics in Mexico in 1968 by a tenth of a second. And then I started to get interested in boys, and I didn't want to get my hair wet anymore." We laugh together at such a common insecurity.

After skipping her sophomore year of high school in Buffalo and graduating at sixteen, she said, "I wanted to go away to school, and the furthest I could get was Boston. Of course, my parents wanted me to be close. I went to Northeastern University as a political science major. I wanted to be a lawyer. And that's when it all happened. I had worked as a swimming instructor part-time at the local YWCA in Roxbury, but that summer there was this big cutback, and there were no summer jobs for college kids. I thought, What am I going to do now?

"There were some girls at school from New York City who became my friends, and they suggested that I become a model. I said, 'Models, what do they do?' So they showed

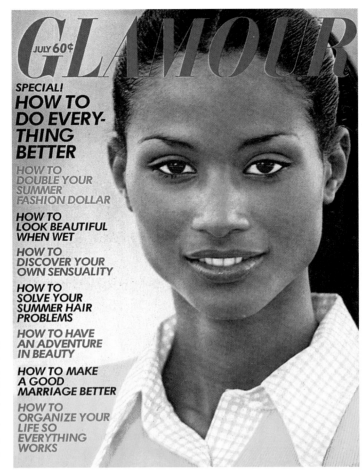

GLAMOUR

JULY 60¢

SPECIAL!
HOW TO DO EVERY-THING BETTER

HOW TO
DOUBLE YOUR SUMMER
FASHION DOLLAR

HOW TO
LOOK BEAUTIFUL
WHEN WET

HOW TO
DISCOVER YOUR
OWN SENSUALITY

HOW TO
SOLVE YOUR
SUMMER HAIR
PROBLEMS

HOW TO HAVE
AN ADVENTURE
IN BEAUTY

HOW TO MAKE
A GOOD
MARRIAGE BETTER

HOW TO
ORGANIZE YOUR
LIFE SO
EVERYTHING
WORKS

While the United States watched **Beverly** grow up inside and on the covers of its magazines, the country was also maturing. Women of all ethnic backgrounds reached past bias and identified with her. *Glamour*, July, 1972. *Vogue*, January, 1981.

me these magazines. I'd never even looked at a fashion magazine before in my life."

With the help of Korby Pleasant, then the manager of the well-known midtown boutique, Jax, she managed to get an appointment at *Glamour* magazine. "I had to convince my mother to come to New York with me. My dad said, 'No, absolutely not, it's prostitution....' But my mother went against my father's wishes, took me to New York, and we went up to *Glamour* magazine. I had my knee socks on, my top knot on my head, and my white gloves, you know, all of seventeen. The editors told us that they liked me. And I said, 'See, Mommy, I told you it's all legitimate. Go back home and tell Dad it's OK.' Then *Glamour* took me on a ten-day assignment to Fire Island."

As for knowing what she was expected to do as a model, Beverly admitted, "I didn't have a clue." But that trip and another one for *Vogue* magazine left her determined to get an agent. Since she'd heard that the best was Eileen Ford, Beverly went to see her at an open interview. The initial meeting was discouraging. "Eileen told me that I was too heavy and that she didn't think I would work as a model. I didn't think to say, Well, you know I'm already working for *Glamour* and *Vogue*. I was naïve. I went to Wilhemina, to Black Beauty. I went everywhere. They all turned me down. Then, about ten days later, I got a phone call from Eileen Ford. The word had probably gotten back that I was free-lancing for *Glamour* and *Vogue*."

Any agent worth staying in business could see that if Beverly was already being booked by the top magazines, there was even more money to be made. What was more difficult to figure was the personality of this new Girl. Beverly signed with the Fords but her relationship with Eileen, who often lodged novice models in her family's East side brownstone, was intense and often contentious. Although Beverly did not live with her, she considered Eileen a surrogate parent. And when she expressed her dreams of being not just inside but on the cover of *Glamour* and *Vogue*, Beverly was rewarded with the hard-nosed realities of the business. "Eileen would tell me that they didn't put Blacks on the cover and that I ought to be glad to be doing what I was doing."

It was 1971. The Black-is-beautiful boom was fading. Although some breakthroughs, changes, and progress had been made, the more conservative decision makers thought those steps were more than enough. Then too, some of the advice Beverly received had nothing to do with color. Models averaged a five-to-seven-year career. Words from the wise about staying in school and saving money were only sensible.

For Beverly, though, the lack of encouragement despite her tangible successes—her first *Glamour* cover came in March, 1972—only "fueled me to really want to do it more. I started investigating and researching and seeing what modeling was really all about. I was reading magazines, and talking to the Girls. I was all wide-eyed and eager to learn. Who's this designer? How does a booking work? How do you do the billing? The bookers

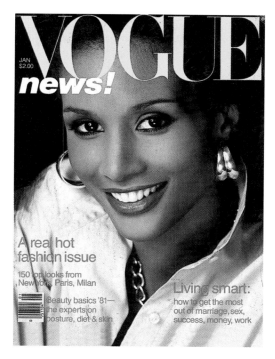

and other Girls were always saying, 'Why do you want to know all this stuff?' I wanted to know. I was always very curious. I wanted to meet the designers and do fashion shows. You know, Girls who did print back then didn't do shows. But I wanted to.

"That's how I first met Naomi Sims, at a show. She was really gracious to me. I already had pictures out in *Glamour*, and she said, 'You're going to do well in this business.' I'll never forget that as long as I live. Everybody was dressing her, because she was the star. I didn't even know how to walk. Others were laughing at me when I came out, because I was like this little hick girl from Buffalo. But Naomi was really so encouraging to me. I said to myself if I ever become a big star I'm going to do the same thing to the other Girls coming up. That's how much impact she had on me. And that year she retired."

While Naomi Sims had done many precedent-setting covers, she had never been on the cover of *Vogue*, which was considered more than a victory. For models, it was a consecration. The fact that Naomi had done many splendid inside spreads and had become an international celebrity made it even more difficult to understand why that particular cover eluded her. One could only speculate on the reasons: racial prejudice, her own too-short hair, a too-strong look…. Whatever the real determining factors were, Beverly won the trophy cover. And by 1975, she had six *Glamour* covers, two *Vogue* covers, the first Black cover of French *Elle*, and a stunning portfolio of other covers, ads, and editorial tear sheets. Her success also attracted an unexpected amount of flak.

With self-confidence bordering on arrogance, Beverly dared to declare to the world that she did not consider herself the top Black model in the business. "I'm the biggest model, period," was her rebuttal to a radio show host, a comment that was later picked up in a controversial 1975 profile by Ted Morgan in the *Sunday Magazine* of the *New York Times*. She went on to elaborate, saying, "I've been in the business four years. There's not a model, black or white, who's done what I've done in such a short time. It's so, and I think I should say it."

The fashion public was furious, and their response to her statements was devastating. Says Beverly now, "People wouldn't even talk to me when I went on jobs after that. The White Girls, the White community, they wouldn't even say Hi. I've always felt that I was misunderstood a lot." Tradition strongly recommended that a Black model appear grateful for her career, humbly ignorant of the extent of her success, and smilingly deferential to the White people who had made it all possible. That Beverly felt confident enough not to act that way was a sign of the times and a symbol that she fully understood her unique status.

Market research discovered that White readers of *Glamour*, even from the South and Midwest, wanted not only to see Beverly Johnson in the magazine, but also to be her in life. She knew her value. She raised her rate to the unprecedented figure of $100/hour when Lauren Hutton, the White star of Revlon's Ultima campaign, raised hers. Furthermore, she articulated the reason why in the *New York Times*. She said that an art director "told me I sold a million dollars' worth of one garment. If you look at it that way, what I'm getting is chicken feed." Never before had a Black model—and perhaps a model of any color—been so candid about the connection between beauty and big bucks.

Although the fiercely competitive nature of the business bothered her, it did not stop her. Beverly continued to do elegant editorial, upscale catalog, designer shows, ads, and television commercials. While she considers Revlon's "Most Unforgettable Women in the World" campaigns her favorites, she claims no preference for a particular branch of modeling. "I got very inspired," she insists, "whenever they were big jobs, big money jobs."

The question of jobs that advertised controversial products—cigarettes, liquor, and fur, for example—was reduced not to principles but to the bottom line. "We're so limited in the jobs we get anyway, that if I didn't do them I wouldn't have been able to pay my rent. I didn't have the luxury to be able to say, 'Oh, I don't do fur ads or cigarette ads or liquor ads.' I mean, I couldn't afford that luxury."

Knowing when and where to compromise came with experience, which Beverly tried to share with others. But solidarity with equally ambitious—if less visibly successful—models was scarce and far from binding. She found herself "really just fighting, fighting, fighting. It was for myself but it was also for everyone. Saying that I would not go on location and do a job for one day, when all the White models were there for a week. Speaking out and encouraging Black Girls to come to the agency. And trying to organize meetings with Black Girls telling them not to cut their rate. The Girls were always asking me, 'Why does it always have to be one Black model at a time?' And I'd say, 'That's what I want to know. Why does it always have to be just one?'"

While Beverly Johnson can be credited with significant professional breakthroughs, she can also be credited with a major personal one. Unafraid of challenging the status quo, in 1978 she became a mother in a business that hesitated to recognize that beauty and babies could go together. "I was always going to disprove everybody. I was at the peak of my career when I had my daughter, Anansa. And afterwards I worked more than I'd ever worked before. I think that really inspired the baby boom in the modeling industry. I couldn't foresee going through my life without having children, but at that time you didn't have kids after thirty, that's what I understood. I was married at the time, although not for very much longer after that. I had someone take care of her, but when she was young, until the age of five, she went everywhere with me. It was only when she got to school age that she had to really settle in."

While Beverly talks with great delight about her daughter, she admits that parenthood did not provide unmitigated joy for her. "I thought that you inherited motherhood. I thought that you innately knew what to do to nurture a child. I didn't realize that that took as much studying and information-seeking as anything else. So, I had a lot of hard knocks at first, because I felt very inadequate as a mother. That was a very frustrating period. Dissolving the marriage made it even more dramatic. Then I went into a very long divorce and custody battle that lasted ten years, which was, I think, the blackest period of my life." She came close to a breakdown.

"Rumors were flying about what was happening with me. It was really, really bad. I was still trying to keep the career together. Iman was coming along. I got into a lot of litigation with modeling agencies and clients about monies that were misappropriated, and I was fighting them. I had to take a two-year leave from the industry to actually fight that case, which turned out very favorably towards me. But, you know, once you

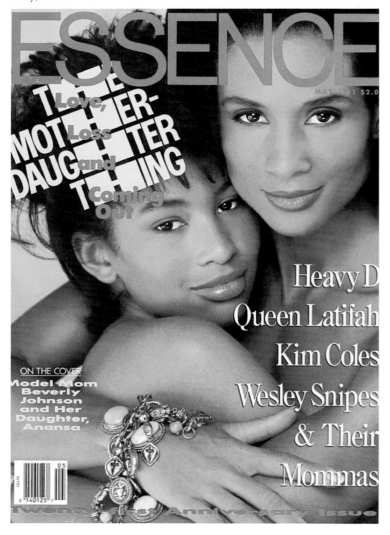

Beverly with her daughter, **Anansa**. At the peak of her career when she first became a mother, **Beverly** worked even more afterward. *Essence*, May, 1991.

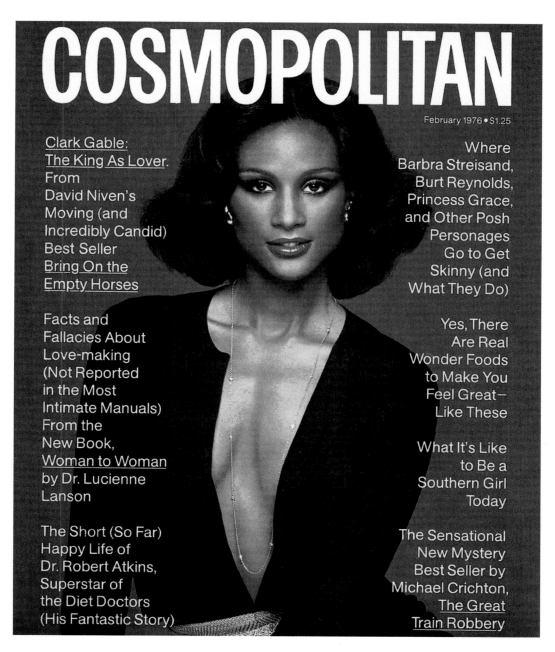

COSMOPOLITAN

February 1976 • $1.25

<u>Clark Gable:
The King As Lover</u>.
From
David Niven's
Moving (and
Incredibly Candid)
Best Seller
<u>Bring On the
Empty Horses</u>

Facts and
Fallacies About
Love-making
(Not Reported
in the Most
Intimate Manuals)
From the
New Book,
<u>Woman to Woman</u>
by Dr. Lucienne
Lanson

The Short (So Far)
Happy Life of
Dr. Robert Atkins,
Superstar of
the Diet Doctors
(His Fantastic Story)

Where
Barbra Streisand,
Burt Reynolds,
Princess Grace,
and Other Posh
Personages
Go to Get
Skinny (and
What They Do)

Yes, There
Are Real
Wonder Foods
to Make You
Feel Great—
Like These

What It's Like
to Be a
Southern Girl
Today

The Sensational
New Mystery
Best Seller by
Michael Crichton,
<u>The Great
Train Robbery</u>

The sensuous side of the goddess next door.
Cosmopolitan, February, 1976.

fight somebody in the business, rumors about drinking and drugs and everything escalate even more.

"I knew I would come back. I just didn't know how to come back. I hadn't given up every ounce of hope, but I was really in despair. I got help. And I realized that all of the pressures and all of the other things that had happened to me were due to self-destructive behavior. I think that happens in a lot of people's lives, and it's very difficult to come back.

"I fought for my respect like you wouldn't believe. I had to put everybody in their place. I fought tooth and nail for people to just respect me, and eventually they did. But it was hell. No one wanted me back. They were trying to eliminate me from the entire business, and I just wouldn't stand for it.

"When you're in the top position, number one, you're a sitting duck. Everybody basically wants to shoot you out of that number one position. They love it when you're down. They can't wait. I've seen that happen to a lot of Girls. But coming back, reestablishing myself, I demanded to be respected. It was easier for clients to think, OK, this Girl isn't finished, so we'd better start being nice to her again.

"Once I really came back and proved myself, I came back stronger, and I came back smarter. I came back right, and I didn't come back bitter. It wasn't easy. It's not that there's no bitterness. But I'm not a bitter person. I felt a huge responsibility to protect and uphold a certain image. I had to protect myself. It's selfish in a lot of respects, but racism also plays a part in there, too. I mean, everybody has skeletons in the closet. But if you were

BEVERLY JOHNSON

229

White and you came out and said, Oh, I was on drugs, people would say, That's great, and they'll give you a job. But you be Black and say you were on drugs and see what happens. It's a different story, totally different standards. It was held against you. It did not propel your career like it did for other people.

"I think it was a mistake at a certain period of time for athletes and entertainers to come out and hang all their dirty laundry on the line. It destroyed a lot of the dreams of young Black children. There were very few positive role models. As a parent, I don't tell my daughter everything just to let her know that I'm honest. I try to set an example. I try to live it, but God knows, I'm not perfect. I don't think she has to know my every imperfection. She's too young. Her mind is too tender.

"I don't feel that it's necessary to bare my soul, particularly at the expense of a nation of people. If I could have avoided going through that period of self-destruction, I would have. I wouldn't wish that on a dog. But I know that you can get help.

"I think my older sister had a lot to do with it. I had become very well-situated through the legal settlements. I was at the point where I could live off the interest for the rest of my life. And my sister, who is a therapist, asked me what would I do if I could do any five things in my life? I thought, I want to be an actress. But how am I going to be an actress? I'm too old. I started with all these negatives. She said, 'Just write them down.' So I did: I wanted to act, I wanted to produce, I wanted to write another book, I wanted to model, and I wanted to produce a TV show. Then I handed them to her on a piece of paper. And she said, 'OK, now I want you to go out and do these things.'

"From that day on my life changed. I started back doing everything I wanted to do. I started to dream again. It's going to be interesting. That's what I try to tell these new Girls coming along. Some of them call me and say, 'I can't do this and I can't do that…. ' And I say, 'Yes, you can.'"

It has been said that the value of our victories is determined by the strength of our opponents. For decades Black models have struggled in non-Black societies like David against Goliath, with no one sling-shot stone delivering an uncontested victory. Beverly Johnson's first *Vogue* cover, however, appeared to be our David's stone. After years of incremental gains, the Goliath of White racism was finally toppled. And we cheered.

Yet when the opponent was more personal, when it became in fact, oneself, victory became more complex. We had to understand what we did to this business as well as what this business did to us. Everyone paid some price. Like innocence, a certain success, once lost, could never be regained. In dramatic cases, the battle was for elemental survival. And we did not always win.

Crowds did not cheer us on during this internal struggle, except, perhaps as Beverly suggested, for one's final downfall. A debilitating double standard did exist. White stars can often rise again, but once Black stars were down, they were often out. And our goddesses were even less likely to be hailed on the comeback trail.

The challenge confronting consumers of Black images was immense. While our inner vision was intricate and subtle, the media offered images sadly lacking in corresponding qualities. Models did occupy a special position. For as much as they were projected at us, we projected onto them. It was largely our dreams that rendered them three-dimensional. But when they no longer rewarded us with perfection, we may have been too quick to deflate and discard them.

The challenge, then, was to recognize that the vulnerable humanity of our heroes and sheroes was much—if not exactly—like our own. We must learn to temper hasty judgments with longer looks in our own mirror. We must decide for ourselves to love our beauty not just when White people told us to, but also when they told us to deny it, to forget it, to reject the honors we were just encouraged to bestow. They told us to forget for centuries. In our hearts we refused to listen. Perhaps because we heard another voice, barely a whisper in all the discordant fanfare of coming and going. That voice kept saying, She is me, and we will survive.

Iman

Picture this: A struggling university student leaves her job in the middle of a bustling city. She is followed by a strange man who asks her if she's ever been photographed before. "Of course," she replies, thinking, What a stupid question. "By whom?" he inquires. "My mother," she answers dismissively.

Fast forward a couple of years to the other side of the globe: A tall, glamorous woman is introduced as the image model for a new cosmetics line. Speculation on the financial terms of her contract merely intensifies the rumors swirling through the business that she was an illiterate tribeswoman discovered tending her family's herd of cattle and sheep on the African plains.

Focus on the relatively here and now: Two women sit in the bright, bamboo-shafted room of a Pacific-rim restaurant in Hollywood where serenity is cheerfully usurped by the high decibels of sophisticated rendezvous. The woman with glasses asks and eats; the other with the big straw hat pressed low on her brow answers, and merely nibbles. Her thin fingers are animated and expressive, speaking a sign language all their own. Bursts of laughter—charmingly cynical and self-mocking—season the conversation with unexpected flavors.

Rumors aside, the college student, shepherdess, and fashion supermodel were all one person, a woman who came to exemplify the prima bitcherina fashion diva of the '80s: Iman Abdulmajid, known, like most stars in the firmament of style by a single name, Iman. Willful, demanding, and superior, her prickly reputation preceded her. The real surprise came in seeing how unseriously she took herself. As Iman filled in her scenes, she seemed to most enjoy recalling the immense hype that surrounded her beginnings.

"I did something that I think worked very well for me when I came to the States. It was rumored that I was, among other things, an African princess found in the jungle amidst people who were illiterate. So I rode with the tide. For three months I didn't speak English. Everybody talked in front of me. That's how I found out how things worked in the business.

"I'd make a great con artist. I can fake my way to the top of anything. You have to be very smart. As you know, as models, we have the reputation that we can't talk and walk at the same time. So you also have that advantage."

Her story began somewhat differently from the fanciful rumors, but it had its own legitimate elements of good fortune, adventure, and intrigue. While Iman, who was fluent in five languages, was attending Nairobi University on scholarship, she was also busily scraping her tuition together by working for the Kenyan Ministry of Tourism. She used her language skills to translate brochures and dispense information from a glass cubicle

Passionate, introspective.
Iman in **Donna Karan**.

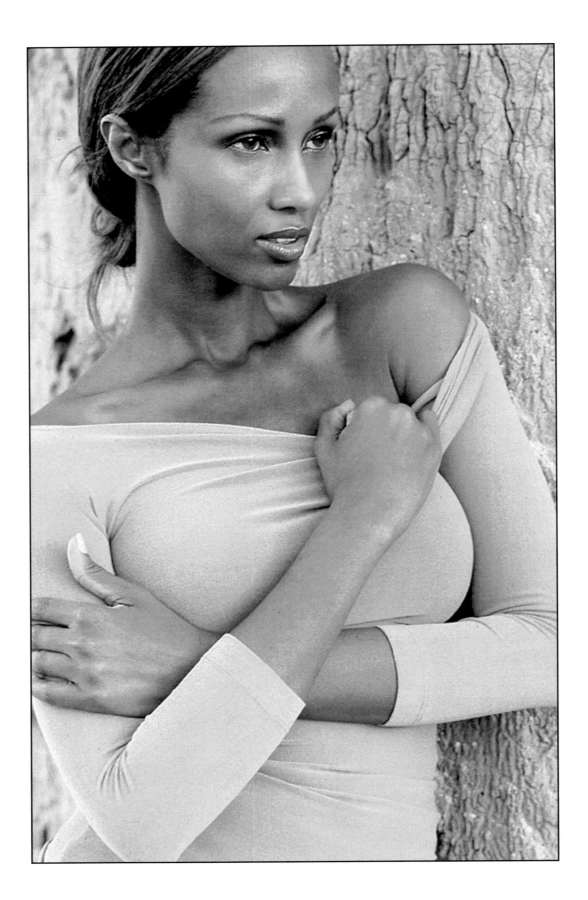

in the middle of Nairobi. Closing the office one day, she was approached by Peter Beard, the internationally acclaimed photographer. He wanted to take pictures of her. Having never been exposed to fashion and fashion magazines, she was reluctant to accept his offer. "He understood that I didn't understand, so he talked to me, showed me magazines, and then said the magic words, 'I'll pay you.' How much? He said, 'What do you want?' I asked him for my tuition. That's how I did it. He took the pictures, gave me my tuition, and that was the end of that. I was going back to school. He left Nairobi a couple of months later and went to New York where he had an exhibition of his pictures in an art gallery. On the invitation was my picture. When Wilhemina saw it, she asked him if he could bring me to New York. The next thing I knew, everybody in Nairobi was looking for me, but they couldn't call me because I didn't have a phone."

It took almost a year for Iman to decide to go to New York. A failing early marriage and other legal constraints made leaving Kenya difficult, if not impossible. "So, ingeniously, I forged my papers. Of course," she asks matter-of-factly, "what else was a girl to do? One morning I had breakfast with my husband, he went to work, I took my suitcase and went to the airport, and I've been gone since then.

"Wilhemina asked me to sign a contract, but I wouldn't sign because I didn't know what a contract meant. The only thing I asked of her was to keep my return ticket open. If and when I wanted to go back home, I didn't want to have to talk to anybody. Just get on a flight and go back, that's it. I still have the ticket.

"The newspapers and magazines started writing about me three months before I even arrived. I felt like the Messiah." She laughed. "She's coming, she's coming. Then when I got to New York, I was whisked off in a limousine, and as I was approaching the apartment on Fifth Avenue and 76th Street where I would be staying, Manhattan looked worse than any Third World country I'd ever seen. There was a garbage strike, so garbage was everywhere. It was a jungle.

"An hour after I got there, they said we're having a press conference. And that's when I found out that everybody thought I didn't speak English. Peter, of course, came up with this Cinderella story, and since I had forged papers, I went along with it." Beard was the one who responded to the sixty-four journalists convened for the occasion. Iman added, "It was a great experience.

"The only person who really suspected and knew from her heart was Bethann Hardison. She was my only confidante. Stephen Burrows called for me to come see him to shoot some pictures, and Bethann was working there, fitting the clothes. I never wore heels before I came to the States. After they gave me a pair of heels, I was having a major struggle trying to put them on and be very graceful at the same time. So Bethann got on her knees and did it for me. Since I didn't speak English, people would talk about me right in front of me. I heard the Girls telling her, 'Oh, don't encourage her, she already thinks she's a princess.' She looked up at me, and said, 'Is that all right?' And I knew that she knew that I spoke English. I said, 'Yes, thank you very much.' She's been a friend from then on. To me she was the Statue of Liberty. That was my welcome to America."

It was 1975. Not everyone received her with open arms. All-American was the most popular model image then, whether White, Black or Other. Exotics, originals, and eccentrics—euphemisms which seemed to include many Black models no matter what their background or projection—were often shunted in the direction of the runway.

Iman entered troubled waters. A rival agency launched "this major campaign" against her which involved alerting immigration authorities about her status. Regularizing her working papers, which normally would have taken only a few weeks, took six months. Then, a political organization threatened to bomb the photography studios where she was scheduled to work, accusing them of "exploitation of the African." Complicating this even further was a prolonged controversy with a top Black magazine in which she refused to appear until a new editor took over.

As a political science major in Kenya, she was aware of the racial situation in the United States and its political complexities. She knew, she said, "not a lot, but quite enough. The reason I say 'not a lot' is because you have to be a Black American to know that kind of injustice. I've never seen the Black population receive injustice in my country, Somalia, because when I was five years old, we got our independence. Everybody has their own kind of suffering. You can't say, 'I know what you feel.' No, you don't. You can empathize, but you don't really know how another person thinks and feels. Since I was in political science I was aware, book-wise, but I didn't *know*.

"Black models at that time were very segregated. They were totally set apart with the mentality that said, We'll only use one Black Girl at a time. A lot of Girls fell for that. I think it's much better now, and I give all the credit for breaking that barrier to *Elle* magazine. I have more fans now among Black models in the business than I would have had before that time.

"I don't mind a Girl competing with another Girl, but if she has to be the same color, there's something wrong with that. If I want to compete, I'll go for the top. Why would I say, 'I'm only going to compete with the Black models?' If the model on top is Black, I'll compete with her. If she's not on top, I don't compete. This is just business, like any other business. You go to do your best."

The question of competition became moot in 1979 when Iman won the first cosmetic contract ever granted a Black model. Polished Ambers, a special line for darker skin tones, was Revlon's first attempt to capture a significant share of the growing market in Black cosmetics. While it traded on Iman's authentic African-ness as well as Afro-centric styling in its ad campaigns, the line lacked something, perhaps a certain African-*American* appeal, and it did not prosper. If Polished Ambers appeared to mark another milestone in recognition of the potential power of Black consumers, in effect, it was merely an updated replay of the old separate-but-equal marketing philosophy. Industry excitement was higher and the dollars were bigger but the print ads' exposure was still limited to the Black press. What seemed like a new commitment folded after a couple of years.

During that time, however, Iman made the most of her personal exposure. Just a few years after she arrived in New York, with editorial spreads, high-paying catalog bookings, and a prestigious advertising campaign to her credit, she was at or near the top of the profession. Then, she was provoked to do fashion shows. "It was like everything else in my life. I stumble into things. Challenged by a colleague, I did the Calvin Klein show, and the rest is history. They wrote about me on the front page of *Women's Wear Daily*.

"What I did and what I still do is that I use my fear and my anxiety while I'm on the runway to work for me. I can only compare myself to a duck. You see it swimming, so cool on the outside, on top of the water. Now look underneath. It's pumping away. You've got to try to keep it inside, and it will work. The other thing that works for me is that I can't let the audience not be a part of me. I pick certain people, and I just beam in on them. So I don't just walk, I have to look. I'll bring that person into me. There will be situations where people can feel the heel of my shoe breaking, and they'll feel it before I do, because I bring them in. It's very exciting to see people coming with you.

"When I do shows, I get the best of clothes and the worst of clothes. Whenever I come on, they say, 'Ah, it must be making a statement because Iman is wearing it.' Sometimes it's not. Sometimes it's a mistake.

"People like to say to me that I'm the best. I don't think so. I think some people have the body for shows, but they don't have the aura. There are people who have the right walk for it, but they don't have the presence. There are people who have the beauty, but they're so bland. They don't have the excitement. The people who can make it work are usually the people who don't have the greatest body, but they have everything else that's needed.

"When I walk on the runway, I think of the desert where I was raised, that vastness. People say to me, 'When you do shows, I wish it were a longer runway.' What a compliment. Some people say, 'What would you like to achieve in life?' Longer runways?" She laughed as if the answer was mindlessly insulting. She is a woman who combines risk and calculation in a constantly changing but ever thoughtful mix.

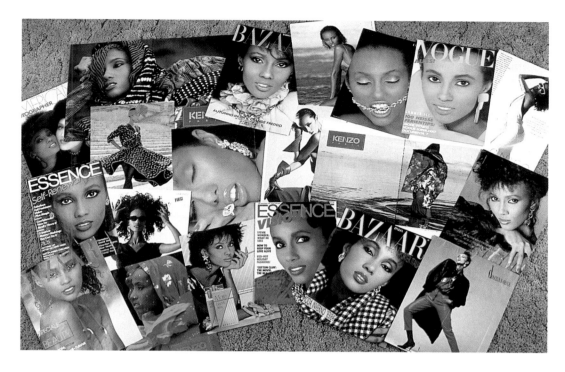

Iman's face covered—and conquered—the world.

"I'm not very business-oriented when it comes to what I want to do. I might do something just to get an ad, but I've never done designers that I didn't think much of. In photography, they can take four or five rolls to get one decent picture out of it. Sometimes the wrong picture out of it. But on the runway, you've got to feel something. You have to feel the clothes. Europe is doing a Broadway show, and New York is showroom, that's what the difference is as far as runway goes. I don't tamper with Japan, it's too far from here. I've been there once for Issey Miyake, but then I'd go anywhere with Issey Miyake."

Claiming that there was "nothing glamorous about modeling," Iman made one important exception. "The money is very glamorous. It's ridiculous. For one year I told the agency to put me on special assignment. Some client called me, it was only a half-day booking, and I said OK, $25,000 for three hours. Maybe I should have asked more?" One million dollars is the most she admitted to making in one year. She coyly added, "If I lie, you know it's more?"

A self-described workaholic, she insisted that "work doesn't rub off. Just because you lie down with someone, talent doesn't rub off. What you are is what you yourself can accomplish. It's not because you're out with someone or you go to bed with someone. I enjoy working because it's good for me, for my self-esteem. It's luxurious to have a lot of money, but I don't want anything. In my young age I lost a lot of sleep over men. I don't want to lose sleep after thirty-five over anything. Have a good night's sleep. That's my philosophy."

A good night's sleep wasn't always so high on her list of priorities, though. "From '77 to '79, it was party time. I was one of those people who would go from work, take a nap for a couple of hours, go to Studio 54 until eight o'clock in the morning, and then go to work again, grab another couple of hours' sleep, and not think about it. There's nothing I haven't done. But basically, it's very simple. I don't have crutches.

"How come every night there's a big party, and when you don't go, the next day everybody calls saying, 'Oh, you missed a great party'? You haven't missed anything. There is no big party to be missed. Isn't it just like the other one I went to yesterday, the same people, the same thing? What'd I miss? You make your own party."

Her marriage in 1978 to basketball star Spencer Haywood added another dimension

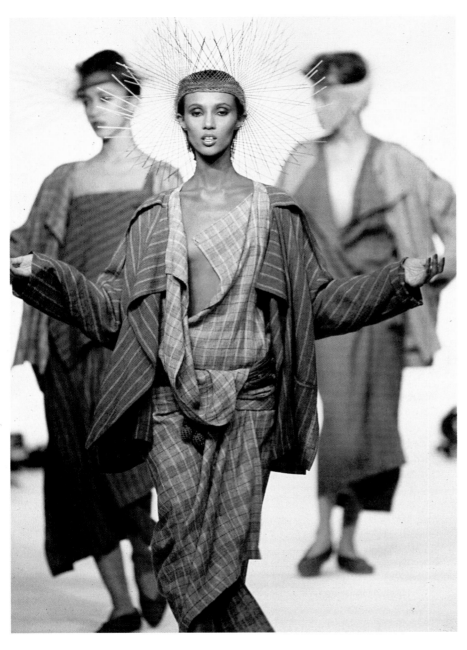

Iman, the runway diva, wearing **Issey Miyake**.

to the on-going fairy tale: the romance of the African princess and the African-American prince. "It was the best of times, it was the worst of times," she recalled. "I remember when I told my parents that I was going to marry an American, they first asked, 'Is he Black or White?' I said, 'He's Black.' The second thing they asked, 'What does he do?' And I said, 'He's a basketball player.' And my mother wanted to know if he was ever going to grow up. We didn't think there were people who played basketball after high school."

She was a proud, protective mother as she spoke about their daughter, Zulekha, born in 1979. "It's difficult for a child to have both parents who are very successful in what they do. She's a smart kid, very street smart. I have protected her to the utmost. Her school is fifteen minutes' walking distance from the house. She would say, 'Mommy, I can walk, please. No, I don't want you to come with me.' So I get into my car with sunglasses and a hat, and follow her. I'm so glad she's spending this year with her father, because being with a man, he's not going to let her date. She can get some leeway with me. But Spencer says he's going to take out a shotgun."

At this point in her life, Iman said, "I want to spend time with myself. I like getting up in the morning, sitting by the pool, making coffee, and getting together with scriptwriters to do the film work I want to do. I want to give myself some time alone instead of always being so involved with people. Otherwise you always consider yourself as a branch of somebody else. I've always been the child of somebody, the wife of somebody, the mother of somebody. Since I was sixteen years old there's always been a man in my life. Men have taken so much of my life. You can't live without them entirely, but you can live without them for a while. Well, how about me? How about Iman, alone, and not the model, just as a person?"

Out of concern for Haywood's privacy Iman refused to talk about her marriage which ended in 1987. Haywood, however, was much more revealing about the environment of their relationship in his 1992 autobiography, subtitled *The Rise, The Fall, The Recovery*. He wrote: "The high-fashion scene is strange and decadent. It is as competitive as the sports world.... The girls not only have to stay thin as greyhounds, but they have to be incredibly hyped up and energized for photo shoots and fashion shows. They have to be on fire, they have to be hot. The sale of a million-dollar line of clothing rests on their ability to make the clothing come alive. What could better accomplish that purpose than our old friend cocaine? And, Valium and Quaalude. Fashion people come second only to athletes in their tendency to use drugs."

Iman did not detail the seamier side to her life and career, but it seemed to play a silent background role in a crisis that challenged not only her image but her life. A taxi cab smash-up left her face a wreck and her career in jeopardy. But it was an accident, she said, "that I knew was coming." Work had been going too well in 1982, so much so that she forgot her principles and succumbed to the hubris of her own image.

"At the end of the year, right before Christmas I started getting depressed. I realized that I had started something that I wanted to stop. I wanted to get out of it, but I knew I would have to pay for it. And I was trying to stop the punishment from coming. So I started not to leave the house. When I was supposed to be going on location, I wouldn't be able to find my passport. I'd look through the whole house. My booker would come over, and my passport would be sitting right there. I'd never done anything like that before. I just thought something bad was going to happen, so I was trying to get out before it did."

A few weeks later, a cab ride home after a dinner date ended in disaster. "At 37th and First Avenue this car hit my cab. I could see my head literally going through the partition inside the taxi. To avoid the impact the cabdriver went up onto the sidewalk, hit a building, and we overturned. I remember I was wearing a white suit. I crawled out of the car, and then I passed out. The next thing I knew I was in an ambulance being taken to the hospital. Finally, the doctor got to me. I said something in my language. The nurse said, 'She's been talking in that foreign language all night.' And the doctor said, 'Does anybody speak Spanish here?' That brought me back. Talking about a sense of humor.

"When I found out what actually happened to me, I thought, Oh, that was close. I looked like the Elephant Man. One whole side of my face was broken. All the bones came out. My eye was intact, but the whole eye socket was broken in pieces. People said, 'You should have died.' Died? That's the easy way out. I could have been totally paralyzed for the rest of my life. I thought, God, forget it. I'll never do this again.

"It was amazing, like a test. I could have been really damaged. I had major plastic surgery. I was supposed to be in therapy for six months. They said I wouldn't be able to finish my recovery program for five years. Three months later I was fine. I didn't go through therapy. Nothing. So all in all, the punishment was needed, and it wasn't even a punishment. It was a scolding."

If the arrogance was chastened, what else changed? What was the lesson learned? "For one thing, I know who I am. I don't say any more, 'Do you know who I am?' You don't have to know who I am. I know who I am. That changed. Also, whenever anything good happened, I learned to say, 'Thanks' and 'Congratulations.' Instead of thinking that I earned it or I deserved it. There are a lot of people who've earned it and deserved it much more, and they still don't get it. I simply say, 'Thank God.' I'm still not a religious person, but the accident just cleared my mind. That blow I needed. My career had gone better than I ever imagined. And with that change in my frame of mind it worked even better.

"For the first time I realized that there is more to my career than just meets the eye. In 1988, Bethann and I started the Black Girls Coalition with a group of models. As you know, the homeless situation is just out of proportion. And being parents, we know that a child born in that environment will almost never get a chance to get out of it. So, it's not just about sending money. It's about actually being on hand and being personally accountable. Every Girl in the Coalition is responsible for five kids; we take them out of the shelters and to the movies or to lunch or to the park.

"The Girls have come a long, long way in becoming a major force for change. Now, it's so good to be Black. No kidding. Before, the people in fashion didn't want to have anything to do with us. Now, it's so chic. Is your father Black? You're in. Everybody who ever had any Black blood in them is now coming out of the closet. It's funny. Black Girls had big lips. Whoever thought they were sexy? Now, there are Black Girls who're getting injections to make their lips fuller. I'm saying, Oh, please, don't go overboard with it.

"I decided a while ago that I'd had it with modeling. After more than a dozen years, I'd had it with New York. And I thought it would be the perfect time for me to get out—at the top of where I am—so I can move into other things and do what I want to do while the doors are open for me.

"Coming from a Third World country, coming from someplace where the opportunities are simply not there, once you do get an opportunity you run with it. And you make sure you don't exhaust yourself on that one opportunity. You can't get too comfortable because things change, people change, ideas change, your time will change. Your time will pass before you've made any other plans.

"So after I moved to L.A. I gave myself one year to re-orient myself, and then I said it's time to hit the books. I wanted to get out there and read and see what was available." Ironically, one of the books she optioned was the autobiography of Elizabeth of Toro, the pioneering Ugandan princess who became a barrister, model, and United Nations ambassador. "It's a risk, but I believe that the best investment you can make in anything is yourself. Invest in yourself, and then back it up. Back it up with what you do."

Iman has appeared in several feature films—among them *Out of Africa*, *No Way Out*, and *Exit to Eden*—and television shows. She has also played an important real-life role in drawing attention to the need for famine relief in war-torn Somalia. There, it is not about gold, glamour or glory. Had she not achieved these things, in this country, however, she may not have become the instantly recognizable face and that identifiable name which have served to personalize such faraway suffering.

Picture this: A desert landscape teeming with collapsed, barely breathing bodies. Wrapped in sexless tatters, an emaciated Black person of indeterminate gender, all hope extinguished except in the eyes, reaches for a package of rehydrating salts. Not even food. In a distant world a striking woman, as articulate she is beautiful, appears on breakfast television pleading for political awareness and concrete aid for her homeland, this same

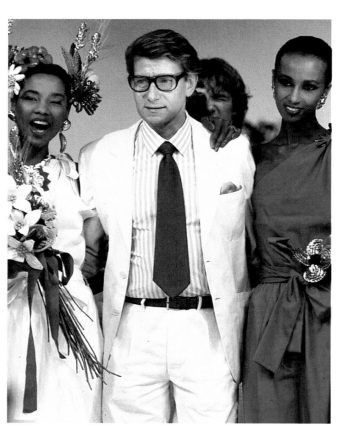

Iman [right] and **Mounia** flank **Yves Saint Laurent** at the end of a show.

desert land. The circumstances could not be more dissimilar. Yet the woman insists on making a connection. We are one, her image says to us. To stop the dying and feed the people, help is needed. It is hardly another cheerful commercial message.

Change of focus: In the spring of 1992, Iman married British rock star, David Bowie, in two ceremonies, one in Switzerland and one in Italy. They lead a well-publicized private life in several homes ranging from a chateau in Switzerland to a Caribbean villa in Mustique. More changes were not only a possibility but a definite.

Fifteen years after she made history as the first Black woman to win a cosmetics contract, Iman continued to break new ground not just as a face and a name but as an entrepreneur. Frustrated that she had "used every brand of makeup on the planet" without finding ones that really worked, she inaugurated her own line of cosmetics and botanically-based skin care products in 1994.

If few celebrities actually control the business attached to their names, it is also true that few images—especially in the fashion world—correspond to an authentic identity. In Iman the convergence of hype and hope reached a level never dreamed of even in her early years as a star model. Using the springboard of American opportunity, she soared from one public success to the next, and perhaps some speculated, with greater ease than if she had been an African American. Becoming blonder with each appearance, she became an international icon, the golden Black woman, as real an image as the many others captured in the lens.

Book

3

Itinerary

I had no nation now but the imagination.
Derek Walcott

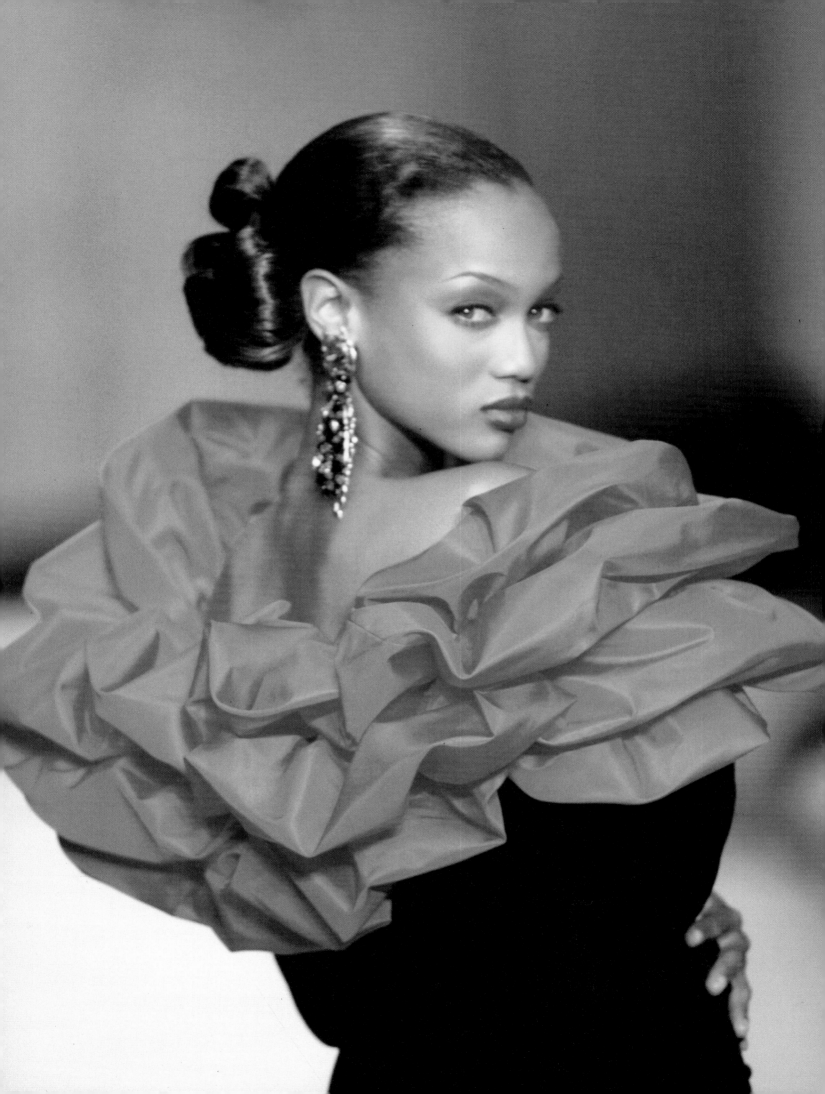

Itinerary

Milan • Paris • Tokyo

In Milan and Paris, October toasts the leaves a crusty brown before they fall limp with the evening rain. There are none of the flashy displays of scarlet maple and gold leaf that adorn more privileged locales. Mother Nature neglects Milan and Paris in October, for this is show season in Europe, and She knows how competitive fashion designers are.

All the colors and color combinations you find missing in the urban wilds you find in the prêt-à-porter collections shown in the fall for the following spring and summer. While swimsuits in hues seen in nature only with the aid of deep-sea diving equipment glide blithely past, the cramped but select hundreds who witness these spectacles are dressed in their own loyalty outfits. One does wear Armani to the Armani show, Chanel to the Chanel show, and Saint Laurent to the Saint Laurent show, although, of course, most everyone wears their Chanel bag most everywhere.

Even in Tokyo. There, at the last stop in the show circuit, even the notoriously chauvinist Japanese bow down to the most coveted European and American labels. Although the foliage in November—when the shows take place in Tokyo—can show a surprising tinge of flame, the year-round barrage of color-saturated neon is enough to make me understand why black is Japan's favorite color.

On October 1, 1992, I set out, minus the Chanel bag that I do not yet own, to cover the summer '93 collections in Milan, Paris, and Tokyo. That is, to see what models were working for which designers, and to find out, in general, how the Girls were doing. I wanted to see who was getting star treatment on the international circuit and who were the newest faces nudging the others off the scene. It was a hard job, but somebody had to do it.

I had my own eye-tinerary. When my vision would start to lose focus after seeing hundreds of outfits, I had to remind myself that I was not there for the clothes. I was there for the people in them, for the personalities and dreams that brought the fabrics and designs to life. I was there for the Girls.

Just getting to see them at work during the shows is a trip in another dimension, and I don't mean geographical. It's not easy. Each fashion capital—in order of '92 show schedules, Milan, London, Paris, New York, and Tokyo—has an organization dedicated to coordinating the presentations of their premier designers to store buyers (who will actually order the merchandise they think their clients will buy) and to fashion journalists (the editors, writers, and reporters who publicize the latest offerings in magazines, newspapers, and on TV). Once you register your credentials with this umbrella organization, next you will need to contact the press relations person at the house of each designer whose show you wish to attend. It is then up to the discretion of each house to send you an invitation with your name handwritten on it.

That is the bare bones of the process. What this does not reveal is the naked ego desire, the muscular tension, the rise in blood pressure, body temperature, and voice level that approach hysteria during show season. For a few weeks twice a year rather normal human beings, the vast majority of whom are members of what used to be called the fair or weaker sex, mutate into snarling, preening, musky, rut-lusting fashion fanatics. Underneath their polished facades nerves are jangling as loudly as their jewelry, making well-dressed adults regress to the prom season jitters of their adolescence.

To be one of the few—from 500 to 1,500 people—present at a major show is to feel tremendously privileged, as if you have been initiated into the most exclusive club in the world, reserved only for the most beautiful, wealthy,

Opposite page:
Tyra Banks

influential, and talented. Although some fashionalities assume that their personal or professional status guarantees them access to the inner sanctum, no one can ever be completely certain. Designers are known to be capricious characters, and accidents do happen.

You do not pass through these doors by just knocking on them. A few seasons ago on the first phase of my book mission, I knocked. A very few houses let me in to their shows. Others I managed to bogart, crash or sneak into. If you understand that there are often more Black people on the runway than there are in the audience, you will understand the precariousness of my unauthorized presence.

But 1992 was different. It was time to be more serious, time to demand more respect. To get into the shows with an invitation—and a seat—you have to know the password: power. And to a place of power, you cannot come empty-handed. You must have some of your own. Why else would a designer want you to be in the audience? For me the power password was *Time* magazine, which was gracious enough to extend its overseas facilities to me.

"The primacy of *Time* was a view I heard expressed again and again on the fashion circuit," writes Nicolas Coleridge in *The Fashion Conspiracy*, a snappy analysis of the international clothing industry. "It still strikes me as odd, in a world awash with fashion magazines, that designers crave to be written about in *Time*, a medium hardly likely to shift clothes and written with far less expertise than the rag-trade glossies. Perhaps it is simply that recognition in *Time* denotes some kind of perm-anence in a hype-ridden industry."

Perhaps. But for me it was clear. *Time* was a means to an end. Because of its clout not only did I get most of the invitations I wanted, but I also got some of the best seats in the house. I was in.

I. MILAN

Serious fashion is not for the faint of heart or foot. No matter what clothes you wear to the shows, no matter what devastatingly simple or outrageously over-the-top outfit, no matter what drape to your shape and the requisite cashmere cocoon, you wear sensible, tasteful, flat shoes. No need to kill yourself looking cute.

That, however, is the voice of experience talking. And it may take a show season or two before you really listen. After all, the models on the catwalk are strutting, slinking, pivoting, and executing various other fancy footwork in spiked heels with the most minimal attachment to the foot or in exaggerated platforms, useful only for staying dry when your palazzo in Venice is flooded. But that is their job. They are paid thousands of dollars an hour to walk convincingly in fantasy footwear, while we are lucky to be paid hundreds of dollars a week to sit and watch what they wear. Although the temptation may arise to compete offstage with what one sees onstage—and you do see intrepid fashion victims in the audience at every show—you learn to squelch that impulse. You learn to save it for people who don't know anything about fashion and will love you for yourself no matter what you wear. These people are certainly not your children. They are more likely to be your mother or your dog.

And though it may be your pride on parade—you are, after all, among the planetary elite simply to be at the shows—it is your feet that do the walking and waiting. However much you resist, you are obliged to heed their sore heels and pinched toes. And, unless you're an editor in chief, whisked by clout and attitudinish subalterns through the crowds, you

admit that flat shoes are a fact of show season survival.

That is no problem in Milan. The Milanese, living in a city whose sidewalks are constantly betrayed by moisture and metal grates and whose streets are subversively paved with ankle-twisting blocks of historic stone, have perfected the flat shoe, the textured loafer, and the sleek stroller. Their Northern sense of being other than Italian reinforces their sense of sophisticated style. Which does not eliminate the fact that some fashionable *signoras* still insist on handicapping themselves with high heels. If they wish to uphold certain traditions, more power to them. Fashion is, lest we forget, all about choice.

A city which prides itself on its dedication to business, Milan makes it easy to enjoy the shows. After La Scala, the Duomo, and Michel-angelo's *Last Supper*, there is little left to see or do. Except for shopping. Window or otherwise, it is splendid. Luckily for my budget and waning self-discipline, the shows are held a decent cab ride away from temptation, in a modern convention center referred to simply as La Fiera.

4 October, 4:15
Ferrè

The room is still pretty empty. Only the camera clans—still photographers and videographers—are more or less installed. The eerie white floor of the catwalk looks like a brightly lit cloud enclosed by rungs of chairs. Now the lights have totally dimmed, and the floor is dawn gold. It still looks insubstantial, as if only angels can tread there.

When I first came to Milan two years ago I was nervous and incredibly lucky. During one crazy, exhausting day in particular I did twelve interviews, snagging as many Girls as I could between shows. It was a festive and unpredictable way to meet, tremendous fun. Now I'm nervous again about going up to strange people and asking to talk with them.

The room's beginning to fill up. Excitement builds with the crowd. Music swells, something with strings, bells, and rock percussion. People around me chat about those they recognize in the audience. I forgive myself for looking for one other Black person. There are several Asian people here but we appear to be nonexistent. OK, the light may be low but still....

Music is breezy, melodic, vaguely Third World. Shows have not only art directors but music directors, too. Man:woman audience ratio? Maybe 1:10. The show's scheduled for four-thirty. Now it's almost five o'clock. They always start late. I'm so busy looking at others. I wonder what they see when they look at me.

Finally, the show begins. A dramatic opening lineup of ten or twelve models, spotlighted in green, is greeted with applause. Bamboo flutes underscore the tropical colors and contrasting textures of a "leaf print on stretch tulle, on organza T-shirts. Leather scarves coming alive in fishnet weaves.... Skirts knotted on a hip in a spontaneous fashion.... Hot sensations for shirts in big orange, mango and passionfruit stripes.... The surprise of a finely pleated scarf enveloping the body like a leaf...."

The Girls are outstanding: Anna Getaneh, Beverly Peele, Katoucha, Naomi Campbell, Roshumba, Sonia Cole. There are lots of Sisters, more than I can count and identify. Roshumba walks alone in a leather bathing suit under a huge straw hat, Katoucha in a royal purple gown with chartreuse heels, Naomi in a blue/black glittery tunic draped over shorts. There are at least twelve Black models out of the thirty-plus Girls in the show. The mix of colors and styles is brought to a dramatic finale in an eco-friendly phalanx of green bathing/body/sun suits.

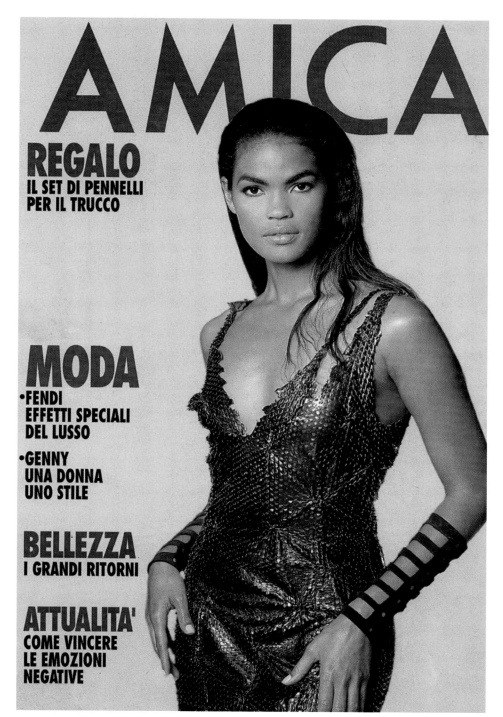

Gail O'Neill on the cover of the Italian fashion weekly, *Amica*. October 12, 1992.

Gianfranco Ferrè walks the runway to enthusiastic applause. In a sober light gray suit and glasses, he looks slightly old-fashioned, like the author of scholarly and personally researched cookbooks, wearing his huge belly before him like the proof of the pudding. Apparently he writes in the same poetics with which he imbues his designs. "All of a sudden... like a modern alchemist who recreated nature technologically dreaming of magic and cunning, I imagined a green summer in the equatorial forest.... I sought out surprising materials with a vague fairy-tale quality.... All adorn a body coming forth forcefully in second-skin clothes.... A collection expressing a firm sense of freedom and energy...of the kind animating woman today...." These notes introduce the press package-cum-program that accompanies the show and the collection. I am delighted with such a promising debut.

5 October, 10:15 pm

Ruminations on what I saw and what's to come:

Show Time and Beyond: A fashion show is a staged extravaganza, a theatre of entertainment where the costumes are character and plot. Behind this purely artistic veil, however, lies a complex production of commercial substance. In Europe, and Italy especially, renowned fabric manufacturers are often the financial backers and/or business partners of the couturiers. Textile designers, shoe designers, and accessory designers are anxiously analyzing fabrics, footwear, and bijoux. Makeup artists and hairstylists elaborate themes complementing the designer's intent.

Since fabrics, accessories, and beauty products are huge markets in themselves, everybody in the audience is looking *at* something *for* something more specific than the general overallness of The Show. What a few dozen women wear for one hour on a spotlit runway can influence businesses affecting millions of people. Beyond the hype of hot new faces, the gears of big business are churning out consumable desires. Next!

Editors, Who, What and Why: Fashion editors may seem to have an enviable job since they have access to visions of non-stop creativity and endless closets, racks, and showrooms. They may not be paid ultraglamorous salaries but often they are treated well, to perks and freebies that to mere mortals seem more than appropriate compensation. That is, however, simplifying their existence. That is dealing only with the fashion part.

The editing part is different. Editors are themselves creative and headstrong individuals. Issues arise: awareness of history and traditions, innovation and originality. There are fine distinctions to be made between one's personal taste and what would look good on one's own body, and then projections onto a wider market of what other—and hopefully many other—women would wear. It can't be easy. My favorite tune may not be

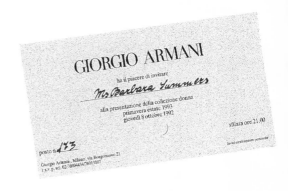

yours. Therefore, what fashion editors report on from a show or, even more immediately, applaud during a show, is extremely subjective.

Along the way to the marketplace, however, designers must pass the test of editors. Hype is a risk, some might say a necessary evil. Thus, the dazzling shows and attention-grabbing editorials. Even so, the true test at the cash register may never happen. What looks good on the stage and on the page may get no further than that. Some design talents may be promoted beyond their capabilities and then dropped and discouraged when they fail to sell.

Also, the editors' selection may have to do with factors unknown to unsuspecting readers: financial pressures, favors received and owed, the swap of editorial pages for ad pages, and other determinants that can influence opinion without showing the strings attached.

6 October, 1:45
La Fiera

Sitting in the press room waiting for the Ferragamo show at two-thirty. Watching folks pass by as one show empties out and another is about to begin, I spot Roshumba and Anna Fiona. Naomi Campbell, dressed in a green pants outfit with a green aviator cap, strides by, followed by two cameramen. There is a sprinkling of Brothers who are

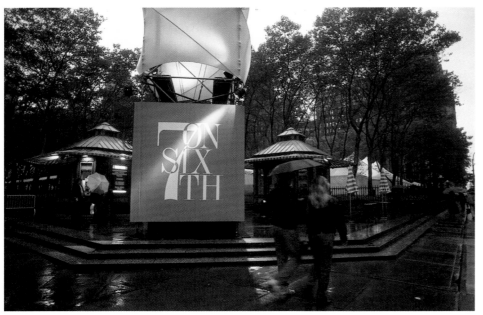

7th on 6th. Starting in 1993, American designers, many of whom were headquartered on Seventh Avenue, presented their collections in large tents set up in Bryant Park on Sixth Avenue behind the New York Public Library. Centralized venues made life easier to organize during hectic show seasons.

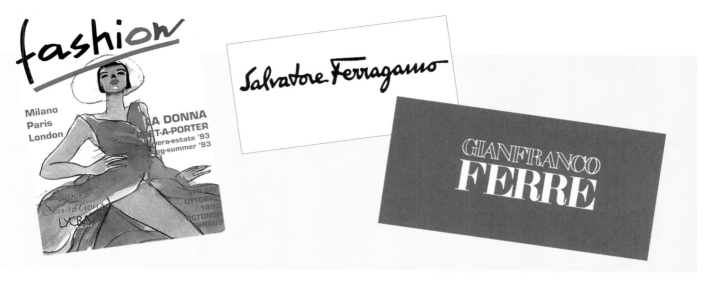

photographers. A Canadian reporter sitting next to me says, "Fashion now is in a zero zone." I think she means unoriginal, uninspired, uninteresting.

In the crowd milling around before seating for the Ferragamo show begins, I kindle a conversation with Miraella Thomas. She's a self-described American army brat who was born in Ethiopia and raised in Germany. She now lives with her family in Connecticut where she has just started college. She talks quickly, vehemently, and being brand new to the business, her impatience can't be concealed.

"You see the other Girls, and you say, I can do that. Then you get in there and discover it's not so easy. It's very hard to break in. I haven't broken in yet. This is my first season in the shows, and I'm doing about three or four. I'm very disappointed, but people are telling me that I'm very lucky to do even that many. You have no idea, because nobody tells the Girls who are White and come over here starting their first season that they can't expect much. No matter what, they are guaranteed to do more than a Black Girl.

"But you wonder just what you have to do to break in. I think it's a matter of timing, somebody's good mood, somebody's whim. If I can't do it the right way then I don't want to do it. I'm in school. I know I have a brain. For a lot of these Girls, this is their life, their dream.

"Being in school keeps me sane; it's something I can depend on for my stability, my foundation. I feel like if I only have modeling, the bottom could drop out at any time. It's such an unstable life to lead. I'm scared of this business but there's something that draws me to it. Sometimes I can earn in a day what it takes my mother two weeks of overtime to make. It keeps me balanced. I know what my mother does and what my friends do. How they work after school and do all that they can to pay for their tuition, books, and all the things they need in the real world. When I say, maybe I'll buy an Azzedine dress, they're like, 'Who's Azzedine?' It's so funny how different the worlds are, but it's the difference that keeps me grounded."

The Ferragamo show has several Black Girls, including a sexy newcomer with strawberry blond hair and hazel eyes, Tyra Banks, and the newest Revlon star, Veronica Webb, wearing the long straight hair so popular this season. Ferragamo is known for well-bred classics, like the sherbet-colored cashmere cardigans knotted over black unitards that open the presentation. Predictable, polished, polite. The clothes, I mean.

The Girls are much more the show, and I observe them more closely. Each one manages to be unique in the minute or two she has to present an outfit. Some walk with an extra-sensual slink, while some glide by cool and detached, and still others appear to be crushing armor-plated bugs at every step. The Girls, most often facially expressionless, direct all of their contact to the cameras stacked at the end of the runway, not to the live audience. This leaves me with a disconcerting feeling similar to that of being in a recording studio. Models, like musicians, are performing for themselves and others not present. Privileged insiders, we are here, and proud to be. Yet, we know that we are only glorified middlemen, not the ultimate object of desire: the cash-carrying consumer.

Afterwards, I sit and talk with Maureen Gallagher, who was just in the show, at her agency's branch office conveniently located right in la Fiera.

Maureen Gallagher

Born in Manhattan, Maureen had an unusual start in a business known for unusual starts. "My family bred dogs, and I would make extra money training people's dogs in Central Park. I'd cut out of high school during lunch time and get business training dogs. When I started training a designer's dog, he asked me to do some pictures. I did, and they were pretty good, so he suggested I go to an agency, and I did. But the first time I went to agencies I was turned down everywhere. They said, 'It's really difficult for a Girl your color to work. You're not really

Black, you're not really White, and you don't really look Spanish.' My mother is White, and my father's half-Black and half-American Indian. But my upbringing was very urban. I don't consider myself locked into one culture, but in the business, I consider myself a Black model."

Once Maureen did join an agency she started working immediately, doing editorial and "money jobs, too. But I didn't have the style, you know? I didn't go any further because I needed to get out of the States and get some pizazz. So, I went to Paris, and I hated it. It was the first time I'd ever been on a plane or out of my own country around people who didn't speak English. It was really tough. You're supposed to be so sophisticated and slick at nineteen. You're supposed to be so aware, especially growing up in Manhattan. But once you get out of New York, it's the devil you don't know. There were a lot of playboys and slick people. I just got caught up in the fast lane. I seemed very mature, but I had no clue. I went through the wringer. After a few months I left and went back home.

"I'd always made money but I didn't get that skyrocket effect that Europe is supposed to give a Girl. Frankly, I wasn't mentally ready for it. I had gone through a really hard childhood, very difficult. I was the kind of girl who was at Studio 54 when I was twelve years old. I went through seeing everybody start to die and overdose and get AIDS when I was thirteen. I had gotten caught up in a big drug scene. It was so easy. There were people who were booking me and giving me drugs at the same time." Running away was the only way she knew to survive. "Now, I make decisions to confront things. Now, I don't run away, but then I did.

"For three years I clung to an Italian man in Milan who taught me to grow up. I stayed here, instead of being in Paris where I probably would have gotten a better hold on

my career. But I learned things that no money can replace: how to take care of myself, how to like myself, how to be responsible. How to have nice times without going to clubs and taking drugs and being so fabulous all the time.

"I watched the fashion business change so much. It used to be about one thing, creativity, and now it's more about money than anything else. Sometimes I regret that I didn't make decisions about my career. I always made decisions about what I could handle, what I needed for myself, because I've been through so much. What keeps me going is the fact that I'm still together. I feel good now. I take really good care of myself."

I'm always so impressed with the speed at which these women travel. From one designer to another, one city to another, one life to another. An hour ago I was watching Maureen on the runway, not knowing a thing about her as a person, and now she's told me details about her life that I can never not know. We all take a tremendous chance on each other, trusting that an open heart will find an open mind.

7 October, 4:15
Palazzo Barozzi,
Via Vivaio 7, Fendi

Leave it to the imperial Karl Lagerfeld, designer in chief of four collections, to present his first of the season in a palace complete with high arched wooden doors, stone columns, and painted portraits in gilt ovals gazing down from distant ceilings. As the show moves swiftly, it is difficult to remember what I see. Horoscope bathing suits to start. Then knitwear, dresses, and suits for city living. Full, fluid, flowing. Long skirts, long jackets. Layers of transparencies, top and bottom. Emphasis, according to the program notes, is on "a new femininity—different, almost abstract—which emphasizes 'being' rather than 'looking.' An elegant and self-confi-

dent woman." Besides basic black and white and "straw and raw colors," preferred shades are "bleached black," "warm brown," and a softly lit "almond green."

Naomi, Veronica, Beverly, Karen, and Tyra, always a frankly sexual vamp, are among the Black Girls. Linda Evangelista, Nadège, and Drena DeNiro are some of the others. At least the Girls smile here. They all wear little tufts of Afro corkscrews pinned on top of their hair, like miniature berets of contrasting color and texture. The show is easy, fun, and feminine. Lagerfeld accepts the closing applause with a bouncy step and a flutter in his fan.

Marva Griffin

After the show I meet Marva Griffin in the courtyard of the Palazzo Barozzi, where everyone greets her with a "Ciao, bella," and a spout of vivacious Italian. Marva is the only other Black woman I've seen in regular attendance at the shows. When she cannot find a parking spot for her big Audi near a chosen café, she invites me to her home for a cup of tea. I am delighted.

Marva is the Italian representative for *House & Garden* magazine. After a quick check with her assistant, we walk down the hallway from her office to her apartment. Her home is lovely, as befits someone in her profession. Over mango tea and cookies, she talks about how she got here. A native of Venezuela, she moved to Italy twenty-three years ago to study Italian in Perugia. Traveling from the New World to "el viejo continente" was an educational must for her. She came to Italy with her son and the idea of going into fashion, a passion since childhood. But studies in fashion design soon gave way to a job with one of the largest furniture companies in Italy.

"Then I discovered," Marva says, "that I also loved furniture and that I also loved decorating. So I was very lucky to come to Italy to work for a

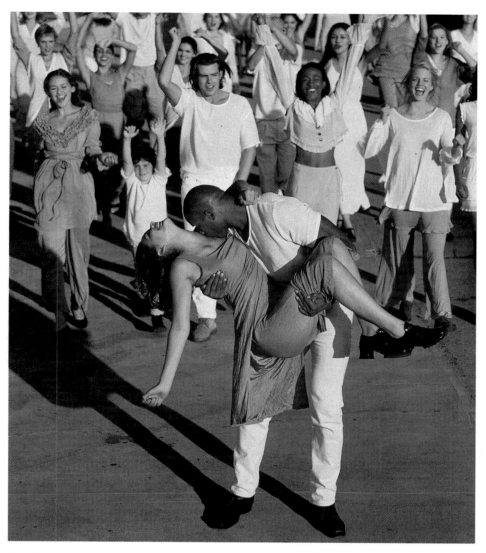

season or two. Look on the runway. All those Girls are foreigners. There's only one Italian model, Carla Bruni, who became really famous. The others are mostly Americans, Brazilians, Norwegians, Germans.

"This year Florence celebrated forty years of Italian fashion, which started in the Palazzo Pitti. In Rome, there is the high fashion, *alta moda*, haute couture which is twice a year, in January and July. But the boom of Italian fashion, which is the ready-to-wear, started in Milan, which is the fashion city for Italy. Florence continues to be part of the fashion world with Pitti Uomo, the men's collections."

Her views on one of the all-time great survivors: "Pat Cleveland was very clever. In this week's issue of *Oggi* they interviewed Pat, with two or three pages on her and pictures of her husband and her children. She's advising young models. I think Pat is great because she's so professional, very serious. Some people continue to ask her to model."

On today's Girls: "I think Naomi's great. When I see her up close and I talk to her, she's like my little daughter. But these young Girls are leading a very intensive life. I think it's too much. Naomi did not have time to enjoy her youth, her teenage years. What's going to happen when she's thirty years old? It's like a tornado. There's simply no time to think or study. If you don't grow into other things, when she becomes older, there's going to be a blank in her life. The risk in this profession is that after," Marva snaps her fingers, "it's over."

From Marva's apartment I take a taxi to the Missoni show on the Via Salvini. Quite a contrast between the modern industrial space at la Fiera, the rich, time-worn palazzo where Fendi presented its collection this afternoon, and this venue, a New-York-style showroom, lined with chairs and chatty women wearing bright diamond rings. I'm in the front

furniture company and to go into interior decorating. I worked there for four years, and then French *House & Garden* wanted someone to represent the magazine, to do their P.R. and be a correspondent for them here. For years I did 'Fabrics for Fashion', a show I organized putting together different companies, and that was how I got into the fashion world. Then I started writing for a Venezuelan magazine on fashion and interior decorating. After *Maison et Jardin*, other magazines from Condé Nast asked me to work: *Vogue Decoration*, American *Vogue*, and now *HG*.

"Although I live here I maintain close contact with my home in Venezuela. I go there whenever I can, about four times a year."

I asked her about the show season and the number of Black Girls working. "I was surprised on Sunday when I saw Ferrè," whose name she pronounces with the high-speed roll of a bullet train. "When he sent out a

group of ten at a time, I was surprised to see them all there. If you've followed the shows, though, you saw that only Ferrè did that. But he always has Black Girls in his shows. Another thing: summer collection. There are always more Black Girls in the summer collection than in the winter. The summer collection is tropics, it's sea, it's tan."

The heyday of Black models in Milan, she explains, was in the late '70s and early '80s, "which was also the boom of the fashion world. It was in fashion to use Black models. It was the fashion also to use Black male models, which you don't see anymore."

She described the backlash against not only Black models but foreign models in general after that period. "The authorities weren't going to give foreign models work permits, and the police were after them. But the Italians could not compete, and it lasted for only one

row, which means just a leg away from the walk space allotted the models. The pre-show mood is casual, very friendly, with the handsome, silver-haired Missonis hugging friends warmly.

In the show there are at least four or five Black Girls, including Miraella, the newcomer I talked with yesterday. Being this close to the models lessens some of their allure, but it is wonderful for the clothes. Missoni is justifiably famous for its knits which have become staples, especially during transitional seasons and for climate-cautious travelers. Simple shapes—long, slim dresses, tube skirts with tunics and vests—predominate.

"Chromatic accents" derive from the ocean ("the chromed green of the damsel fish"), the desert ("Touareg blue"), and the land ("suitcase stickers with names of touristic locations"), writes style maven Anna Piaggi in her emphatic notes for the collection. Although they may veer dangerously close to being corny, such catchwords help busy observers define what we're looking at. It's one thing to put attitude into clothes while you're wearing them; that's the model's job. It's another to put attitude into words about clothes; that's the editor's. Whether aiming to sell the clothes or trying to understand the Girls, we are all working to share a vision. We make use of whatever tools are at hand.

9:10 pm
Palazzo Rovero, Via
Borgonuovo 21, Armani

The Via Borgonuovo is very narrow and very dark. The moon, just three days short of being perfectly full, hangs high in the night sky like a mobe pearl in a velvet box. Wan street lights are suspended above the pavement on wires, strung like laundry lines from one side of the alley to the other. Serious construction reduces the one-lane traffic to a

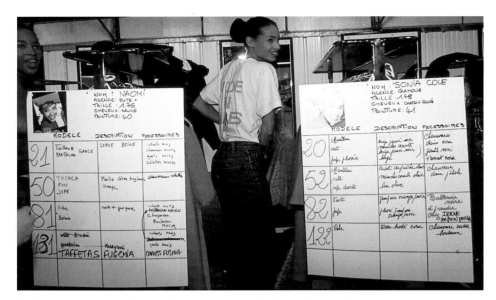

Backstage at a **Chloé** show with **Naomi Campbell** and **Sonia Cole**.

snarl of taxis and pedestrians, all honking together in this holding pen.

This is the hot ticket, along with Versace who showed earlier this evening (and which I, uninvited, did not see), the last show of collections week: Giorgio Armani. The name alone conjures up contradictory images of shoulder-padded power suits and laid-back Italian luxe. The scene right now, though, is unambiguously mad, frenzied, feverish. The fashion herds are being corralled. While five hundred buyers are leaving, five hundred members of the press are waiting to enter Armani headquarters, a low-storied palazzo whose centuries of history lie discreetly behind a modern glass entrance. I feel vulnerably American, that is, too young, too new, raised in a rapidly changing but constantly present tense.

I tap André Leon Talley on the arm, introduce myself to him, and ask to talk with him in Paris where he is headquartered as creative director for American *Vogue*. He nods from his great height, 6′7″, and replies that he hopes he can make time. He says it in a gentlemanly way that gives absolutely no prospect of success, but I am impressed by his politeness. He has worked in the fashion industry

for twenty years, and as one of few Black males—perhaps the only one present at this show—he knows everyone and probably most everything worth knowing.

After we are finally shunted inside we find in each seat a tiny shopping bag with a bottle of the new Armani fragrance, Giò. Nice touch.

The show is achingly simple and beautiful. Long, easy layers in his signature cloud and earth tones, wet and dried and still perfectly clean. Sand, dust, clay, bone. Lots of pants suits, then wrap gowns with gauze underskirts or underpants, pareo waists on skirts and trousers. Head hugging pillboxes like prayer caps, and long black scarves tied severely around the head and left to drift down the back. Forms and fabrics seem influenced by dreams and myths of North Africa and Polynesia. Sequins and beads add evening shimmer to his muted sunset colors. Each piece calls for applause but each one comes and goes before I can close my mouth and put my hands together. Anna Fiona, Lu Sierra, Roshumba, and Sonia Cole are some of the Black models in the show. Paulette James, Armani's long-time fitting model and favorite, presents a classic outfit in her classic walk.

There is none of the erotic hype here and thus, more of a secure femininity. Armani's new citizen of the world is described as a woman unfettered by trends and remakes, a woman who travels freely and borrows liberally from other cultures to create her own. Where some designers may overwhelm with gorgeous but unwearable theatrics, Armani underwhelms with a credible, almost chaste elegance. It is a heavenly finish. Before I can levitate to Cloud Nine, Armani with his silken, silver hair takes his bow in a *terra firma* workshirt and jeans.

The night is quieter now, maybe not in the bright and noisy places some models will retreat to so as not to decompress too quickly from the high of the show and the Italian season as a whole. But somewhere, maybe just in my memory imprinted now with Armani's final tableau of an Eden from Gauguin, a pacific swell washes over me. I feel as if I can float home. But a cab appears—surprise—and I take a less mystical means of transportation.

10 October, 10:15
After breakfast in the
hotel lobby

Reading the European edition of the *Wall Street Journal* Friday/Saturday 9-10 October '92. A front-page article by Lisa Bannon is headlined "Some Fashion Houses Tighten Belts, Try Models of Austerity," with the sub-head, "In Milan, Fewer Superstars Grace Catwalks This Year; Armani Turns Up Nose."

Bannon writes, "As the world's most sought-after supermodels are suddenly discovering, not everyone is willing to fork over $9,000 for a few two-minute jaunts down the runway." She continues, "Runway fees shot up from an average $5,000 in 1989 to between $9,000 and $10,000 today, while second-tier models are commanding $5,000 to $6,000 and even unknown faces charge $2,000.

One supermodel can pocket more than $100,000 in a week.

"Designers now complain that prices are too high, and that overexposure of the models is blurring the designers' distinctive images."

Bannon makes very real and pertinent points, but I am glad that my perspective helps me see what she doesn't or can't. The concept of a "well-known face" selling clothes on the runway is a phenomenon less than a decade old. The unvarnished truth is that until recently most Print Girls—and particularly the superstars—did not know how to walk. Their photographic success, however, preceded them, protected them, and persuaded designers to use them. Just like producers casting a film, some designers now feel that the audience recognizes—and is charmed by—the faces of the moment and is therefore more likely to confer star status on their collections if they hire stars to show them.

Let it also be understood that on the show circuit there are many Girls who are proud to specialize in runway work. While top Print Girls are encouraged to cross over into shows, few top Runway Girls manage to do the reverse. They are, nonetheless, stars in their field. Instantly recognizable in their own right, they are the consistent—and slightly less expensive, but hardly cheap—*corps de mode* on which designers depend. In this group there are many Black women. Some of the stars of this fashion generation would include Sonia Cole, Anna Fiona, Katoucha, Rosalind, and Lu Sierra. They may not receive the extensive press write-ups and the exaggerated paychecks, but they often get the important outfit, the immediate audience applause, and the return booking.

4:00

Carol Hobbs

I arrive at the apartment of Carol Hobbs and her husband Giorgio Reineri just a few minutes after she has returned home from an exercise class. I'm impressed. On a dark, cold, rainy day like today I would be reluctant to leave the bed, let alone the house. And for a session of jaunty aerobics? Absolutely out of the question. But that is why, after many years out of the business, she is her same modeling size, a perfect eight, and I am a twelve and impressed.

Born and bred in Manhattan, Carol was part of a small band of Black Girls who made Europe their base in the late '60s and '70s. Two years of college in New York City made her eager to try something more stimulating.

"The idea of going to France and doing something sounded better than knocking around New York and not doing anything. So I went to Paris in January, 1968, and stayed there until they had the famous strikes in what is now called the May Revolution. While I was stranded in Paris, one day I walked over to the American Express office to find out if I had any mail, and on my way back, I saw a sign for a bus that left for Milan. I took that bus to Milan carrying my *Europe on $5 a Day* with me.

"When I got to Milan, I was completely lost. But that first night I met some of the nicest people I'd ever met in my life. It was a time when Italy was completely different from the way it is now. It was the last leg of an old era, the development of Italy after the war. In '68 everything changed, and I was very, very lucky to have been there then. I also started working then. I had my first fashion pages, and I did a couple of shows. Since I had never done runway before, I had to learn how to walk. I was the world's worst. For photographs, I was good. Put me in front of a camera, great. But put me in front of a whole bunch of people, and I just never seemed to have all that much grace.

"Maybe that was another reason why I was not steered toward fashion in Paris. There I saw a lot of model agents and advertising agents, and I did a lot of work, but it was always for coffee or chocolate, product ads, not a lot of fashion. Perhaps it was because the agency wasn't fashion-oriented or maybe they just didn't think that I could do it.

"In Milan I met Riccardo Gay, the agent, and he's the one who introduced me to Biki. She was one of the top designers of the period. I did the entire photographic campaign for Biki in 1968 with the understanding that I would do the show. So she would have somebody come in twice a week and teach me how to walk and have the jackets slide off my shoulders." Carol laughs recalling her awkwardness but she also understands that she was a pioneer in Italy.

"I was the first Black American, in the sense that I was a Black woman, not mixed, with dark skin, who did fashion photographs here. After I did my first spread, I stayed and spent the next two months waiting for those pages to come out. I figured if I went back to New York, I would probably never see the prints which were supposed to be in the September issue of *Vogue*.

"I finally went back to New York, but on the way I picked up the coffee shot that I had done in Paris and some other advertising pages. The big thing, though, was the Biki campaign because that was a lot of tear sheets. When I was in Paris, I had read about Naomi Sims, and I knew that she worked with Wilhemina in New York. When Willy accepted me, I was delighted. I did some work, and eventually I did more work, and then I went back to Europe in 1970. In New York I wasn't doing much fashion. I knew that the fashion season was coming up in Europe, and I thought it would be nice to go back.

"Then, too, there was a big boom for American and foreign models. I think I was still at that

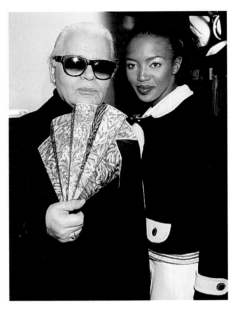

Fashion royalty. **Karl Lagerfeld** and **Naomi Campbell**.

point the only Black American. When I came back in 1970, I worked a lot for some of the most mundane magazines, *Gioia* and *Grazie*. They weren't prestigious magazines, but it was even better for me because it meant that I was being accepted as a model. I also did a fashion spread for Italian *Vogue* for lingerie. But working for these other magazines was, in a sense, even more of a coup than doing lingerie for *Vogue*. Even if it was just doing two pages here, and one page there, regular people saw your face, and you had tear sheets to bring home. I never really did big things like covers for magazines, but I worked.

"Back in the States I did a lot of advertising. One time I did test prints for leg shots for a big panty hose campaign. Finally it narrowed down to three of us. Another Girl got the campaign, but as it turned out, they used her head and my legs. The person who shot it told me they were my legs, but they never paid me for the campaign. Had I been smarter, I would have done something about it.

"As a photographic model I had about six or seven good years, and

then I started working as a photographic assistant to Les Underhill. If he had catalogs to shoot, he would give me one page or a couple of hours, a half-day or whatever. His clients were always very good about that.

"I enjoyed photography, but at the same time I hated it. Not having studied formally, I had to learn everything on the job. I used to spend hours in the darkroom, hours printing photos. It was like an obsession with me. I loved doing portraits of people. But fashion photography was almost a torture sometimes. You have such a big responsibility, unlike modeling, where all you have to do is go in and look good. You never really lost any sleep over that. But I wasn't used to having the responsibility of What's going to happen if this person doesn't show up? Or if the Girl doesn't work out well? Or this or that? I mean, I had my act together. I always went and checked out my locations and tried out my lights and did tests beforehand. But there were all kinds of variables that could and would enter into a situation.

"After a while in New York I realized that I was getting bogged down. I could have gone to the magazines, and they wouldn't have looked at me because I had no connections. But Paris was more open to foreigners, somebody different doing something maybe a little bit different. They were more receptive to me in Paris and Milan, and so it worked out.

"But that first year I went back to Europe was the worst year of my life. I hated living in Paris, I hated the French. There's one thing I'll always remember about the first time I was in Paris in 1968. A French woman told me, 'Ah, you are so beautiful. I don't understand the American people, why they don't like Black people. They are so beautiful. Your color is so beautiful,' she kept saying.

But I knew that every nation had its prejudice, so I asked her, 'What about the Arabs?' And she said, 'Ah, that's another story.' As it turned out of course, two years later, the French had an influx of Blacks. No matter where they came from, they were no longer 'so beautiful.' Now they were 'too many.'

"I did a lot of work, though, as a photographer. I started with *Dépêche Mode*, and that was pretty lucky. But since I hated living in Paris, I thought I would try Italy again. I'd always loved coming here. After that I had three or four good years working as a photographer.

"I had been a gypsy for so long until I came to Italy. Then I started living here with Giorgio. He's a sports journalist, and his hours were so different from mine. I decided to put more of myself into our relationship. I also got tired of lugging all that photographic equipment around from place to place. So I started to do showroom modeling, fitting. It was something I had never done before, and I worked for one client for five years. It was only twice a year but I had eleven good seasons.

"I knew I wasn't built for New York fashion designs. They wanted bigger shoulders and taller bodies. By their standards, I was pretty short. But by Italian standards, I was tall. They would make clothes on somebody my size, which meant that the Girls who did the shows could fit them and the people they really made clothes for could wear them, too. So I was perfect!"

Now that she has retired from her work as a fitting model, Carol lives a comfortable life with homes in Italy and California. She sparkles as she talks about her husband, their life together, and especially their wedding day. "The day I got married, I must say, was the happiest day of my life." Carol makes me feel like throwing rice. I love happy endings, and many others must feel the same way, for even in the hard-boiled world of fashion, the bride—all promise and love and beauty—is the last figure in the show.

11 October, 2:00
Linate Airport

Mission accomplished. Arrived in the rain and left the same way. One clear blue day in a week. The only other spots of color and excitement came from fashion, food, and folks. I'm so happy to be returning to Paris.

II. PARIS

Paris is grand. It has been the undisputed heavyweight champion of world capitals for so long that I, a veteran fan, am always anxious to know if it still retains the title or if New York, the only real contender, has trounced it. Paris is still the fashion champ, or in its own terms, the queen, beautiful, graceful, rich and inviting, the City of Light, lanterns, and luxury. But the fact is that New York is the capital of capital, and the United States, the market excelsior. The planetary dream still wears an American label, not French or German or Japanese. That, however, may be just a matter of time.

Like all royals of a certain age and habit of power—although they may be effectively power-less—Paris knows how to look good from the outside. There the ready-to-wear collections are not relegated to a convention hall, comfortable though it may be, as in Milan. No less a venue than the Louvre, the ancient royal fortress-palace started in the 13th century, is considered an adequate showcase for one of France's leading industries.

Inside the courtyard, imperial grandeur confronts the media circus. Literally. For the Cour carrée is taken over by tents, four huge, drab pre-fab constructs. The center tent is a press room, complete with pay phones, lounge chairs, and a tiny coffee shop. The three others, equipped with long runways and cramped bleachers of plastic chairs, wear auspicious names: the Salle des Arts, which fashion is supposed to be a wearable form of; the Salle Sully, named after the 16th century Duke of Sully; and the Salle Perrault, in honor of Claude Perrault, one of the leading architects of the 17th century Louvre and brother of writer Charles Perrault, best known for the Mother Goose stories. Art and finance, creativity and practical construction, beauty and business: that is what we are all here for, and the names pointing the way to our destinations never let us forget it.

This season, however, is historic. It is supposed to be the last one that will see the prêt shows in the tents. For some years construction has been going on underneath the Louvre which will provide modern theatres and exhibition space. A scale model of the new Maison de la Mode is on view in the press tent. When I see it I am surprisingly nostalgic for the Good Old Days that are not quite over. The mushy moment is thankfully brief, because this season is historic for me also. Now, I, too, can swagger past the swarms of design students and fashion fans who plaintively beg outside the courtyard for permission just to peek. I've been where they are. And I know that a mere slip of paper makes the only difference.

14 October, 1:00
Yohji Yamamoto

My first show of the Paris season. Do not ask why it is a Japanese designer. All right, ask. The answer is simple: Paris is the biggest showcase, the most prestigious, the most creatively important. Economic restrictions being what they are—tight—

this particular concentration works to everyone's advantage. No matter what, everyone wants to be in Paris, showing somewhere, during the season. And it feels like it. Expectation builds with a self-righteous intensity, as we all assume the role of ballet impresario Sergei Diaghilev demanding of writer Jean Cocteau, "*Etonnez-moi*!" Something astounding must follow. Yet, stepping from a sun-bright October day into this dreary mechanical cave of fluorescent tubes, metal supports, cold plastic chairs, and rickety wooden floorboards feels crazy, as if I'm going in the wrong direction to get to the right place. But this *is* the right place.

At one-thirty-five the music starts, the gross fluorescents go off, and black-flagged spots come on. Girls in long dresses with even longer trains sweep slowly down the runway, the bright orange fabric quickly giving way to black. Ingenious layers, folds, and wraps of material play hide-and-seek with arms and legs,

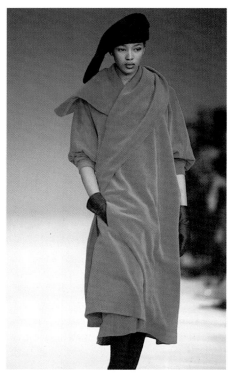

Naomi Campbell wearing **Yohji Yamamoto**.

shoulders and necks. Anna Getaneh, Beverly Peele, Gail O'Neill, Karen Alexander, and a couple of other Girls make up about one-fifth of the total model contingent for the show. There is no sexy fashion walking.

It is not about a model's personality here at all, rather, the sublimation of it, the distillation of distinctive beauty into a basic neutrality, all the better to show the clothes. Which are now draped and bowed and billowing, in pastels, caramel, and sand. Now black again with dangling threads, now black and white with one tail of a morning coat cut short at the waist and the other left long to waft behind a slim dress. With knits unraveling into webs and fabrics enclosing and extending the body, Yohji's clothes appear part of an intellectual discourse on the construction and, of course, deconstruction of apparel, appearance, and eventually, the world. In a kind of post-nuclear aesthetic, the models wear matte makeup with a pale metallic streak under one eye and damp-looking hair pinned into long false queues. During one sequence they wear pointed and intricately jeweled headdresses, perhaps from some isolated ethnic group documented by *National Geographic*.

These models seem to comprise the entire number of women in the world who could or would wear these clothes. I find them, nevertheless, appealing in their exaggerated unconventionality. The show ends with an enormously wide-skirted bride in a black dress. The Girls are smiling now, still dressed in Yohji's clothes but in their own character. In flat shoes they tower over Yamamoto when he appears—in black—to take his bow.

2:30
Junko Shimada

Pillars garlanded with pink roses set the tone for this défilé which sounds an unchic but also unconflicted note: middle C, as in cute. As

abstract and sculptural as Yohji's clothes were, Junko Shimada's are just as practical and wearable. There are figure-hugging outfits in giraffe prints, and jungle themes, and white, of course. There are about four or five Black Girls, each able to strut her stuff and more. The finale presents a parody of a Miss Universe contest with models parading in bathing suits and satin I.D. ribbons. Ms. Cuba puffs on a cigar, Ms. Jamaica on a spliff, Ms. Austria carries a bow and arrow, Ms. Japan sports tattoos, and Ms. France, wearing a courtly white wig, provides a big concluding laugh. The clothes may not have moved design mountains but the show broke through an icy layer of seriousness, reminding me that fashion can be about something as simple as lighthearted fun.

4:00
Chloé

For this show, marking Karl Lagerfeld's return to the Chloé line which he designed from 1965 to 1985, I'm armed with an invitation but no assigned seat. This means Standing Room Only, and what a mob to have to stand in. Outside the Salle Sully there are big crowds pushing in on all sides trying to squeeze past the paper checkers. Once inside there is zero visibility and the kind of close, surreptitious sexual contact permissible only during Carnival.

Clothes look insubstantial and floaty—*le flou*, the French call it—à la late '60s and early '70s, suspiciously macramé-d and empire-waisted. The soundtrack even features Jimi Hendrix's "Crosstown Traffic," one of my personal favorites, and the Beatles' "You Put a Spell on Me." But it is not just personal memories that make it difficult for me to focus. The shorter and longer and numerous layers of gossamer fabrics in dusty pastels tend to trick the eye and the tongue into a nervous What is it?

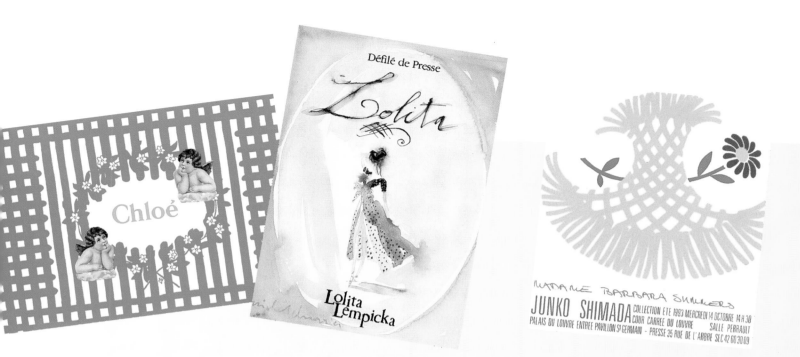

And, of course, all the miniscule details of what is probably fine workmanship are lost in this kind of mammoth presentation.

Models appear under a white arbor trellised with spring flowers. Naomi, Beverly, and Veronica are some of the memorable faces. Naomi is a special stand-out in a mammoth russet Afro wig studded with blossoms that plunge down her back. It is a challenge, but one quality of a good model is the ability to convincingly inhabit a look and not necessarily identify with it.

At the end Karl Lagerfeld bounces out on stage to applause that was missing during the show. Fashion audiences always applaud the designer even if they don't do the same for the work: an A for effort until the real judgment is in.

5:45
Lolita Lempicka

My last show of the day. I will not be doing this again, seeing four shows in one day. I'm not really seeing them. The buzz after Chloé was especially unnerving. It left me with a lot to digest. Everything is at least a half hour late. Thank God, I'm sitting, in what is to me a great seat, right at the gateway between backstage and onstage.

Janis Joplin's gritty version of "Summertime" launches Lolita Lempicka's series of floaty chiffon dresses, mixed prints, collages of flowers and lace. It's feminine, cute, and wearable. There's only one Black Girl in the show: a blonde with a mole.

16 October, 11:00
Karl Lagerfeld

There is no such thing as a show that starts on time.

Check out this seating: fourth row at the very end of the runway—the chic neighborhood—between the *New York Times* and the *Tobé Report*, the director of which, sleek but non-plussed, asked me more than once and rather cuttingly, if I was in the right seat. She's probably not a prejudiced person, just not used to some unknown individual sitting next to her. Shows are basically for insiders only.

Karl Lagerfeld generates excitement no matter what he does for any label. It matters little what you like in which collections or individual outfits. Indeed, it matters little if you like them at all. The anticipation of some fresh burst of creativity charges the air around all of his shows—Fendi, Chloé, his own, and Chanel—with a special current. The press packet for this one has notes and photographs by KL himself:

"Transparent like glass, romantique and severe at the same time, with a poetic expressionism mixing the urban and the playful, this is the spirit of the summer to come…. Fashion ignores equality, it also refuses legality…. Fashion does not lack logic nor comic twists. But it does not lecture. It says: 'To each his own.'"

And in today's womanist world, that means: To each *her* own. The show opens with a statement by Miss Thing that "there is no guest list tonight."

This stylistic open house starts with sheer black and white tops over black shorts. There are sheer double-layered skirts over chiffon pants worn with socks and flats or flat boots; pale leather long coats; hip-hugging skirts with bustiers or short vests; long net skirts and head ties; prints floating over stretch tight-bodied two-pieces. En Vogue's pulsating lyrics, "You're never gonna get it," puts a hard-edged bop in the models' walk. Veronica, Karen, Beverly, Stephanie Roberts, Lana Ogilvie, and a few other Sisters are there: a great group. It is a sexy show, upbeat, contemporary. A much more modern mood than the Chloé show. The cameramen stacked behind me are as loud in their catcalls as a stereotypical construction crew on a lunch break. The truth is, we're all uplifted, relieved that Lagerfeld came through.

As Suzy Menkes writes in the *Herald Tribune*, "Karl Lagerfeld stitched together fashion's generation gap, and credibility gap in the powerful but light-handed collection he sent out Friday. It closed with models in black bodysuits with transparent inflatable life belts gyrating around their hips—a fitting symbol for the airy transparency of the show and because Lagerfeld is viewed by retail bosses as the designer keeping high fashion afloat."

Money is one of those massively unmentioned details, sitting like an elephant with a blond wig under the tent with the rest of us, who pretend that talking about the wig is important while talking about the elephant is bad manners.

4:00
Paco Rabanne

My friend, Ernest Anderson, who has worked with Dior and Georges Rech among others during his decade in Paris, joins me to see Paco Rabanne. In the background John Coltrane plays "All Blues" as we wait for the show to start. Again there are diaphanous layers and shimmering colors befitting the four major groupings: City of Sky, City of the Sands, Optic City, and the City Lost in the Jungle. Pearlized silk, laser ciré, and holographic jersey are some of the innovative fabrics Rabanne uses in shifting cloud colors of rose, lilac, and blue. Iridescent pants and skirts and silver-spangled two-pieces parade by, along with his signature astronautical styling.

Many garments are shiny and look like plastic. Ernest, who loves fine natural fabrics, gets grouchy and says, "Now you know what to do with your old linoleum. Melt it down, stretch it, and then cut it asymmetrically." And make sure to wear it with espadrilles on three-inch platforms.

5:00
Cirque d'Hiver, Jean-Paul Gaultier

We leave Rabanne early to dash through the métro—it is rush hour and a cab would be too slow—crosstown to the Winter Circus (really, no fashion pun intended) where Jean-Paul Gaultier's show is slated to begin at six. We have no tickets but since Ernest, who usually does, has many friends who work for Gaultier and who have promised to get him in, we just need to be there early enough to catch the attention of one of them. When we get there, early, only a few hopefuls are standing near the barricade in front of the entrance.

Gaultier, himself and his style, is much, much funkier than the Louvre shows. That tends to arouse the fashion rebel in all of us. While we wait outside we read people's outfits, attitudes, and personalities in the suddenly cold October air. The meta-show never disappoints. We spot Ernest's connection once but somehow never manage to connect with her again. We grow nervous and uncomfortably chilly. A friend of Ernest's with whom we successfully rendezvous outside, whispers ominously, "If those drag queens get in

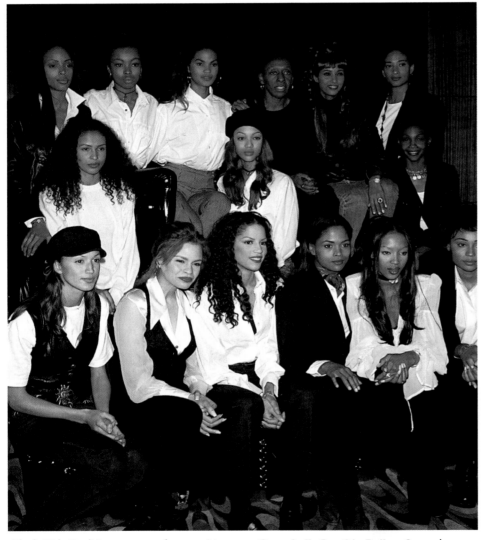

Black Girls Coalition press conference, New York City, December 14, 1992. Front row: **Carla Otis**, **Kersti Bowser**, **Veronica Webb**, **Karen Alexander**, **Naomi Campbell**, **Cynthia Bailey**. Second row: **Akure**, **Tyra Banks**, **Roshumba**. Third row: **Coco Mitchell**, **Phina**, **Gail O'Neill**, **Bethann**, **Iman**, **Peggy Dillard**.

before we do...." And sure enough, a raucous covey of bald, painted, and overly-breasted transvestites who have been camping it up for the crowd does make it in. And we don't.

Reports rave about the Gaultier show and always mention his sense of humor, or as Carrie Donovan of the *New York Times* put it, "Gaultier's penchant for wit." "Just when you thought there was nothing else to be done with the mannish pinstriped trouser suit, he made the pants empire-line, flowing from the bosom.... Gaultier's Adam and Eve scene of wigs made into clothing—including a beard on the male chest and locks curling round the body—brought the house down," wrote Suzy Menkes in the *International Herald Tribune*.

Wish I had seen for myself. Regrets are not profound, however. Lock-outs and standing-only tickets keep alive the insider-outsider feeling of special privilege. On one hand it leaves me frustrated, but on the other hand it makes me satisfyingly proud and even more appreciative of what I do have: tickets to, among others, the heavyweight shows of Lacroix, Chanel, and Saint Laurent, thank you very much.

17 October, 11:00
Espace Jeu de Paume,
Katharine Hamnett

The Jeu de Paume is an indoor tennis court famous in the annals of the French Revolution. It was there that the Declaration of the Rights of Man and Citizen was adopted in 1789. Along with the rights of freedom of speech and freedom of the press, the inalienable rights to liberty, property, security, and resistance to oppression were guaranteed.

What's the meaning of this little historical preamble? A mildly ironic context for Katherine Hamnett's show whose pinkish invitation reads loudly WOMEN, and softly 66% World's work, 10% Income, 1%

Assets. In other words, the revolution isn't over yet.

This small tent on the edge of the Place de la Concorde is the most tightly cramped show space yet. The morning is crisp and gorgeous, and the crowd is young and enthusiastic. Hamnett is a British designer who, acceding to market realities, shows in Paris. As well-known for her political slogans as for her wear-with-all jackets, she presents a casually underwhelming collection in attention-getting ways: on lots of Black Girls.

A new British Sister, Lorraine Pascal opens the show. She has a flawless ebony complexion, short hair, a long, lush body, and definite potential. Three Black Girls in a row, at the beginning, too, and still more to come. Stephanie, Lana, Gail, among them. They wear short jackets in menswear gray and pinstripes with sequined tanks or bustiers. There are long flowery shifts with pale chiffon scarves at the hips or on the shoulders. Bull's-eye targets are strategically placed on shiny stretch pants and T-shirts; bleached stars and stripes figure on denim jeans. A lot to see in a little space, but easy to look at and easy to listen to, especially Aretha's all-time goodie, "Respect." At the end Hamnett takes her bow in jeans and a black T-shirt reading "Use Democracy." She and Lorraine hold hands high, like co-champions at the end of a grueling tag team match.

5:30
Issey Miyake

Even though I did not have an invitation for Issey's show, I thought I would be able to get in for at least the last part of it. No such luck. Begging and pleading with the forces of order outside the tent had no effect. When a guard happened to crack open the door, I tried to brazen my way through and was pushed in the chest and rudely shoved back. I was stunned by the ferocity of his gesture.

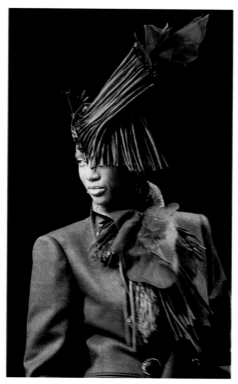

Naomi Campbell in **Dior.**

Fashion may be a passionate endeavor but does protecting it lead to near-brutality?

After Issey's show is over—and the doors are no longer guarded—I go backstage where everyone is euphoric, the sound of a standing ovation still ringing in their ears. My friend and stalwart fashion insider, Walter Greene says this was the best show he's seen this season. Issey always uses a large number of Black Girls, and I say Hi to all of them whether I know them or not. Karen, Gail, Beverly, and Aria are some of the ones I know. I stand in line to greet Issey, and when I tell him my name, he cries, "Barr-bar-rah!" We hug excitedly. It's the first time I've seen him in too many years to remember. I am pushed along by others equally as excited, but not before hoping that we will see each other again soon.

7:00
Martine Sitbon

Waiting. A seven-foot-tall Black giant in a blond Marie Antoinette wig and a tiny black sheath pushes me through the gate. "Can you get me on the cover of *Vogue*?" s/he asks. "Any time," comes the reply from someone who obviously cannot.

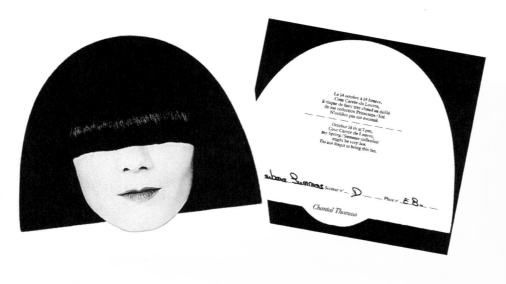

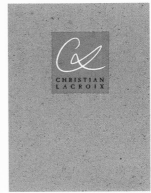

Inside, a coterie of drag queens takes turns vamping on the runway. A handful of people in the audience, maybe their own claque, laugh and applaud. But after a few minutes their show grows tiresome, tasteless, and boring. I am quite ready for the real thing. The crowd makes the room too hot and smoky. Two German women are sharing one plastic chair next to me. None too soon the runway is cleared of impostors, and the real Girls step out.

To a music of eerie voices and weird strings, they move under huge hats swathed with netting. A long coat is held closed by filaments. Pin stripes mix with black leather. There are lots of sheers and visible breasts. The camera crews are move vocal than the audience. Beverly wears a pretty brown slip dress that is backless before it ties at the base of the spine. There are tight lace knits layered in black; long, long jackets worn with long, long ropes of beads; and breast saucers, not big enough to be plates, worn as part of an evening ensemble. Models carry a cigarette holder with a lit cigarette trailing smoke. This startles me. Are cigarettes to become a cool fashion accessory now that anti-smoking restrictions are going into effect?

A key song repeats this line: "I wanted to be a hippie again, a Dadaist hippie in my own style, with short hair and a good fitting suit, but a hippie anyway." This is an appro-priate theme for many of this season's shows: dressing from the past, living in the present, dreaming of the fu-ture, and somehow embracing all the contradictions in between. Sitbon, a waif in a bright red pageboy haircut, accepts the audience's applause, and I'm glad to be outta there.

Gail O'Neill

I'm surprised to see Gail, a print star, on the runway here. To the ultra-sophisticated circus of the shows she brings a kind of quiet, nat-ural innocence which is both pro-vocative and refreshing. Raised in the Westchester suburbs, she graduated from Wesleyan with a major in English literature, and then worked for Xerox in New York. On her way back from a vacation in San Francisco, she had a fortuitous encounter with photographer Chuck Baker and his wife, Martha, a stylist.

"Chuck," Gail explains over sushi, "is very shy, so it took him the entire flight from California all the way back to New York before he finally got up the courage to talk to me just as I was about to leave the airport. Martha sent me over to a friend at *Self* magazine and then to Click. Alan Mandell was at the agen-cy then, and he was very flamboyant. He said, 'Oh, you're fabulous. When are you going to stop working at Xerox? We'd love to work with you!'

"I didn't know if he was sincere, because I was used to working with very sedate people who would take the time to carefully examine a situation and only then make a decision. I really didn't know enough to be nervous or to try and impress anyone, but I was meeting all of the right people.

"When I first started working, I was twenty. I was doing editorial, a lot of jumping, very youthful things. But I was dying to wear a long gown with red lipstick and be very sophisticated. I had a very easy start, and I didn't even have a fantasy like that. I never had to come to Paris to start a book or anything. A lot of women would come up to me and ask me how could they get started. You could really see stars in their eyes. It happens that way in life so often though, that things will come to the people who are just ambling along, and the people who are seeking will have a lot of difficulty."

Encouraged by her mother and warned by her father not to be come spoiled or jaded, Gail said, "It's been very professional all the way. No hitches, no hassles, nobody trying to come on to me. I wouldn't call myself anti-social, but I don't like going out with the express purpose of rubbing elbows."

While Gail never felt pressured to socialize in ways she didn't want to, she understood that others were not so free. And not just models. "You learn that photographers have to rub elbows with the right editors, and

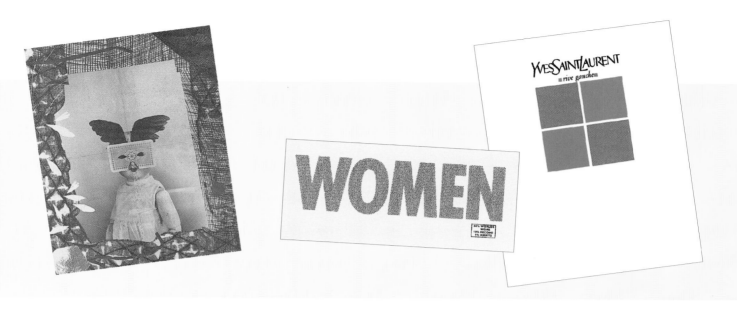

they have to keep current, and they worry about how good their competition is. But while you're in the midst of it, those things don't occur to you. They didn't occur to me.

"I did a lot of British *Vogue*, *Glamour*, *Mademoiselle*, and then *Elle* magazine came to the States. A whole new thing was happening there: the first time you had two Black models in the same issue of a magazine, and maybe in the same spread. It was really an exciting time. No other magazines were doing that.

"When I'd see a Black person on a catalog job all of a sudden I'd get excited because I realized that I hadn't worked with another Black person in months. And that's because when you do catalog, they have their quotas: minorities maybe one-fourth of the time. It's not determined just by race; it's also a matter of being a blonde, brunette or redhead. It dawned on me that this was really systematic. An *Elle* booking was the only time that I could actually work with another Black model.

"When I first started, I felt that this was some kind of fantasy world. It all happened so quickly. How long could it possibly last? I guess I was superstitious, too. This was too good to be true. So I told myself that I'd stay in it for two years and then go to law school or go back to Xerox. Within two years, I had no desire to do anything like that. I was enjoying myself. I was making a good living. I

had freedom. I looked forward to going to work in the morning. I was happy. So I decided to ride with it."

It takes more than that happy-go-lucky kind of attitude to land you on the runways, though. Gail started doing shows in New York very early in her career. "When I started out, nobody told me how to act on the runway. I had a lot of ballet training, so I walked very correctly. Good posture. Then when I began to watch other models, I realized that they weren't always smiling like I was. I saw that they had a little swagger to their walk or some funkiness. All of these things began to dawn on me over the years. I've never copied other people. I'm in my own world a lot of the time. But seeing videos helped me with my walk because I've learned what the choices are out there."

After about three years she went to Paris because people kept telling her that it was so much fun. Fun was not exactly what she found. "I didn't enjoy going on all the castings. People could be very rude, for no reason. Once you got to the designers, they were fabulous. But getting up the rungs of the ladder? You run across some pretty nasty people. After the first time I vowed I would never do the shows in Paris again. I worked then, and I worked well. But it just wasn't worth it to me, the emotional expense and its toll.

"I've gone on castings, and I've

been requested for movie roles and that type of thing. I never say no to an opportunity. Once I stepped into modeling and made a living at it, it taught me that you never know what your limitations are. And if there are any, it's because you've created them. I'm taking acting lessons, and I try. I'm not so devoted to it that I'm pining for my big break. But if it happens, I would be excited. I mean, when you walk on the runway, you're really acting. That's what I enjoy most. I enjoy being sexy, because in real life, I don't wear makeup. I don't wear tight-fitting clothes. I'm pretty conservative. It's such a departure from how I really am."

Not that how one "really" is always stays the same. One of Gail's most identifiable characteristics is her mane of naturally long wavy hair, which many Black women would envy for its texture and length. Her mother is half Chinese, and both of her parents, who are from Jamaica, have the same kind of hair. Growing up, Gail admits, she had not come to terms with its own natural beauty. "I had no appreciation for my hair being washed and then dried naturally in ringlets. I used to think that unless my hair was washed and set and underneath the dryer and really tame, that it was basically a mess. When I first started out in the business, clients wanted to straighten it. But that's not good for your hair.

It causes a lot of damage. Then some hairdressers, English hairstylists as well, taught me, and I realized that my natural hair was an acceptable look. They're the ones who acclimated me to the idea and taught me.

"And this is where the role model thing comes in. With models like myself coming in who are portrayed with their natural hair, little Black girls began seeing images that reflected themselves. Roshumba coming in with her own short hair, unprocessed. I think that's so beautiful. I'm not putting down people who have weaves and everything. Having a range is what's important."

In a world where ego and artifice are essential tools of survival, Gail seems a model of prudence and poise.

Anna Getaneh in **Yves Saint Laurent**.

"I have to thank my family for everything that's really good in my life. For keeping me centered. For keeping my clothes on, even. I don't judge people who decide to pose nude or anything, but it would never be a consideration for me. Unless you're the type of person who lives in a limousine, who never lives in the real world, you're never exposed to anything, and you're protected. But that's not me. I take the subway when I'm home. I look like any student going to school. People think that a model should live a certain kind of life, and taking the subway is definitely not a part of this program.

"But if you look to other people to determine how you should live your life, for one thing, I'd have no money. I would have invested it in an expensive wardrobe and drugs. Instead, I invest it in real estate, retirement accounts, really staid, safe things. I mean, I have gone shopping here in Paris. I have gone crazy. I got some beautiful shoes." She shows me a pair of impeccably-made but plain black oxfords, not exactly what I expect, but then again… "I have fun with my money, but I don't live like I'm going to be earning this kind of money for the rest of my life. Now I'm thinking about going into broadcast journalism, whether it's with a talk show or news, something to do with the media."

Gail O'Neill is far from needing—or even wanting—to make dramatic changes in her career at this time. She could be one of those long-distance runners, staking out new territory for herself while consolidating terrain that is already familiar. From huge Benetton billboards I saw in Milan to the newly released Revlon ColorStyle ads, from the pages of *Elle* to the pages of the *Sports Illustrated* swimsuit issue, she has been out there and back. Although she does not know what her next step will be, she insists, "If I do make a decision, it will be my decision, and not something that's forced upon me."

Gail is active in the Black Girls Coalition—founded by Bethann Hardison and Iman—and looks forward to the more political stance the group will soon be taking. "It's time that we have a press conference to address the issue of the marketplace and demographics. We're not being represented, and it's time that we are. We have such a voice in New York, but we're not really making use of it. We'll still give money to people in need, but now let us have something to say, too, and make people answer to us.

"There's a lot involved in putting on that pressure. It's got to be a united, group effort, not only individuals. If we pay attention to designers with our dollars but never hold them accountable for their decisions, why should they spend the extra money? They'd be fools, or Gandhi. And people who are Gandhi don't make it on Seventh Avenue.

"We're business people. I'd like to have a million-dollar contract. That's the American way. So I have no hesitation in saying that not only do I want there to be positive role models for young kids because I take that very personally, very seriously, but also that I want to make as much money as I can before I go.

"Friends are always encouraging me to talk to students in high school because they feel that I'm someone young people could look up to, especially young girls. But I'm reluctant to do that in the capacity of a model because I don't think that this is something a young girl should aspire to. There are so many other things that you have to develop inside.

"Maybe that's what my goal would be, to impress this message on the children that education is very important. Having integrity, having character is so important. The emphasis on family. Then again, if you're not from a close-knit family, it may sound like Fantasy Island to a lot of kids. You talk to them about following good role models. What if there are none where they are? What if I'm the role model, a pretty face who's making money? They'd probably do anything to get where I am when what they want is just some acknowledgment and respect. That's what you hear all the time from young people. They're out there killing each other because 'You stepped on my shoes' or 'You didn't respect me and looked at my woman.' Seeking these things in all the wrong places."

We finish our dinner in a mellow mood and walk back toward the Palais Royal and the Louvre, passing a small group of Americans obviously on vacation. Something about Gail registered in the tourists' eyes but they could not place her immediately, and she gave them neither the time nor the opportunity to do so. It was a naturally self-protective reaction, avoiding any trespass on her privacy. While models have little say in how they are shown to the public, the best do establish their own rules about how they are known in private. I got just the tiniest glimpse of that self-preservation in action.

In front of the Hotel du Louvre we catch separate cabs. Gail heads to her sister's apartment on the Right bank and I'm crossing the Seine to the Left. It's been a good, long day.

18 October, 9:00
Hotel St. James and Albany

While I was letting off steam in the press tent last night during Issey's show, I met Stella Larby, an enterprising Sister, and we agreed to meet this morning to talk at her hotel.

A native of Elkhart, Indiana,

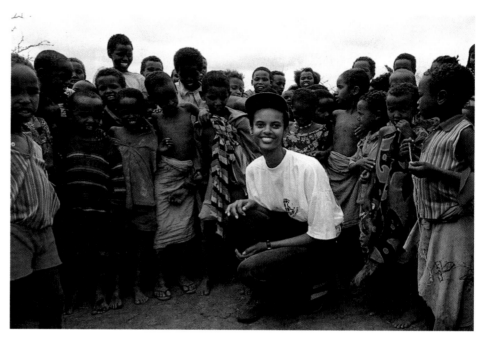

Anna Getaneh with refugee children in her homeland, Ethiopia. Although she traveled the world, she never forgot where she came from.

Stella moved to Zurich, Switzerland eight years ago and now runs her own hair and makeup firm called Supreme, which employs about twenty people. After she learned German, she worked first as a credit secretary for an American bank, and then moved into advertising. "I started doing model bookings for campaigns there. Next, I got an offer from a modeling agency in Zurich, where I worked for a couple of years. Then I got an offer from someone to open the first hair and makeup agency in Zurich. And I did it, but after two years I quit and opened up my own business.

"We do live productions, a lot of shows in Milan, seven shows in Paris this season. Soon we will be doing whole productions. That means I'm given the entire budget from the client. I get the layout person, I book my own photographer, I book my own hair and makeup, and I do my own model castings. If we're talking photos, I do everything and deliver the finished product to the client. If we're talking fashion shows, we're talking the whole production. You

take care of the whole team, and you're responsible when something goes wrong.

"Zurich is very commercial and located right in the center of Europe. From Zurich you can work anywhere in the world. I book Black Girls constantly, and I have two Blacks working in my agency. In the very near future, I'd like to open a second office in Miami for the catalog season—October to April—and get jobs there. I try to work as internationally as possible through computers. You've got millions of agencies who are happy doing low-level things. That's not me."

2:00
Christian Lacroix

Lacroix hails from Arles in the south of France, and part of his charm lies in the exuberant mix of colors, patterns, and textures considered characteristic of sunny Provence. His collection is always one of the most eagerly anticipated. The tent is packed, the audience in a festive mood. Now I see why he has scheduled three shows today, at ten, two, and four-thirty. To accommodate the converted and the curious in this, the smallest of the three tents, two shows were originally scheduled on the Chambre syndicale's calendar. Obviously, they weren't enough, and a third was added. The Girls will be working hard for their money today.

The wonderful thing is that they appear to enjoy it tremendously. Nadège, the French superstar of North African heritage and the bright tan good looks found in almost every ethnic group on the planet, opens the show. Second is Lana Ogilvie, the green-eyed Black beauty from Toronto who just signed an exclusive cosmetics contract with Cover Girl, the company which inaugurated the contract model thirty years ago.

Embroidered black denim gives way to hot, fruity colors. Orange,

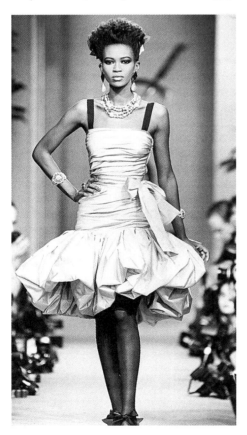

Amalia wearing **Yves Saint Laurent**. In photography and shows she projected a compelling gravitas.

yellow, green, and blue, all at once. Lacroix dips into so many cultural barrels: Mexican, with striped knit ponchos over striped knit sheaths; Indian, with mirrored inserts; Provençal, with summer flower prints; African and aboriginal prints in earth tones.

The multitude of garments is incredible. And so are the Girls. Katoucha, Karen, Sonia, Aria, Anna, Roshumba, and they keep on coming. They get by far the most applause. Is it because their outfits are better or because these Girls are simply outstanding? Katoucha receives the loudest applause for a golden breast plate worn over a sheer black sheath. At the end she is the one who walks out with Lacroix to the final ovations.

On my way backstage I manage to penetrate the frenzy, shake Monsieur Lacroix's hand, and thank him for using so many beautiful Black women. He responds with a solid burst of laughter, and we are both pushed in opposite directions by the noisy crowd. Once I finally reach backstage it seems as if a party is going on. Instead of rushing off to their following assignments, the models are able to relax right where they are in preparation for the next show. They smoke, nibble on hors d'oeuvres, and drink mineral water, orange juice or champagne. Friends and fans of Lacroix are cheerfully busy congratulating him and his *responsables* on the collection. Everyone speaks more than one language and at the same time, it seems.

I spot Anna Getaneh, sitting alone on the makeup table. She is one of the most sought-after Girls in the world of fashion, and I jump at this opportunity to talk with her. I ask her point blank if she likes Lacroix. She answers just as directly. "Do I like him? He's my favorite designer. He's just wonderful to work with. I love his clothes. I love the atmosphere. I love everything about the show. Over the years—and

I've been doing it for four and a half years now—you begin to attach yourself to certain houses because you like the ambiance, the way they treat you, the way they treat the other Girls, the outfits they give you, the music, and everything. To me that's how I judge a designer. It's not just what I'm wearing."

Originally from Ethiopia, Anna Getaneh was the daughter of a career diplomat, and used to traveling with her parents. She explains, "I came to Paris to study French, and then I started modeling. I was twenty-one, so I was old enough, but to my parents I was still a baby. Finally, I hooked up with an agency here, and at the same time, I finished school and got my degree, a BA in Marketing. I took an interpreting course, so I'm bilingual in French and English. Then when I got all that out of the way, I moved to New York. And I've been living in New York for two and a half years, working full time now."

If she surprised people by making the move to the States, Anna had another surprise in store for her fashion clients. She did the unthinkable; she cut her hair. "I'd always had long hair, even until twenty-one I wore braids. I didn't want to straighten it or use relaxer, so it was very difficult to get through my hair. With the slightest humidity, it would frizz, and people were constantly complaining. I was already feeling very self-conscious about my hair and all. So about a year into the business, I decided to just cut it all off. I didn't tell anybody. Since it was myself and my body I didn't think that I had to ask my agency. I just went to a hairdresser in New York, and said that I wanted my hair cut in a small Afro. The immediate reaction was, 'Ohhh, you'll never be able to do your classic couture shows.' But they're still loyal to me."

The haute couture shows in January and July, the ready-to-wear shows in March and October, plus the photography shoots all year round keep her on the go. "When I started out, I was doing runway, because it was seasonal and it gave me time to continue my studies. Once I graduated, I realized that I was more of an expert, if I could say that, in the runway business than I was in print. I had no problem with this because I do shows in Japan, Spain, Germany, London, New York. I don't do all the shows everywhere, but I still do five or six countries which means that I work eight months out of the year just doing shows. Over the years I realized that you need to do print, too. That's when I started doing editorial. But I must say that it's not what I enjoy doing most. I love doing the shows."

Feeling and looking relaxed on the runway is how Anna earns her income. It is in a far distant world — Ethiopia—that she spends it. "I never forget where I'm from. Even though I work here, when I go to Ethiopia, that's home, that's reality for me. That's where I come from, and I never forget that. I try to help as much as I can back home." I leave her to try to relax and recoup for the next show.

Then I seat myself at Roshumba's table where she's taking a breather. The necessary catch-up facts: nine shows in Milan and ten shows in Paris. "It was a pick and choose season." And who does the picking and choosing? "Me. After five years, I should hope so," she declares. Feedback form the *Sports Illustrated* swimsuit issue? "It was really, really good. Now when I'm in the airport, people point and say, 'Look, it's Roshumba.'"

Edouard Saint-Bris, an executive with Pierre Cardin, comes to sit with us. He is smiling and voluble as he describes Roshumba's popularity with French designers. It is her gaiety, energy, and spontaneity that set her apart from most European models, and most models in general, he states emphatically.

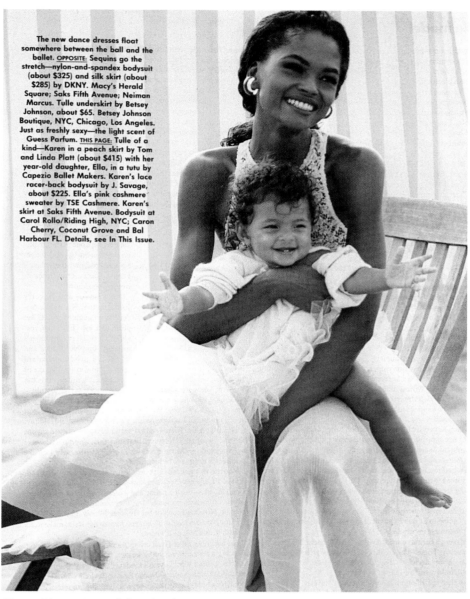

The new dance dresses float somewhere between the ball and the ballet. OPPOSITE: Sequins go the stretch—nylon-and-spandex bodysuit (about $325) and silk skirt (about $285) by DKNY. Macy's Herald Square; Saks Fifth Avenue; Neiman Marcus. Tulle underskirt by Betsey Johnson, about $65. Betsey Johnson Boutique, NYC, Chicago, Los Angeles. Just as freshly sexy—the light scent of Guess Parfum. THIS PAGE: Tulle of a kind—Karen in a peach skirt by Tom and Linda Platt (about $415) with her year-old daughter, Ella, in a tutu by Capezio Ballet Makers. Karen's lace racer-back bodysuit by J. Savage, about $225. Ella's pink cashmere sweater by TSE Cashmere. Karen's skirt at Saks Fifth Avenue. Bodysuit at Carol Rollo/Riding High, NYC; Caron Cherry, Coconut Grove and Bal Harbour FL. Details, see In This Issue.

Karen Alexander with her daughter, **Ella**.

She invested in her career by learning the language and the culture, and the French have repaid her interest in them. They love her, he says. And I ask her why.

"Because if you know the people, you know their spirit, you know their feelings. You make it work. I like to take situations and make them work. Get inside the culture, learn the language, and make friends. That's what makes me different."

It's so easy to get carried away and start hearing exclamation points punctuating my very thoughts. Rubbing shoulders with glamorous people tends to polish every perception to a higher gloss. But there is always another side, a scruffier, darker side that is never far away.

A New York journalist tells me a story that's making the rounds this season. One of the hottest and youngest Black Girls was accused of stealing another star Girl's credit cards and running up a big bill. She's a klepto, my informant says, "too much, too soon. She's been engaged two or three times. She's had an abortion. And now her agency has repudiated her." I shake my head in disbelief. Why would she want or need to do something like that? She's been everywhere, she's making a fortune, and she's not even old enough to vote! More than anything she needs help.

I chat with Sonia Cole and tease her about her plans—which she told me in Milan two years ago—to move back to the States. "I was going to," she says with a laugh. "I had found an apartment in New York and everything. But then I met a Frenchman, fell in love, moved in with him, and stayed." She seems very happy with the direction her life has taken. When a mutual friend mentions the model scandal, Sonia asks me, "You heard

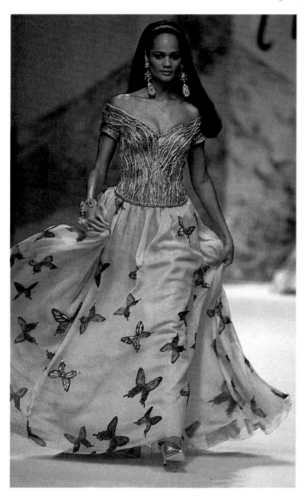

Michele in a **Hanae Mori** gown with signature butterflies.

about it, too?" Then she shakes her head and points her finger to it. "The Girl is sick," Sonia says, and moves off cheerfully, as if to emphasize that she, for one, is not.

6:00
Sonia Rykiel

The music for the Sonia Rykiel show runs the gamut from European classical to classic American soul. And why not? This is my last show for the day, and if the clothes are unremarkable, they are nonetheless very wearable. Sonia Rykiel is renowned for unpretentiously elegant knits, classic long cardigans over classic long skirts. There are blue and white stripes, solids and plaids. Anna, Roshumba, Katoucha, Lana, and Karen are among the Girls on the runway. Even though they've had a long day with the other shows beforehand, they still make their presentation seem graceful and effortless.

Karen Alexander

After the Sonia Rykiel show Karen and I search with little luck for a cab. It is Sunday evening in Paris, and according to the strict but unwritten rules of French timing, everybody should already be where they wish to go. Luck finally smiles on us with the arrival of a taxi *libre*. We arrive at the Ritz Hotel and take seats in the lounge at a tiny table next to the harpist. Leave it to the Ritz to regale one with such heavenly sounds after an exhausting day. The only drink to order is champagne. We do, and, for our own private reasons, we celebrate.

Karen's motivation for going into the modeling profession seems as far removed as possible from outsiders'

notions of youth, beauty, and oversized ego. "I've always loved older people," she says. "All my grandparents died when I was very young. So I thought, Why don't I work in a nursing home? I can be around all the older people that I'd like." While working in an institution in New Jersey where she was raised, she dreamed of what she could do with money earned from modeling. But all the agencies she went to in New York said no to signing her.

"It's not like I ever wanted to be a model because I was so beautiful or so amazing. It had nothing to do with looks for me or having my picture on a magazine cover. The only reason I kept going and trying and trying was because I wanted to build a nursing home. It's only in the last few years that I've been able to think, All right, maybe you're pretty. But it's taken me a long time to sort of accept it.

"I beat the pavement for more than a year. And that's when I met my agent, Pauline. My first big job, I mean *big* job, was in Paris. I did ten days with Oliviero Toscani for French *Elle*. I had no idea what I was doing. I had this orange thing on and high heels, and I thought I was going to die. I cried the first day and the second day. But by the third day, I got it.

"I'd never heard French before. I had no idea. That's why I work with young Girls now. I say to them, 'Look, here's my number. If you have a question, call me. I don't care what time it is.' I think that in the beginning, you need someone else to say, 'It's scary.' I'm not too proud to say to new Girls that I still get nervous.

"I take my job very seriously. If *Vogue* chooses me over a million Girls—Black, White or green—and they decide that they want Karen Alexander for ten pages, I feel a lot of pressure. I mean, I know that I'm not a brain surgeon. When I do a catalog, I take that seriously as well. There are a lot of other models in the world. The thing that I love most, my best compliment, is a good catalog client

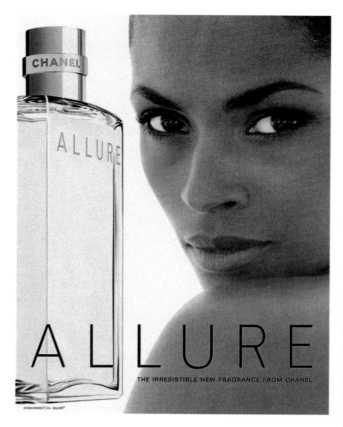

ALLURE

THE IRRESISTIBLE NEW FRAGRANCE FROM CHANEL

Karen Alexander for **Chanel**'s newest fragrance, Allure.

or an art director who'll say to me, 'Hey, we know this piece is a dog, but Karen, we know you can sell it.' What else does a model want to hear?

"When I went to Paris for the collections, I must have been eighteen or nineteen. It was great. I did thirteen shows my first season. It really hit me that for a designer to choose you to do his show is a very personal thing. I mean, that's why we're models, for the designers. I'm really honored to be here."

But when she started out, she had an entirely different attitude. "I didn't like shows. My first show was for Ralph Lauren at the Hotel Pierre. I guess I was about eighteen. I was feeling so nervous. And Ralph takes both of my hands and says to me, 'You're going to be fine. You're beautiful.'

"Now, this man was in the middle of all this serious stuff, and he took the time to say this to me. So obviously, I'm very devoted to Ralph Lauren. But, you know, I really never take anything for granted."

Karen Alexander is one of the few top Girls in her generation to be a mother. "The shows came around when I was four months pregnant. I worked a lot, and I felt beautiful and strong. I sailed through Paris, but when I showed up in New York, I'd had enough. I was pleased with my career, and I just wanted to stop. I felt that motherhood would be my next thing and that I would retire."

But the fashion industry was not ready to let her quit. When her daughter, Ella, was only two weeks old, the Gap wanted to do an ad with Karen and her baby. And during the eight months she stayed home to breast-feed, Karen came to realize that the new career of motherhood was not enough for her. Her old career beckoned.

"To be perfectly honest, I missed it. I missed having something that was mine. During pregnancy my body was not my own anymore, and I needed my own thing again. After eight years of covers and pictures and articles and stories and pretty clothes and pretty people, I missed it. My ego was addicted. So I came back little by little. I dragged Ella around the world with me, and I had a great time traveling with her, but finally I really had to commit to her and say, 'Wait a minute. Real life isn't like this.'

"It's real because I'm doing it. But I need her to know that not everyone wears Chanel every day. Not everyone has her makeup put on for her and has someone do her hair and powder her nose and ask if she's hungry. I want her to know that there are a lot of jobs and all kinds of kids in this world. And this isn't a job where she could ever see that.

"I felt that she needed some stability. Finally, I had to decide what's best for Ella and what's best for me. At what point am I being selfish by having her around? It's easier for me to have her with me so I don't miss her and I'm not sad. But what about her? Her friends and her toys and her crib and her father and grandmother?

"Well, I'm a big girl, and I can take care of myself. But for children, their surroundings are so important. I think she's had a great time. But I'm learning to let her go, and it's hard. I miss her. When I'm not with her, I feel like my arms are missing."

Although Karen's favorite magazine story was a *Vogue* spread with photos of her with Ella and an article on her family, Karen has decided not to do any more pictures with her daughter. "I think that it's an invasion of her privacy. She's not an accessory. She's not a handbag. When she's old enough and she'd like to be a model and be in a picture with me, I'd be more than happy. But I don't feel that because she's my child, she's my possession. I have a lot of respect for her. I don't feel that it's my right to subject her to that."

Karen's efforts to achieve stability and security for her family and self-satisfaction for herself involved a constant balancing act. She maintains two homes, one in California where her husband, screenwriter Adam Kidron, is based, and another in New Jersey. She checks in twice a day, knowing that long-distance conversations are emotionally risky, but she insists on confronting the challenge to intimacy and honesty by being as present as she can.

"I don't want Ella thinking that I'm going out only to make money. That's not why I'm working. I know how kids are. 'If Mama is working for money, then I don't want anything, so we don't have to spend any money, and we don't need any more.' But it's not about money. It's for me. I need it. It makes me a better mother, I think. I hope."

19 October, 10:30 Chanel

It is wild and noisy in the outer courtyard of the Louvre. The guard insists that identification is required.

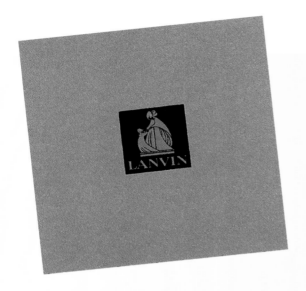

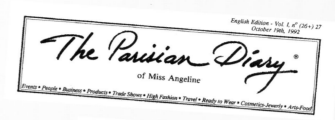

But I snort my way past, almost slapping him on the wrist with my precious invitation. It's true, though, the fine print does say that the card and I.D. are required. Still, I attitudinize my way through and end up, thanks again to *Time*, in the prize section right in front of the camera crews at the end of the runway. In the aisle a television interviewer is holding her passport and talking about showing I.D. to get an assigned seat that's probably occupied by someone else anyway. Roy Campbell, the savvy fashion columnist at the *Philadelphia Inquirer*, stops by to chat with me. He says he's doing an article that takes people step-by-step through a fashion show. He chose to base it on Chanel, the epitome of that madness, so his report should be fun.

The backdrop for the show resembles a marble bathroom with big square bottles of perfume on the counter. When we entered the tent, we were greeted with a gift of Chanel No. 5 Eau de toilette. What kind of thank-you note do you write for that?

"Success, we've got it" is the opening song. Claudia Schiffer, the bubbly blond megamodel, leads the show, followed by Nadège, Naomi, Linda Evangelista, Stephanie Roberts, Beverly Peele, Lorraine Pascal, and several more Black Girls. They wear bolero tweed jackets over longer tweed tanks in pastel colors. There are bell bottoms in black and white and hi-top basketball shoes à la Converse. The music gathers speed like a runaway train. "My name is Prince" comes on at the same time that Sandra Bernhard, the comedienne, comes out. The audience laughs—possibly in nervous recognition—but she looks mean and angry and carries her arms in a simian swing. Whatever joke she's a part of is lost on me.

The joke that everybody gets is the underwear. White jockey briefs with the Chanel name on the elastic waistband are worn to be seen underneath open trench coats, as the Weather Girls sing, "It's raining men," and also under sheer black skirts and wide pants. At $160 a pair, these panties seem to be the last laugh of label lunacy. As Stephanie strides to the end of the runway, her bright smile is turned down at the corners as if she's trying to control a full-throated laugh.

Less hilarity follows. There are embroidered pastels, sequins on sheer silks, pale suedes, bandanna head ties. Then handkerchief whites, like milkmaid costumes, with eyelet and embroidery complete the show, which has been fun and bright.

Sandra Bernhard is the bride. Although Lagerfeld has designed collections for four houses this season, he seems to appear at the end of each show in the same frumpy-looking clothes, a gray striped jacket with dark gray pants. I am obviously missing something here. I do not miss, however, his number one accessory, his fan.

12 noon
Hanae Mori

My dear friend, Dr. Esther P. Roberts takes a break from her schedule as the resident psychiatrist at the American Embassy and meets me for the Hanae Mori show. It's crowded and hectic, and we have only standing invitations. But somehow Esther manages to finagle an impossibly decent seat, while I remain slapped up against the wall, glaring holes through the back of people who crowd me and narrow my view.

Madame Mori, the doyenne of Western design in Japan and arguably Japan's best-known female export, presents a line of sophisticated, feminine, and extremely wearable clothes. Georgiana, Beverly, and Anna Getaneh open the show in swimsuits. Well-bred suits, dresses, and tuxedos follow in a reassuringly respectable manner. Here no one has to decipher the hidden import of women flashing jockey shorts. We tread a familiar path even as we are treated to jungle prints and animal patterns.

Ironically, I note only one Asian model in the line-up. I'll be interested to see how the personnel changes for the Tokyo show.

My next show is not until two-thirty, so Esther and I hop on the métro to the Marais where she steers me to lunch at Le Coude fou, a tiny restaurant suffused with the old-fashioned charm of aged wood and attentive gourmands.

2:30
Christian Dior

How divine! Chanel No. 5 for breakfast, and now Miss Dior *après* lunch. And perfume, this time.

The show is a huge operatic production costumed by the Italian Gianfranco Ferrè, design head of the House of Dior as well as his own line. Scenes of Venice set the place while an aria from *Don Giovanni* with a modern rock beat sets the mood. Opening outfits are variations on a theme of black and white stripes. Sonia, Roshumba, Beverly, Katoucha, Maureen, and others work the combinations of leggings, white organza shirts, silk tunics, short skirts, long dresses, and black lace bodysuits. Four Black models appear on stage together in sand tops and white pants. In another grouping of four, Katoucha, in a long coat of black and white diagonal stripes over a short white skirt, is the only model to do dramatic double spins, showing the full effect of the garment.

It is a lush and elegant collection, more shapely than the transparent fluidity on display elsewhere during this season. Ferrè's theatricality is in full force during the finale when ballet dancers from the Paris Opera leap down the runway in wild carnivalesque gestures. A harlequin offers a big bottle of perfume to the bride, actress Isabelle Adjani, masked in black and glitter, her neck tied with a huge black satin bow. Ferrè enters the ball to great applause. On one hand, the festivities of the show seem to be over; on another, they are just continuing.

If the designers, their backers and assistants can now celebrate a finished production, the models cannot. In the back courtyard between tents, I have only a minute to salute Katoucha. Dressed now in black work clothes and boots, and clutching a cigarette and a glass of champagne, she limps across the cobblestones to the next tent. She's had an operation on her foot, she tells me, but no one would ever know that from her performance on the runway. Unstoppable stamina. Dedication. Endurance. Unflagging good humor. The Girls have to have those qualities—or at least project them—to make it through show season. I'm getting ready for my fourth show of the day, and I'm exhausted just from watching.

4:30
Balenciaga

The collection of this traditional couture house is being designed by a new, young talent, Josephus Melchior Thimister. Program notes highlight "a collection of contrasts; the extremes come together in a combination of structured and unstructured." We see that "the opacity of wool crepe or double linen is offset with chiffon or gauze. Suede

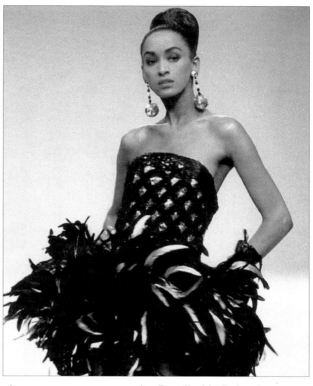

A consummate runway artist. **Rosalind** in **Balmain**.

and sable are perfectly matched. Suits with long jackets and chiffon skirts or silk jogging trousers for the evening. Everything is fresh, humorous, but also disciplined."

Indeed. The strict, clean, straight lines of the clothes are partnered by a most unusual hairstyle worn by all the Girls. Sleek in front, the hair is parted in the middle in back and twisted like twin tornadoes into two vertical rolls. The effect of futuristic science fiction reminds me at the same time of some ancient, pre-literate style.

Katoucha appears, followed by Sonia, Georgiana, Tyra, and others. Three Black Girls together show black suede tunics over black silk pants. Another grouping places Black Girls in black outfits and White Girls in the same outfits but in white. The most amusing accessories are hats with wings in neon pink. The bride appears in white gazar and organza as "Ave Maria" plays. Then James Brown cleans up the finale with "I Feel Good."

Talking about contrasts! The delightful thing is that it works.

20 October, 10:30
Guy Laroche

Another classic couture house in its ready-to-wear incarnation, but I am bored by the clothes, and resentful to be so so early in the morning. The Girls perk me up. Roshumba and Tyra and Rosalind, whose runway style is the epitome of sophisticated restraint. Outfits in reptile prints and safari suits receive applause. Why, I do not know. The evening clothes resuscitate uselessly imprecise words like cute and lovely, and I am peevish about my limited vocabulary.

11:30
Emanuel Ungaro/Parallèle

This is an unexpectedly rowdy crowd, noisy and good-humored, but I see that it's really the press folks who are causing the commotion. Photographers are busy shooting French screen star Alain Delon in the front row. His once dark hair is silver now, and he has those interesting lines in his face that in a mature man equal enhanced character.

Women were—and still are—often penalized for those same lines. Naturally, the evolved among us are changing that ridiculous double standard.

The show finally starts with Sonia, Anna Fiona, and another model in a fabulous mix of prints and patterns anchored by black. There are jackets with everything. They can be in broad stripes paired with thin stripes in the trousers and worn with a brightly flowered shirt; in black and white checks over a flared skirt with multi-colored polka dots and a Matisse-inspired scarf; and of course in prints with varying backgrounds (black, green, and rose) worn with jersey dresses in contrasting colors. Fuchsia and orange, lime and raspberry, beige and saffron are some of the color couplets that combine the "rigor and baroqueness" and the "simultaneously suave and sour" elements of Ungaro's signature lush, relaxed, and feminine designs.

While some fashion folk consider Ungaro a pretty, but ultimately safe bet for ladies who lunch, his own notes indicate otherwise. In a tart comment on this season's major trends echoing the '70s, Ungaro writes: "When history repeats itself, it stutters. So why attempt to revisit the past, which, though it teaches us much, has poor intentions.

"This collection claims appropriateness to the savageness of the time...."

"Don't cry for me, Argentina" brings the show to a close and the petit Ungaro to the stage and high-calorie applause.

1:00
Issey Miyake showroom, 5 Place des Vosges

This morning I called Bethann at her hotel. She woke up quickly, said she'd been out all night dancing in her chair at the "Balade de l'Amour," an AIDS benefit held last night at the Folies Bergère. We decided to meet at Issey Miyake's showroom at one o'clock this afternoon to talk.

While I'm waiting for her, I get a chance to watch a video of Issey's show that I missed a few days ago. It is delightful. Augmenting the regular model corps, members of the Frankfurt Ballet leap, twist, and burst into all kinds of surprising moves while just happening to present the collection. The most touching moment of the show—and of the entire season, I feel—comes at the finale, traditionally reserved for the bride. In this passage, called "Sand cocoon," six Black women command the stage. They seem appealingly natural, in loose, coarsely woven linens and flat shoes. Their spirit seems humble and yet transcendent. As they walk off the runway to climactic applause, five of them are linked arm-in-arm. In a beautifully impetuous movement, Roshumba looks back and beckons the last Girl to join them. She does, and the six Black Girls stride off, united and powerful in Sisterhood. Issey receives a standing ovation, the first—and almost the last—of the season.

Even for me, distanced by size (the small screen) and time (three days later), especially for me, it is a tumultuous moment. That one scene symbolizes the beauty, strength, resilience, and generosity of Black women in fashion. That one scene captures the essence of *Skin Deep*.

Part of the ambivalent magic of video is its ability to retrieve the real thing and at the same time reduce its emotional impact. Massaged by repetition, I can begin to focus on other things besides my feelings. For example, the clothes. From the roving camera's perspective, however, it's difficult to concentrate on a single element. Mostly I see layered blocks of color and large, loose shapes in innovatively pleated fabrics. People like to say that Issey makes art to wear. But art still has to sell. Thus, the showroom.

When Bethann arrives, I turn on my tape recorder. She needs no prompting, and Q & A is unnecessary with her. It's all answers to questions I don't have to ask.

First, she updates me on the Black Girls Coalition. The group will be holding a press conference before the end of the year to speak out about politics, racial representation, and advertising in the '90s.

Bethann remembered the lessons of the '60s and '70s. "I kept thinking that the upsurge of Black models was going to die at any minute, because I don't trust this industry. I know how it is: here today, gone tomorrow. We knew that what happened for us was the result of a strong political effect."

While the current generation of

Girls has rekindled that old success, Bethann thought, "These kids don't know the struggle. My point was to celebrate them but also to remember that we're fortunate and that there are a lot of people who are not. And that's how we came up with benefits for homeless children. We've raised lots of money, but we're really trying to raise consciousness.

"Now the Girls are so strong in number that they start straying. One's pitted against the other. They fight with each other. So we need to give them a purpose to come together. For their own sake, they have to learn to take responsibility and learn how to become a unit. I want them to see how they can be known for something more than being just a pretty Girl.

"We happen to be in the business of advertising images. Minority money is being spent, and minority images are not being made. I'm coming from the premise that we're not just talking about us being Black. We're talking about, Where's the Asian? Where's the Greek with the broken nose? I don't see any Puerto Ricans. We're just using our Blackness because we have the strength to do it.

"I tell the Girls, If you're afraid to lose a client by speaking out, don't be, because clients feel more guilty than you think."

Bethann Management has been in business since July, 1984. Managing models has always been difficult, but Bethann says it's even more difficult now. "I seem to be running out of gas. I just kept going because I'm strong. I learned a lot from my mistakes, and that's good. But I'm just going to keep helping these Girls, and people can say anything they want."

Ever the entrepreneur, Bethann talks of opening a shop on the island of Anguilla where she and her husband have a home. She wants to stock it with baskets, paintings, artifacts, and furniture: beautiful, inanimate objects. So different from the beautiful, highly animated subjects of

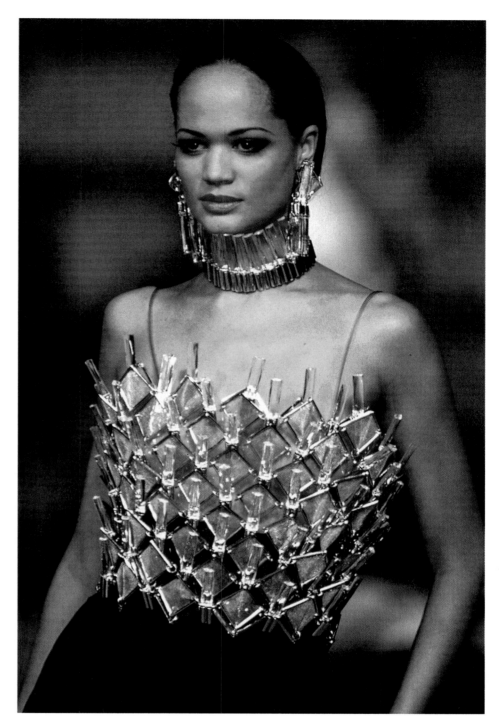

Classic plastic by **Paco Rabanne** worn by **Michele**.

her model business. "I'm looking forward to the next fifty years," she says. If the past is prologue, they will be active, involved ones, and any snoozing will still take place close to the hippest dance floor in town.

21 October, 11:00
Yves Saint Laurent

Saint Laurent traditionally has this last day to himself. There may be a whiff of *primus inter pares* about it,

but then again, it's the Chambre syndicale's schedule, and the Chambre syndicale was founded and headed (until 1993) by Pierre Bergé, chairman of Saint Laurent. By this time buyers and journalists are tired, and the models completely exhausted. But everyone pumps their spirit up for this last show.

My seat is in the second row, absolute paradise. I am the only Black woman in the neighborhood, although there are several in the audience, and I am ferociously proud to be here. I like to feel that even the faintest presence of Black people in the audience reminds us all that Black models do not exist isolated in a world of power, prestige, and all-pervasive Whiteness. There are more where these Girls come from. Saint Laurent, born in North Africa, has long made a point of using high percentages of Black models. The feeling among us was always that the best use the most.

The show starts with a fabulous line-up of twelve Girls, more than half of whom are Black and Brown. There is nothing like seeing so many Girls of color on the runway at one time. It looks like victory. This sensation of rightful authority can be applied to Saint Laurent as well. People are always nervous about YSL. Each collection is burdened by the necessity of competing with contemporary designers as well as with his own glorious past. Today the Saint Laurent legend looks healthy and strong. An old-timey voice-over counts the outfits off just as in the traditional couture shows: *Numéro un*, Number one; *Numéro deux*, number two; and

When I design and craft my dresses, I need a living model, a moving body. I could never work with a mere wooden dummy because for me clothes must live. I need to work with a woman's body before sending out my clothes into the real world.

Black models are graced with particulary modern proportions and motions. They are perfectly suited to my needs and have always inspired me enormously. I love the luminosity they lend to fabrics. I feel the depth of colour of their skin brings added intensity to colours.

They have never disappointed me. I love their expression, the lustre in their eyes, their long lines and the irresistible suppleness of their movements.

For me they possess that most magical of a woman's qualities : mystery. Not the outworn mystery of the "femme fatale" but the dynamic mystery of the woman of today.

Yves Saint Laurent

so on. Music, including Michael Jackson's "Keep it in the Closet," is layered on top of that.

The bold opening line-up highlights accessories worn with serenely simple black body suits. These are followed by navy ensembles with trousers and wrapped or pleated skirts. Mixes include brights with white, small patterns, and contrasting textures such as leather and silk. There are short straight skirts, loose long ones, tailored trousers, and soft wide pants slit to the thigh. Jackets of several lengths and shapes go with them. Long golden sarongs, like molten metal, are paired with

colorfully beaded and sequined halters, also inspired by Eastern cultures. The bride wears black, her bodysuit edged with gardenias whose white is reprised in her veil. Applause erupts often during the show and Saint Laurent himself—sometimes so ill or nervous that he does not even appear—receives a standing ovation. Exultation mixes with relief as the official season comes to a close. How can I feel fired up and burned out at the same time?

26 October, 6:00

Carol Mongo

Talking with Carol Mongo is therapy for the over-stressed of fashion. Illustrator, journalist, teacher, and long-time observer of the French scene, she provides a refreshing, penetrating, and often humorous perspective on What This All Means. But after fourteen and a half years in Paris, after twenty-four seasons of fashion shows, even she is shaking her head in bewilderment.

"My eyes got really cluttered with all this season's hippie stuff. Of all the years to go back to, the '70s were just the ugliest period. And for very good reasons. We're talking about the drug culture and a generation protesting against Vietnam.

"I wasn't really that against people re-doing the '60s, because the '60s were almost the modern-day version of the '20s. It was short and fun, and it was a livelier time. And when they were doing the '60s in the '80s, they put in padded shoulders and stuff, so it looked updated. But the way some are presenting the '70s turned me off. I talked to a lot of people who felt the same way. So I came down really heavily on designers who were going back to the '70s."

Where she critiqued them is in *Le Carnet Parisien d'Angeline de Monthurban von Shtupp y Fuentes*, translated with a noticeable diminu-

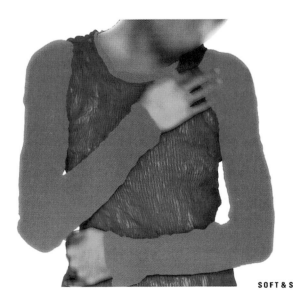

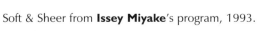
SOFT & SHEER

Soft & Sheer from **Issey Miyake**'s program, 1993.

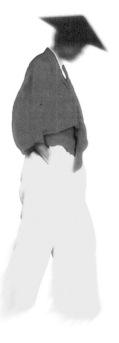

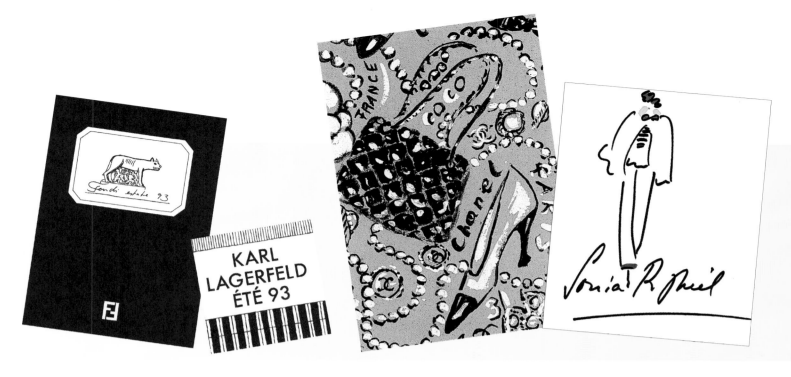

tion of society satire as *The Parisian Diary of Miss Angeline*. This unique four-page journal is published—without advertisement—in French and English daily during show season and distributed gratis at the Louvre gates. Carol and a small staff write idiosyncratic reviews of the collections in the voices of a trademarked list of dubiously titled international ladies. Mildred Frozenfrog Bottomlyne, Abigail Stitch, Lady Washingsocks, and Delores de la Huerta—"the whammy of Miami"—are a few of the cast of characters in the English edition.

In one column, after Angeline finishes an early-morning phone call with her friend Kanga Rue in Sydney, she "thought once again about what a miraculously beautiful city Paris is…and. how successfully the city continues to modernize without losing its soul. And then the thought struck her, 'Why isn't fashion doing the same thing?' How, in fact, had everyone become so short of imagination, since it's not only fashion designers that are swimming in schools, but car designers, magazine editors, everyone. Was this the normal reaction of people threatened and perplexed by the need for the new? She decided it was and that the whole world is suffering from creative gridlock at the turn of the century."

In her own voice Carol Mongo is just as acerbic. For example, "this hemline debate," she says heatedly, "seems to be quite ridiculous. I just don't believe that women are such sheep anymore. I'll wear long when I feel like wearing long and short when I feel like wearing short. That leads me to the other reason I was disappointed with the season. It seems like the designers are grasping at straws to get women to buy things, but I think the real problem these days is cost. The winners are the people who can produce well-made clothes that are comfortable to wear and that are priced right.

"I also write for a little paper called the *Paris Free Voice*, and with that paper I write for real people. One story we did was on the resale shops. I guarantee that you can go down the Faubourg St. Honoré, Avenue Montaigne or Place de la Victoire, and even on a Saturday, you would be hard-pressed to see many people in those stores. Do you know where all the French women are? They're lining up in the resale shops. Women are still interested in clothes. They're always going to buy things. But what's wrong are the prices.

"The shows cost these designers anywhere from a half-million to a million francs—$100,000 to $200,000—each. The cost of the tent, the cost of the models, maintenance, choreography…. Just the shows, not the clothing samples. That means you have to make all that back, and it's going to be reflected in the price. Regular customers end up paying for all the hype and the models. I just think that the whole business has gotten out of hand. In talking to other journalists I found that a number of us were wondering the same thing: Is it time for me to stop for a while? Or is it the season?

"When you get away from the tents and the journalists, nobody really cares. They just want to know what colors are important and what the hemlines are like. Every summer when I go home to Detroit, they say, 'Where are the hemlines?' and basically that's it. So it's coming to terms with this: Is it really important what a handful of so-called fashionable women are wearing? We've got a whole new generation that doesn't care.

"You can't discount the American market because we are the customer who buys more clothing than anyone else. We're a bigger country to begin with. Americans are conditioned from birth. You have to shop for Easter, which really doesn't exist here. Then you buy something for graduation, and then you have summer clothes, and then you're going to buy back-to-school clothes, then you're going to buy holiday clothes, then you're going on a trip, and you're going to buy resort clothes. In France, there isn't this constant change every couple of months where you buy something for a certain time of the year.

"A journalist pointed out to me

that the only real trends moving fashion forward—whether you like them or not—are coming from poor, violent neighborhoods. It kind of makes sense. When you're poor, you don't have anything, so you have to take a look and make it work. But when you have everything, you get lazy. What we're looking at in fashion—and it's very disturbing—is something that parallels music. There's not a lot of new things coming out. We're looking at the remix.

"Right now, the only part of fashion that is looking toward the future is the textile industry with all of the experimentation in fabric. In Patrick Kelly's last few shows, people thought that he was going to have to do something else besides stretch fabrics. Now, suddenly, there's this whole big industry that's booming by doing brand new things with stretch. They're putting Lycra into cotton piqués or denim or traditionally very rigid fabrics. I don't know if all this just happened by accident or if he was a catalyst.

"Today we're looking at fibers and materials that act like holograms, that give you a feeling of body heat. You've got fabrics being mixed with metallics. I've seen copper materials that are incredible. But it's getting to the point that you wonder who is the real creator of the piece. Who do you give the credit to: the textile designer or the clothing designer?

"I have done twenty-four show seasons. When I began in 1980, it was easy to get tickets to the shows. There weren't as many people, and they just gave us tickets. Then they became these huge productions. More and more people came over, and shows became more and more elaborate. Our generation has seen everything—from Cardin's space age to Lacroix's bustles. So, where do you go from here? We're all getting a little blasé. I'm beginning to wonder if it's time for fashion to

take a different form. My feeling about this season was that I was happy when it was finished. It was the first time I ever felt like that. Today there is no big star that's knocking everybody's socks off. And frankly, I don't know what anybody is going to create to knock anybody's socks off. I hope we'll pull out of it. How people dress and what people say they want are really two different things. We say we want to wear something exciting, but what we really want is something comfortable."

III. TOKYO

There are three things not to do on arriving in Tokyo. #1 Do not take a taxi from Narita airport into Tokyo. #2 Do not tip the driver. Those two no-nos cost me about $250, making the 60+ kilometer ride into this city of 12,000,000 people one of the most expensive trips of my life. #3 Do not be afraid. That is, you can feel it, the fear of the unknown— the "foreign" language, the "different" people, the "other" place. But you can't live in fear. It may sound silly to sing a Bob Marley song in Tokyo, but a line kept dancing around my lips anyway: "Everything's gonna be all right." And it was.

A packet from Hiroko Tashiro at *Time* was waiting for me at the hotel. She has listed three shows for me to see: Issey Miyake, Mitsuhiro Matsuda, and Yohji Yamamoto. Kenzo and Comme Des Garçons are already over. Kansai Yamamoto has no show this autumn. And Hanae Mori's show takes place on the 16th, after I leave. Too bad. The Tokyo shows are not nearly as concentrated time-wise as they are in London, Milan, Paris, and New York. I was not able to get a

complete schedule before the season started, so I am not surprised that I won't see everything I wanted. Still, I am not disappointed. Far from it. I have not been in Tokyo in sixteen years, and I've never been here on my own. I will rise to the occasion.

5 November, 4:00
Issey Miyake

I've been anxious to see this show ever since I missed it in Paris. How will it compare to that enormous production, which included ballet dancers among the models? When Hiroko and I arrive at the Hamilton Place Building, I immediately scale down my expectations. The space itself, an industrial room with black pipes visible overhead, is stacked with rough wooden platforms in the center. Rows of benches angle around the perimeter of this "stage." I feel as if I'm in a SoHo loft, but pre-renovation and sky-high prices. There is the usual stand of photographers and cameramen and a crowd of maybe two hundred people, mostly young. Women are casually dressed; men are suited and tied. Issey's posse wears great "Splash" outfits, jumpsuits in a fabric that looks artfully painted. The actual cloth of clothing has always been the strong point of his designs.

The show begins. Three video screens replay the Paris défilé while a half-dozen live models step up and over the platforms. The clothes are rigorously no-iron with themes like "Airbrush," "Smooth & Shrunk," "Linen Petals," "Rhythmic Contrast," and "Matte & Sheer." Forms are loose, sizes approximate. Seaming is minimal, darts nonexistent. The fit is an active interplay between breathing body and breathable fabrics, wherein lies most of the fun.

The show, however, is not fun. Garments blowing on hangers would have had more appeal than this presentation. The Girls, Asians, are emaciated, pale, unattractive, and spiritless. I am disappointed. Comparison with the lively video show is unbearable. There is applause afterward but Issey does not appear to take a bow. Hiroko introduces me to Midori Kitamura, Issey's director of public relations. She is tall, thin, and very pretty, with long hair hanging straight down her back. She should have done the show. Merely looking at her makes it easier to accept her frustratingly polite explanation that Issey is unavailable for an interview. He is to be in New York shortly, working on another book collaboration with Irving Penn. Maybe then. We complete a Japanese ritual by exchanging business cards.

6 November, 1:00

Sanae Sasahara

Unknown to each other, Sanae Sasahara and I sit on opposite sides of my hotel lobby for fifteen anxious minutes before we finally meet.

Working thirty years ago as an interpreter for English-language newspapers, Sanae interviewed an American, Patricia Salmon, the first woman to open a modern charm school and modeling agency in Japan. That initial interview led Sanae to work with Miss Salmon's school as a teacher and secretary, and eventually, as a translator for artists, athletes, and entertainers. For six years she worked with Elsa Klensch, host of the popular cable television show on fashion.

Sanae explains the big difference in models working now in Japan compared to the ones working ten or fifteen years ago. Previously, they were European Girls, twenty-five and older who had "used up their clients abroad" and were moving toward the end of their career. Now, she says, "young kids, fourteen, fifteen, and sixteen years old, without a chaperone, come from Canada and Brazil to work. When business is slow they don't work much. Waiting creates so many problems. If a Girl

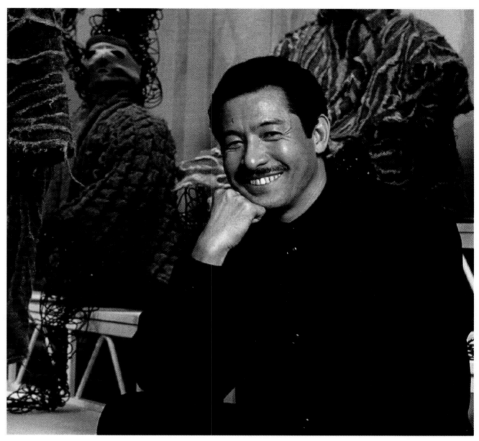

Issey Miyake at an exhibition of his designs. The Museum of Decorative Arts, Paris, 1982.

goes out at night and comes back in the morning with circles under her eyes, she is not going to work. It's a vicious cycle."

Despite the recession, foreign models are still in demand for fashion shows and photography shoots in Japan, says Sanae. Typically, a model comes on a contract basis with a minimum salary guaranteed. Leaner production budgets, however, have siphoned off business from the major professional modeling agencies to the benefit of less expensive foreigners moonlighting from their regular jobs as teachers or military personnel.

Sanae's work brought her into close contact with many Black Girls modeling in Japan. When she first saw Terri Coleman, she says, "Everything about Terri enchanted me. I went back

to my agency and said, 'We must have her.' Sanae continues, "Rebecca Ayoko, the model from Senegal, wasn't that tall, and she wasn't all that pretty. But when I would visit designers with other models, all the top designers said they were waiting for Rebecca to come. Everybody wanted her." There are Black Girls who are or were real stars in Japan. "Everybody loved Pat Cleveland. And Katoucha was really funny."

Sanae considers that Tokyo's fashion scene was born just about thirty years ago. "Not only fashion, but what we include in that whole industry: advertising, commercials, art designers, art directors, and everything. It's a very comprehensive field. Many of the people who started out small thirty years ago are big people today." When I suggest that similar changes have taken place in other countries, especially the United States, she hastens to add, "We think

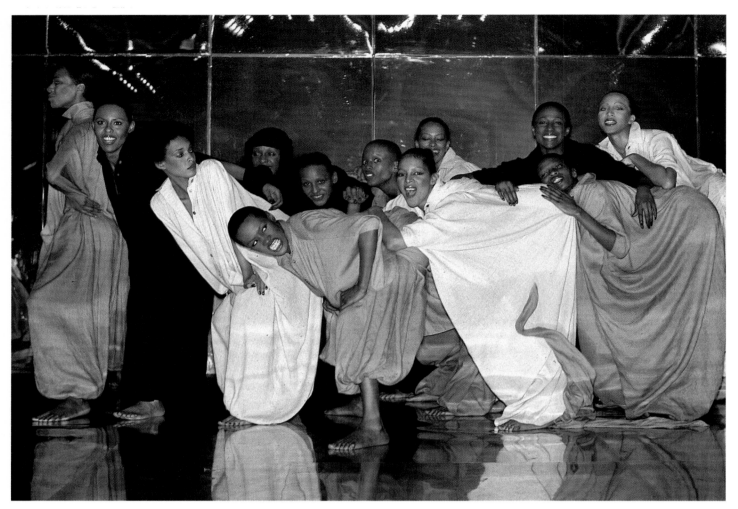

A memorable tour: Twelve Black Girls in Japan with **Issey Miyake**, 1976. **Karen Wilson**, **Carol Standifer**, **Barbara Summers**, **Jessica Brown**, **Grace Jones**, **Barbara Jackson**, **Toukie Smith**, **Ramona Saunders**, **June Murphy**, **Esther Kamatari**, **Paschal**, **Jan Maiden**.

that whatever happens in the United States will happen in this country, but maybe five or ten years later. There's even a saying: When America sneezes, Japan catches cold."

6:30
Madame Nicole aka Matsuda, with Terri Coleman

Terri Coleman picks me up at my hotel and drives us to the district of Akasaka. She is tall and gracious, and I immediately sense what Sanae Sasahara was trying to describe about her approachable kind of elegance. What truly impresses me, however, is her driving. Behind its broad boulevards, Tokyo is threaded with exceedingly narrow, hilly back streets that seem to belong to an era preceding the wheel, not to mention the motor car.

Tokyo is, in fact, comprised of many ancient villages now linked together by necessity and modern avenues. These villages evolved into distinct neighborhoods and have come to symbolize certain qualities. Our destination, Akasaka, the location of huge, elegant hotels, many foreign embassies, and exclusive private clubs, is considered the capital of conspicuous consumption. "My" neighborhood, Harajuku Aoyama, is probably the pleasantest in all of Tokyo, says a guide book. Maybe it has something to do with the trees, many of which are still optimistically full and green in the daylight.

Tonight though, between Aoyama and Akasaka, neighborhoods whiz by as Terri navigates their dark twists and turns with nonchalant skill in her right-hand drive Toyota. She used to ride a motorcycle until she had an accident. Now it's safer driving, she says. I take her word for it while managing to hold my breath and a tight-lipped smile on my face.

LaForêt Museum in Akasaka has a real, international-style runway room. There's a sizable crowd which seems to include more men than in the European shows. While we wait for the Matsuda show to begin, Terri and I talk.

In the early '80s, a handful of avant garde Japanese designers helped to shift the world's fashion compass toward Tokyo. "There is no excitement around fashion now," Terri laments. "Now things are more matter-of-fact. There is a lack of innovation in design and in the economy. The talent is there but the Japanese are not putting their money into the fashion business anymore."

Press coverage of the shows is also limited, she complains. Too polite to be interesting let alone challenging, Japanese journalists never write opinionated commentary. "There is no one here like Suzy Menkes, who keeps designers on the edge and forces them to do something creative." As for foreign reporting, most American publications never cover the Tokyo shows, although "Tokyo does the world."

At seven-forty the lights dim, and soft bells signal the start of the show. The clothes are lovely and graceful, simple but tasty, like vanilla ice cream on a hot summer day. There are about twenty-five Girls, the first dozen of whom are White. I count a few Asians, zero Black Girls. Their makeup is very pale with streaks of color—red, white, blue—in their hair. Their presentation is basic, straight walking, no posing, no extra body attitude. Flat shoes and no accessories combine with the garments' neutral colors for an understated, relaxed look.

The audience, as is customary in Japan, is silent until the end of the show when applause emerges from its cocoon. Terri explains that she used to do the Matsuda show but that he has stopped using Black Girls. Maybe it was bad for his image, she suggests and shrugs her shoulders as if refusing to speculate any further.

8 November
Sunday afternoon,
The Almond Café

The Almond Café et Patisserie sits on the corner of Roppongi Crossing. Its candy-striped awning seems incongruous at this grimly bustling intersection where traffic is raised to new heights—literally, to an express roadway roaring over an already congested avenue. Innovation is Tokyo's middle name. Large numbers of people living in a very limited space demand it. Relative financial prosperity makes it possible.

It's been said that Roppongi has more night spots per square inch than anywhere else in the world. It doesn't exactly sleep during the day either. In front of the Almond Café hip little hustlers with reddish, streaked hair or wide-shouldered double-breasted suits flit between girls modestly dressed in their pastel Sunday best and young women in brazenly thigh-

high suede boots. I realize that this is a serious rendezvous spot. And with the Japanese penchant for punctuality, a big Seiko clock on the corner reads 1:51 for Tokyo; 12:51 for Peking and Hong Kong; and 5:51 for Paris and Rome. I don't even try to calculate what time—or day—it is in New York. I simply observe and enjoy this scene while I wait for Terri Coleman and Khadija. They end up arriving an hour late.

Trialogue at the Almond Café

We are three Black women: one African, one West Indian, one North American. We are in our 40s, our 30s, and our 20s. We are or have been fashion models. We are drinking tea and hot chocolate in a Japanese coffee shop with a half-English name that serves French pastries. Despite our differences and similarities and the singularity of our location, we are together, and glad to be.

"I was a beauty queen," starts Khadija, who originates from Nairobi, Kenya. "In 1985, I was Miss Africa, and I went to London to do the Miss World pageant, where I was one of the finalists. When I was there, Peter Beard, whom I've known all my life, called up and told me that I should go to Paris and meet Yves Saint Laurent. I got intimidated, and I didn't want to go through that whole scene, so I said No. But I did go to Paris to have a drink with Peter, and while I was there he brought some people from Saint Laurent with him, and we met for five minutes. Then, when I arrived back in Nairobi, there was a ticket waiting for me to return to Paris. So, I started at the top, and then I worked my way down." She punctuates this introduction with a bruised laugh, which I soon learn is one of her trademarks.

Her debut with Saint Laurent led to the cover of *Cosmopolitan* magazine in 1986 and tremendous exposure in the world of fashion and

beauty. But Khadija claims that she "was also misused. I didn't know anything about business. You pay a young woman from Nairobi $100 for just sitting there, and will she take it and run or what? One hundred dollars is what an average person in Nairobi makes in a month. This young Girl accepts the money, which was a lot in her eyes, but in reality another Girl in Paris doing the same job would have gotten $1,000. I had no concept of money. When they paid for my dinner, I was happy. I wasn't brought up to be materialistic, so I wasn't able to ask for anything. I didn't have an agent. I had nobody to speak for me. They had control over me."

"You were under exclusive contract with Saint Laurent?" I try to clarify.

"Yes, completely. After the newspapers wrote a lot of stories about me, my grandmother asked me, 'So, daughter, who are you working for, and what are you doing? What are all these things that people are reading in the newspapers?' I said that I was working for a designer. And she said, 'What is a designer?' 'Grandmother, this man designs clothes. He creates them, and they're sewn up on you.' Then she says, 'So, I worked all those years getting you up early in the morning and sending you to school so you could work for a tailor?' I said that he was not a tailor, that he was an haute couture designer. Try explaining to a grandmother in Africa what haute couture is!"

Terri and I laugh. Every model should have such problems. "You're under contract to Saint Laurent," I repeat. "That means you're not beating the pavement looking for a job. You're dressed in the most beautiful clothes. You go to the most wonderful parties…"

"…Where I don't even know if I should eat with my gloves or without," Khadija breaks in. "That's my first question. Who do I ask? They are all strangers expecting this diva to walk in. So I walk in and hold my head real high. But at the table I slide down in my seat and whisper to the guy sitting on my left. 'I'm sorry. Can you tell me, do I eat with the gloves on or the gloves off?' You should have seen his face. Then he said, 'You're Khadija! You can eat any way you want. I can feed you if you'd like.' And this is Alain Delon speaking, the movie star. You can't get any more 'mega' than that. And I'm, like, Hello! This is it, Grandma, I've made it."

"But how does that hit you?" Terri asks. "The reality of someone saying that, then finding one day that it's sinking in because everyone is treating you like 'You're Khadija, you can do whatever you want to do.'"

"When you work with ten models day-in, day-out in the *cabine* of Saint Laurent, you get wise pretty quick," she responds crisply. "And when you're new you get scared. But whatever is written for you in the business is yours. Just eliminate negativity. That's what helped me survive in this business."

In 1986, she won an exclusive makeup contract with Saint Laurent cosmetics, the first transracial line to feature a Black model and the first to be named after an individual, Khadija. The deal was not to last long, however. Khadija admits, "Sales went down because I was a Black Girl. People wrote nasty letters."

"I think that's bad marketing," Terri Coleman insists. "If the campaign had started in America, with the right marketing...."

"It sold very well in the Middle East, in other countries, in France. But in America, somehow, the sales went down. And for that reason, they didn't renew my contract."

Khadija counts her blessings, though. "I have too many people I'm responsible for before I go into the politics of fashion. I'm sure most of the Girls who do the rounds make $350,000 a year or more. That's the least you'll make. Now, why do I need more money than that a year? It pays for eleven kids to go to university. It pays for my mother and my grandmother. It pays for my uncle and his kids. So, thank God, I just do my business."

When I ask her about aspects to the down side, Khadija says, "The down is that if you are not careful, because of the pressure, you get sick a lot. Physically, you get completely drained."

"It starts here as well," adds Terri, pointing a finger to her head.

Khadija agrees. "Mentally, you become funny. I never looked in the mirror. Suddenly you become very vain because you're constantly looking in the mirror, and if there is a pimple or a little line, sirens start going off in your head, whereas in real life you probably wouldn't even notice. In our business, you become obsessed with looks.

"The other down side is that you

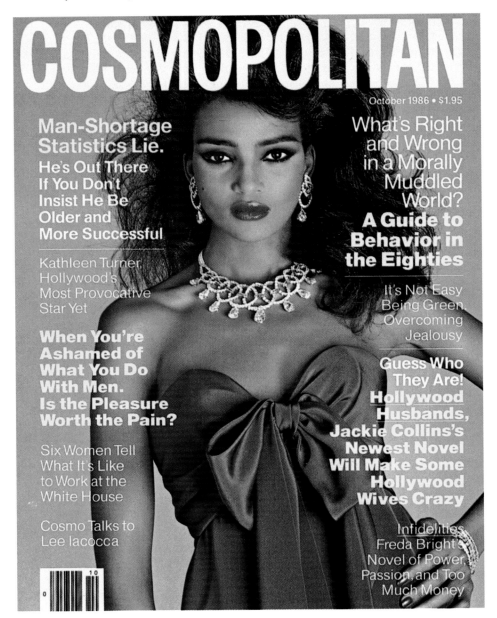

Khadija. *Cosmopolitan*, February, 1986.

cannot have a regular family life. The worst part is that traveling so much puts a lot of strain on relationships."

Next, Terri recounts her experience. "I'm from St. Kitts, a little island in the West Indies. I started modeling when it was suggested to me by Carlos Falchi, the designer, who was a passenger on an airplane where I was working as a flight attendant. I had no experience, no book, no pictures, not even a snapshot. But I sort of forced my way in, and they liked me because in Japan at that time, there were no Black models. This was in 1980. I found my niche by pursuing it and hanging in there.

"I used to go to Paris twice a year, but I always made my base in Tokyo. Why? Because I felt secure. I felt welcome and wanted. Unless you've been invited to Paris, you have to go and knock down those doors and give attitude and take s--t to get somewhere."

"Thank God, I didn't have to," Khadija interjects.

"You were lucky," Terri says simply. "I really don't know another Black model who had it so easy."

When I ask Khadija and Terri about their preference for shows or photography, I get, not surprisingly, two different answers.

"I do both," Khadija says, "but I personally prefer photography, because you don't have to deal with too many people. You do your job very quietly with the makeup artist, the hairdresser, the photograper her, and you. It's very tranquil. With fifty models in a show there's a lot of noise and always some kind of drama brewing somewhere. You may try and hide in a corner but it doesn't work."

Terri's perspective is quite dissimilar. "I was never really a print model. I didn't have any rapport with the camera. I prefer doing shows. I love the people contact. I like being with the Girls. For me, it's been like a study of women's behavior. You meet so many different nationalities, so

many different levels of education, so many different classes. I was fascinated by all the different types of women I could meet and the things I could learn about the way women react not just to beauty, but to life circumstances. How a woman handles a crisis. How a woman handles a man walking out on her. How a woman handles rejection from a client. How a woman handles being a friend with someone who's made it very big, when you have been trying to do the same thing for so long, and you never will, and you know it. These things I find fascinating. You pull out pieces that you can apply to your life and say this is what will hold me together. I just love being backstage."

"And I just hate it," says Khadijah. "Just like you learned a lot and learned it positively, I faced that and unfortunately, I could only see the deterioration of women. So you were much stronger than I, because you would look for what you could apply. I looked at those people and said that this was something I didn't want to deal with."

"Also, in my experience," Terri continues, "I find that a lot of the Girls are very late in finding out who they are. Late, meaning that they don't start that search until they are near thirty, when I think that the average person does it a lot earlier. With modeling, you can just sail along without having to face life as a woman, as a responsible individual."

"You wear rose-tinted glasses," Khadija agrees. "Unfortunately, some people take that for reality. But you and I," she says to Terri, "were already exposed to it. In the Third World, you're taught to take care of children and newborn babies, when you're eight. You get trained to be a wife at nine. In a way, I feel sorry for myself because I didn't have very much of a childhood. On the other hand, I was very well prepared for life. I'm happy with what I have."

"Sometimes," Terri says dreamily, "I sit and think about the girl that

I was when I lived in the Caribbean, running backward on the beach. And I think about the woman that I am now and the differences. Sometimes I reflect, Had I not had all this, what would I have been like? I'm not saying that I don't like who I am now. I'm quite content with my being. But I think I would have been a different person without these kind of influences."

"We would have children," states Khadija.

"I would have six," says Terri, who has one.

I can't quite believe what I'm hearing. "You're talking as if your life is over," I object. "Come on. You can still get married. You can still have families. You can still pursue other careers."

"But it's not the same anymore," Terri says wistfully.

"How would I be able to change from having my shoelaces tied for me to tying my shoelaces myself?" Khadija asks. "That's the question." Our laughter is spontaneous response and necessary release.

9 November, 6:30
Yohji Yamamoto

Yohji's show takes place at LaForêt Museum, but in a different room than the Matsuda show. It's still set up in the international style with gray industrial carpeting, padded—a nice touch—folding chairs, and lettered seating sections.

There is already a long line of standees waiting to get in. Naturally, black predominates in this audience's attire, although I do see one bright yellow jacket and a spattering of beige, maybe from raincoats since it is drizzling tonight. Observing the fashion crowd is always interesting. Lots of Tokyo women are coiffed with crinkly permanents and softer body waves. The blondest are auburn, almost russet, with flagrantly dark roots. Always, lots of bowing.

There are three or four White people here. Behind me a tall blond girl, perhaps a model, says to her companion, "I'm the only blonde here." I think to myself that I'm the only Black person here.

Once the standees are let in, the room is packed. Although there must be over 500 people here, they're all amazingly low-volume. There are few talkers, and even they are whispering.

The room goes black, and then the lights come up. Music similar to the theme from *2001* plays but it sounds somehow abstracted and strangely bopped up. The show opens with the same paprika red dress that appeared in Paris. The second model, Nina, is Black. She did the show in Paris, and I find out later that she was flown in for this one job. Anna Getaneh is also in the line-up. The Girls wear the same hairstyle— long, twisted queues—and makeup— stripes of iridescent color under the eye—that they wore in Paris. There are very few Asian Girls and a handful of Girls of indistinguishable ethnicity. They all move in a stilted, expressionless way. The clothes are wearing the Girls.

By some accident the music goes off, but the show goes on, in silence. The loudest noises in the room are the clicking of cameras, the footsteps of the Girls as they maneuver the metal stairs, and the jingling of coins and chains on the spectacular head-dresses that accessorize some of the outfits. The audience is entirely silent except for one person who has dared to clap because, I think, he thought the show was over.

Although there were fewer Black Girls, I am encouraged to see that Yohji's Paris and Tokyo shows were basically the same. Once again, fashion leaps across national frontiers, shrinking differences and expanding similarities. Maybe it's just that Yohji is well-financed enough to mount big productions wherever he wants. Afterward, I shake his hand and thank him for using Black models.

Kohei Katsura

Kohei faxed me a hand-drawn street map to show me how to get to his apartment. It is a five-minute walk from my hotel, but without names and numbered buildings, I still get a little lost. Not a lot, though, because I arrive only a few minutes late.

Kohei is charmingly voluble— unlike most Japanese men, he admits—with the kind of sensibility that can conceive of grand interna-tional projects and still handle frail individual egos with care. He entered the fashion business through the side door of music. As a young person he was interested in making under-ground movies and music, "private style" like Andy Warhol, and event-ually he started arranging music for fashion shows. After working success-fully free-lance, he formed his own company, The Directors' Workshop, where he produces and directs fas-hion shows. As he explains, however, his work "is not like a regular fashion show. A regular fashion show is actually a designer's show, just clothes and models." What he adds is a more theatrical dimension, as I see from watching video tapes of some of the extravaganzas that he has mounted.

In 1986, he produced and directed a spectacle for the house of Christian Dior entitled "One Night's Dream," based on the Cinderella fable and staged at Japan's Disney World. A television special was made of the entire production, detailing highlights onstage and backstage. Thus, the general public could wit-ness the less glamorous preparations of castings, fittings, and rehearsals as well as the actual presentation of the clothes. A surprise thank-you to the models took the form of brilliant fireworks at the show's finale.

It was then that I understood what Kohei meant when he said, "I am not a fashion person. I am not a fashion victim. People like that are crazy. I love fashion, but I'm not crazy for fashion. I'm looking for style."

It was during pre-production of a show called the "History of *Vogue*" that he auditioned Terri Coleman for the role of Josephine Baker. "Josep-hine Baker was very important for her time, and the Black influence has always been very important for fashion. I had met Josephine Baker, and I wanted a Girl like her, with a nice body. Terri did an excellent job that gave her a start in Japan.

"Before, it was very hard for Black Girls in Japan. Japanese people like Black Girls but what they really think is that Black Girls have nice bodies. Real foreign Girls are ones with blond hair and white skin. My favorite Girls have a mixture.

"As for Japanese models, after Hideko and Sayoko, I don't know. Japan has only one race. In Europe, in the States, they are mixed. I like it like that, scrambled."

11 November, 1:00

This is my last full day in Tokyo. I walk around Parco, which com-prises at least four huge branches of the department store, and I find the Tobu Hotel where we Twelve Black Girls stayed in '76. The aerobically hilly neighborhood is congested with shops and shoppers. "Our" street is now called Via Parco. The glazed brick pavement looks familiar, but nothing else feels the same. Taller, closer, worldlier, everything has grown up. I have, too. Ralph Lauren is on the corner where I thought I re-membered "our" theatre. Issey has a shop nearby where a dancing pleated dress in the window draws crowds of amused teenagers. Only one salesgirl is inside. I go in, look through the scanty racks and leave. Issey's clothes require bodies to make them come truly alive. I remember when I was one of those privileged bodies, and I am pleased to see that I have no nostalgic regrets. I'm happy to be heading home at last.

Right: **Anna Getaneh**.

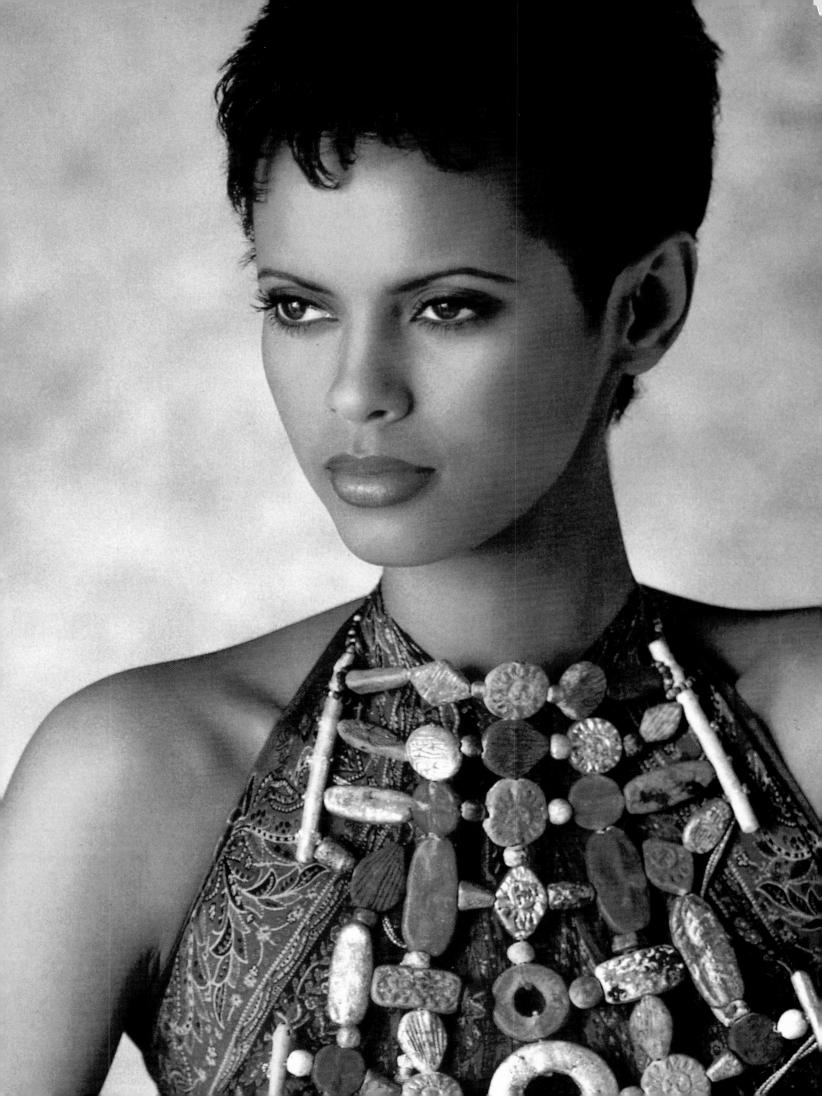

ACKNOWLEDGMENTS

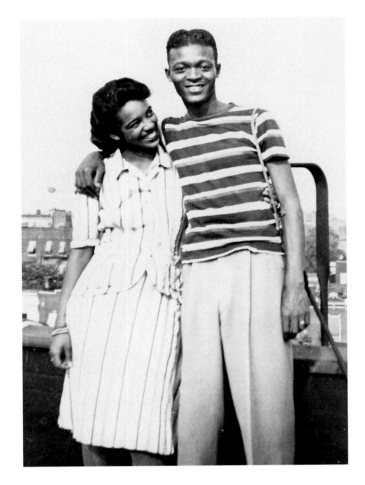

Deepest love and gratitude to my parents, **Lucy** and **Don Summers**, seen here as newlyweds, June, 1942.

Director of Art and Design: Gilbert D. Fletcher
Picture Editor: Suzanne Volkmann Skloot

I am indebted to Gail Kinn and Della Smith for insightful editorial assistance; to Ernest Anderson for documentary research in Europe; and to Nancy E. Brown for steadfast production management.

I would like to thank everyone mentioned in *Skin Deep* for contributing to this epic endeavor.

I would also like to thank many people who are not mentioned but who contributed in their own way. Among them are: Malaika Adero, Marc Albert, J Alexander, Rufus Barkley, Maïté Battini, Jodye Beard, Rafiq Bilal, Anne Boyd, Enoch Buckery, A'Lelia Bundles, Mark Buxton, Tonia Carter, Leah Clendening, Ornette Coleman, Paola Comolli, Mamie Vick Cooper, Charissa Craig, Derek Daniels, Helen and Harold Doley, Daria Dorosh, Eric Fletcher, Deirdre, Marian, Rusty, and T from the Ford Agency, Raoul Jean Fouré, Dee Gibson, Sherry Gordon, Alonzo Grundy, Myrna Stevens Haigh, George Hartman, Frances Hathaway, Lynell Hemphill, Shelya Huff, Ingrid Isaacs, Jun Kanai, Deborah Kidd, Grace and John Oliver Killens, Ida Lewis, Edie Raymond Locke, Eleanor Lofton, James Malone, Michele March, Mirella Moretti, Gordon Munro, Jennifer Noble, Gilles Rosier, Dee Simmons, Arlice Sims, Andrea Skinner, Alice Jackson Stuart, the Tagliatella Family at the Old Saybrook Inn, Betty Terry, Gay Thomas, Pat Tracey, Tony Verga, Pat White, Sylvia Berthena White, Karen Williams, Troy Word, Bani Yelverton, and Pauline A. Young. Thanks also to Alexandre Boulais at Paco Rabanne; Christiane Bourlon at Givenchy; Bérangère Broman at Christian Lacroix; Emmanuelle at Guy Laroche; Séri Kimura at Jean-Louis Scherrer; Philippe Salva at Lanvin; and Gabrielle Buchaert at Yves Saint Laurent.

PHOTO CREDITS

p.143: © Charles Tracy
p.144: Sveva Vigeveno/Gamma
p.146: Photography by Douglas Dubler
p.149: Photography by Anthony Barboza
pp.152, 153: Photograph and card courtesy of Helen Williams
p.154: Photography by Michael Thompson. Courtesy of Iman Cosmetics, Inc.
p.155: © Valentino
p.156: Photograhy by Gilles Bensimon. Courtesy of *Elle* © Copyright 1997, a publication of Hachette Filipacchi Magazines
p.158: Photography by Avedon. Courtesy *Vogue*. © Copyright 1984 by the Condé Nast Publications, Inc.
p.159: Guy Webster/Gamma
p.162: Photograph courtesy of Essence Communications, Inc.
p.164: © Antonio/Paul Caranicas
p.165: Eric Robert/Sygma
p.166: Daniel Simon/Gamma
p.169: © Philip Morris 1989
p.170: © 1996 Revlon
p.173: © 1994 Revlon
p.174: Composite courtesy of Sebastian Cardin
p.175: Russell James/*Sports Illustrated*
p.176: Matthew Jordan Smith/Gamma
p.177: Photograph courtesy of Rampage
p.178: Left: Marcel Thomas/Sipa Press right: Photography by Bruce Weber. Courtesy of Polo Ralph Lauren
p.179: Photography by Bruce Weber. Courtesy of Polo Ralph Lauren
p.180: Photography by Herb Ritts for Nine West, Spring 1997
p.181: Popperfoto/Archive
p.182: Photography by Anthony Barboza
p.183: Thierry Orban/Sygma
p.184: J. Donoso/Sygma
p.184A: Courtesy of Yves Saint Laurent
p.184B: Photography by Walter Chin. Courtesy *Mademoiselle*. © Copyright 1988 by the Condé Nast Publications, Inc.
p.184C: Daniel Simon/Gamma
p.184D: Paul Massey/Spooner/Gamma
pp.186, 188: Photography by Gösta Peterson
p.191: Photography by Anthony Barboza
p.192: Photography by Mel Dixon
p.194: Composite courtesy of the author
p.196, 201, 202: Photographs courtesy of Dorothea Towles (p.196) Photography by Maywald
p.198: Schomburg Center for Research in Black Culture
p.199: Photography by Howard Morehead
p.205: D.Fineman/Sygma
p.206: Photography by Douglas Dubler
p.207: © Charles Tracy
p.208: © Unilever
p.211: Daniel Simon/Gamma
p.212: B.Edelhajt/Gamma
pp.214, 215: Materials courtesy of Patrick Kelly
p.217: P. Vauthey/Sygma
p.220: Illustration by Antonio/Paul Caranicas
pp.221, 222, 223: © Charles Tracy
p.225: Photography by Scavullo. Courtesy *Vogue*. © Copyright 1974 by the Condé Nast Publications, Inc.
p.226: Photography by Susan Wood. Courtesy *Glamour*. © Copyright 1972 by the Condé Nast Publications, Inc.
p.227: Photography by Avedon. Courtesy *Vogue*. © Copyright 1981 by the Condé Nast Publications, Inc.
p.228: Photography by Charles Bush. Courtesy of Essence Communications Inc. © 1991
p.229: Photography by Scavullo. Courtesy *Cosmopolitan*. © 1969 The Hearst Corp.
p.232: Photography by Peter Lindbergh. Courtesy of Donna Karan
p.235: F.Meylan/Sygma
pp.236, 238, 240: Daniel Simon/Gamma Liaison
p.243: Photography by Michael O'Brien. Courtesy of *Amica* magazine © 1992
p.244: Bottm: Jeff Christensen/Gamma Liaison; top: © Armani
p.245: © Salvatore Ferragamo, © Gianfranco Ferrè
p.247: Courtesy of Bisou-Bisou
p.248: Abbas/Magnum
p.250: Stephane Cardinale/Sygma
p.252: Daniel Simon/Gamma
p.253: © Chloé, © Lolita Lempicka, © Junko Shimada
p.254: Steve Allen/Gamma
p.255: Daniel Simon/Gamma

p.256: © Chantal Thomass, © Christian Lacroix
p.257: © Martine Sitbon, © Katharine Hamnett, © Yves Saint Laurent
p.258: Thierry Orban/Sygma
pp.259, 260: Daniel Simon/Gamma
p.261: Photography by Patrick Demarchelier. Courtesy *Vogue*. © 1991 Copyright by the Condé Nast Publications, Inc.
p.262: Daniel Simon/Gamma
p.263: Photography by Patrick Demarchelier. Courtesy Chanel. © 1996 Chanel Inc.
p.264: © Lanvin, © *The Parisian Diary*
p.265: Composite courtesy of Rosalind
p.267: Thierry Orban/Sygma
p.268: Top: © Yves Saint Laurent. From Personal Notes, *Le Nouvel Observateur*, 8-14 Nov. 1990 bottom: © Issey Miyake
p.269: © Fendi, © Karl Lagerfeld, © Chanel, © Sonia Rykiel
p.271: F. de Lafosse/Sygma
p.272: © Hajime Sawatari
p.274: Photography by Scavullo. Courtesy *Cosmopolitan*. © 1969 The Hearst Corp.
p.277: Photography by Robert Whitman. Courtesy of Flori Roberts.
p.281: Greg Gorman/Gamma
p.282: Left: © Harvey Boyd. Courtesy of FIT; center: Photography by Irving Penn. Courtesy *Vogue*. © 1988 Copyright by Condé Nast Publications, Inc.; right: Alexis Duclos/Gamma
p.283: Left: © 1977 Eve Arnold/Magnum; right: © Charles Tracy
p.284: Left: © Karen Pugh; right: Ferdinando Scianna/Magnum

We have endeavored to obtain the necessary permission to reprint the photographs and drawings in this book and to provide proper copyright acknowledgments. We welcome information on any error or oversight, which we will correct in subsequent printings.

SELECTED BIBLIOGRAPHY
All-Consuming Images: The Politics of Style in Contemporary Culture, by Stuart Ewen, Basic Books, 1988
Appearances: Fashion Photography since 1945, by Martin Harrison, Rizzoli, 1991
Arthur Elgort's Models Manual, by Arthur Elgort, Grand Street Press, 1993
Backlash: The Undeclared War Against American Women, by Susan Faludi, Crown, 1991
The Beauty Myth: How Images of Beauty Are Used Against Women, by Naomi Wolf, Morrow, 1991
Black Looks: Race and Representation. by bell hooks, South End Press, 1992
Blacks in the History of Fashion, by Lois K. Alexander, Harlem Institute of Fashion, 1982
Bulletproof Diva: Tales of Race, Sex, and Hair, by Lisa Jones, Doubleday, 1994
Catwalk: Inside the World of the Supermodels, by Sandra Morris, Universe, 1996
Chic Savages, by John Fairchild, Pocket Books/Simon & Schuster, 1989
The Color of Fashion, conceived and edited by Lona Benney, Fran Black, and Marisa Bulzone, Stewart, Tabori & Chang, 1992
Couture: The Great Designers, Caroline Rennolds Milbank, Stewart, Tabori & Chang, 1985
East Meets West, by Issey Miyake, Heibonsha, 1978
The Fashion Conspiracy: A Remarkable Journey Through the Empires of Fashion, by Nicholas Coleridge, William Heinemann, 1988
Model: The Ugly Business of Beautiful Women, by Michael Gross, William Morrow, 1995
Négripub: L'Image des Noirs dans la publicité depuis un siècle, Bibliothèque Forney, 1987
The Power of Style: The Women who Defined the Art of Living Well, by Annette Tapert and Diana Edkins, Crown, 1994
Princesse Mounia, by Mounia and Denise DuBois-Jallais, Editions Robert Laffont, 1987
Scenes from the Fashionable World, by Kennedy Fraser, Knopf, 1987
Style Noir, by Constance C.R. White, Berkley, 1998
Tar Baby, by Toni Morrison, Knopf, 1981
True Beauty: Secrets of Radiant Beauty for Women of Every Age and Color, by Beverly Johnson, Warner Books, 1994
Tyra's Beauty: Inside & Out, by Tyra Banks, HarperPerennial, 1998
Veronica Webb Sight: Adventures in the Big City, by Veronica Webb, Hyperion, 1998
Women of Fashion: Twentieth-Century Designers, by Valerie Steele, Rizzoli, 1991
Women Who Run with the Wolves: Myths and Stories of the Wild Woman Archetype, by Clarissa Pinkola Estés, Ballantine, 1992

Opposite page: **Grace Jones.**

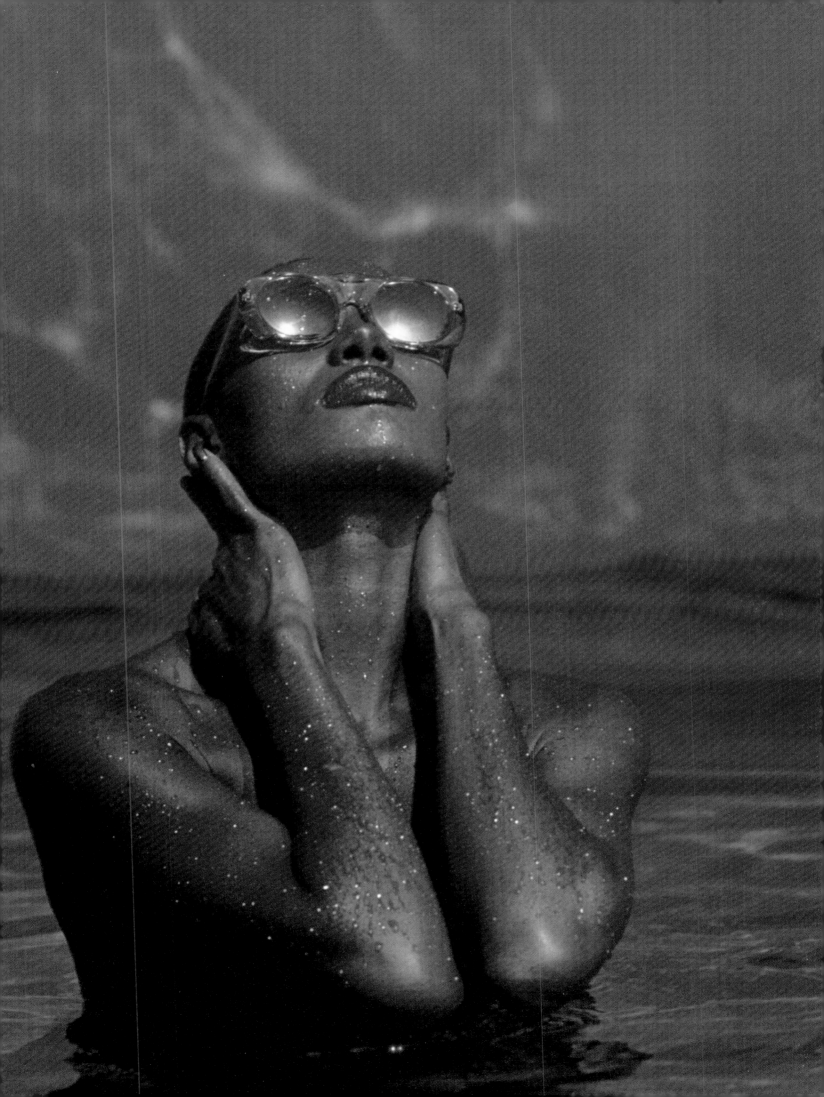

INDEX

Adams, Elaina, 49
Adjani, Isabelle, 265
Adolfo, 78-81
Ailey, Alvin, 72
Akure, 84, 254
Alaïa, Azzedine, 83, 93, 177, 245
Alex, Joe, 6
Alexander, Karen, 84, 127, 167, 207, 246, 252-255, 260-263 [daughter, Ella, 261, 263]
Alexis, Kim, 207
Allen, Billie, 31
Altman, Robert, 167
Amalia, 84, 260
Amelan, Bjorn, 211, 218
Anderson, Eddie "Rochester", 198
Anderson, Ernest, 260
Anderson, Sheila, 123-127
Anna Fiona, 97, 99, 118, 244, 248, 249, 266
Antonio, 49, 58, 164
Aria, 84, 129, 210, 255, 260
Armani, Giorgio, 93, 97, 241, 244, 248, 249
Astrid, 157
Atchison, John, 204, 205
Aya, 110
Ayoko, Rebecca, 84, 86, 211, 271
Bailey, Cynthia, 84, 260
Bailey, Laura, 177
Bailey, Pearl, 37
Baker, Chuck, 256
Baker, Josephine, 3, 5-10, 45, 87, 100, 101, 182, 198, 202, 212, 213, 220, 276
Baker, Martha, 256
Balanchine, George, 7
Baldwin, Duke, 21
Baldwin, James, 224
Balenciaga, 85, 265
Ball, Lucille, 213, 214
Balmain, Pierre, 49, 200, 201, 265
Bandy, Way, 206
Banks, Tyra, 115, 167, 174-176, 241, 245, 246, 254, 265, 266
Bannon, Lisa, 255
Baptiste, Angela, 22, 23, 171
Barboza, Anthony (Tony), 16, 43, 66
Barnes, Byron, 157, 209
Barrie, Scott, 77, 145
Basie, Count, 37
Bass, Sandi, 89, 95, 103, 122
Beard, Peter, 233, 273
Beauvais, Garcelle, 167
Beavers, Louise, 198
Beckford, Tyson, 176, 178

Beene, Geoffrey, 79
Belafonte, Shari, 157-159, 167
Bell, Lois, 29
Bennett, Barbara, 102-104
Beretta, 83
Bergé, Pierre, 214, 215, 274
Bernhard, Sandra, 270
Berry, Halle, 115
Bethune, Mary McLeod, 10, 198
Biki, 256
Blair, Billie, 4, 67, 109, 118, 120, 121, 158
Blake, Eubie, 6
Blanchard, Nina, 87
Blass, Bill, 3, 38, 79
Bohan, Marc, 3
Bouvier, Jacqueline, 48
Bowie, David, 238
Bowser, Buddy, 122
Bowser, Kersti, 260
Boyd, Harvey, 49, 85, 213
Bradshaw, Carmen, 54
Brandi, 144
Breedlove, Sarah Jane, 9 (see Madam C.J. Walker)
Brewer, Sherry (Bronfman), 20, 71, 72, 171
Brice, Fannie, 7
Brooks, Donald, 38, 39
Brown, Charlotte Hawkins, 45, 46
Brown, Jade, 92, 93, 98
Brown, Jessica, 278
Brown, Marie D., 195
Bruni, Carla, 253
Burgess, Gloria, 95, 96, 210, 211
Burrows, Stephen, 3, 4, 57-59, 63, 70, 77, 220, 221, 233
Cain, Harriet, 189
Callendar, Eugene, 218
Callendar, Rupert, 27
Campbell, E. Simms, 39
Campbell, Liz, 39
Campbell, Naomi, x, 20, 21, 85, 113, 114, 141, 160, 167, 177-179, 184B, 208, 243, 244, 246-248, 250, 252-255, 264
Campbell, Roy, 264
Cardin, Pierre, 3, 73, 261, 270
Carnegie, Hattie, 58
Carson, Johnny, 40
Carter, John, 122
Carter, Lady, 122 (see Sara Lou Harris)
Casablancas, Johnny, 25
Cassandra, 69
Catano, Elizabeth, 283

Chanel, 98,134, 144, 241, 253, 255, 263, 269
Chanel, Coco, 212
Cheeseboro, Barbara, 69
Chinn, Alva, 4, 5, 59, 69-72, 152, 155, 158, 165
Chinn, Henry, 70
Chirac, Jacques, 211
Chloe, 252, 253
Chrystèle, 138, 144, 160
Church, Thomas, 122
Clark, Nancy, 88, 89, 104
Clarke, John Henrik, 60
Cleveland, Ladybird, 219
Cleveland, Pat, 4, 67, 71, 131, 135, 152, 153, 155, 158, 213, 219-223, 247, 271
Cole, Carole, 45, 139
Cole, Nat "King", 45, 139
Cole, Natalie, 139
Cole, Sonia, 85, 91, 184, 243, 254, 255, 266, 268, 271, 272
Coleman, Terri, 100, 102, 271-276 [sister, Greta, 102]
Coleridge, Nicholas, 242
Comme des Garcons, 101, 270
Conrad, Robert, 168
Cooper, Cecilia, 27, 28
Cooper, Fran, 157-160
Cooper, Ralph, 27
Cosby, Bill, 91, 137-139
Cunard, Nancy, 45
Cuington, Phyllis, 158
Cunningham, Bill, 4, 49, 70, 88
Cusseau, Bernadette, 206
Dali, Salvador, 56
Dandridge, Dorothy, 13, 30, 207
Darden, Norma Jean, 4, 20, 21, 44, 53, 77, 82, 135, 160, 161 [sister, Carol, 160]
Darden, Walter T., 44
Dash, Charlene, 4, 5, 53-55, 66, 135
Davenport, Jane Hoffman, 111, 120, 154 (see Hoffman, Jane)
Davis, Angela, 105
Davis, Bette, 213
Davis, Miles, 124-127
Davis, Sammy, Jr., 32, 44
de Gaulle, Charles, 8
DeKnight, Freda, 154
de la Renta, Oscar, 3, 38, 79, 105, 155
Demarchelier, Patrick, 206
Denby, Michele, 89
Deneuve, Catherine, 207

DeNiro, Drena, 252
DeVore, Ophelia, 17, 23, 25-28, 32, 153, 203
Dillard, Peggy, 93-95, 122, 144-147, 149, 178, 254
Dior, Christian, 3, 83, 184, 197, 199, 254, 255, 265
Dobson, Tamara, 66
Donghi, Alessandra, 152, 153
Donovan, Carrie, 255
Douglas, Mike, 206
Douglass, Frederick, 78
Dream, 222
DuBois, W.E.B., 10
Duke, Vernon, 7
Dunaway, Faye, 208
Dunham, Katharine, 30, 220
Edia, 211
Eggers, Tanya, 106, 121, 130
Eisenhower, Dwight D., 5
Elizabeth, princess of Toro, 59-61, 65, 83, 238
Ellington, Duke, 37, 45
Emilia, 210
Erasme, Marguerite, 67
Estés, Clarissa Pinkola, x, 84
Evangelista, Linda, 113, 246, 264
Evans, Elaine, 140-142
Evans, Pat, 19, 20, 62, 63, 122, 153, 182
Factor, Max, 13
Fairchild, John, 72, 73
Falchi, Carlos, 275
Farrabee, James, 157
Fellini, Federico, 116
Fendi, 246, 253, 269
Ferragamo, 251
Ferre, Gianfranco, 242, 243, 245, 247, 265
Fields, Mike, 176
Fine, Sam, 209
Flowers, Yvette, 67
Ford, Eileen, xi, 25, 86, 178, 189, 226
Ford, Jerry, 25, 178
Fornay, Alfred, 209
Fox, Sonny, 40
Fredericks, Connie, 137-139
Freeman, Peggy Anne Donyale Aragonea Pegeon, 49 (see Luna, Donyale)
Galanos, James, 38
Gallagher, Maureen, 245, 265
Gamiliana, 18, 98
Gaultier, Jean-Paul, 92, 260, 261
Gay, Riccardo, 152, 256
George, Victor, 79
Georgiana, 166, A2, 264, 265

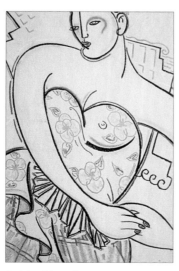

Spirit of love by **Harvey Boyd.**

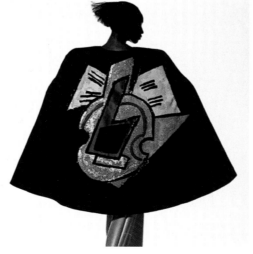

Katoucha.

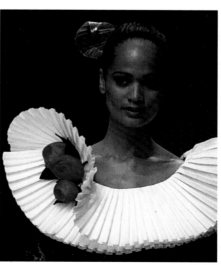

Michele.

INDEX

Gershwin, George, 7
Getaneh, Anna, 243, 252, 260-262, 276
Getz, Stan, 44
Gibson, Charles, 211
Gillespie, Marcia, 66
Gillett, Judy, 99, 100
Givenchy, Hubert de, 3, 20, 83, 87-91, 119, 134
Goldberg, Whoopi, 142
Goodrum, Liz , 216, 218 (see Miss Liz)
Graham, Martha, 21
Graham, Virginia, 40
Green, Amy, 64, 65
Green, Edward S., 14
Green, Pita, 69
Greene, Walter, 255
Griffin, Marva, 246, 247
Guyse, Sheila, 126
Hack, Shelly, 73
Haggins, Jon, 77, 78
Halsey, Margaret, 108
Halston, 3, 58, 120, 220, 223
Hamnett, Katharine, 255
Hampton, Lionel, 122
Hardison, Bethann, 4, 20, 21, 42, 55, 80, 81, 107, 153, 233, 237, 254, 258, 266, 267
Harris, Ann, 29
Harris, Charles F., 195
Harris, Sara Lou, 20, 21, 122
Harth, Ellen, 145
Hawkins, Arlene, 62, 157
Hawkins, Marie (Maria Cole), 45, 46
Hayatt, Lester, 145, 158
Hayes, Dor-Tensia, 91, 92
Hayes, Lor-Tensia, 91, 92
Haywood, Spencer, 235, 236
Head, Sandy, 188, 189
Headley, Shari, 164
Heilbrun, Caroline, 69
Henry, Pal (Palmira), 78-81 [daughter, Lisa, 78, 80]
Hicks, D'Atra, 218
Hideko, 276
Hilton, Shari, 112, 113
Hobbs, Carol, 68, 249-251
Hoffman, Jane, 65, 66, 111 (see Davenport)
Holly, Ellen, 28
hooks, bell, 1
Hope, Bob, 7
Horne, Lena, 8, 11-13, 30, 32, 37, 45, 213
Houston, Whitney, 167, 209
Howard, Chuck, 34, 37

Hundley, LeJeune, 27, 30
Hunter, Maurice, 30
Hunter, Rene, 39, 116, 122, 131, 152, 154
Hutton, Geneva, 158
Hutton, Lauren, 157, 227
Iman, 20, 85, 98, 112, 113, 131, 133, 154, 157, 178, 207, 228, 231-238, 254, 258 [daughter, Zulekha, 236,
Ishioka, Eiko, 195
Jackson, Barbara, 4, 194, 272
Jackson, Warren, 95-97, 123
James, Paulette, 93, 97, 154, 248
January, Barbara, 31
Jean-Louis, Kathy, 57
Johnson, Beverly, x, 16, 33, 69, 85, 107, 110, 135, 142, 147, 157, 160, 167, 178, 207, 224-230 [daughter, Anansa, 224, 228]
Johnson, Eunice W. (Mrs.), 40, 155, 219, 220
Johnson, John H., 28, 29, 33, 40
Johnson, Lyndon, 38
Johnson, Sheila, 16, 17, 20, 92, 114, 120, 164, 165, 169
Jones, Ann, 66
Jones, Grace, 67, 164, 165, 194, 204, 213, 272, 281
Jones, Jolie, 54, 65, 67, 116-118
Jones, Quincy, 65, 117
Joplin, Scott, 12
Jordan, 153
Jordan, Magic (Sharon), 18, 119, 154
Jordan, Michael, 139
Kabukuru, Kiara, x, 182
Kaiserman, Bill, 206
Kamatari, Esther, 83, 132, 133, 272
Karan, Donna, 232
Katoucha, 85, 90, 91, 96, 97, 119, 243, 249, 260, 262, 265, 271, 282
Katsura, Kohei, 100, 101, 104, 276
Kawakubo, Rei, 98
Keckley, Elizabeth Hobbs, 47
Kellie (Wilson), 54, 56, 66
Kelly, Grace, 206, 207
Kelly, Patrick, 210-218, 270
Kendrick, Gail, 69
Kennedy, John, 48
Kenzo, 89, 98, 270
Khadija, 85, 113,184, 207, 273-275
Kidron, Adam, 269
Kilgallen, Dorothy, 32
King, Bill, 177
King, Cynthia, 69

King, Ruth, 28, 29, 108
Kironde II, Katiti, 64
Kitamura, Midori, 271
Klein, Anne, 3
Klein, Calvin, 207, 234
Klensch, Elsa, 91, 92
Koshino, the sisters, 101
Kruger, Barbara, 33
LaBrie, Carol, 20, 21, 68, 87, 88, 122, 135, 168, 169-171
Lacroix, Christian, 89, 134, 255, 256, 259, 260, 270
Lagerfeld, Karl, 93, 134, 246, 250, 252-254, 264, 269
Lambert, Eleanor,155
Landis, John, 165
Lanker, Brian, 195
Lanvin, 83, 264
Larby, Stella, 259
Laroche, Guy, 60, 70, 211
Laug, Andre, 155
Lauren, Ralph, 129, 145, 176, 179, 262, 276
Lawrence, Martin, 167
Lee, Spike, 167
Lempicka, Lolita, 253
Levine, Bob, 218
Lewis, Edward, 65, 68
Liberman, Alexander, 185, 206
Lincoln, Abraham, 47
London-Johnson, Carolyn, 175
Louis, Marva (Mrs. Joe), 30
Lowe, Ann, 47, 48
Lumet, Gail, 12
Lumumba, Patrice, 132
Luna, Donyale, ix, 42,43, 46, 47, 49, 50, 52, 56, 116, 131, 157, 222
Mackie, Bob, 38
Macpherson, Elle, 178
MacGil, Gillis, 37, 79
Maiden, Jan, 69, 158, 272
Mandell, Alan, 256
Manin, 221
Marshall, Tina, 31
Martin, Richard, 59
Martin, Sandra, 158
Matisse, Jacquelyne, 85
Matsuda, Mitsuhiro, 270, 272, 273
Maxwell, Daphne (Reid), 64, 67
Mayer, Louis B., 12
McBroom, Marcia, 66
McCarther, Avis, 65
McDaniel, Hattie, 198

McDonald, Maria, 69
McKinley, Barry, 223
McKinney, Nina Mae, 13
Menkes, Suzy, 253, 255
Michele, 262, 267
Miles, Carol, 71
Miles, Emily, 24, 25
Miller, Jacqueline, 89
Miller, Robert, 218
Mills, Joey, 73, 158, 204-209
Minelli, Vincente, 7
Ming (Smith), 109-111, 140 [son, Kahil, 109]
Miss Liz (Goodrum), 210, 211, 215
Missoni, 247, 248
Mitchell, Candy, 66
Mitchell, Coco, 210, 212, 254
Miyake, Issey, 42, 75, 98, 193, 194, 235, 255, 266, 268, 270- 272, 276
Mobutu Sese Seko, 132
Mongo, Carol, 119, 268-270
Montana, 83
Moore, Nonnie, 189
Moore, Rashida, 67
Morehead, Howard, 157
Morgan, Ted, 227
Mori, Hanae, 90, 101, 262, 264, 270
Mouchette, 69, 73
Mounia, 133-136, 207, 213, 238, 283
Mugler, Thierry, 83, 224
Murphy, Al, 27
Murphy, Eddie, 164
Murphy, June, 40, 55, 69, 131, 132, 194, 272
Nadege, 246, 260, 264
Newton, Helmut, 66
Nicholas Brothers, 7
Nixon, Pat, 54
Nixon, Richard, 54, 69
Norell, Norman, 38
Norford, Thomasina, 17
Norman, Jessye, 213
Ogilvie, Lana, 113-116, 127, 253, 255, 260, 262
Olatunji, 62
Oliver, Andre, 3
Oliver, Sy, 21
O'Neill, Gail, 85, 110, 174, 243, 252, 254-259
Otis, Carla, 85, 254
Pagano (Studios), 32, 108
Parkinson, Norman, 60
Parks, Gordon, 30, 34, 39, 49, 66
Parks, Rosa, 48

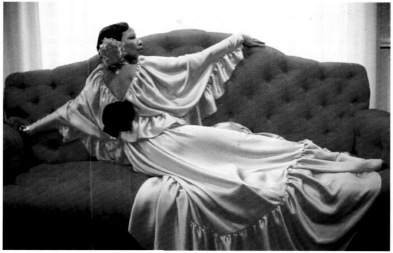

Mounia.

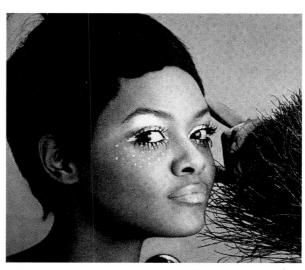

Elizabeth Catalano.

Pascal, Lorraine, 261, 270
Pascale, 210
Paschal, 278
Patou, Jean, 89, 90
Patterson, Rene, 211, 212
Pauline, 268
Peele, Beverly, 85, 149, 150 , 243, 246
    252, 253, 255, 256, 264, 265, 284
    [daughter, Cairo, 150]
Peele, Lucia Beverly, 149, 150
Penati, Gianni, 53
Pendarvis, Janice, 218
Perez, Jua, 116
Peterson, Gus (Gösta) 51, 66, 188, 189
Peterson, Pat, 51
Petit, Roland, 85
Pfeiffer, Michelle, 208
Phina, 260
Piaggi, Anna, 248
Picasso, Pablo, 6
Piercy, Marge, 172
Piguet, Robert, 197, 200
Pleasant, Corby, 226
Poitier, Anika, 146
Pollard, Fritz, 21
Poteat, Julie, 66
Powell, Adam Clayton, Jr., 28, 104
Powell, Maxine, 24
Powlis, LaVerne, 4
Princess Di, 213
Pucci, Emilio, 155
Pugh, Karen, 284
QuietFire, 209
Rabanne, Paco, 56, 57, 83, 211, 254, 267
Rafelson, Bob, 87, 89
Rashida, 218
Reagan, Caroline Dudley, 7
Reagan, Ronald, 94
Rech, Georges, 260
Reeves, Jackie Booker, 112, 135, 136
Reid, Daphne Maxwell, 167
Reid, Tim, 168
Reineri, Giorgio, 249, 251
Rhodes, Zandra, 71
Richards, Beah, 14, 17
Richardson, Regina, 89
Roberts, Esther P., 270, 271
Roberts, Mozella, 34-38
Roberts, Stephanie, 85, 142, 147-149,
    253, 256, 264
Robeson, Eslanda Goode (Mrs. Paul), 30
Robinson, Elizabeth, 66
Robinson, Etta Mae (Mrs. Sugar Ray), 44
Rodgers, Carolyn, 136
Rodgers, Melonee, 141
Rosalind, 249, 265, 266
Rose, Uli, 169
Roshumba, ix, 85, 142, 143, 144, 174, 243,
    244, 248, 254, 258, 260-262, 265, 266
Ross, Diana, 75, 76, 164, 167
Rossellini, Isabella, 207
Ruffin, Thomas, 105
Russo, Rene, 86
Russo, Romney (Williams), 69, 158
Rykiel, Sonia, 83, 214, 262, 269
Saint-Bris, Edouard, 261
Saint Laurent, Yves, 3, 22, 83, 85, 87,
    134, 135, 177, 184, 207, 215, 238,
    241, 255, 260, 267, 268, 273, 274

Salmon, Patricia, 271
Sanchez, Fernando, 87
Sanders, Madelyn, 65
Sands, Diana, 139
Sangare, Yahne, 34
Sasahara, Sanae, 271
Saunders, Ramona, 4, 67, 194, 272
Sayoko, 276
Scaasi, Arnold, 36, 38, 49
Scavullo, Francesco, 66, 204
Scherrer, Jean-Louis, 83, 93
Schiaparelli, Elsa, 108, 199, 200
Schiffer, Claudia, 178, 264
Schumacher, Joel, 58
Scimone, Carlo, 102
Sebastian, 174
Selenow, Kari Page, 168
Seydou, Chris, 133
Shange, Ntozake, 106
Shakespeare, William, 64, 128, 179
Shepard, Von Gretchen, 69
Shields, Brooke, 207
Shimada, Junko, 101, 252
Sierra, Lu (Lucelania), 20, 22, 109, 151,
    172, 211, 248, 249
Silvera, Rashid, 176
Simonelli, Don, 79
Sims, Naomi, 46, 48, 50-54, 57, 65, 69,
    70, 77, 87, 131, 135, 147, 151, 152,
    157, 160, 178, 195, 207, 227, 250
Singleton, John, 167
Sissle, Noble, 6, 12
Sitbon, Martine, 261, 262
Smaltz, Audrey, 14, 17, 122, 154-157, 216
Smith, Barbara, 23, 69, 112, 131, 160,
    161-163

Smith, Toukie (Doris), 42-45, 76-78, 167,
    194, 218, 272
Smith, Will, 167
Smith, Willi, 44, 45, 76-78
Standifer, Carol, 272
Steinem, Gloria, 213, 215, 218

Stevens, Sandra, 104, 105
St. Jacques, Sterling, 158, 222
Strasberg, Lee, 15
Strayhorn, Billy, 37
Stutz, Geraldine, 58
Summers, Barbara, 187-195, 272
    [son, Kimson, 188, 191, 192]
Summers, Don Alphonso, 187, 278
Summers, Dona, 188
Summers, Lucy Cooper, 140, 187, 278
Talley, André Leon, 248
Tara, 98
Tashiro, Hiroko, 276
Taylor, Mikki, 46, 66, 67
Taylor, Millicent, 29
Taylor, Susan, 67, 68, 158
Teasdale, Sara, 121
Terada, Minoru, 195
Terrell, Mary Church, 122, 198
Thé, Christine, 116
Thimister, Josephus Melchior, 271
Thomas, Darnella, 72-75, 163, 164, 207
Thomas, Miraella, 245, 248
Thomass, Chantal, 256
Thompson, Kevin, 218
Tiegs, Cheryl, 86
Tiffeau, Jacques, 39, 220
Tomba, Jany, 15, 16, 54, 65, 69, 140, 168
Toone, Lloyd, 147
Toscani, Oliviero, 223, 262
Towles, Dorothea, 14, 23, 44, 86, 87, 108,
    121, 122, 195, 197-203
Towles, Lois, 199
Townsel, Rudy, 211, 215, 218
Townsend, Robert, 137
Townsend, Robin, 16, 17
Tracy, Charles, 59, 70
Trigerè, Pauline, 34, 49
Trotter, William Monroe, 10
Trump, Donald, 155
Turbeville, Deborah, 66
Turlington, Christy, 113
Turner, Tina, 93
Turnier, Marcia, 69, 157, 208
Underhill, Les, 256
Ungaro, Emanuel, 3, 83, 85, 134, 266
Valdes, Beverly, 34
Valentino, 70, 155
Versace, Gianni, 40, 96, 178, 248
Vivian, 92, 103
Vodi, 81

Vreeland, Diana, 53, 221
Vyent, Louise, 85, 107, 137
Walcott, Derek, 239
Waldron, Rose, 66
Walker, A'Lelia, 10
Walker, Alice, 215
Walker, Charles Joseph, 9
Walker, Joyce, 60-62, 69, 108, 109
Walker, Madam C.J., 8-11, 30, 113, 140
Walz, Barbara, 224
Wanakee, xiii, 85, 157
Warhol, Andy, 131, 220, 276
Waris, 110, 170, 184D
Warsuma, Amina, 4, 71
Washington, Booker T., 10
Washington, Diane, 60, 89
Washington, Fredi, 13
Watson, Albert, 158
Watson, Elizabeth, 158
Watts, Lynn, 87, 89-91, 123
Webb, Veronica, 15-17, 24, 25, 85, 93, 110,
    113, 167, 173, 245, 246, 253, 254
Weinberg, Chester, 56, 79
Weiss, Adele, 104
Wek, Alek, 156, 160
Wells, Reggie, 209
Wells-Barnett, Ida B., 10
West, Mae, 133
Wheeler, Jacob, 89
White, Renauld, 176
Whitney, Ruth, 64
Wilhelmina, 18, 51, 77, 112, 226, 233, 250
Williams, Billy Dee, 76
Williams, Helen, 27, 28, 32, 33, 44,
    49, 108, 116, 122, 152-154, 168, 195
Williams, Vanessa, 18
Wilson, Earl, 32
Wilson, Karen, 278
Wilson, Woodrow, 10
Winfrey, Oprah, 213
Wolfe, George, 41
Woodson, Julie, 69, 70
Worth, Charles, 200
X, Malcolm, 78, 109
Yabro, Marie-Louise, 30
Yamamoto, Kansai, 98, 276
Yamamoto, Yohji, 98, 251, 252, 270, 275, 276
Yancy, Emily, 27
Young, Kara, 48, 85, 121, 184D
Zoli, 18, 22

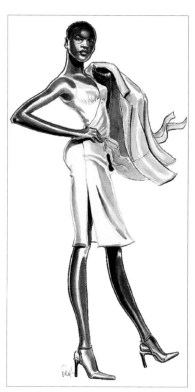

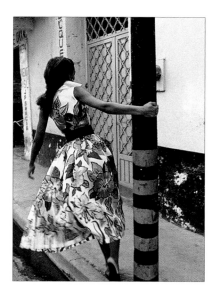

Left: Spirit of the '90s by **Karen Pugh**; right: **Beverly Peele.**

DATE			

60.00   4-5-00

BAKER & TAYLOR

FREEPORT MEMORIAL LIBRARY